D0079732

SECOND EDITION

INTERNATIONAL ORGANIZATIONS
PERSPECTIVES ON GOVERNANCE
IN THE TWENTY-FIRST CENTURY

Kelly-Kate S. Pease

Webster University–St. Louis

Prentice
Hall

UPPER SADDLE RIVER, NEW JERSEY 07458

Library of Congress Cataloging-in-Publication Data

Pease, Kelly-Kate S.
  International organizations: perspectives on governance in the twenty-first century/Kelly-Kate S. Pease.—2nd ed.
    p. cm.
  Includes bibliographical references and index.
  ISBN 0-13-045427-3
    1. International agencies.   2. International organization.   3. Regionalism (International organization).   I. Title.

JZ4839 .P43 2003
341.2—dc21   2002075230

Senior acquisitions editor: Heather Shelstad
Associate editor: Brian Prybella
Editorial assistant: Jessica Drew
Marketing manager: Claire Bitting
Marketing assistant: Jennifer Bryant
Editorial/production supervision: Kari Callaghan Mazzola
Prepress and manufacturing buyer: Ben Smith
Electronic page makeup: Kari Callaghan Mazzola and John P. Mazzola
Interior design: John P. Mazzola
Cover director: Jayne Conte
Cover design: Bruce Kenselaar
Cover art: Keith Ballinger/Masterfile Corporation

This book was set in 10/12 New Baskerville by Big Sky Composition
and was printed and bound by Hamilton Printing Company.
The cover was printed by Coral Graphics.

Printed in the United States of America
10   9   8   7   6   5   4   3

ISBN 0-13-045427-3

Pearson Education LTD., London
Pearson Education Australia PTY, Limited, Sydney
Pearson Education Singapore, Pte. Ltd
Pearson Education North Asia Ltd, Hong Kong
Pearson Education Canada, Ltd., Toronto
Pearson Educación de Mexico, S.A. de C.V.
Pearson Education—Japan, Tokyo
Pearson Education Malaysia, Pte. Ltd
Pearson Education, Upper Saddle River, New Jersey

CONTENTS

CHAPTER 5
INTERNATIONAL SECURITY   97

CHAPTER 6
REGIONAL SECURITY   128

CHAPTER 7
TRADE   155

CHAPTER 8
DEVELOPMENT   177

CHAPTER 9
THE ENVIRONMENT   208

CHAPTER 10
SOCIAL AND HUMANITARIAN ISSUES   234

CHAPTER 11
GLOBAL GOVERNANCE IN 2075   261

APPENDICES

PREFACE

I WROTE THIS BOOK out of passion and frustration. International organizations are fascinating objects of study. They are almost organic entities—evolving, changing, adapting, even dying. However, many texts on international organizations tend to view the lives of international organizations through liberal lenses. Liberal lenses are not exactly rose-colored, but they are colored by the implicit assumption that international organizations are inherently "good" and that their "good" efforts are often thwarted by organizational weaknesses, world politics, or self-interested governments. Liberalism has contributed much to our understanding of global politics, but it has its blind spots. Examining international organizations solely from a liberal vantage does a disservice to the study of international organizations and to its development as a discipline. It unnecessarily narrows analysis; worse, it suggests that just one view of the world exists. The September 11, 2001, attacks on the United States and the response of the "international community" highlight the need to understand the world from different perspectives in order to understand and manage complicated problems. This text brings other theoretical perspectives to bear on the study of international organizations. It integrates international organizations with international-relations theory by showing how international organizations matter in the worlds of the realist, the Marxist, and the feminist, as well as the liberal.

Several people have contributed to the development of the second edition of this book. First, I thank the four reviewers who provided valuable insights and criticism: Timothy Nordstrom, University of Mississippi; Miriam Elman, Arizona State University; Lawrence LeBlanc, Marquette University; Ali R. Abootalebi, University of Wisconsin. I would also like to thank Bethany Keller, a graduate student in Webster University's International Relations Program, for her research on Indonesia. I thank my parents for their emotional support, and I would also like to acknowledge Webster University, which provided some financial assistance for research through its Faculty Research Grant Program.

Finally, I would like to dedicate this book to Casey, Kelsey, and Ryley Pease.

Kelly-Kate S. Pease

INTRODUCTION

A RENAISSANCE IS TAKING PLACE in the study of international organizations. International organizations like the United Nations (UN), the World Trade Organization (WTO), and the International Monetary Fund (IMF) are playing greater roles in the governance of the international and domestic affairs of many societies. Scholars, politicians, and citizens worldwide have renewed their interest in questions that address the nature and behavior of international organizations. Who created international organizations and why? Whose interests do these organizations serve? How do their activities affect individuals, groups, and societies? What is the future of international organizations in the twenty-first century? In this textbook we examine the theory and practice of international organizations, recognizing that international organizations are part of a complex web of relations that can have subnational, national, international, and transnational ties. To trace the patterns of this complex web, we employ four competing theoretical frameworks—realism, liberalism, Marxism, and feminism—as a means of approaching the subject. Technically speaking, a theory is a set of generalized principles that have descriptive, explanatory, and predictive value (Bennett 1995, 15). Thus, we can think of international relations theory as a way of systematizing and understanding world politics.

Theoretical frameworks are based on organizing assumptions that simplify the world and guide analysis. In many respects, theoretical approaches are quite similar to "world views" (sets of widely held beliefs): Both serve as mental maps, providing a guide as to how the world works. However, world views are more informal. They are clearly shaped by values, norms, and culture. Theoretical frameworks build upon world views, yet are more rigorous in that they become mechanisms for methodically generating hypotheses, explanations, and predictions about world politics.

Another way to think about theoretical frameworks is to envision them as a pair of glasses whose different lenses allow us to view the distinct political, economic, and social characteristics and processes that shape world politics. These lenses act as filters, directing attention toward (and away from) certain kinds of actors and focusing discussion on certain kinds of questions. Through these theoretical lenses, we see different reflections, different explanations regarding which actors—states, individuals, class, gender—should figure most prominently in our understanding of international relations. And these lenses guide our analysis, allowing us to examine particular kinds of international dynamics—anarchy, interdependence, capitalism, and patriarchy. Thus, our theoretical lenses, which reveal different patterns, also provide divergent interpretations regarding the nature and roles of international organizations in international politics. They also prescribe different strategies for solving international problems.

Theoretical frameworks allow us to organize and simplify such complex subjects as international relations in a systematic way. They also remind us that there are differing views about how the world works. Thus, former President George H. Bush (R) could see the UN as a pillar of a "new world order" while Senator Jesse Helms (R-NC) could insist, with equal confidence, that the same institution is a threat to the national security of the United States. Similarly, while the leaders of the world's nation-states meet to strengthen the WTO or IMF, mass protests (many of which have turned violent) have erupted around the world. Unfortunately, the development of theory is not a neat and tidy process. Scholars and practitioners do not always fit squarely into one framework, nor are the lines between theories clear and distinct. In fact, the lines are easily blurred, and this, in turn, increases complexity and contributes to conceptual confusion. But despite their formal shortcomings, theoretical frameworks are both necessary and useful. And such frameworks can help students understand the intricacies and diversity of today's international organizations.

Prior Studies of International Organizations: An Overview

What is an international organization? The history of international organizations as a field of study suggests no clear answer. The analytical shifts from "formal institutions" to "institutional processes" to "organizational roles" to "international regimes" have expanded the concept of international organization to include almost any type of patterned, repetitive behavior (Kratochwil and Ruggie 1986, 753–775; Rochester 1986, 777–813). Traditionally, international organizations have been conceived as formal institutions whose members are states. Such organizations are called intergovernmental organizations (IGOs) because the governments of nation-states voluntarily join, contribute financing, and make decisions within the organization. IGOs are easily identified because their purpose, structures, and decision-making procedures are clearly spelled out in a charter or treaty. Examples of IGOs include the UN, the North Atlantic Treaty Organization (NATO), the European Union (EU), and the League of Arab States (the Arab League).

All IGOs have governments as their formal members. IGOs can be further categorized by membership rules. IGOs can have universal membership whereby all states are allowed to join. For example, all states may become members of the United Nations, at least in principle. Chapter II, Article 4 (1) states that UN membership is open to all peace-loving states "which accept the obligations contained in the present Charter, and, in the judgment of the Organization, are able and willing to carry out these obligations." States seeking UN membership must petition the UN Security Council, which then makes a recommendation to the General Assembly. The General Assembly then makes the final decision. While membership decisions can be quite political, the UN has, for the most part, practiced an open-door policy.

IGOs may also have limited membership. Participation in IGOs is restricted by some objective criteria. The Arab League, for example, is a voluntary association of states whose people mainly speak Arabic. This association seeks to strengthen Arab ties and promote common political and economic goals. NATO, a security alliance, limits its membership, restricting it by a combination of specific political, geographic, and military considerations.

IGOs are also categorized by their purpose. IGOs can be multi- or general-purpose organizations, which means they can take up any international issue. An example of a general-purpose IGO is the Organization of African Unity (OAU). Founded in 1963 and consisting of fifty African states, the OAU was created to help with the decolonization of the African continent and to promote national self-determination. The OAU has addressed African security issues as well as economic and social development. The OAU has publicly and systematically challenged white, racist rule in the southern part of the continent. It has politically and diplomatically (and perhaps militarily) supported Black Nationalist movements and has organized economic and social policies that address human rights and migration/refugee issues. General-purpose IGOs, such as the OAU, consider a variety of international issues that affect their members.

IGOs can also have narrow mandates. Thus, they may focus on specific military, economic, or social issues. The Australian, New Zealand, and U.S. alliance (ANZUS), for example, is a narrow, tripartite security organization. Other examples include the International Labor Organization (ILO), which is charged with setting international labor standards, and the World Health Organization (WHO), which is responsible for addressing health issues ranging from child immunization to cholera outbreaks and AIDS. These specialized IGOs provide focused and expert analysis to very specific international issues.

Traditional studies of international organizations, especially during the first half of the twentieth century, tended to focus solely on the institutional framework and norms of IGOs in order to explain their roles and behavior in international relations. This legalistic and descriptive approach to IGOs has proved inadequate for understanding the behavior and function of international organizations. It fails to explain, for example, why the activities of IGOs do not usually square with their stated missions. Charters may detail goals, objectives, and procedures; yet the practices of international organizations can be quite different. For instance, the UN Charter charges the UN Security Council with maintaining international peace and security and countering aggressive war. But during the Cold War, the UN Security Council did little to fulfill that mission. In the 1960s, scholarly research shifted to trying to understand the institutional processes and the organizational roles of IGOs. Scholars sought to understand how the interests of states enhanced or interfered with the purposes of international organizations. Faced with the incongruence between the written purposes of international organizations and their practices, scholars were compelled to address the "politics" and the "economics" of international organizations.

At the same time, scholars also sought to explain why international organizations seemed to function well in nonpoliticized issues areas. These functionalist analyses showed that cooperation in the nonpolitical (economic and social) spheres could "spill over" into highly politicized areas such as security. Spillover is thought to foster the integration of societies into a single economic and political community (Mitrany 1948, 1966; Haas 1958, 1964). The focus on institutional processes and organizational roles showed the duality between the interests of states and the idea that IGOs could also become important actors in their own right, even though states were the principal members.

Since the 1980s, the study of international organizations has seen an explosion in analyses of international regimes. The study of international regimes concentrates on other types of international interactions that occur either in conjunction with, or independent of, IGOs. An international regime is defined as "sets of implicit or explicit principles, norms, rules and decision-making procedures around which actors' expectations converge in a given issue area" (Krasner 1983, 2). Regime analysis extends analysis to include other actors beyond states and IGOs, such as nongovernmental organizations (NGOs), multinational corporations (MNCs), and even individuals.

NGOs are essentially nonprofit, private organizations that engage in a variety of international activities. NGOs can be oriented toward a single issue or they can have a multipurpose agenda. NGOs participate in international politics by defining goals, providing information, and giving expert advice. They also pressure governments and IGOs through direct and indirect lobbying techniques. NGOs such as Amnesty International, Greenpeace, and the International Committee for the Red Cross are instrumental in setting international norms and executing international policy. While most NGOs receive some funding from governments, their activities can be autonomous and are often coordinated with IGOs. MNCs are for-profit firms that have subsidiaries in two or more countries. MNCs engage in transnational activities that involve the movement of goods and services across national boundaries. IGOs, NGOs, and MNCs are the kinds of international organizations that are examined extensively in regime analysis.

Regime analysis delves into the tangible principles and rules that are codified in charters, treaties, and international law. Informal principles, rules, norms, and decision-making procedures are also examined (presuming that they are identifiable) even though they are not spelled out in any formal sense. Regime analysis seeks to explain and model the complicated nature of international relations in which multiple actors engage in a variety of international and transnational activities. It seeks to understand the very complex web of international relations that invariably develop through some kind of international organization.

The analytical shifts that have occurred in international organizations as a field of study in no way suggest that one type of analysis is superior to another, nor do they suggest that earlier research on formal institutions is obsolete in the face of regime analyses. In fact, the complexity and imprecision of regime analysis have led many to view the entire endeavor as a passing fad or "intellectual chaos" (Rochester 1986, 800). To assume that the history of the discipline represents an evolution into a higher state of knowledge is misleading. Rather, traditional and contemporary research on international organizations represents the work of scholars from diverse theoretical backgrounds, backgrounds that shape their conception of international relations and the role of international organizations within those relations. The conceptual confusion surrounding what an international organization is stems from the differing theoretical orientations. Hence, international organizations are many things. International organizations are IGOs (like the UN), NGOs (like Greenpeace), and MNCs (like General Motors). International organizations are also institutions, processes, laws, and regimes that consist of state and nonstate actors.

ORGANIZATION OF THE TEXT

The central purpose of this text is to explore the nature, role, and behavior of international organizations in world politics. In order to achieve this purpose, international organizations are analyzed using four theoretical perspectives. No attempt is made to rank these theories in terms of importance; nor are their underlying assumptions challenged. Theoretical approaches are generally evaluated on the quality of their explanations, descriptions, and predictions, not on the accuracy of their assumptions (Lakatos 1970, 91–138). Individuals often end up talking past one another when theoretical orientation is ignored or essential assumptions are challenged. Students must determine for themselves the utility of a particular explanation while recognizing that one theoretical approach may be useful for analyzing one kind of organization or situation, but not another. Students are also cautioned against dismissing descriptions, explanations, and insights generated by a theoretical approach that is incongruent with their own world views.

Chapter 2 provides a nuts-and-bolts overview of three kinds of international organization: the IGO, the NGO, and the MNC. The structure and the principles of three IGOs—the UN, the EU, and the Organization of Islamic Conference (OIC)—are detailed. NGOs are examined generally in terms of their roles and functions. MNCs are analyzed in the context of their activities and goals. The purpose of Chapter 2 is mainly informative. It is designed to give the student an idea of the basic composition of certain IGOs and functions of NGOs and MNCs. International relations theories are used in subsequent chapters to interpret the activities of international organizations in world politics.

International organizations do not exist in a vacuum. They are part and parcel of the world's political landscape—a landscape in which scholars and observers disagree about the relative importance of certain actors and dynamics. As Wolff and Resnik (1987, 10) have argued, the differences between theories are not minor. Theoretical differences amount to profound disagreements as to how the world works and what ought to be changed. Differences about policy are differences about theory. The priorities and actions of international organizations cannot be adequately understood unless considerable attention is paid to the theories that provide meaning to their activities.

As a field of study, international organizations can be thought of as a well-shuffled deck of playing cards. In this text, we sort out the cards by suit or theoretical approach. Realism, liberalism, Marxism, and feminism—respectively described as spades, diamonds, clubs, and hearts—are used as mental maps that help make sense of contemporary relations and international organizations. Then we apply these theoretical approaches to substantive issue areas addressed by international organizations—security, economic relations, development, the environment, and human rights. Realism, liberalism, Marxism, and feminism posit different conceptions of states and of international organizations; therefore, they have different conceptions of international governance. Predictions regarding the nature of international governance in A.D. 2075 are offered to demonstrate that each of the theoretical approaches contributes to a more comprehensive understanding of the role of international organizations in international relations. As in solitaire, all of the suits are necessary in order to win the game.

SPADES: REALISM

Chapter 3 discusses realist theory, the oldest theoretical approach in international relations. Also known as statist, mercantilist, and nationalist theory, realism as a world view conceives of world politics as essentially conflictual. International relations center around sovereign nation-states seeking power and exercising power against each other. Nation-states exist in a hostile and dangerous world that forces them to be prepared for war and other forms of violent conflict. This general world view informs the realist theoretical framework, which is based on four assumptions. First, the state is the principal unit of analysis. While realists recognize that nonstate actors do exist, nonstate actors are not as important because, ultimately, they are responsible to the state or, at least, are vulnerable to state action. Relations between states are international relations for realists. Second, the state is a unitary and rational actor. The state behaves as if it were a single entity capable of engaging in a cost-benefit analysis when selecting courses of action or policy. While realists recognize that a nation-state consists of people, interest groups, branches of government, and bureaucratic agencies, the state ultimately speaks with one voice. Furthermore, the state is rational; that is, it seeks to survive and to maximize its national interest. This assumption allows realists to simplify analysis considerably by conceiving of states as if they were individuals making rational choices. Third, international relations are essentially conflictual relations. The darker side of human nature and the constant threat of a violent attack guarantee that the relations between states will be contentious. Fourth, international issues are divided between "high" and "low" politics. High politics include geostrategic and military issues while low politics involves economic and social issues. States seek power, control, and autonomy in order to maximize their security and national interests. Security issues dominate, and will continue to dominate, the international agenda and the agenda of all individual states. International economic issues are important only inasmuch as they relate to a state's relative power capabilities. Social and environmental issues are not nearly as important to states because they do not directly correlate with national security.

The concept of anarchy is critical to an understanding of the realist view of international relations. Anarchy is defined as the absence of a higher authority or world government. The international system is organized around sovereign states. Sovereignty means that the state, or its representatives (the government), has the final say within its territorial jurisdiction. This means that no higher authority exists in international relations than the state. This condition requires states to engage in "self-help" in order to secure their security and other national interests. International relations are essentially conflictual because states, each pursuing a particular self-interest, often collide with each other. This collision can very easily result in violence. With no world government, no referee exists to settle disputes or prevent war. States, therefore, must seek power because it is through power that states can maximize their interests and guarantee their security under the condition of anarchy.

The realists' emphasis on anarchy does not mean that they see the international system as chaos. On the contrary, they point to the distribution of capabilities, or the balance of power, as a source of order in the international system. While there is no higher authority in international relations other than the state, there is a hierarchy of power. Through this hierarchy of power, realists explain the creation of international organizations and their role in maintaining international order and cooperation. According to proponents of hegemonic stability theory, world order is established by a single, dominant power that creates and administers international organizations. These organizations serve the interests of the hegemon and legitimize its dominant position. The hegemon will maintain and support international organizations as long as the gains outweigh the costs. Other states join these organizations even though they serve the interests of the hegemon because the hegemon, through its power, is able to provide positive incentives and inducements. The hegemon also bears the costs of maintaining international organizations. International organizations, therefore, are created by and serve the interests of the dominant states. States will belong to and use international organizations if it is in their interest to do so. However, they will also ignore or even undermine them if that is in their self-interest.

Order and stability in international relations is based on a hegemon's power. As that power declines, so does the world order and the international organizations that provide the foundation. Hence, most realists are very pessimistic about the independent role of international organizations in fostering cooperation among sovereign states. Rather, it is the hegemon's power reflected in international organizations that facilitates international cooperation. Realists tend to view international organizations as extensions of the great powers or as great-power directorates. The interests and behavior of international organizations must be understood in the context of the interests of dominant states. Conceptually, international organizations are IGOs, which are no more than the sum of their member states. For realists, governance of international relations is a great-power concert facilitated by international organizations.

DIAMONDS: LIBERALISM

Chapter 3 also examines the liberal theoretical approach to international relations and international organizations. Liberalism is often associated with pluralism and neoclassical economic theory. As a world view, liberalism maintains a strong belief in the value of the individual, the idea of limited government, and the market. The liberal tradition in international relations, which grew out of a critique of realism, draws heavily upon the economic theory of Adam Smith and the political theory of John Locke. Liberals tend to be more optimistic about the prospects for cooperative relations between societies. They point out that much of international relations is based on the peaceful exchange of goods, services, and ideas among societies. While war is a major problem, it does not define international relations. International relations are also shaped by important economic and social transactions.

The liberal theoretical framework rests on several simplifying assumptions. First, liberals argue that nonstate actors, such as multinational corporations and international organizations, are also important actors in international relations. This is not to say that states are unimportant, only that other actors can exercise a significant amount of influence that may even equal that of states. Strictly speaking, most liberals see individuals as the most important unit of analysis because they make up households, firms, governments, societies, and international organizations. It should also be noted that some liberals take a state-centric approach to international relations and see the state as a unitary and rational actor.

Second, liberals see the state as a more fluid entity, an aggregation of competing individuals and interests within a society. Many of these interests have transnational ties that extend beyond a state's borders. The governments of states can also be composed of executive, legislative, judicial, and bureaucratic agents that have personal and sectoral interests. These domestic factors can influence the decision-making process as much as international considerations. Understanding the individuals and types of groups that compete for control of the government is necessary in order to understand how a state behaves in international relations, as is understanding the domestic political system that frames the competition. Rationality cannot necessarily be assumed, given that the different influences on the government can lead to suboptimal decisions.

The third assumption of the liberal approach is that international relations are a combination of cooperation and conflict. Human beings are self-interested, but they are also cooperative, economic creatures. The natural instincts of humans to "truck, barter, and trade" draw individuals together in a market. The market that generates wealth and prosperity also creates complex interdependence. The expanding global market brings societies together, connecting them through international trade and finance. Societies come to rely on each other for security and economic well-being, and that reliance provides incentives for actors to cooperate with each other. Even when conflict arises, complex interdependence reduces the likelihood of that conflict turning violent. To use military force against a society that provides you with investments, goods, and services is like shooting yourself in the foot. Complex interdependence promotes more peaceful relations between societies.

A fourth assumption of the liberal theoretical approach is that a variety of issues can dominate international politics. States seek a variety of goals other than security. They seek wealth, development, prosperity, and environmental health. Social and economic issues are also important when studying international relations because they are part and parcel of global society. In fact, they may even be the principal sources of international conflict in the twenty-first century.

Liberals see international organizations in one of two ways. Some see international organizations as the early institutions—precursors—of world government. That is, they are the foundations of a nascent "new world order." International organizations are evolving into supranational organizations that exercise authority and jurisdiction over nation-states. Others see international organizations as mechanisms that assist governments in overcoming collective-action problems and help them to settle conflicts and problems peacefully. International organizations are important in their own right, cooperating with governments and also acting independently. For liberals, international governance is based on the interaction of several kinds of actors—individuals, interest groups, government agencies, IGOs, NGOs, and MNCs—competing and working together to define and promote the "international collective good."

CLUBS: MARXISM

Chapter 4 is devoted to critical approaches to international relations and international organizations. Critical approaches challenge the "conventional wisdom" and provide alternative frameworks for understanding the world. The first critical approach examined in Chapter 4 is Marxism. The Marxist perspective is distinguished by its attention to modes of production (the manner in which goods and services are produced) and economic forces that shape international life. The Marxist approach is considered a "critical" theoretical approach because it systematically challenges the "mainstream" traditions of realism and liberalism while offering a different perspective regarding the dynamics of international relations. The Marxist approach emphasizes economic and political inequality in international relations, an inequality that leads to superior-subordinate relationships. Such relationships result in both violent and non-violent international conflict.

The first assumption of the Marxist approach is that capitalism as a mode of production is the defining feature of the international system. Capitalism is a way of producing goods that is based on four attributes—private property, profit motive, wage labor, and the market. Capitalists seek to maximize profits in a very competitive global market. That competition creates winners and losers and determines the position and behavior of actors in international affairs. The capitalist accumulation process and the exigencies of the market affect individuals and societies in ways that are not always positive or constructive.

The second assumption of the Marxist approach is that economic class is the principal unit of analysis. Class is defined by Marxists as a person's relationship to the means of production. Actors in international relations are distinguished by their role in the production of goods and services worldwide. Capitalism spawns two primary, yet unequal, classes: the bourgeoisie (owners of the means of production) and the proletariat (salaried and wage-earning workers). Class analysis includes these economic classes as well as economic classes of nation-states. Core states (advanced industrialized countries) provide capital and finance. Periphery states (Third World countries) provide cheap raw materials and unskilled labor. Semiperiphery states (newly industrializing countries) provide offshore sourcing and inexpensive skilled labor. The economic interaction of core, periphery, and semiperiphery results in the production of goods and services for global markets.

The third assumption of Marxism is that international relations is essentially conflictual because capitalism is based on exploitation. Capitalists seek to exploit resources, markets, and labor in order to maximize profits. In other words, capitalism exploits people and breeds social, political, and economic inequality. The nature of economic relations is essentially a zero-sum game in which one player wins while someone else loses. The core exploits the periphery and the semiperiphery, benefiting at their expense. Hence, international relations are conflictual, divided between rich and poor. The division between rich and poor exists both between nations and within societies. In a global context, the experience of most of the world's population with capitalism is one of violence and poverty.

The fourth assumption of the Marxist approach to international relations is that economic factors are most important for understanding both domestic and international politics. Governments are reflections of the dominant economic class and this dominant class formalizes its interests as the interests of society as a whole. Wars and other forms of violent conflict are rooted in class exploitation and issues that seem to be geostrategic are really economic in nature. Economic factors must be addressed in order to understand the dynamics of contemporary international affairs. In other words, if you want to understand the nature of contemporary international conflict, you have to understand the nature of contemporary capitalism.

For Marxists, the nature of international organizations is determined by the underlying economic order. Contemporary international organizations reflect, legitimize, and promote global capitalism. International financial institutions, such as the World Bank and the IMF, are mechanisms of capitalist domination. They pry open markets, forcing privatization and encouraging foreign investment. MNCs entangle societies in a malignant web of dependency that causes underdevelopment and a gross maldistribution of wealth within and between societies. International organizations and law further the interests of capitalists, particularly capital that is transnational rather than national in nature. Capitalism expands under the guise of promoting global economic and social welfare.

HEARTS: FEMINISM

Chapter 4 also presents the feminist theoretical approach. This approach examines international relations and international organizations through the lens of gender. Like Marxism, the feminist perspective is a critical approach; it challenges conventional understandings by examining world politics in terms of how it affects women and how gender-biases influence contemporary international relations theory. Feminists seek to understand what it means to be "feminine," both in theory and practice of international organizations. That is, the feminist approach examines the status, roles, and contributions of women in international organizations and seeks to understand how the actions and policies of international organizations affect women. Feminist analyses also highlight the gender-bias of the realist, liberal, and Marxist perspectives.

The feminist theoretical approach is organized around four interrelated assumptions. First, gender matters. Conventional scholarship regarding international relations and organizations either minimizes gender or assumes universality. Feminists argue that contemporary explanations are inadequate because the experiences of women in war, politics, markets, and class are not addressed. With gender as the principal unit of analysis, new insights into world politics become possible. Gender is not simply the sex of an individual. Gender is associated with social expectations about what it means to be masculine and feminine.

Second, international relations are conflictual. Conflict results from the superior-subordinate nature of gender relationships. Biology may account for many differences between men and women, but whether "masculine" and "feminine" differences are considered superior or inferior is socially constructed. This assumption extends the analysis of international conflict to women in order to understand how their experiences differ from that of men. It also allows scholars to examine exploitation that extends beyond the market or economic class.

Third, patriarchy is the main feature of the international system. Patriarchy means "male dominance." Most of the edifices of international relations (states, international organizations, firms) are either masculinist in nature or they are dominated by men. Feminists argue that ignoring this feature narrows analysis to principally masculine issues that are the domain of men. Also, scholars implicitly assume universality when they ignore gender, thereby making masculine issues, traits, and behavior universal.

Fourth, the hierarchy of contemporary international issues is ordered on the basis of masculine preferences, marginalizing many "feminine" issues. The priorities of governments, heads of states, decision makers, ambassadors, and senior-level bureaucrats of organizations such as the UN and WTO are masculine, not because they are evil men, but because they conceptualize and understand the world in a masculine way. Those who attempt to address feminine issues or consider feminine approaches are faced with the unfortunate reality that feminine attributes and issues are of a lower status and are even the subject of ridicule.

These interrelated assumptions provide an alternative framework for systematically criticizing realism, liberalism, and Marxism, and offer an alternative lens for viewing international relations and international organizations. The feminist theoretical approach brings the issue of gender to the study of international organizations by highlighting and evaluating the role of women in international organizations. This kind of gendered analysis examines the employment practices of international organizations to see what kinds of positions women occupy and to assess the status of those positions. Feminist scholarship emphasizes the exclusion of women from important decision-making positions and also seeks to value the contributions of women in their traditional gender roles as caregivers, nurturers, and supporters.

The feminist approach also explores NGOs in considerable detail because they are, arguably, more "feminine" in nature and empower women to take more control over their lives. NGOs tend to be more horizontally structured, and they often work with IGOs to provide aid and relief to the "victims of world politics." NGOs challenge traditional (masculine) approaches to international problems by focusing on grassroots and community-level efforts to ameliorate poverty and check human rights violations. Traditional analyses of international organizations mention NGOs but rarely detail their activities because their bias is toward the more hierarchically structured IGOs. The activities of NGOs are trivialized as a result.

Realism, liberalism, Marxism, and feminism provide different ways of understanding international organizations in terms of their nature and the role they play in world politics. Table 1.1 (on page 12) summarizes the different approaches in terms of their key theoretical features.

THE GAME

This text also examines international organizations in practice. Chapters 5 through 9 are organized around three sections. The first section introduces the international issue and provides a brief overview of some of the relevant international organizations in terms of their charters, operations, and mandates. The second part outlines the relevant facts of a case study. The third section then examines case studies using the different theoretical approaches. Borrowing from Graham Allison's (1971) classic case study of the Cuban Missile Crisis, *The Essence of Decision*, international events are examined using the different theoretical perspectives to guide the analysis. This technique provides the student with multiple and often competing interpretations of the same event. This method yields improved explanations regarding the nature, behavior, and role of international organizations in world politics.

Chapter 5 examines the issue of international security and the role of the UN Security Council. The history of the UN Security Council and its role in collective security are analyzed in the context of the Cold War while the structure and decision-making procedures of the Security Council are detailed. Chapter 5 also explains why the Cold War paralyzed the Security Council, but shows, as well, how the UN adapted to that paralysis by developing peacekeeping as an alternative to collective security. The immediate post–Cold War era is addressed in terms of the case study of the Persian Gulf War, a crisis precipitated by Iraq's invasion of Kuwait in 1990. The case study is presented in terms of the chronology of events and the international community's response to the crisis.

TABLE 1.1   COMPARISON OF THEORETICAL APPROACHES

	REALISM	LIBERALISM	MARXISM	FEMINISM
Unit(s) of analysis	States	Individuals, groups, and states	Economic class or economic classes of states	Gender
Nature of international relations	Conflict	Cooperation and conflict	Conflict	Cooperation and conflict
Principal feature(s) of international system	Anarchy and balance of power	Complex inter-dependence	World capitalism	Patriarchy
Nature of international organizations	Principally IGOs; extensions of great-power interests	Regimes; mechanism for collective action and international problem-solving	IGOs, MNCs, TNEs; reflections of the underlying economic order	Varied: IGOs are patriarchal; NGOs are more horizontally structured
Behavior of international organizations	Nonautonomous; determined by great-power interests and the underlying distribution of capabilities	Foster cooperative relations among states and nonstate actors; autonomous	Promote and reinforce capitalist production; tools of capitalist domination	Varied; reinforce and challenge patriarchy

The UN Security Council's response to the Persian Gulf crisis is interpreted using the different theoretical approaches in the first case study. Realists tend to interpret the UN action as a mask or tool for United States or great-power intervention. Key strategic interests were at risk, namely oil and oil access, which compelled the United States and its allies to act. Had this land grab occurred where no great-power interests were at stake, the action would not have elicited such a global response.

The liberal interpretation is that finally, for the first time in its forty-five-year history, the UN Security Council performed as it was intended to. The Security Council was an important instrument for collective action. It signaled the start of a New World Order where the rule of international law would prevail and aggression would not be tolerated. The UN provided a very important mechanism that helped egoist states overcome collective-action problems and counter international aggression. It demonstrated that competitive states can find common interests and act collectively, absent serious ideological differences.

Marxists highlight the role of economics and the role of economic class in shaping international organization and international politics. The Persian Gulf War accents the differences between rich and poor not only between North and South, but also between small oil sheikdoms and large Arab states. It illustrates how the concept of neoimperialism shaped the international debate as to how to counter Iraq's aggression. Marxists argued that the exploitation of wealth, labor, and value by the United States and its friends in the Middle East was a direct cause of the war. The West has never understood or respected the position of states in the Middle East. The West has historically relied upon its privilege and its control to promote its interests at the expense of most Arabs. The gall and the brutality of Saddam Hussein were not so much in question. After all, the United States has supported President Marcos of the Philippines, the Shah of Iran, "Papa Doc" Duvalier of Haiti, and President Pinochet of Chile. The crimes of these leaders rival, or pale in comparison to, the crimes of Saddam Hussein. Saddam Hussein's crime was to overtly attack the West's puppet, threatening the resource that sustains capitalism and the West's entire way of life.

The feminist interpretation of the Persian Gulf War criticizes the realist, liberal, and Marxist interpretations of the world and examines the impact of the war on women. Feminists argue that women are virtually excluded from the decision-making process of states and of international organizations. They argue that the policies that emanate from international organizations, particularly IGOs, ignore or dismiss policy impacts on women. They also point out that collective security is carried out against those who are too weak to defend themselves.

The second case study of the chapter examines the UN actions in Srebrenica, a small city in Eastern Bosnia that was the site of Europe's worst massacre since World War II. This case study explains the UN engagement in the former Yugoslavia. The theoretical approaches are then applied to explain why the UN behaved in the manner it did in Bosnia. The realist approach highlights the unwillingness of the United States to get involved in the conflict and Europe's inability to generate a common foreign policy. It also points out that military capability is the final arbiter of disputes, whether it be Serb military capability in Bosnia or U.S. capability in Kosovo.

The liberal approach shows that while the UN was incapable of preventing the massacre, it was able to alleviate the suffering of many in the Balkans. The UN's shortcomings must be analyzed and addressed; however, they should not detract from the good the UN has done to help all the ethnic groups in the Balkans. The UN is learning from its mistakes and even if it cannot prevent all atrocities, it at least attempts to counter them in both traditional and innovative ways.

Marxists show how the UN biases against non-Western issues influence its decision making. Most of the Bosnian victims were Muslim. This, coupled with Europe's historic suspiciousness of Islam, contributed to the paralysis of the UN. The eventual salvation of the Bosnian Muslims was not the result of UN concern with their plight. Rather, their persecution and murder took place in Europe, which threatened to destabilize the rest of Europe. This is what prompted UN protection efforts, such as they were. The feminist perspective shows the unique role of women in the aftermath of a crisis and their willingness to challenge the status quo of the UN. It shows how violence affects women differently and also shows how violence against men and women is treated differently by the UN system.

Chapter 6 examines the issues of regional security and the nature of military alliances. It details post–World War II regional security arrangements such as the Warsaw Pact, ANZUS, and NATO. Special emphasis is placed on NATO history and structure as the case study examines issues and controversies surrounding NATO expansion. Realists tend to see NATO expansion as weakening the credibility of the alliance. They question the wisdom of extending solemn security guarantees to countries that most people cannot locate on a map. Realists also worry that NATO might become a collective security arrangement, prone to the same political problems faced by the UN Security Council. Liberals, on the other hand, argue that NATO can help stabilize Central Europe politically and economically. The fledgling democracies of Central Europe are part of Europe and should be part of European institutions. NATO is a military alliance, but it is also a political institution that has denationalized the defense policies of Western Europe and fostered economic and political integration. NATO expansion projects the stability and prosperity of Western Europe eastward. Marxists see NATO expansion as an effort on the part of the West to stabilize markets and guarantee the capital investments. NATO is a tool for political and economic intervention by the West, enabling Germany to conduct an aggressive foreign policy and to extend its influence in the former Eastern Bloc states under a multilateral cloak. NATO was created to threaten and contain Russia, and the end of the Cold War has done nothing to change that central mission. NATO expansion is provocative and threatens to bring about another Cold War in Europe. In contrast, feminists favor a multilateral alliance over unilateral security. Yet they remain concerned about the status of women in NATO and the impact of NATO expansion on host communities. The feminist lens focuses on the superior-subordinate relationship within any alliance as well as the effects of NATO on the lives of women.

The second case study examines the Arab League and its impact on the Middle East crisis. It details the role of the Arab League with the Palestinian Uprising in 2000. Realism shows how the power politics of the region, specifically the relationship of the United States to Israel, Egypt, Jordan, and Saudi Arabia, are determinative of Arab League action. The liberal approach shows how the competing interests in the region are balanced in the international arena. Liberalism also shows how nonliberal values can contribute to the conflict, rather than resolve it. The Arab League's clear and unwavering bias against Israel makes it an unsuitable candidate as a major player in the peace process.

The Marxist approach emphasizes how the legacy of colonialism continues to exacerbate the tension in the Middle East. It shows that the history of colonial domination is still fresh in the minds of the indigenous peoples and shows why they suspect UN solutions. The Marxist approach also illustrates how the elites in oil-rich Arab states are bought off by their former and their neocolonial benefactors. The feminist world view questions the virtual domination of men in the Arab League and whether they can reach a lasting peace without the inclusion of women. While Arab and Israeli women participate through NGOs, their voices are muted in IGOs such as the Arab League and the United Nations.

Chapter 7 examines international trade in terms of the origins and principles of the post–World War II trading order. It details the General Agreement on Trade and Tariffs (GATT), the failure of the International Trade Organization (ITO), and the creation and structure of the World Trade Organization (WTO). This chapter places special emphasis on the impediments to free trade, including tariff and nontariff barriers. The case studies explore the U.S. Clean Air Act and genetically modified foods as they relate to international trade. The WTO ruling that declared certain provisions of the U.S. Clean Air Act as impermissible barriers to free trade is examined in detail. Many realists see the ruling as a clear violation of U.S. sovereignty, although in this particular instance the ruling is actually good for the United States because it gives the United States additional sources of gasoline. Realists point out that the WTO ruling undermines national industries because they have to meet higher environmental standards than their foreign competitors. Liberals saw the decision as a victory for free trade and praised the WTO for rooting out sophisticated forms of protectionism. The

WTO is an example of how technical experts can assist states in achieving free trade and promoting market efficiency.

Marxists see the WTO as guided by neoclassical economic thought. This ideology favors transnational capital at the expense of national interests because it employs market solutions and reforms to address economic, political, and social issues. Unfortunately, the WTO undermines the bargaining power of labor and marginalizes the environment. States are forced to reduce their labor and environmental standards in order to compete internationally, and efforts to protect labor or the environment are interpreted as unfair barriers to international trade. Profits and quarterly returns are favored at the expense of everything else. Feminists contribute to an understanding of the ruling by accentuating the masculine bias of the realist, liberal, and Marxist views of the WTO. Feminists take a more general approach to the ruling by analyzing the impact of free trade on women. The reorganization of economies toward export-oriented industries displaces women and undermines their livelihoods.

Trade in genetically modified foods and organisms has become a contentious international issue and serves as the second case study of Chapter 7. Realism explains why food security is so important to states and why genetically modified foods are distrusted. The United States, through its MNCs, could come to control the world's food supply, which would give it enormous leverage in bargaining situations. Some realists question whether genetically modified foods are even safe for human consumption. Liberals spotlight the role of technological innovation. Genetically modified foods can help feed the world, increase crop yields, and enhance nutrition. International organizations can help assess the safety and the efficacy of genetically modified foods. Marxist approaches are critical of the scientific process. The ability of MNCs to influence scientific studies and independent NGOs through their financial backing raises serious questions regarding the validity of the science that says that genetically modified foods are safe. Marxist approaches show how MNCs are able to interlock farmers in the developing world in a web of technology that forces them to purchase from MNCs in the future in order to survive. The feminist approach casts the debate in gendered terms. Feminists question the willingness of international organizations to really inquire into the safety of genetically modified foods. They also see the resistance of the industry to labeling such food as effectively disenfranchising women (who do the shopping) of their right to make consumer choices.

Chapter 8 examines the issue of economic development. The controversies surrounding the nature and efficacy of development are detailed in terms of orthodox and critical perspectives. The international organizations that are involved in economic development are discussed at length. These include IGOs like the World Bank, the IMF, the UN Development Program (UNDP), and the UN Conference on Trade and Development (UNCTAD). The Mexican Peso Crisis and the Indonesian economic collapse serve as the chapter's case studies. The crises are analyzed using the different theoretical approaches to interpret the cause of the crises and the response of the IMF.

Realists see the Mexican Peso Crisis as the result of irrational state policies on the part of Mexico and the United States. The economic policies of Mexico are irrational because the government allowed the market to determine the value of the peso, causing its value to plummet as foreign investors panicked. U.S. policy was irrational because officials had unwisely tied the dollar and U.S. economic health to Mexico through the North American Free Trade Agreement (NAFTA). The IMF intervention and structural adjustment programs place extensive burdens on Mexico and have allowed for direct U.S. control of Mexico's oil profits. Liberals, on the other hand, place responsibility for the peso debacle squarely at the feet of Mexican officials. Their corrupt and questionable policies contributed to economic instability. The artificially high peso skewed investments and caused a favorable, but unsustainable investment environment. The market reforms required by the IMF as the condition for assistance are in the long-term interest of the Mexican economy.

Marxists argue that the IMF conditions are favorable to capitalists seeking access to the Mexican market. The IMF action also amounts to a bailout of capitalists and investors who made risky and speculative choices. The mobility of capital and its abandonment of the Mexican economy show the true power of transnational capitalists. The structural adjustment programs of the IMF amount to passing the cost of financial instability onto the working class while capitalists get unprecedented access to Mexican assets. Feminists point out that the IMF policies have more severe effects on women. Once again, women are excluded from high-level decision making and they bear the brunt of policies in which they have no voice. The chapter concludes with a brief discussion of the ongoing Southeast Asian currency crisis.

Similarly, the Indonesian crisis illustrates the effects of different actors and influences on international organizations. Realism suggests that the geopolitical position of Indonesia had changed and, as a result, the choices of Indonesia were limited. During the Cold War, the IMF and the World Bank treated Indonesia with "kid gloves" because it was a strategic partner of the West during the Cold War. After the Cold War, the United States was less tolerant of the Indonesian kleptocracy and its corrupt practices. When the crisis began in Thailand and then spread throughout the Southeast Asian region, the Indonesian government made poor choices that made it vulnerable to the IMF and its controlling shareholders. The liberal approach shows how the IMF helped avert a deeper crisis and obtain the necessary reforms for a full Indonesian recovery. While painful, the IMF-mandated market reforms will stimulate economic growth and create jobs for Indonesians in the long run.

Marxist approaches question who actually suffers and benefits from IMF reforms in Indonesia. The banks and investors are bailed out while working people pay for these bailouts with their tax dollars. The IMF creates the conditions that allow Indonesian assets to be sold to foreign MNCs at bargain-basement prices. Feminist critiques of the IMF in Mexico are also applicable to the Indonesian crisis. In addition, they add that the IMF has never made the equal treatment of women in the workplace a condition of their loans. The ideological bias of the IMF sees market reforms as the key to the liberation of women and not the cause of their plight.

Chapter 9 addresses the environment. Specifically, it examines the problems of environmental degradation and economic development. The chapter reviews the role of the UN and NGOs in promoting conferences to manage the Earth's resources, protect the environment, and achieve sustainable development. The case study centers on the Global Warming Treaty negotiated in Kyoto, Japan. The causes of global warming are addressed and possible solutions are investigated. Realists are not very optimistic about international cooperation to curb global warming. The causes of global warming go right to the heart of economic development and the West's way of life. The only way an agreement might be reached is through the lowest-common-denominator approach. Any agreement made in this manner is weak and ineffective.

Liberals argue that a flawed agreement is better than none and environmental governance without government is possible. Liberals also stress that the market can provide innovative solutions to environmental problems. Marxists stress the incongruence between capitalism and the environment. The global economy is based on the burning of fossil fuels, and industries are not going to change just because the atmosphere is a few degrees warmer. Efforts to arrest global warming are efforts on the part of the advanced industrialized countries to pass the costs of their capitalist development onto the poorer, developing world. Feminists accent the roles of women as environmental managers and reproducers of the human population. Any effort to curb global warming must address the issue of population growth and consumption patterns. A split between feminists of liberal and socialist bents is evident. Liberal feminists argue for market solutions to global warming and do not see authoritative curbs on consumption as the solution to global warming. Socialist feminists charge that the liberal feminists ignore the environmental harm caused by capitalist development. All of the theoretical approaches recognize that any international agreement regarding the causes and the effects of global warming is difficult to achieve.

The International Whaling Commission and the issue of whaling is the second case study of Chapter 8. The case study examines whaling as a commercial enterprise and an environmental issue. The realist approach points out that whaling is a very low priority of states; however, it is fundamental to the national identity of some states. In order to understand the International Whaling Commission, one must study the relationship between powerful conservationist states and whaling states. The liberal approach shows how the International Whaling Commission is able to balance the interests of conservationists and whalers by promoting the voluntary cooperation of members. The liberal approach also shows how the International Whaling Commission as a scientific body has been able to save the whale populations. The Marxist approach suggests that as long as there is a market for whale products, the International Whaling Commission will be unable to protect the whales, as whalers have a rational self-interest in continuing the hunt. The feminist approach emphasizes that whaling is almost exclusively a masculine pursuit. The International Whaling Commission and the whaling industry are controlled by men. Women, on the other hand, are at the forefront of NGO efforts to save the whales.

Chapter 10 focuses on social and humanitarian issues. It examines refugee and human rights. The Office of the United Nations High Commissioner for Refugees is examined in terms of its mandate and role in refugee crises. The chapter also details international efforts to promote and protect human rights. It defines what human rights are and reviews the major human rights agreements and organizations. Special attention is paid to the UN High Commissioner for Human Rights and NGOs that are actively involved in human rights issues. The first case study examines the UN response to the genocide in Rwanda. Realism explains that genocide will go unchallenged if it occurs in an area where the great powers have no important national interests. Liberalism shows that even though mistakes were made, the UN took responsibility for its inaction and documented the horror for future generations. Marxism focuses on how Belgian colonial policy created a rigid class system, based on racial superiority, that contributed to the genocide. The feminist approach focuses on the role of women in the genocide. Liberal feminism explains that both men and women are capable of horrific violence and women played an active, direct role in committing genocide.

The second case study concentrates on the Yugoslav War Crimes Tribunal and the efforts of the international community to enforce human rights in Bosnia-Herzegovina. Realists criticize the creation of war crimes courts as a violation of sovereignty and as a bad idea, pointing out that only the vanquished are prosecuted and other, more immediate interests take precedence over morality and justice. Liberals stress the moral interdependence of gross violations of human rights, arguing that the international community has every right to insist upon good governance. They emphasize that other principles challenge state sovereignty, and that sovereignty as a principle is no longer sacrosanct.

Marxists counter that human rights have given the capitalist powers the excuse to intervene in the internal affairs of developing states. The war crimes tribunal is another mechanism of domination that holds weak states accountable to strong ones. Marxists note that the West is not interested in ensuring that economic, social, cultural, and collective rights are enforced; nor do they seem particularly interested in arresting indicted war criminals in Bosnia. Feminists argue that one of the few good things to emerge from the Bosnian crisis is international recognition that rape is a war crime and a clear violation of the human rights of women. Violence against women during peace and war has long been ignored by the international community. The human rights of women have taken a backseat to the rights of men for too long.

Chapter 11 describes the nature of international governance in the year 2075. The theoretical approaches are used to make projections regarding the nature of governance late in the twenty-first century. Multiple futures are predicted regarding the status of states and international organizations. More important, all of the theoretical approaches have something to say about the quality of life for human beings now and in the future.

This text combines international relations theory with the study of international organization in order to provide a comprehensive explanation of the nature of international governance. Currently, more than 185 nation-states and self-governing territories exist on the planet. The human population is more than five billion people. The complexity of contemporary world problems and their elusive solutions are the result, at least in part, of competing world views about how the world operates. The first step in addressing this dilemma is to understand and explore world views other than one's own. To help students in the exploration, this text integrates foreign media reaction to the activities of international organizations. The U.S. Information Agency provides a digest of the editorial and op-ed reactions from the world's major newspaper, magazines, and broadcast media. Looking at an issue from a different perspective or world view creates an expanded knowledge base and assists in resolving disputes in a fashion that is acceptable to all parties involved. The international media reactions show how the paradigmatic cuts are manifested in real-life situations.

INTERNATIONAL ORGANIZATIONS:
NUTS AND BOLTS

A VARIETY OF DIFFERENT INTERNATIONAL ORGANIZATIONS actively participate in contemporary world politics. This chapter has a dual purpose. First, it details several major intergovernmental organizations (IGOs) in terms of their structures and functions. These IGOs were selected on the basis of their significance to world and regional politics and their geopolitical orientation. Although other IGOs are discussed in later chapters, the purpose here is to provide an abbreviated overview of some of the IGOs central to international relations.

Second, this chapter examines nongovernmental organizations (NGOs) and multinational corporations (MNCs) in terms of their broad, general characteristics. These kinds of international organizations number in the tens of thousands, so an extended classification scheme is presented in order to sort them out in a meaningful fashion. It is important to recognize that, while international organizations do not exist in a political vacuum, sometimes "the devil is in the details." That is, the structures and procedures of international organizations can, and often do, affect international political outcomes.

INTERGOVERNMENTAL ORGANIZATIONS

HISTORICAL ANTECEDENTS

The idea of international organization has probably been around since the advent of the first governments. From the writings of ancient Greek philosophers, for example, we learn of military alliances and international trading agreements. And we know that the early Greek city-states Athens, Sparta, and Macedonia once employed a common currency, which required a high degree of international cooperation. Most contemporary scholars, however, point to the Congress of Vienna (1815–1822) as the earliest modern precedent to today's IGO. The Congress of Vienna, a multipurpose IGO, was created by the European great powers to reestablish order and stability on the continent after the Napoleonic Wars. The Congress of Vienna was a forum for international collaboration on European security and commerce. It also strengthened the Rhine

River Commission (1804), a bilateral IGO between France and the German confederation. This Commission established navigation rules for the Rhine River and an adjudication board to prosecute individuals accused of violating those rules. Similar river commissions were subsequently created for the Danube and Elbe rivers in central and eastern Europe.

The next important IGO to emerge was the League of Nations (1919–1939), which was established after World War I. The League of Nations was the first twentieth-century multipurpose IGO to have universal membership. The League was organized around three bodies: the Council, the Assembly, and the Secretariat. The Council was the chief executive organ of the League. It consisted of the victors of World War I, together with any four lesser powers that they chose to invite. The Council was mainly responsible for addressing issues relating to international war and threats to international peace. In addition, according to the League's Charter, the Council could "deal at its meetings with any matter within the sphere of action of the League" (Article 4, Section 4). The Assembly functioned as a quasi-legislative body; it, too, was entitled to address any matter within the purview of the League. All members of the League of Nations belonged to the Assembly, and each member could have up to three representatives. The Secretariat served as the League bureaucracy, which was responsible for carrying out League policies and mandates.

In addition to the League's three principal organs, several autonomous and semi-autonomous organizations were established under the League Charter. The Permanent Court of International Justice and the International Labor Organization were created to help member states meet their obligations under the League Charter. Article 13 committed members to submit any matter unsolved by diplomacy to international arbitration or judicial settlement. The Permanent Court of International Justice was established to consider disputes that might arise regarding treaty interpretation or breaches of international obligations assumed under international law. The International Labor Organization (ILO) was created, in part, to help member states meet their social responsibilities. Article 23(a) stated that members of the League "will endeavor to secure and maintain fair and humane conditions of labor for men, women and children, both in their own countries and in all countries to which their commercial and industrial relations extend, and for that purpose will establish and maintain the necessary international organizations." The ILO, one of the few surviving League institutions, remains the central IGO responsible for setting and preserving international labor standards.

The League of Nations, although widely considered a failed experiment, was based on three important principles, which have since been incorporated by its successor, the United Nations. First, the League of Nations embraced the idea of collective security where international security is directly tied to the security of member states. Second, the League established as a norm the peaceful settlement of disputes through such nonviolent measures as mediation, negotiation, arbitration, and adjudication. Third, the League was founded to foster international cooperation in the economic and social realms. The ideals of the League were both novel and innovative. They were also heavily influenced by American values, as one of its principal architects was President Woodrow Wilson. Ultimately, however, the U.S. government chose not to join the organization—a decision that is widely considered to have compromised the League's effectiveness during the interwar period. The League was politically challenged by the

Japan–China conflict in Manchuria (1931) and the Italy–Ethiopia conflict (1935). The outbreak of World War II spelled the demise of the League as a viable international organization. However, its legacy lives on.

The post–World War II era has witnessed a massive proliferation of IGOs, as well as other types of international organizations. Active IGOs now number well over 20,000, while nongovernmental organizations (NGOs) number more than 100,000 (Runyan 1999, 12). In the following section, we outline three representative IGOs, organizations that feature prominently in contemporary world and regional politics—the UN, the EU, and the Organization of Islamic Conference (OIC).

THE UN SYSTEM

The UN system was created in 1945 following World War II. The founders of the United Nations sought to strengthen the idea of the multipurpose, universal IGO first envisioned by the League of Nations. The UN was designed to be the center of multilateral diplomacy in postwar world politics. Its central purpose is manifold: to maintain international peace and security; to develop friendly relations among nations; to address economic, social, cultural, and humanitarian problems; and to promote respect for universal human rights. The UN retains the age-old principle of the sovereign equality of all states; however, it also commits members to the non-use of force and the peaceful settlement of disputes.

The UN is a comprehensive IGO to which, effectively, any state can belong. The UN system is structured around six principal organs—the General Assembly, the Security Council, the International Court of Justice (ICJ), the Economic and Social Council (ECOSOC), the Secretariat, and the Trusteeship Council. These organs serve as an umbrella to other UN agencies and autonomous bodies (see Figure 2.1 on page 22). The six principal organs of the UN, together with its several agencies and autonomous organizations, comprise the UN family of IGOs; collectively, they address just about every conceivable global issue, including war, civil disorder, arms control, trade, development, the environment, and human rights.

The General Assembly   The UN General Assembly serves as a quasi-legislative, deliberative body. Its principal, de jure functions are assigned by the UN Charter (Chapter IV) and are fivefold. First, the General Assembly may deliberate and consider any issue or questions that may arise under the Charter. While its resolutions are nonbinding, the General Assembly may address issues that relate to international peace, security, and disarmament, and it may bring to the attention of the Security Council any matter that may cause a breach of the peace. Second, the General Assembly is responsible for initiating studies and making recommendations for promoting political cooperation and the progressive development of international law. Third, the General Assembly is responsible for promoting international cooperation in the economic, social, cultural, educational, and health fields. Fourth, the General Assembly is charged with drafting and approving the UN budget. And fifth, it oversees the UN bureaucracy.

The General Assembly is based on the liberal democratic principles of political equality and majority rule. It is a plenary body, meaning that all member states may attend and fully participate in General Assembly meetings. Originally, the General Assembly consisted of 51 nation-states. Today, 189 states are represented. Decisions are

PRINCIPAL ORGANS OF THE UNITED NATIONS

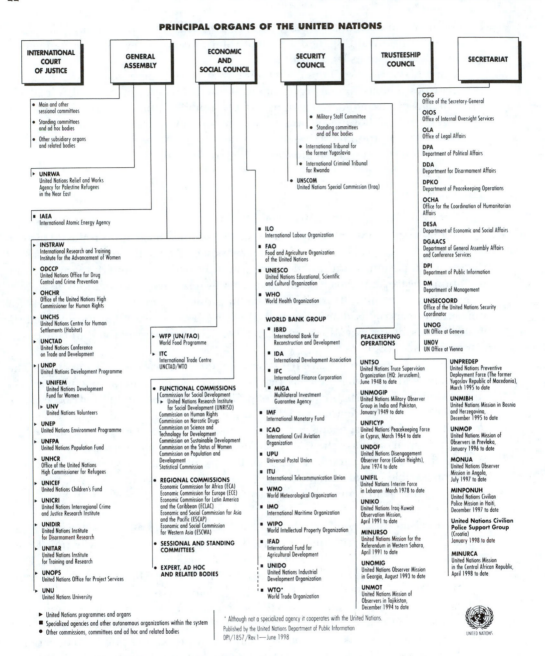

FIGURE 2.1   THE UNITED NATIONS SYSTEM

Source: Courtesy of the UN Publications Office.

made on a one-state/one-vote basis, with a simple majority deciding most issues. A qualified majority of two-thirds is required for important questions, such as recommendations made with respect to the maintenance of international peace and security or the election of the nonpermanent members of the Security Council. The General

Assembly operates much like a congress or parliament, although the General Assembly does not produce binding law. Rather, General Assembly resolutions function as an expression of general legal principles, often forming the basis of the "hard" international law, which is created through treaties. The General Assembly, through its activities and its resolutions, best approximates the priorities and sentiments of the "international community."

The Security Council   The UN Security Council (discussed in more detail in Chapter 5) is the organ whose primary responsibility is maintaining international peace and security. This task is quite complicated because it involves identifying threats to international peace and security, crafting an appropriate international response, building international consensus, and carrying out collective security actions. Unlike General Assembly resolutions, Security Council decisions are binding on member states, and members are obligated to abide by and help carry out these decisions. It should be noted that not all Security Council resolutions are binding, only those in which a formal "decision" is issued.

The Security Council has limited membership. It is composed of both permanent and nonpermanent, elective members, and is headed by a president, an office that rotates among all the members. The permanent members include the five great-power victors of World War II while the ten elected members are selected from and by the General Assembly. Each of the Security Council's permanent members possesses an absolute veto over substantive Security Council decisions. This veto allows one member to kill Security Council actions (excluding procedural questions), and it cannot be overridden. Absent a veto, Security Council resolutions are passed by an affirmative vote of nine members.

The International Court of Justice   The International Court of Justice (ICJ), also known as the World Court, was created to be the principal judicial organ of the UN. Incorporating much of the Statute of the League's Permanent Court of International Justice, the ICJ has semiautonomous status within the UN family. Chapter XIV of the UN Charter authorizes the ICJ to adjudicate disputes arising under the Charter and international law. It is also responsible for providing advisory opinions on legal questions to the Security Council or the General Assembly, upon their request. Other agencies of the UN, when authorized by the General Assembly, may also request advisory opinions on any legal question that may arise in the scope or course of their activities. To date, the ICJ has issued advisory decisions for a variety of UN agencies ranging from the ILO to the IMF to the World Meteorological Organization (WMO). The ICJ statute mandates that the court consist of fifteen justices, no two of whom may be nationals from the same state. The justices of the Court are elected for nine-year, staggered terms by the General Assembly and the Security Council through a complicated nomination and selection process. These justices hear cases submitted to it by member states, and decisions are reached through a majority vote. A quorum of nine justices is required for the Court to hear a case; however, the Court does not have compulsory jurisdiction over all cases. Article 36 of the ICJ Statute, often referred to as the "Optional Clause," allows parties to decide whether they want to give the Court blanket jurisdiction over their current and future international legal disputes. Very few states have given the Court this kind of jurisdiction; thus, states usually consent to the court's jurisdiction on a case-by-case basis. Access to the ICJ is also limited to states. That is, only states may be parties in cases before the court. Private individuals are barred from bringing cases to the ICJ and the court has refused to consider private petitions and requests. States must be parties and all the states involved in a legal dispute must be willing to have the ICJ hear the case before the Court will consider the merits. As a result, the ICJ hears only one or two cases a year, and it is generally considered an ineffective mechanism of international adjudication. The ICJ remains "marginal to most of the structural issues of international relations" (Forsythe 1998, 385).

The Economic and Social Council   The Economic and Social Council (ECOSOC) was established under the UN Charter (Chapter X) to promote economic and social cooperation among member states. It is actively involved in the substantive issue areas of economic development, human rights, and social welfare. The ECOSOC consists of fifty-four members elected by the General Assembly for three-year, staggered terms. Each member has one vote and decisions are based on majority rule. Retiring members are eligible for immediate reelection.

The ECOSOC has several important functions and powers. First, the ECOSOC "may make or initiate studies and reports with respect to international economic, social, cultural, educational, and health and related matters and may make recommendations with respect to any such matters to the General Assembly, to the Members of the United Nations, and to the specialized agencies concerned" (Article 62, Section 1). Second, the ECOSOC may make recommendations for promoting and protecting human rights. Third, the ECOSOC may prepare draft conventions relating to economic and social issues. Finally, it may call international conferences on matters falling within its competence.

The ECOSOC is a collaborative body with authority to create commissions to promote human rights and economic and social cooperation. The ECOSOC invites all UN members and representatives of the specialized agencies and certain NGOs to participate in ECOSOC activities. While these non-ECOSOC members do not have a vote in ECOSOC decisions, they provide perspective and expertise to ECOSOC proceedings.

The Trusteeship Council   The Trusteeship Council was created to oversee the transition of colonies into self-governing territories. The Trustee Council's mandate is to ensure that the interests of the inhabitants of these non–self-governing territories are placed at the forefront of the decolonization process. Among the members of the Trusteeship Council are UN member states that administer trust territories. These members take an oath to respect the cultures of the people involved and to respect their political, economic, and social development. The Trusteeship Council also includes permanent members of the Security Council that are not administering trust territories. In addition, the Trusteeship Council is balanced; it must consist of "as many other members elected for three-year terms by the General Assembly as may be necessary to ensure that the total number of the Trusteeship Council is equally divided between those Members of the United Nations which administer trust territories and those which do not" (Article 86, Section 1c). Decision making is based on a one-member/one-vote, majority-rule arrangement.

The Trusteeship Council, while pivotal in the 1960s, is largely obsolete today. All the original UN trusts have become autonomous or self-governing, and there is little left for the Trusteeship Council to do. Its historical legacy is its oversight of the volatile decolonization process, a process for which there have been as many critics as champions. The

Trusteeship Council's role in this process has been to debate and deliberate different strategies for decolonization, as well as to monitor the effects of the process on trust populations. It has also supervised the process by issuing binding decisions on members that were not permanent members of the Security Council and making recommendations to those that were.

The Secretariat   The Secretariat serves as the UN bureaucracy. It consists of the Secretary-General and the bureaucratic staff necessary to carry out the UN's complex tasks and functions. The Secretary-General (discussed in more detail in Chapter 5) is the chief diplomat, whose task is to represent the UN to member states. The staff of the Secretariat is supposed to be recruited on the basis of efficiency, competence, integrity, and geographic diversity, although political patronage is not unknown. The bureaucratic agencies of the Secretariat are created by the General Assembly; however, both the ECOSOC and the Trusteeship Council are explicitly assigned their own staffs. The size, expense, and priorities of the UN bureaucracy are widely criticized today; yet most agree that some kind of bureaucracy is necessary to carry out the large, complex tasks that characterize today's global issues.

THE PRINCIPLES OF THE UNITED NATIONS

The UN is based on several complementary principles. First, the UN is founded on the principle of the sovereign equality of all members. This simply means that each state, at least in legal theory, retains the right to determine its own internal and external affairs. Second, UN members voluntarily accept responsibility to carry out certain international obligations upon joining the UN, one of which is the obligation to settle disputes peacefully. Thus, the third founding principle of the UN is the peaceful settlement of disputes. Fourth, member states agree not to threaten or use force in their international relations. Fifth, the UN is enjoined from intervening in the domestic jurisdiction of member states. The principles of sovereign equality, the peaceful settlement of disputes, non-use of force, and nonintervention are companion principles critical to the maintenance of international peace and security.

The UN Charter attempts to strengthen international peace and security by permitting regional arrangements. Chapter VIII recognizes that regional and local solutions to regional and local problems are often preferable to UN attention. However, the UN Charter does require that the UN be kept informed of regional activities and events that may threaten international peace and security. Furthermore, the Charter seeks to restrict regional enforcement activities by stating that "no enforcement action shall be taken under regional arrangements or by regional agencies without the authorization of the Security Council" (Article 53). The architects of the Charter wanted to balance the benefits of regionalism with the need for universal approaches to international problems. The post–World War II era has witnessed an explosion of regional organizations. Two of these organizations, both multipurpose, are the European Union (EU) and the Organization of Islamic Conference (OIC), discussed below.

UN AMBITIONS AND CHALLENGES

The UN of the twenty-first century will continue to have a role in preventive diplomacy, peacekeeping, peacemaking, conflict resolution, and economic and social development. However, several challenges threaten to derail or restrict UN activities in these areas. First, the UN suffers from resource difficulties. The United States, which is the UN's largest contributor, is also its largest debtor. The United States owes approximately $1.6 billion to the UN and continues to balk at paying, for political reasons (Wren 1999, A6). In 1999, a deal was struck between the UN and the United States that broke the impasse which might have led to the loss of the U.S. vote in the General Assembly (Schmitt 1999, A18). The impasse was between the UN and the United States over exactly how much is owed (the United States rejects numerous UN assessments) and between the then–Clinton administration and the Republican-controlled Senate over the financing of international organizations that provide abortions or promote abortion rights. The United States agreed to release $1 billion in UN payments and a ban on financing abortion rights groups would be implemented. The Bush administration continues the ban; however, the Republican House of Representatives continued to hold up the payments to the UN until September 2001 and released them only after the World Trade Center and Pentagon bombings. The U.S. arrears account for approximately 60 percent of what is owed to the UN.

Second, the UN has had enormous difficulties in protecting its personnel. Throughout the 1990s, UN workers have been assaulted, kidnapped, and killed in record numbers in hot spots such as Lebanon, Mozambique, Afghanistan, Angola, Sudan, Cambodia, Somalia, Rwanda, and Iraq. Given the crisis of resources and the reluctance of member states to commit militarily, UN personnel remain at risk while attempting to deliver humanitarian and development assistance.

Third, the UN is suffering from a lack of leadership. The United States, under the Bush administration, has demonstrated its preference for unilateral approaches by withdrawing from the Kyoto Protocol and the International Criminal Court (discussed in Chapters 9 and 10, respectively). The attacks on the United States in September, 2001, have further complicated the political landscape and have raised questions about the appropriate role of the UN in the "war on terrorism." Secretary General Kofi Annan has argued that only the UN could give "global legitimacy" to the war on terrorism (Schmemann 2001, B3); however, the United States appears to consider the UN a minor partner to this most recent threat to international peace and security. In spite of these challenges, the UN is sure to play an influential, if not controversial, role in contemporary world politics.

THE EUROPEAN UNION

The EU is a comprehensive, multipurpose regional organization that has been under construction since the end of World War II. The goals of the EU revolve around the economic and political integration of fifteen European states—France, Great Britain, Germany, Italy, Belgium, the Netherlands, Luxembourg, Denmark, Greece, Spain, Portugal, Ireland, Austria, Sweden, and Finland. The EU demonstrates how a series of IGOs can be tied together to create a supranational organization, albeit one in its nascent stages, which combines the interests of diverse nation-states. The EU represents the highest degree of economic, political, and social integration found in a contemporary international organization.

The construction of a united Europe has been a long and arduous process, and it continues today, as twelve of the fifteen EU members seek to implement a common currency, the "euro." The process began with the Paris Treaty (1951), in which Germany and France agreed to merge their steel and coal industries. Then, in 1952, the

European Coal and Steel Community (ECSC) was created as Italy and the Benelux countries (Belgium, the Netherlands, and Luxembourg) joined with France and Germany to coordinate steel and coal policies. Later, the Treaty of Rome (1957) extended ECSC cooperation to atomic energy with the creation of the European Atomic Energy Community (EURATOM). The Treaty of Rome also established the European Economic Community (EEC), which was committed to formation of a common market. The three communities—ECSC, EURATOM, and the EEC—had separate commissions and councils but shared the European Parliament and Court of Justice in common (Noel 1993, 5). Since 1967, however, the three communities have shared the five institutions that now comprise the EU.

Eventually, the three communities evolved into a single organization, called the European Community in 1979, then the European Union (EU) in 1992. EU membership expanded gradually: Great Britain, Ireland, and Denmark joined in 1973; Greece in 1981; Spain and Portugal in 1986; Germany in 1990; and Sweden, Austria, and Denmark in 1994. And, as EU membership expanded, its institutions became more powerful and formalized through a series of multilateral treaties. In the following sections, we look at the five institutions of the EU and outline the treaties designed to integrate the nation-states of Europe.

The European Council The European Council, which consists of the heads of state/government of EU members, represents the political leadership of the EU. The European Council was formally established by the Single European Act of 1985 and was strengthened by the Maastricht Treaty of 1992; however, the Council has existed informally since 1974. The European Council meets twice a year with representatives from other EU institutions in order to coordinate EU policy with national policies and interests. The European Council is playing an increasingly influential role in EU affairs as most political and military (and some monetary) decisions are still made at the national level. The European Council is crucial for constructing the long-term plan of the EU.

The Council of Ministers The Council of Ministers, which is made up of the relevant ministers from the governments of EU members, is the chief decision-making body. According to Noel (1993, 6), each national government sends one of its ministers to the Council; which minister usually depends on the subject matter of the Council meeting. The Foreign Minister is usually considered the principal representative to the Council, but a variety of ministers, ranging from the Minister of Agriculture to the Minister of Transportation, regularly attend Council meetings. Formally, decisions in the Council are made through a weighted voting system with a qualified majority rule. Informally, most important policy decisions are made on the basis of unanimity (Noel 1993, 28–29). The Council of Ministers is a fluid body whose composition changes depending on the issue area. Members of the Council represent their national governments to the EU; consequently, the Council is an inherently political institution, often influenced by individual national interests.

The European Commission The Council of Ministers is only part of the EU decision-making process. Most EU proposals and initiatives emanate from the European Commission, the bureaucratic arm of the EU. While the European Commission formally reports to the Council of Ministers, it exercises a great deal of autonomy. The

Commission consists of twenty members who are appointed for four-year terms and maintain a staff of approximately 5,000 people. Commission members are expected to further the interests of the EU as a whole as opposed to the interests of their own countries—hence Commission members and staff are often referred to as "Eurocrats" because of their priorities and allegiances. Commission members tend to be highly trained techno/bureaucrats who are skilled, complex-problem-solvers. They are often technical experts and adept administrators in the areas of energy, trade, transportation, finance, and agriculture, rather than politicians with national constituencies.

The Commission has several important powers that help it develop common policies for the EU. The Commission has the power to initiate policy proposals. While proposals are often initiated by the Council of Ministers or the European Parliament, the Commission has the authority to investigate strategies for addressing the problems it identifies. The Commission also has the power to execute EU policies. The European Parliament and the Council of Ministers generally approve broad policy goals, leaving it up to the Commission to create the specific rules, regulations, and procedures for reaching those goals. Coupled with the authority to set budgeting priorities, the execution of EU policies gives the Commission a great deal of influence over those policies. The European Commission has also emerged as the "Guardian of the Treaties." It is given the responsibility for implementing the multilateral treaties creating the EU and for building confidence among EU members.

The European Parliament   The European Parliament is mainly responsible for overseeing the Commission, although its legislative powers are limited. The Parliament can advise both Council and Commission on proposals, and it must approve the Commission's overall budget. It does not have the right of line-item approval. Even so, the Parliament is an important part of the co-decision process by virtue of its input in EU policy development. The co-decision procedure is a complex one, involving two readings and seven steps. First, the Commission develops a proposal. Second, the Parliament advises the Commission on other considerations and suggests revisions. Third, the Council of Ministers brings national concerns to the table, presenting their positions on the proposal. Fourth, the Parliament votes yes or no. Fifth, the Commission issues a second opinion of the now-revised proposal. Sixth, the Council issues its secondary opinion. Seventh, the European Parliament either accepts or rejects the final proposal. If a proposal reaches the seventh stage, it is almost always approved by the Parliament.

The co-decision process perhaps overemphasizes the legislative role of the Parliament. The Commission and the Council exercise the most influence over the formulation of common EU policy. The Parliament's influence remains largely deliberative and symbolic. The European Parliament consists of 626 members, each of whom is directly elected by voters in Europe. And, as with national legislatures, political parties feature prominently in European Parliament elections and operations. Europe's political parties reflect a broad political spectrum; they include, but are not limited to, the European Socialists, the Christian Democrats, the Greens, and the Democratic Alliance. Seating within the Parliament is based on political party sections; however, the members of the parties sit alphabetically in order to reduce any nationalist sentiments that may arise among the party members. The complicated composition of the Parliament is a surprising, yet effective, formula for projecting an image of European unity.

The European Court of Justice The European Court of Justice was created in 1958 to adjudicate any legal disputes arising under the Treaty of Rome involving ECSC, EEC, and EURATOM activities. Over time, the jurisdiction of the Court has expanded to include disputes arising under later treaties such as the Single European Act (1986) and the Maastricht Treaty (1992). The Court is composed of fifteen justices who are appointed by national governments for six-year terms. The justices are assisted by advocates-general to handle the Court's expanding caseload. The Court functions much like the U.S. Supreme Court in that it interprets whether EU policies and national laws are congruent with EU treaties. But unlike the U.S. Supreme Court, the European Court is permitted to issue preliminary or advisory opinions that are referred to it by national courts.

The European Court of Justice is different from other international courts in that it may be used by individuals as well as governments. Traditionally, only states are subjects of international law, which means that only states may make claims in international courts. Individuals, though, are traditionally objects of international law, which means they must have their governments make claims on their behalf. The European Court of Justice is unique because individuals have standing to bring some cases before the Court. The Court has heard EU employment cases, for example, and has addressed such issues as job discrimination and equal pay for equal work.

EU Ambitions and Challenges

The impressive institutional structures of the EU indicate its ambitious goals. Current EU goals have been outlined in the Single European Act and the Maastricht Treaty. The Single European Act was designed as a capstone of the Treaty of Rome, putting the final touches on a true European common market. The Single European Act called for the final elimination of all internal barriers to trade in goods and services by 1992. This is a critical step to ensuring the free movement of goods, services, persons, and capital within the EU. The Maastricht Treaty is even more ambitious, calling for the final step of economic integration—the implementation of a common currency, known as the euro. The euro has been the European currency for international transaction since 1999 and it is set to replace the domestic currencies of EU member states in January 2001. The transition to the euro has been rocky. When put to a popular vote via a referendum in Denmark, citizens voted against the euro by a significant majority (Kuchment and Beith 2000, 5). The UK, which represents a significant proportion of the European economy, has yet to indicate that it is ready for monetary union. For those states that have adopted the euro, public opinion polls suggest that their citizens are at best indifferent to the euro and at worst, would reject it if the decision were put to a public vote (*European Report* 2001, 102). Concerns also remain about the value of the euro relative to the U.S. dollar, the security of the euro from theft and counterfeiting, and the loss of millions of dollars worth of undeclared income from Europe's underground economy. In spite of these challenges, the implementation of the euro proceeds on schedule.

The Maastricht treaty also called for serious steps toward political and military integration. The Maastricht Treaty obligates EU members to begin the process of formulating a common foreign policy and providing for a common European defense. Both ambitious and controversial, the Maastricht treaty has been slow in achieving ratification. Great Britain and Denmark have ratified the treaty but retain severe reservations that allow them to opt out of monetary and political union. Currently, just twelve of the fifteen EU members are experimenting with the euro, and no member is taking serious steps toward political and military integration. To complicate matters further, a crisis of confidence occurred in 1999 with the resignation of the entire European Commission. The Commission was formally linked to mismanagement and fraud by European auditors with more than $1 billion in EU expenditures lacking adequate accounting. Critics of the Commission have charged that it lacks democratic controls, transparency, and financial rigor (Cohen 1999). The resignation of the Commission has caused further uncertainty within the EU.

In addition to the challenges relating to deeper integration among current members, the EU faces several problems relating to EU expansion. Many European states are seeking inclusion in the EU; however, they bring with them significant economic and political baggage. Turkey, Cyprus, and Malta are seeking full EU membership, but their political and economic differences with Greece and the rest of Europe hinder negotiations. Turkey, for instance, presents several, seemingly intractable, problems. First, Turkey's geopolitical situation renders it technically ineligible for EU membership: Only a small part of Turkey is actually on the European continent. Second, Greece, Turkey's historical adversary, is adamantly opposed to Turkey's inclusion. Third, Turkey's population is Muslim, which contrasts with Europe's predominantly Christian population. Nevertheless, Turkey's membership is a major sticking point among EU members, largely because it has been a pivotal NATO ally and has a democratically elected, secular government.

Membership issues are further complicated by the bids of Poland, the Czech Republic, Slovakia, Hungary, and Romania. The EU has negotiated several European Association Accords involving trade, the environment, culture, and future EU membership. Expansion of the EU into Central Europe threatens to make the EU cumbersome and unwieldy. Many specialists argue that the current members of the EU need to concentrate on deeper integration before extending EU membership to the potentially unstable Central European states. States seeking EU membership can participate politically in the Organization for Security and Cooperation in Europe (OSCE). The OSCE is a universal regional organization open to all states in Europe (and the Euro-Atlantic world). It is also a multipurpose organization that can address a vast array of European problems.

The future of the EU is uncertain, and whether further economic and political integration takes place depends on the success of the euro. The EU has created a European System of Central Banks and a European Central Bank. The strength of these institutions has yet to be determined, and observers question whether European monetary stability will take precedence over immediate national interests. Regardless of the future, the EU remains the most remarkable of international organizations because of its success in uniting the diverse cultures and politics and creating a European identity.

THE ORGANIZATION OF ISLAMIC CONFERENCE

The Organization of Islamic Conference (OIC) was created in 1969 by twenty-four Islamic states to safeguard the well-being of their peoples and of Muslims in general. According to Article II of the OIC Charter, the OIC seeks to strengthen Islamic solidarity, consolidate cooperation among member states in the economic, social, cultural, and scientific fields, safeguard the Holy Places, support the struggle of the Palestinian people, and eliminate racial discrimination and all forms of colonialism. Currently, it is a fifty-seven member IGO that is based on the following principles:

1. The full equality of member states
2. The observation of the rights to self-determination and noninterference in the internal affairs of member states
3. The observation of the sovereignty, independence, and territorial integrity of each state
4. The settlement of any dispute that may arise among member states by peaceful means
5. A pledge to refrain, in relations among member states, from resorting to force or threatening to resort to force against the unity and territorial integrity or the political independence of any one member state

The OIC principles are similar to most post–WWII IGOs in that they recognize the sovereign equality of members, nonintervention, and the peaceful settlement of disputes. Its membership is open to all Islamic states that seek to uphold the principles of OIC. States wishing to join may submit an application to the OIC and membership is decided on the basis of a two-thirds vote of the member states. The OIC is neither as comprehensive nor as institutionalized as the EU; however, it does seek to organize a very diverse group of states that govern well over one billion Muslims. Its goals are the promotion and protection of Islam as a religion, as well as Islamic cultural values. The OIC is financed by member states and each member's assessment is based proportionally on their national income.

The birth of the OIC was turbulent. Its creation in 1969 was a unified Muslim response to the Israeli policies after the 1967 Arab–Israeli war, including the occupation and annexation of Jerusalem. Known as Al-Quds to the Muslim world, Jerusalem is home to one of Islam's most holy sites, the Aqsa Mosque. The Aqsa Mosque sustained extensive arson damage while under Israeli control, and the subsequent Arab and Muslim outrage prompted the formation of the OIC (Ahsan 1988, 23). The OIC was created to safeguard Muslim holy sites and to be a voice for the Palestinian people.

The OIC is structured around four major components. At the top is the Conference of the Kings and Heads of State and Government which is also known as the Islamic Summit Conference. According to Article IV, the Conference of Kings and Heads of State and Government is the supreme authority of the OIC and, with an amendment to the Charter in 1981, it meets once every three years or when the vital interests of the Muslim nations warrant. Next in the hierarchy is the Conference of Foreign Ministers, which meets once a year or when the need arises. According to Article V, the Conference of Foreign Ministers shall be held for the following purposes:

1. To consider the means of implementing the general policy of the Conference
2. To review the progress in the implementations of resolutions adopted at previous sessions
3. To adopt resolutions of matters of the common interest in accordance with the aims and objectives of the Conference set forth in the Charter
4. To discuss the report of the Financial Committee and approve the budget of the Secretariat-General
5. To appoint the Secretary-General, the four assistants to the Secretary-General on recommendation of the Secretary-General

6. To fix the date and venue of the Coming Conference of Foreign Ministers
7. To consider any issue affecting one or more of the member states whenever a request to that effect is made with a view to taking appropriate measures in that respect

Meetings at the Foreign Ministerial level require a quorum of two-thirds of the member states and resolutions and recommendations are adopted on the basis of a two-thirds majority. Voting is based on a one-state, one-vote basis; however, the norm is that members proceed on the basis of consensus (Ahsan 1988, 26). Decisions and resolutions adopted with a two-thirds majority are not binding on members that either abstained or voted against (Moinuddin 1987, 106). In addition to the Conference of Foreign Ministers annual meeting, which is rotated among members, it has held regular sessions in New York during UN General Assembly sessions since 1980.

The OIC political leadership is supported by an elaborate bureaucracy called the Secretariat-General. The Secretariat-General is headed by the Secretary General who is appointed for a nonrenewable four-year term. The Secretary General is the chief bureaucrat and represents the OIC to member states and other states and international organizations. Article VI commits the Secretary General to political neutrality in that "in the performance of their duties, the Secretary General, his assistants, or the staff of the General Secretariat, shall not seek to receive instructions from any government or authority other than the Conference. Member states undertake to respect this equality and the nature of their responsibilities, and shall not seek to influence them in any way in the discharge of their responsibilities." The Secretary-General, with the assistance of his staff, is responsible for executing OIC decisions and resolutions, as well as monitoring and drafting reports on existing operations and programs.

OIC AMBITIONS AND CHALLENGES

The OIC is the principal forum for Islamic cooperation; however, cooperation has been difficult to achieve. The OIC is not a regional organization in that the geographic location of member states extends from Africa to southeast Asia. OIC also includes observer states that have large Muslim populations, like Bosnia-Herzegovina, Central African Republic, and Thailand. Not only does the OIC represent geographic diversity, it also represents political diversity. Members are Islamic republics, monarchies, military dictatorships, national democracies, and democratic socialist republics (Ahsan 1988, 19). National income among IOC members is also unevenly dispersed. Some states are among the wealthiest in the world like Oman and Saudi Arabia, while others are among the poorest, like Mali and Afghanistan. Cooperation is further complicated by the fact that while all members share a colonial past, not all have shed the colonial yoke. "The alien structures implanted in the member states of the OIC during the colonial period have failed to cater to the needs of the majority of the people; the colonial system of education and administration which introduced alien values and outlook has estranged the majority of the masses from their rulers" (Moinuddin 1987, 69). As a result, dissension within the OIC was evident during the Lebanese Civil War, the Iran–Iraq War, and the Persian Gulf War.

In spite of all the differences between OIC members, its single unifying force is Islam. This religious commitment also involves protection of the Holy Sites and fostering the self-determination of Muslim people, including Muslims living in non-Muslim countries. This has placed the OIC squarely in the middle of some of the most explosive conflicts in contemporary world politics: the Palestinian–Israeli crisis, the Arab–Israeli crisis, the Bosnian crisis, Kashmir, and Afghanistan. In addition, the OIC has sought to protect Islamic culture from Western secular materialism. The heads of state of the OIC have declared that "Strict adherence to Islam and to Islamic principles and values as a way of life constitutes the highest protection for Muslims against the dangers that confront them. Islam is the only path that can lead them to strength, dignity, prosperity, and a better future. Islam is the pledge and guarantee of the authenticity of the *ummah* safeguarding it from the tyrannical onrush of materialism" (Ahsan 1988, 19). The OIC represents a challenge to the West's liberal world order in that it articulates a different view of the relationship of religion to politics, private property, and human rights. Some even view the OIC as a subversive transnational religious actor undermining state sovereignty in order to further the goal of creating a pan-Islamic religious community (Haynes 2001).

Currently, the greatest challenge for the OIC is how to respond to the September 11, 2001, attacks on the United States and the U.S. retaliation against Afghanistan. The Taliban government only has observer status in the OIC because only three states (Pakistan, Saudi Arabia, and the United Arab Emirates) had recognized the Taliban as Afghanistan's lawful government. On October 9, 2001, the Secretary General of the UN, Kofi Annan, called upon the OIC to take a central role in devising a strategy to combat terrorism (SG/SM/7989). The OIC condemned the attacks on the United States, but Iran, Iraq, and Syria have also condemned the U.S. military response. Other OIC members wanted to see the evidence against Osama bin Laden and the Al Qaeda network. A communiqué issued on October 10, 2001, stated that "the conference also expressed its concern that confronting terrorism could lead to casualties among innocent civilians in Afghanistan and asserted the importance of assuring the territorial integrity of Afghanistan and its Islamic character" (www.cbsnews.com/now/story). The OIC also warned against the targeting of other Muslim states. The OIC is in the difficult position of trying to balance a desire to have a cooperative working relationship with the West and the UN with anti-U.S., anti-Western sentiments among large sections of the Muslim population.

Multipurpose IGOs like the UN, the EU, and the OIC play pivotal roles in contemporary world politics. They have been formed, in part, to meet and further the common goals of their member states. IGOs can have universal or limited membership; they can be specific- as well as general-purpose organizations. But regardless of their function, intended or otherwise, IGOs are inherently political institutions operating in an inherently political environment with other actors beyond states. In the following section, we explore another kind of international organization that has attracted considerable scholarly attention of late—nongovernmental organizations (NGOs).

NONGOVERNMENTAL ORGANIZATIONS

NGOs are, for the most part, private, nonprofit organizations that have international as well as subnational ties. When the first NGO was founded is a matter of considerable debate. Some observers date the first NGO back to 1674 when the Rosicurian Order, an educational fraternal order, was founded (Jacobson 1984, 10). Others date the first NGO back to 1846 with the formation of the World Evangelical Alliance (Feld,

Jordan, and Hurwitz 1994, 25). Still others think bigger, arguing that the Catholic Church, with its associated orders, represents the first NGO. Whatever the founding date, classifying NGOs is exceptionally difficult by virtue of their multiple origins, purposes, and resources. Some NGOs might be social welfare organizations, such as World Vision and Doctors Without Borders; or they might be professional organizations, such as the International Studies Association and International Chamber of Commerce. NGOs can serve specific purposes, such as the International Olympic Committee and Amnesty International, or they can be multipurpose organizations, such as the Catholic Church. NGOs, whose membership can be either compulsory or voluntary, currently number more than 100,000. Their financing comes from private sources, including membership dues, income from investment earnings, and charitable contributions from individuals and businesses. NGOs may also receive financing from public sources, such as government agencies, and IGOs, which usually comes in the form of contracts and/or grants. Some NGOs, such as Doctors Without Borders or World Vision, command budgets in excess of $200 million (Donini 1996, 91).

NGOs interact with a variety of international actors, ranging from states to IGOs and MNCs. NGOs attempt to influence the activities and the decision making of these actors with a view to getting their help in achieving some or all of NGO goals. This means that NGOs may employ both direct and indirect lobbying techniques. Direct lobbying techniques involve contacting officials (and their staffs) in order to persuade them to adopt appropriate initiatives or policies. Such contact can also involve attempting to educate officials and staff. This entails addressing the IGO, state, or corporate agency directly or submitting relevant documentation. Indirect lobbying techniques involve multinational advertising campaigns aimed at shaping or mobilizing public opinion. These techniques also include executing grassroots campaigns that take place at the international and national levels. Such campaigns consist of encouraging members and others to write letters or otherwise contact national and international public officials. NGOs even use national courts to achieve their aims. They may bring cases directly, file briefs, or provide legal representation to individuals or groups. NGOs utilize both human and capital resources to further their respective aims. Success tends to depend on NGO objectives and resources. NGOs with more resources and narrower goals tend to be more effective than those having fewer resources or those seeking to change policy in some broad or fundamental way. Those that lack resources or seek substantial change may even employ alternative participation strategies such as civil disobedience that involves peaceful, but illegal behavior and violence.

NGOs play three interrelated roles in world politics. The first revolves around information-related activities. Many NGOs are actively engaged in gathering information, as they have people on the ground who are directly involved with an issue or a problem. In addition, NGOs share information with states, IGOs, MNCs, and each other. Fact-finding is crucial for identifying and managing problems. Another aspect of NGO information activity is providing expert analysis. NGOs often employ highly qualified individuals who are widely recognized experts in their respective fields. They bring their education and experience to bear on defining and addressing global issues. This involves publishing studies and articles and issuing documentation. NGOs are even responsible for establishing standards, guidelines, and regulations.

A second role of NGOs in world politics involves carrying out the policies of states and IGOs. Implementing policy is largely the domain of social-welfare NGOs which are, in effect, "subcontractors." Working in conjunction with states and IGOs, many social-welfare NGOs serve as vehicles for delivering immediate humanitarian assistance to persons displaced by natural disaster, civil disorder, violent conflict, or war. In addition to responding to crises and emergencies, these NGOs work on a continuous basis with populations mired in poverty and afflicted by disease and starvation. They distribute medicines and medical care. Some NGOs are specifically involved with women's health issues. They provide information on birth-control methods, dispense contraceptives, and deliver, pre- and postnatal care. Many NGOs are also involved with elementary and secondary education as well as providing technical and skills training. In many respects, the web of social-welfare NGOs and IGOs provides the only safety net that many people have. The works of NGOs are so important that many have formal consultative status with the UN.

The nongovernmental delivery of social-welfare services encounters numerous obstacles, which can emanate both from governments and from nongovernmental, domestic groups. For example, NGO relief activities in war zones can run afoul of government wishes, and NGO access to populations at risk can be restricted (Duffield 1998, 139–147). NGOs are, for the most part, respectful of sovereign prerogatives, but problems can arise when a government does not control all the territory within a state. NGOs that deliver humanitarian assistance to populations in rebel-held territory can easily be seen as subversive, in effect "giving aid and comfort" to the enemy. Negotiating NGO access to war-torn areas is an arduous and tedious process—one that involves strategic and military calculations as well as humanitarian concerns.

Religious groups in both developed and developing countries may oppose NGO activities relating to reproductive rights. They may see NGOs' activities in this area as sinful or disruptive of traditional family values. NGOs that monitor human-rights compliance are seen as threatening the sovereignty of states and undermining governmental stability. As with all international issues and problems, disagreements about definition and implementation exist. NGOs seeking to deliver social-welfare services may actually be exacerbating or creating problems rather than solving them.

A third role that NGOs play in world politics revolves around private interactions. International relations is no longer solely the domain of states. NGOs are involved in a variety of private international transactions that bring together groups and individuals. This includes student and faculty exchanges and study-abroad programs. NGOs often host conferences that facilitate the exchange of ideas. In many cases, such conferences are held jointly with conferences sponsored by IGOs. Some NGOs, such as the Ford or Rockefeller Foundations or the Pew Charitable Trusts, award huge grants for the research and development of projects that promote international cooperation. Many observers see the dramatic increase of private NGO interaction as critical to the formation of global civil society (Yamamoto 1996). This civil society is based on shared ideas and values that can be quite removed from governments and IGOs. NGOs are seen as "the conscience of the world," influencing the moral development of states and IGOs, as well as civil society (Willetts 1996).

While NGOs can play constructive roles in world politics, their activities, like the activities of other international organizations, can generate controversy. NGOs often represent particular interests that can conflict with other powerful interests. NGO antiglobalization efforts in Seattle, Prague, Davos, Genoa, and Washington, and their willingness to challenge status quo politics, have made them targets of criticism by businesses, governments and IGO officials (McFeely 2000, 14). NGOs can also complicate the policy- and decision-making processes of governments and IGOs. NGOs have long sought transparency in and access to UN agencies. However, when granted access to agencies and conferences, problem identifying and solving can become intractable. For example, when the WTO invited NGO comment on a trade dispute between Canada and France (regarding a French ban on a type of asbestos), the dispute settlement process of the WTO was reduced to a muddled mess (*The Economist* Dec. 9, 2000, 6). Apparently many developing states claimed the WTO had overstepped its authority and demanded that the WTO must rescind its invitation, which the WTO did, based on an obscure technicality. The result was a lack of confidence in the WTO on the part of NGOs and developing nations.

Are NGOs "friends or foes"? The answer to the question depends on your world view. Some NGOs complain about "pretender NGOs" (see Fowler 1991, cited in *Foreign Policy* 2001, 18). There a CONGO, a commercial NGO, is "set up by businesses in order to participate in bids, help win contracts, and reduce taxation" (*Foreign Policy* 2001, 18). Businesses then claim they are participating in cooperative partnerships and are being good global and local citizens. Another type of "pretender NGO" is called a MANGO: a mafia NGO that provides services "of the money laundering, enforcement, and protection variety; prevalent in Eastern Europe" (*Foreign Policy* 2001, 18). Still another type is the PANGO, or party NGO, which is an "aspiring, defeated or panned political party or politician dressed as an NGO; a species of Central Asia and Indo-China" (*Foreign Policy* 2001, 18). Many businesses, government officials, and social conservatives complain that many, if not most, of the NGOs accredited by the UN are either radical, leftist, feminist, pro-abortion, pro-environment, or pro-homosexual, whose politics are disruptive and unrepresentative of the mainstream. In other words, the so-called civil society can be decidedly uncivil.

Regardless of the divergent views, NGOs are increasing in prominence as international actors and as objects of study (see, for example, Weiss and Gordenker 1996). These private, nonprofit international organizations serve as information gatherers and providers; they help carry out the policies of states and IGOs; and they serve as the building blocks of global civil society. NGOs offer vehicles for individuals and groups to participate in international politics outside of their respective nation-states. In other words, NGOs enable a broader range of participation beyond the usual foreign policy elites. NGOs allow the average individual the opportunity to shape and influence the international political landscape, albeit in small, incremental, and often controversial ways.

MULTINATIONAL CORPORATIONS

Multinational corporations (MNCs) are private, for-profit organizations that have commercial operations and subsidiaries in two or more countries. As Gilpin (1987, 231) so aptly states:

> [N]o aspect of the political economy has generated more controversy than the global expansion of multinational corporations. Some consider these powerful corporations to be a boon to mankind, superseding the nation-state, diffusing technology and economic growth to developing countries, and interlocking national economies into an expanding and beneficial interdependence. Others view them as imperialistic predators, exploiting all for the sake of the corporate few while creating a web of political dependence and economic underdevelopment.

These views of MNCs, while opposite, indicate the significance of MNCs to world politics. These international organizations command huge resources and can influence entire national economies. In subsequent chapters of this text, we explore why these divergent views of MNCs exist. But for our purposes here, we define MNCs and look briefly at their historical evolution.

The origins of the first MNC are difficult to pinpoint in part because of the confusion attending their definition. Many companies engage in international activities. They may import goods or buy raw materials from foreign sources. They may export products and engage in a variety of trading activities. Multinational corporations are different from companies that engage in international transactions in that ownership, management, and sales activities of MNCs extend beyond several national boundaries. MNCs are usually headquartered in one country with subsidiaries in secondary countries. The expansion of MNCs into other national jurisdictions is called foreign direct investment (FDI). FDI is distinguished from other types of investments because MNCs retain ownership and managerial control over subsidiaries. The principal economic objective of MNCs is to produce goods and services for world markets at the least possible cost (Gilpin 1987, 232). MNCs, at least in economic theory, seek to maximize their profits and their shareholders' returns. MNCs may also engage in portfolio investments in which they purchase shares in national companies and other MNCs.

One of the earliest MNCs was the East India Company, which was founded in the late seventeenth century. Involved with the production and distribution of tea, spices, jewels, and textiles on a global basis, the East India Company was headquartered in London, with offices and operations in the Netherlands, the Americas, China, Southeast Asia, and India. It was a private, joint stock company that was chartered by the British Crown (Ralph et al. 1991, 628). In fact, the Company helped the British government administer much of India when it was a colony during the nineteenth and early twentieth centuries. The Company's trading posts evolved into political administrative units used by Great Britain to govern India (and to protect company interests).

Today, there are more than 37,000 MNCs with 170,000 foreign subsidiaries (Balaam and Veseth 1996, 340). The proliferation of MNCs has changed the nature of international trade and international relations in general. MNCs fall into four broad categories. The first category includes MNCs involved in agriculture and extractive industries. Multinational agribusinesses, like Archer Daniels Midland (ADM) and Dole, produce and process a wide variety of agricultural products for stores and supermarkets around the world. MNCs engaged in extractive industries control and process natural and raw materials used for manufacturing. This extractive category also includes powerful petroleum MNCs such as British Petroleum, Royal Dutch Shell, Exxon, and Amoco. These MNCs control not only the means of access to the vast majority of the world's oil supply, but the processing and refining of crude oil as well.

A second category of MNCs centers on the provision of financial services. Financial MNCs include multinational banks, brokers, and insurance companies. Multinational banks provide hundreds of billions of dollars in venture capital and loans to businesses and governments. They engage in international currency exchange and trade. International brokers buy and sell securities in most of the world's stock markets. Global insurance companies insure everything from the legs of international supermodels to loans made by multinational banks. International financial services are the grease on the axles of the global economy.

A third category of MNCs is industrial corporations. These MNCs are involved in the manufacture of durable and other kinds of goods. The most famous of the industrial MNCs include General Electric, Motorola, Sony, and IBM. Included in this category are the global automobile manufacturers such as Ford, Volkswagen, General Motors, Toyota, Honda, and Daimler-Chrysler. Industrial corporations have workforces that number in the hundreds of thousands, and they own production facilities and sales activities that extend all over the world. A subcategory is retail corporations such as the Coca-Cola Company, the GAP, TieRack, and Eddie Bauer.

A fourth broad category of MNCs is general service companies. These companies sell everything from fast food to telephone and Internet services. The golden arches of McDonalds are symbols of the global expansion of MNCs. Burger King, Pizza Hut, and Starbucks are common in urban areas everywhere. AT&T, Sprint, and MCI are global telecommunication giants, providing local, cellular, and long-distance telephone services to individuals around the world, however remote their locations. America Online, CompuServe, and Prodigy provide Internet access to both individuals and firms. Information and technology firms link the world with instantaneous communication capabilities.

The proliferation of MNCs has been accompanied by a "trimming down" of certain kinds of operations and the "megamergers" among others. In addition, MNCs have entered into intercorporate alliances with other firms in order to spread risk and gain access to national markets (Gilpin 1987, 255). Almost all MNCs are headquartered in developed countries, and their national origins tend to be American, European, and Japanese. Their owners are shareholders from all over the world, although the vast majority are from the advanced industrialized countries. They are one of the many different kinds of international organizations that participate in world politics.

CONCLUSION

Today's international organizations are diverse and complex. IGOs are organizations for states. Some IGOs, like the UN or the OIC, promote cooperation among sovereign nation-states. Others, like the EU, foster the economic, political, and social integration of diverse societies. But world politics involves more than just the affairs of states. The activities of NGOs and MNCs show the interconnectedness of private and public international relations. The activities of IGOs, NGOs, and MNCs overlap, complementing and challenging one another. Their activities influence the lives of billions of people.

International organizations do not exist in a vacuum. They are part of a complex political world that is shaped by a variety of actors, processes, and events. Scholars and observers of international politics disagree about which actors, processes, and events are important for understanding the world. Consequently, they disagree about the nature, the roles, and relative importance of international organizations. These differences are the result of divergent world views, which condition their knowledge of the world. In Chapter 3, we examine the mainstream theoretical approaches to international relations—realism and liberalism. These approaches approximate widely held world views about the central influences of international politics and the role of international organizations within those politics.

3

MAINSTREAM APPROACHES

REALISM AND LIBERALISM represent the mainstream approaches to international relations and international organizations. Often thought of as the "conventional wisdom" in international governance, realism and liberalism approximate widely held world views about how the world operates and what the role of international organizations should be within the broader context of world politics. Both approaches are rooted in rich intellectual traditions, and each describes different actors and dynamics in international politics. Not surprisingly, a fierce academic debate has been raging between realists and liberals about their relative importance to international organizations in global governance (see, for example, Barnett and Finnemore 1999; Baldwin 1993). In this chapter we examine realism and liberalism systematically in terms of their philosophical roots and organizing assumptions. Then we apply those theoretical frameworks to explain the creation and maintenance of international organizations. We also look at the role international organizations play in the governance of international affairs.

REALISM

Realism is one of the oldest theoretical approaches to international relations and is widely held as a world view. Often referred to as power politics or realpolitik, realism's central focus is the acquisition, maintenance, and exercise of power by states. Power can be "hard" in that it is identified in terms of tangible military capabilities such as tanks, planes, troops, and missiles; or power can be "soft," meaning that it stems from the influence that results from ideas, wealth, or political/economic innovation. The realist lens focuses on nation-states and directs analysis toward particular sets of international issues—security, war, and other forms of violent conflict. Realism also asks certain kinds of questions. What accounts for order and stability in international relations? How does order deteriorate and why does stability break down? Thus, realism analyzes the perennial issue in international relations—the use of violence.

Generally speaking, realism as a world view and as a theoretical approach has grown out of European historical experience and scholarship. Even in the United

States, the best-known realists in American politics, Henry Kissinger and Zbigniew Brzezinski (the national security advisors for Presidents Nixon and Carter, respectively), were born and brought up in Europe. Why the preoccupation with security and war? The European continent has witnessed some of the world's more destructive and brutal conflicts, from the Thirty Years War (1618–1648) to the Napoleonic Wars (1803–1815) and from World War I (1914–1918) to World War II (1939–1945). European states have also engaged in the violent endeavor of imperialism, which is the quest for colonies and empires. Beginning in the fifteenth century, European expansion brought violence to every region of the world. The United Kingdom (Great Britain) once controlled so much territory that "the sun never set on the British Empire."

The European experience of war and imperialism has shaped the realist framework for understanding international relations. Many outside Europe have embraced this framework and its world view because it generates valuable insights and lessons regarding world politics. Realists are generally pessimistic about the independent role of international organizations, arguing that international organizations can neither constrain state behavior nor prevent war. After all, many of the aforementioned wars ended with the creation of international organizations—organizations that were supposed to keep the peace. When the Napoleonic Wars ended, for example, the Congress of Vienna and Concert of Europe were created. But the Concert of Europe could not prevent World War I. And in the ashes of that war, the League of Nations was formed. Then, when the League of Nations failed miserably in its task of promoting international peace, the world again slid into global conflict. After World War II, the United Nations was established, yet another organization charged with maintaining international peace and security. Yet war is still with us and violent conflicts abound. Why?

Many realists see war as the inevitable result of uneven power distributions among states, in which case international organizations can do little in the face of state power. International organizations are, for all intents and purposes, tools that powerful states use to control weaker states. And if international organizations are largely extensions of the great powers, they respond only to great-power interests and direction. That is, international organizations are important only as reflections of great-power values and norms regarding appropriate state behavior in international relations. Hence, governance in international relations boils down to a great-power concert, which is thinly veiled by international organizations. When the security interests of the great powers conflict, international organizations are either discarded, ignored, or rendered impotent by the states that created them.

How did realists come to such conclusions regarding the role of international organizations? In the following section, we detail the philosophic underpinnings of realist theory in order to gain historical insight into contemporary realist thought.

PHILOSOPHIC ROOTS OF REALISM

The philosophical tradition of realism is a rich one, dating back before Plato and Aristotle. Contemporary realists owe a particular intellectual debt to the great historian of Athens, Thucydides (ca. 460–401 B.C.). Thucydides, a general in the Peloponnesian War, analyzed the exercise of power by the city-states Melos, Athens, and Lacedaemonia (Sparta) in his *The Peloponnesian War*, covering the period of conflict from 431 to 411

B.C. In this tome, Thucydides offered many insights regarding the role of fear, power, and alliances among competing city-states.

In one of his most dramatic and influential passages, "The Melian Dialog," Thucydides shows that power is the final arbiter of disputes in international relations. In this passage, we see the politics of power in action after Athens has militarily surrounded Melos and demanded the Melians' surrender. The Melians argue, assuring the Athenians that they pose no threat to the security or well-being of Athens. They plead that they are neutral in the conflicts between Athens and the surrounding city-states, so that attacking them would be immoral and unjust. The Athenians respond by insisting on the total surrender of Melos. Failure to do so would result in their destruction. According to the Athenian representatives, "You must act with realism on the basis of what we both think, for we both alike know that in human reckoning the question of justice only enters where there is equal power to enforce it and the powerful exact what they can and the weak grant what they must" (Thucydides 1963, 181).

The first realist lesson is clear: Might makes right. What is just and moral is relative and usually defined by the powerful. It is, after all, the victors who write the history books, and they are not going to portray themselves as brutal, violent oppressors. The victors in any war are always just and righteous liberators.

The second realist lesson is equally clear: The strong do what they have the power to do and the weak accept what they have to accept. This statement is self-evident, yet has implications: "Good" does not always triumph over "evil," hence the only way to escape the fate of the weak is to join the ranks of the strong. Unfortunately, the road to the ranks of the strong is paved with murder, cheating, stealing, and lying. Those who wish to be strong must put aside their moral or religious beliefs and be prepared to engage in the same kind of behavior. The acquisition and maintenance of power must be of overriding importance to the state, given the consequences of being weak. Not only is the very survival of the state at stake, but also the right to establish international rules, values, and norms.

Thucydides also questions the usefulness of alliances, a type of international organization. A security alliance is predicated on the notion that an attack on one member of an alliance is an attack on all members of the alliance. By joining together in an alliance, members seek to deter potential aggressors (usually a common enemy) from attacking any member of an alliance. This also enables members to divert resources away from security—i.e., maintaining a large standing military—to other pursuits such as economic or social welfare.

In Thucydides' account, the Melians had an alliance with the Lacedaemonians; thus the Melians cautioned the Athenians that an attack on Melos would provoke a response by Lacedaemonia. The Athenians responded, "When you imagine that out of very shame they [Lacedaemonians] will assist you, we congratulate you on your blissful ignorance, but we do not admire your folly. . . . The path of expediency is safe, whereas justice and honor involve action and danger, which none are more generally averse to facing than the Lacedaemonians" (Thucydides 1963, 184).

Thucydides shows that alliances can lull states into a false sense of security. In spite of its advantages, an alliance is valuable only if it is credible that the allies will stick together. The problem is a classic catch-22. I (and my enemies) cannot know whether an ally will actually come to my aid until I actually need their aid. However, I joined the alliance in the first place so that I could deter potential aggressors from attacking.

Potential aggressors also know that allies are not likely to risk themselves unless it is in their immediate self-interest to do so. Hence, alliances are of questionable value when it comes to national security. The Melians banked on their alliance with Lacedaemonia, rendering themselves vulnerable. Their only hope was for Lacedaemonian intervention, an intervention that was not to come. Since the Melians could not defend themselves, they really had just two choices: surrender or be destroyed. The end of the story is not pleasant. The Melians chose not to surrender and the Athenians attacked. The adult males were massacred and the women and children were enslaved.

The lesson of the Melian story is that states must guarantee their own survival through their own military power. What is perceived to be right, just, or moral will not guarantee survival. An alliance will not necessarily deter an aggressor nor does it necessarily mean an ally will help. Power is the only thing adversaries will understand. On a side note, Thucydides wrote *The Peloponnesian War* in part as a scathing critique of Athenian and Greek foreign policy in general. Today, however, Athens is remembered neither for its violence nor its crimes against its neighbors, but as the birthplace of democracy. And the Greek civilization is known more for its brilliant philosophers, stately architecture, and breathtaking sculpture than for its wars. In effect, the Greeks won.

Niccolo Machiavelli (A.D. 1469–1527), the Florentine author and statesman, was another early realist. His *The Prince* is a classic analysis of statesmanship and power, well known as a guide for acquiring and maintaining political power. In a word, Machiavellianism. While Machiavellianism has assumed negative connotations owing to the cruel tactics advocated in *The Prince*, Machiavelli is very clear in showing how the accumulation and judicious use of power are necessary for political survival and for attaining social and political goals. Issues of justice, right, and wrong are negligible to the prince [ruler] and to the survival of the state. Rather, the prince must be willing to use violence and cruelty to maintain power.

Machiavelli asks the legendary question: Is it better to be loved or feared? And his answer is, it is best to be both loved and feared; but if just one choice is possible, it is better to be feared. Feelings of love are likely to be fleeting, but fear make foes and friends (potential foes) cautious in their dealings with the prince. Machiavelli thus advises against relying on idealistic notions of true friendship or shared values as a shield against potential aggression. Power and the fear of power are the prince's ultimate defense. But we cannot interpret *The Prince* to mean that statesmen should constantly seek raw power, aiming to dominate or destroy adversaries through brute force. Machiavelli maintained that such actions are shortsighted and ultimately self-defeating. If he could speak today, he might say something like this: When push comes to shove, power gives you an edge. You have to have the tangible capabilities to impose your wishes and to eliminate your opponents. If you have that capability, others will think twice before challenging you. And if they do challenge you, you can crush them.

Like Thucydides, Machiavelli was deeply suspicious of alliances: "When one asks a powerful neighbor to come to aid and defend one with his forces, they . . . are as useless as mercenaries" (Machiavelli 1952, 77). Machiavelli and Thucydides stress state self-reliance as the decisive factor to survival, particularly as it relates to military defense. There is no guarantee that allies will do what they pledge to do. Furthermore, Machiavelli argues that relying on allies makes the prince a prisoner of those allies. The prince becomes vulnerable to the interests and desires of his allies and the prince's own interests become compromised. Hence, the prince should avoid entangling alliances and pursue his own power.

Thomas Hobbes (1588–1679), a British philosopher, contributed to realist theory through his conception of the nature and the condition of man. Heir to Puritan notions of human nature, Hobbes conceived of men as essentially selfish and evil creatures. In a state of nature, man is pitted against man and the only rule is survival of the strongest. Writing in the *Leviathan*, Hobbes characterized the state of nature as "continual fear and danger of violent death; and the life of man [as] solitary, poor, nasty, brutish, and short." Hobbes argued that one way to overcome the unsavoriness of human instincts and escape the state of nature is to vest power and authority in a leviathan—an absolute state, particularly a sovereign or king—that can enforce human agreements and protect citizens from each other. This so-called leviathan uses power to control the baser human instincts, allowing citizens to live civilly in a social environment relatively free from violence.

Realists have drawn upon Hobbes's state-of-nature theme, characterizing the international system as anarchy, or absence of higher authority, lacking a world government to enforce agreements or prevent aggression. Without a world government, or in Hobbesian terms, an overall leviathan, international relations can be very dangerous, so states must be prepared for war. Thus, the law of the jungle applies to nation-states existing in this international state of nature. The essence of interstate relations is conflictual and often violent.

Carl von Clausewitz (1780–1831), in *On War*, sees war as the "continuation of political activity by other means." Von Clausewitz, a Prussian general who fought in the Napoleonic wars, stresses the importance of military power for achieving political aims. Military power is an appropriate tool of states to accomplish their goals, especially when political pressure and negotiation prove ineffective. Twentieth-century heads of state have also noted the importance of military power. When told by aides that the pope was displeased with the Soviet treatment of Christians, Joseph Stalin reportedly responded, "How many divisions does the pope have?" And Mao Zedong, the leader of the communist revolution in China, is credited with the saying that "power comes from the barrel of a gun." Realists are noted for their emphasis on military means to coerce others and secure their interests in the international environment.

Realism also has economic implications. Alexander Hamilton (1755–1804), for example, argued for the primacy of politics over economics in his "Report on Manufactures." Hamilton's view is considered an intellectual precursor to economic nationalism or neomercantilism (discussed later in this chapter) in its advocacy of economic self-sufficiency. He asserted that the U.S. government should actively promote a highly diversified economy based on industrial production. A strong, diverse domestic economy is crucial to a nation's security because it enables a state to be self-reliant in times of crisis. Economically, it might be less costly to get goods and services from abroad. However, the United States should avoid becoming dependent on others for the goods and services that are necessary for the nation's security and economic health. Hamilton advocates a central role for the state in the development and protection of key national industries and the management of the economy. He argues that political considerations such as state-building and national security must take precedence over strictly economic interests and the state must be willing to intervene in the market to secure state interests.

Thucydides, Machiavelli, Hobbes, von Clausewitz, and Hamilton are representative of realism's rich intellectual and philosophical heritage. Contemporary realism builds upon their insights, accepting them as foundational assumptions for a theoretical framework that analyzes, explains, and predicts international relations.

CONTEMPORARY REALISM

Contemporary realism embraces many variations—traditional realism, neorealism, structural realism, mercantilism, and neomercantilism. But whatever their differences, each of these variations rests on four organizing assumptions from which hypotheses, propositions, and generalizations may be deduced regarding the nature of international relations. Let's look at these assumptions in turn.

1. The state is the most important actor in international relations. Since the Treaty of Westphalia (1648), international relations have been based on political units called nation-states. That treaty marked the fact that the transnational authority of the Roman Catholic Church (which had long been fading) was displaced by distinct territorial entities unified by monarchs who asserted absolute sovereignty within a defined territory. That is, the states, or representatives of states (the government), have the final say regarding policy within their territorial jurisdictions.

Realists are quick to point out that while sovereignty and autonomy may be considered rights in legal theory, in practice that "final say" within a territory requires the power to deter outside intervention. In other words, autonomy stems from capability. The recognition of the sovereign nation-state in 1648 fundamentally changed the character of international relations. The Church no longer had even the nominal capability to maintain a transnational sovereignty, while monarchs were able to militarily establish territorial states where they exercised jurisdiction. For realists, international relations since 1648 principally concern the activities and interactions between territorial nation-states.

2. The state is a unitary and rational actor. This is a simplifying assumption, but it is analytically helpful for understanding international relations. Realists recognize that states are not, literally, unitary; they are composed of individuals, groups, and even diverse governmental actors such as legislatures and bureaucracy. However, all of these differing views are ultimately integrated through state structures so that the state speaks with one voice (Viotti and Kauppi 1993, 35). And that single voice speaks for a rational state—a single actor capable of identifying goals and preferences and determining their relative importance. The state is also capable of engaging in a cost-benefit analysis and choosing optimal strategies for achieving its goals.

The realist image of the state as an integrated unit possessing rationality has two advantages. First, analysis of international relations becomes less complicated if the state is viewed as a single actor that interacts with other actors. After all, the goal is to make generalizations and predictions, a goal that cannot be achieved unless the complex set of associations comprising international relations is simplified. Second, it allows analysts to paint the big picture, without getting bogged down in the minutiae of who said/did one thing or another in international relations.

3. International relations are essentially conflictual. While all realists accept this assumption, they differ in assigning reasons for it. Traditional realists see international relations as inherently conflictual because they are pessimistic in their assessment of

human nature itself. Traditional realists, such as Hans Morgenthau and E. E. Carr, are largely Hobbesian. Human beings are, at bottom, selfish, aggressive creatures prone to base behavior. States are human creations; therefore, states must possess these same characteristics. While some states may strive for goodness and peace, they must always guard against aggression, arming themselves to defend against other states owning less virtuous motives.

Structural realists point to structural, or systemic, attributes which contribute to international conflict and condition the behavior of states. The international system, according to structural realists, is characterized by anarchy and the balance of power—both of which shape state actions. Kenneth Waltz (1959), for example, argues that anarchy is a permissive cause of war because there is no higher authority or world government to prevent aggression. States must resort to "self-help" in order to secure their survival and their national interests. All states want to continue to exist regardless of government type, ideology, or demographic characteristics. All are subjected to anarchy. All behave in the same predictable, rational ways as a result. As Waltz (1959, 201) points out, "States do not even enjoy an imperfect guarantee of their security unless they set out to provide it for themselves. If security is something the state wants, then this desire, together with the conditions in which all states exist, imposes certain requirements on foreign policy that pretends to be rational. The departure from the rational model imperils the survival of the state."

Anarchy compels states to arm themselves for self-defense. However, the acquisition of arms is itself a provocative act. Other states must respond in kind or risk attack or destruction. This response leaves the first state no better off than it was before, so it must acquire even better weapons to counter the threat. Then the other states must respond in kind. And so on. Anarchy leads to arms-racing and arms-balancing behavior on the part of states. States with good and kind leaders will engage in the same kind of behavior as selfish and evil leaders because they exist in the same international environment.

States must also contend with another systemic feature, the distribution of capabilities. More commonly known as the balance of power, the distribution of capabilities affects the power calculation of states. According to structural realists, order and stability are maintained through a balance of power whereby states seek military and other capabilities in order to deter each other from attacking. States may also form alliances; however, those alliances are rarely permanent. For the realist, order and stability mean the absence of war or at least a reduced likelihood. This is achieved through a relatively equal distribution of power. If all states possess enough military capabilities to credibly defend themselves and inflict significant damage on an aggressor, then potential foes are discouraged from making war. Furthermore, the possession of capabilities, both military and economic, often translates into influence that can enable states to get other states to do things that they may otherwise not do.

The distribution of capabilities in the international system is not static, and shifts in the balance of power can threaten international stability. Several factors can disrupt the status quo. Technological innovations can very quickly give one state a significant military or economic advantage over others. The United States was the first to develop and deploy atomic weapons and after using atomic weapons against Japan during World War II, it became the undisputed military power in the world. But that advantage was short-lived. The Soviet Union exploded an atomic bomb in 1949, and Great Britain and France followed suit shortly thereafter. For those few years, however, every state in the international system was vulnerable to a nuclear attack because they had no credible deterrent.

Uneven economic growth rates can also disrupt the status quo, causing shifts in the balance of power. States and their economies grow at different rates. Some states are rising powers while others are declining. Consider contemporary China for example. China's potential for economic growth and development is staggering. China is likely to grow at a faster rate than most other states; this growth can lead to international instability and conflict as other states increasingly feel threatened. States must adjust their policies to account for changes in the balance of power.

Security and geostrategic issues, or high politics, dominate the international agenda. Given the hostile international environment and the dire consequences associated with international war, national security is the top priority of states. Traditional realists see the acquisition of power as the principal strategy for achieving national security. States will engage in power-maximizing behavior, particularly as it relates to their military capabilities. Other international issues, including economics, the environment, human rights, and poverty, occupy the realm of low politics. States may address these issues but by no means treat them as priorities.

Neorealists modify the traditional realist position by ascribing greater importance to economic issues. Neorealists emphasize economic issues because they relate to national power and security. The neorealist's economic counterpart is the neomercantilist. These economic theorists evince a realist orientation in their focus on states in the international economy. International political economy is a subfield of international relations that centers on the relationship between markets and societies. Neomercantilists see participation in a highly interdependent world economy as necessary for attaining and maintaining great-power status. However, interdependence, of necessity, limits the autonomy of the state because states are reliant on each other to varying degrees. Neorealists and neomercantilists argue that interdependent relationships are rarely symmetrical. States foster dominant, asymmetrical interdependent relationships with others and manipulate these relationships to their advantage. States also seek to minimize interdependent relationships in which they are vulnerable. Furthermore, states intervene in the domestic and international economy to protect industries that contribute to the wealth and power of the state.

Neorealists/neomercantilists see certain types of economic activities, especially industrial production, as crucial to the power and security of the state. They also recognize that quests for military power and economic development are not necessarily compatible. The trade-off hypothesis posits that spending in the military sector can compromise economic health. Also known as the "guns v. butter" hypothesis, the trade-off hypothesis suggests that states will seek to maximize security, not power. The acquisition of power is not the principal goal of states, as traditional realists suggest. Rather, neorealists/neomercantilists argue that states are often willing to satisfy, not maximize, military security, exchanging some power for robust economic health.

It is important to note that neorealists do not consider all types of economic activity to be equally important. They are not concerned with the international trade in potato chips or shoes or basketballs. Neorealists are interested in industries in leading sectors of the economy—those sectors that spur economic growth and generate spin-off industries. In the past, leading sectors included textiles, steel, durable goods (refrigerators, stoves, etc.), and automotives. Durable goods and automotives remain important today, but computers, technology, and telecommunications have also emerged as leading sectors. Neorealists/neomercantilists advocate industrial policies that promote a state's competitiveness in leading sectors because they foster diversification and development, thereby enhancing state wealth and power.

In sum, contemporary realism is a mixture of variations of political realism and economic realism (mercantilism and neomercantilism). This world view shapes the way realists see international organizations in international relations. In the next section, we examine realist explanations for the nature of international organizations—why they are created and how they work—in the context of sovereign states struggling for power in a hostile international environment.

REALISM AND THE NATURE OF INTERNATIONAL ORGANIZATIONS

Realists argue that no hierarchy of authority exists in international relations. The international system is characterized by anarchy, where authority resides with each individual state. No international entity exercises jurisdiction over states or reviews their domestic or foreign policy decisions. Anarchy, however, does not mean chaos. The international system is, in fact, quite orderly because a power hierarchy does exist among states. Some states are endowed with a plentitude of resources and, through design or chance, have attained great-power status. Realists tend to classify states in terms of this hierarchy as super-, great, middle, or lesser powers. And it is through this power hierarchy that the creation and nature of international organizations is explained.

Hegemonic stability theory is a widely accepted explanation for the creation and behavior of international organizations. According to Robert Gilpin:

> An international system is established for the same reasons that any political system is created; actors enter social relations and create social structures in order to advance particular sets of political, economic or other interests. Because the interests of some of the actors may conflict with those of other actors, the particular interests that are most favored by the social arrangements tend to reflect the relative powers of the actors. (Gilpin 1981, 9)

International organizations and law thus represent the social arrangements among states whereby the interests of the powerful are institutionalized.

One type of power distribution is a unipolar, hegemonic system in which "a single powerful state controls and dominates lesser states in the system" (Gilpin 1981, 29). The dominant state, or hegemon, creates international organizations and regimes to further its own interests and values in the international system. The hegemon uses its wealth and dominant power to create international organizations and bears the costs of maintaining them. The hegemon also provides incentives, such as security guarantees or economic assistance, in order to get other states to join. Once the international organization is established, the dominance of the hegemon and the tangible incentives it offers encourage other member states to defer to the hegemon's leadership.

Realists tend to focus on international organizations that are intergovernmental and public in nature. Since states are the most important actors in international relations, the organizations to which they belong become the subject of analysis. Adherents of hegemonic stability theory see international organizations as an extension of the hegemon. The effectiveness of international organizations is directly related to the hegemon's power. As the power of the hegemon declines, so does its support for the international organizations it has created. The diffusion of the hegemon's power also emboldens those who stand to benefit from a change in the status quo. These states will challenge existing institutions and norms, and ultimately seek to overthrow the existing order. For many realists, hegemony is required for the formation of international organizations, and their maintenance requires continued hegemony (Keohane 1984, 31).

In a similar vein, long-cycle theory posits an international order provided by a world leader. George Modelski (1978) argues that the international system can be understood in terms of recurrent historical patterns, or cycles, of world leadership. Each cycle of world leadership, lasting approximately 100 years, can be characterized by four distinct phases—global war, world leadership, delegitimation, and deconcentration. The first phase, global war, is a military conflict among states to determine the nature of world order. Global war is a "crude selection mechanism" of the state that gets to decide the rules and norms of the new system. For example, World War II was a global war in that it pitted liberal, capitalist democracies against fascist, imperial dictatorships. Usually, global wars are great ideological struggles between groups of states with markedly different views as to how the world ought to be ordered.

During the second phase, world leadership, the "winner" of the global war consolidates its power and establishes international organizations. Through the creation of international organizations and international law, the world leader's vision of world order is institutionalized and its dominant position legitimized. However, as the world leader's power capabilities decline, it enters the third phase, delegitimation. During delegitimation, rising states challenge the world leader's authority to lead. This greatpower competition, also known as oligopolistic competition, erodes the foundation of world order the world leader has created. The fourth phase in the long cycle of world leadership is deconcentration. During deconcentration, the world leader resorts to domination by force rather than domination by nonmilitary means. This further erodes the order and the power to maintain that order because such territoriality is a much more costly endeavor. The weakening of the world leader sets the stage for the next global conflict.

Gilpin and Modelski are similar in that they see world order as the creation of a single dominant power that is subject to decline. The decline of the dominant power leads to an erosion in the importance of international organizations and their activities. And both argue that the decline of the hegemon or world leader is not sufficient for the breakdown of world order. For that, a desire to change the existing system is required. That is, a revisionist power must be willing to challenge the status quo. In addition, the existing order must have weaknesses that the revisionist power can exploit. As leading states decline and other states rise, the international organizations comprising that world order are either rendered obsolete or are reshaped to reflect the new power distribution.

Consider the creation of the United Nations in 1945. Its principal sponsor in terms of political leadership and finance was the United States—the only victor to emerge from World War II virtually unscathed, both geostrategically and economically. Moreover, the United States was in sole possession of atomic weapons. Clearly, it was the most dominant state, a hegemon, a world leader. The UN Charter outlines several purposes for the institution, purposes that were directly linked to U.S. interests. First, the UN was charged with maintaining international peace and security. This task was given to the UN Security Council, which then consisted of five permanent and six nonpermanent members.* The permanent members were the World War II victors, the United States, Great Britain, France, the Soviet Union, and China, each of which had an absolute veto over Security Council decisions.

During the early years of its operation, the Council both considered and adopted U.S. initiatives. And, in its first three years, when the Security Council held more than 130 meetings, it was widely considered to be an effective instrument of international governance (Bennett 1995, 63). In 1949, however, two events signaled a dramatic shift in the global balance of power. First, the Soviet Union exploded an atomic bomb. Second, control over mainland China was seized by communists led by Mao Zedong. The nationalists, led by Chiang Kai-shek, were exiled to Taiwan, an island off the coast of the mainland. This shift in the global balance ended the effectiveness of the Security Council in international security affairs.

Tension between the communist, totalitarian Soviet Union and the capitalist, democratic United States was evident prior to 1949; however, the power differential minimized the likelihood of conflict. After all, the Soviet Union had been ravaged by war. It had lost more than 25 million people and was economically devastated. But a few years of relative peace and the acquisition of nuclear weapons put the revisionist Soviet Union in a position to challenge U.S. world leadership. The Soviet veto made it difficult to reach UN collective security decisions. The Security Council also lost credibility in the developing world because the United States refused to recognize communist China. Until 1971, it was Taiwan that represented China on the Security Council. The idea of UN collective security under U.S. leadership was dead. Thus the United States turned to the North Atlantic Treaty Organization (NATO), which was created that same year. Used as a limited collective security provision for western Europe, NATO was dominated by the United States.

Collective security under the UN Security Council between 1949 and 1990 was virtually nonexistent, with one notable exception. In 1950, the Security Council authorized the use of force by member states to repel a North Korean attack on South Korea. The Security Council resolutions passed only because the Soviet Union was boycotting the Council in protest against communist China's being denied UN membership and a permanent seat on the Council. During this Cold War period, threats to international peace and security came largely from one or more permanent members of the Security Council, each of which could impose unilateral force. Moreover, these members could veto any condemnation or response to their action. The British/French/Israeli invasion of Egypt (1956), the Soviet invasion of Afghanistan (1979), and the U.S. invasion of Grenada (1984) illustrate the signal failure of UN collective security to deter aggression and maintain peace and security. If great powers wish to use force, no organization is going to stop them.

The UN's failure was rooted in power politics and the underlying political order. That is, UN collective security measures work only when the powerful states want them to work. Recent UN successes in collective security (discussed extensively in Chapter 5) are no more than the result of a congruence of great-power interests, a congruence that is likely to be short-lived. The balance of power in the post–Cold War era is changing rapidly. The United States is widely considered a declining hegemon and has been

---

*In 1965, the nonpermanent membership in the UN Security Council was expanded to ten to reflect the overall increase in UN membership.

unwilling or unable to provide financial support for the UN or its activities. It is slow to pay its dues and often seeks to use its financial contributions as leverage to manipulate the UN. The United States, for the most part, fought the Korean War and paid for it. Forty years later in the Persian Gulf, the United States was forced to go, hat in hand, to its allies and ask them to pay for the use of U.S. military force. The decline of U.S. capabilities undermines its ability to lead. In other words, the United States either cannot or will not bear the costs of supporting its own creation.

Realists also recognize that international organizations can be formed without the benefit of a hegemon or world leader. International organizations can be created when states have common interests or common problems. For example, after the end of the Napoleonic Wars, the Congress of Vienna (1815) established the Concert of Europe in an effort to keep the peace in Europe. The great powers were willing to collude because each had an interest in avoiding war with the other, and hence in preventing any single state from gaining too much power. Europe in 1815 was a multipolar system; but instead of generating conflict, the great powers cooperated to avoid another continental war. And, arguably, the Concert of Europe succeeded in keeping the peace until World War I. However, when the balance of power shifted, the great-power interests changed, too, together with the efficacy of great-power cooperation.

Contemporary realist analyses of international organization and cooperation often employ game theory as a tool to explain why cooperation is difficult under conditions of anarchy. Since game theory is utilized by both realists and liberals to explain cooperation, or the lack thereof, it deserves a brief overview here.

ON GAME THEORY

Game theory, which is a variation of rational choice theory, originated with economists who were trying to explain choices among actors participating in a market. Although game theory employs jargon that can daunt nonspecialists, that jargon can readily be translated into more familiar language. Students, then, need not fear the logic of game theory, nor shy away from some of the explanations that logic generates. In simple terms, game theory seeks to explain economic and political choice by placing that choice in the context of a game—a game based on several governing rules or assumptions.

The first of game theory's assumptions is that rational actors seek absolute gain when choosing among strategies. That simply means that actors choose the best possible outcome for themselves, no matter what other actors might gain. This assumption is important for game theorists because they expect egoistic actors to think only in terms of their own gains—and not to think in relative terms, weighing their gains against those of others. Another assumption, at least for a simple game, is " perfect" information. This means that all the actors know all the payoffs (the possible outcomes) and all the possible strategies of other actors. In more complex games, this assumption is relaxed to include imperfect information. In this case, payoffs and actors may not be known, so probabilities have to be assigned. Fortunately for us, simple games are most often utilized to explain the behavior of states in international relations.

Many traditional realists and mercantilists see international relations and economics as a zero-sum game. In a zero-sum game, the interests of players are diametrically opposed and one player's gain is balanced by another player's loss (Binmore 1992, 237). Chess is a zero-sum game, as is backgammon: One player wins while the other loses. What does this mean in the context of international relations? When one state gains a greater degree of security, the security of other states is lessened by that degree. That's a zero-sum game. Under such conditions a state has no incentive to cooperate with others or even modify its behavior. The state's goal is to maximize its own power and security even if it is at the expense of other states.

Traditional realists and mercantilists are criticized for characterizing all international relations as strictly zero-sum. International relations may be competitive, but they need not necessarily be zero-sum. In fact, incentives to cooperate often exist. Realists respond that the security dilemma that states face in an anarchical environment is a Prisoners' Dilemma. The Prisoners' Dilemma is a simple game, but it clearly shows why cooperation is difficult to achieve even in non–zero-sum situations.

The Prisoners' Dilemma works like this. Two armed-robbery suspects, A and B, are in police custody. They have, in fact, committed the crime, but the only evidence is a gun the police found in their car. The police separate the prisoners and then question each one in a separate room—"the box." There, the police present each one a choice among four possible scenarios:

Scenario 1:
> Confess to armed robbery and rat out your buddy. Then you walk and your buddy goes up the river for twenty years.

Scenario 2:
> Clam up and let your buddy rat you out for armed robbery. Then you go up the river for twenty years and he walks.

Scenario 3:
> You both confess to armed robbery. Then you both get a deal—just ten years.

Scenario 4:
> You both clam up. Then the armed robbery goes away, but you both get three years for illegal possession of a firearm.

Surprisingly, Scenario 3 is the option of choice. Both prisoners confess to armed robbery and each receives a ten-year sentence.

What? Wouldn't it make more sense if both remained silent? Surely, being convicted of illegal possession—and getting a three-year sentence—is more rational than confessing to the greater crime. But the decision to confess is rational. Here's why. Recall that the rules of game theory say that each player is seeking absolute gains. That is, each player wants to get the best possible outcome for himself. The other rule is that each player knows all the possible strategies (moves) the other player can make. Not that each player knows what another player will actually do—but each player can predict the move based on what is rational from the other player's standpoint. Now consider the logic from Prisoner A's standpoint. "If I clam up and my buddy rats me out, I get the worst possible outcome—twenty years. If I rat him out and he clams up, then I get the best possible outcome—the walk. So Prisoner A has an incentive to confess. But what Prisoner A gets depends on what Prisoner B does. Prisoner B is going through the same rational, clam/rat thought process. So Prisoner B has an incentive to confess, too.

At this stage, each prisoner is inclined to confess, even though the outcome—ten years for armed robbery—is clearly not the best possible for the two of them. In fact, it would be optimal for both if each were to remain silent; that way, each would get just three years. So why wouldn't both prisoners just keep mum? The trouble is, that choice is not rational. If Prisoner A knows that Prisoner B will stay silent, then Prisoner A could "cheat," or defect: He could confess and get the walk. After all, a walk would be

optimal for A, much better than serving three years. But that option isn't available because Prisoner B is considering this same strategy . . . and Prisoner A knows that. So the
only solution to the Prisoners' Dilemma is for both suspects to confess, each one an-
ticipating the other's confession.

The Prisoners' Dilemma demonstrates how rational behavior can lead to suboptimal outcomes, and why cooperation is difficult to achieve. This is why realists argue
that even in positive-sum games, where all parties can achieve gains, cooperation remains unlikely. The security dilemma faced by states is quite similar to the dilemma
faced by the suspects in the box. Consider the case of Iran and Iraq for example. Each
seeks security in order to ensure its own survival. Both are rational and egoistic actors
seeking to maximize their national interests in a competitive, anarchical environment.
Iran and Iraq, then, are faced with a decision: Should they cooperate with each other
in order to meet their respective security needs, or should they defect from each other,
unilaterally arming themselves and risking a potentially expensive arms race? Cooperation could include both sides agreeing not to acquire sophisticated weapons, even
though those weapons might give them a strategic advantage over foes or be useful in
achieving foreign policy goals. Cooperating would also be beneficial because the government could divert resources usually targeted toward the military to the economic
base of the state. However, not cooperating, or defecting, also has advantages, especially
if the other side adheres to the cooperation course. The advantage gained by defecting provides incentives for cheating. Like Prisoners A and B, Iran and Iraq are faced
with four basic scenarios that have different outcomes. And, as for the prisoners, it is
rational for both Iran and Iraq to defect and engage in an expensive arms race, the worst
possible outcome for both states.

Realists have never argued that international cooperation does not occur. Situations
do exist in which states must coordinate their policies by agreeing on international
rules to avoid undesirable outcomes (Krasner 1991, 338). However, these situations
tend to reside in the realm of low politics. While cooperation may occur in such international issue areas as transportation and telecommunication, international and
national security are not conducive to such cooperation. The overriding significance
of security, together with rapid technological developments, forces states to be vigilant. Furthermore, as Susan Strange (1983, 345) states, "All those international arrangements dignified by the label regime are only too easily upset when either the balance
of bargaining power or the perception of national interest (or both together) changes
among those states who negotiate them."

For the realists, international organizations are either created by a hegemon or
formed through great-power cooperation. Realists tend to conceive of international organizations as IGOs that serve as extensions of the hegemon or function as great-power
directorates. Their activities are directly tied to the powerful states that control them.
As a result, international organizations are no more than the sum of their member
states; hence their behavior can be explained by the underlying power distribution in
the international system.

REALISM AND THE ROLE OF INTERNATIONAL ORGANIZATIONS

The explanations generated by realism regarding the creation of international organizations suggest that international organizations play one of two roles in the realist
world. One role is a marginal one. International organizations matter only at the

fringes of world politics (Mersheimer 1994/95). They may foster cooperation in non-controversial issue areas where states have common interests. However, they rarely constrain state behavior in issue areas where interests are diverse and opposed. In other words, international organizations play little or no role in maintaining international peace and security. Rather, balance-of-power realities dictate whether or not war will break out.

International organizations can also play an intervening role in great-power calculations. International organizations are used by the hegemon and great powers to further their interests in the international system. Other, non–great-power states may also use international organizations to attain goals and to have a voice within the existing system. But, in terms of constraining state behavior, international organizations have little influence. States will bypass or ignore international organizations if their immediate security or important national interests are at stake.

In spite of this rather pessimistic view, international organizations do matter in the realist world. Schweller and Priess (1997) point out that international organizations perform several important functions. First, international organizations provide a mechanism for great-power collusion. Great powers usually benefit from the existing order and have an interest in maintaining it. After all, the fact that they are great powers suggests that they are doing well under existing rules and institutions. International organizations may not be useful if great-power interests collide, but do permit great powers to control other states in international systems. Second, international organizations are useful for making minor adjustments within the existing order while the basic underlying principles and norms remain uncompromised. An enduring international order must be flexible to account for changes in national interest and for rising and declining states. Third, international organizations can be agents of international socialization. International organizations legitimize the existing order, thereby gaining the acceptance of the status quo by those who are dominated. Finally, "international institutions are the 'brass ring' so to speak: the right to create and control them is precisely what the most powerful states have fought for in history's most destructive wars" (Schweller and Priess 1997, 13).

CRITICISMS OF THE REALIST APPROACH

Realism as a theoretical approach has several advantages. It is parsimonious, which means it is a simple and lean framework. At the same time, realism has extraordinary explanatory power regarding international relations and world politics, particularly as it relates to war and violent conflict. Given the complexities of world politics, realism's parsimony and insights have contributed to its popularity and longevity.

But realism is not without its critics. Liberalism, Marxism, and feminism mount challenges to many realist explanations of international relations and analyses of international organizations' behavior. However, a specific criticism of realism is its conceptual imprecision. Realism is based on the concept of power. After all, realism is power politics. But what is power? Very little consensus exists regarding a precise definition of power. Some see power as tangible, concrete military capabilities. Power is measured by the number of tanks, planes, and nuclear weapons a state has. Others see power as including potential. Japan and Germany are considered powerful, even though they do not possess any significant military capability. Their economic and technological prowess indicates that they could put forth a formidable military. And what about states that do have formidable militaries, but do not have the will to use them? Thus, many realists conceive of power as a thing—a thing that includes both tangible and intangible elements.

Power is also conceived of as influence. Influence means the ability to get other actors to do what they would otherwise not do. This definition of power is problematic because we rarely know what an actor would have done in the first place. Analysis also becomes complicated because power is linked with authority. The pope is a powerful man, not because he has any divisions but because he commands moral and religious authority. Is U.S. hegemony based on its tangible capabilities, or has it been able to influence others through the power of its ideas regarding democracy, equality, human rights, and self-determination?

Realism is based on a concept that is so imprecise that it raises questions regarding other key concepts. If we do not know precisely what power means, then how do we know what balance of power means? How can we determine whether a balance of power exists among states, whether a state is revisionist or status quo, or whether a state is a rising or declining power? How, then, do we know that international institutions reflect the underlying power distribution?

Another imprecise concept bandied about by realists is national interest. States seek power in the international system to secure their national interests. States create international organizations to further their national interests. States make political calculations based on their national interests. Outside of state survival, defining the national interests of states is next to impossible. Interests vary, and claims of national interest have been used to justify almost every kind of state behavior. This leads to a circular logic. Realists assume rational states act in the national interest. Yet, national interest is measured by state action. Hence, anything the state does is, by definition, in the national interest. So, when the United States participates in the UN, it does so because it is in the national interest to do so. And if the United States ignores the UN, it does so because it is in the national interest to do so. Realism, thus, becomes one big tautology: Because the national interest can be construed to mean anything, it explains nothing.

In spite of these conceptual shortcomings, realism retains a great deal of value in explaining international relations and the behavior of international organizations. Realism paints a rather bleak picture of international relations as hostile, conflictual, and warlike. Realists are not very optimistic about the role international organizations play in preventing war and violent conflict. International organizations are tools of the great powers to control lesser states without dominating them by force. They are agents of the dominant power(s) and serve great-power interests at the expense of others. International organizations do not promote some idealized notion of the "collective good." For realists, the so-called collective good is defined by the dominant power(s)—in effect, what is good for me is good for the collective. The behavior and priorities of international organizations are to be understood in terms of the motivations and priorities of leading member states.

LIBERALISM

Liberalism challenges the pessimistic world view of realism by painting a more encouraging picture of the relations between societies. Liberals see international relations as a mixture of cooperation and conflict and argue that international organizations can play a positive, constructive role in promoting international stability and global welfare. For liberals, the nature of international relations has fundamentally changed during the latter half of the twentieth century for three substantive reasons. First, the importance of military force in international relations has waned. Conventional weapons have evolved, becoming so destructive that their usefulness for achieving foreign policy goals has declined. Weapons of mass destruction (chemical, nuclear, and biological) function as effective deterrents, but are not practical for war fighting. Second, the spread of democracy has instilled values of compromise and the rule of law in governments—values that inhibit decision-makers from resorting to war to settle disputes. Third, societies are not as isolated from each other as they were in the past. Societies are linked together by global markets and global production. Nation-states are linked together by instantaneous mass communication, rapid transportation, and emerging technologies such as the World Wide Web. Societies are increasingly seeing themselves as part of a greater whole rather than as ships of state navigating the treacherous waters of war. International relations today is significantly different from the geostrategic power game played earlier in the twentieth century on the European continent. Liberals, then, are much more optimistic about the prospects for international peace.

Liberalism is a term that has different and often contradictory meanings. Many journalists use the word "liberal" to indicate a position along an ideological spectrum. Liberals on this spectrum are to the left of conservatives and tend to favor government policies that promote social welfare, health care, and civil rights. Conservatives, on the other hand, tend to favor government policies that promote business, prisons, and military spending. Hence, Senator Edward Kennedy (D-MA) and Jesse Jackson are considered liberals while former Representative Newt Gingrich (R-GA) and Senator Jesse Helms (R-NC) are considered conservatives. This common usage of liberalism suggests a political position that is rather leftist in nature. Given the political environment since the 1980s, to be liberal often has meant being out of sync with mainstream America.

Liberalism means something quite different to economic and political theorists. Liberalism in economics refers to a belief in capitalism and its emphases on profit, private property, and a free, self-regulating market. In political theory, liberalism means a belief in individual equality, individual liberty, participatory democracy, and limited government. Both of these definitions represent classical liberalism. Former Presidents Ronald Reagan and George Bush, both conservatives in a journalistic sense, are classical liberals. The conceptual confusion surrounding liberalism has prompted many scholars to adopt the term pluralism to distinguish between journalistic and scholarly uses. In this text, however, we'll retain the term liberalism and use it in its classical sense. Students should recognize that the majority of policymakers in the United States have a liberal world view because they have been socialized by liberal ideas. The political and economic systems of the United States are based on liberal principles that are institutionalized in the U.S. Constitution and in the nation's laws. As a result, most citizens in the United States, including policymakers, have a liberal orientation.

Liberalism has emerged out of the Anglo-American experience of political and economic development. Both Great Britain and the United States have evolved into capitalist democracies and both have been the world leader or the hegemon in international relations. Both Great Britain and the United States have promoted a liberal vision of world order (limited politics/emphasis on free trade) since 1850, largely because of their disillusionment with the politics and economics of continental Europe. The United States found the politics of Europe distasteful and dangerous and sought to isolate itself from the realpolitik of the day (Ambrose 1988). U.S. isolationism did not mean the United States was totally inward-looking. The United States was more than willing to challenge the European powers in the Western Hemisphere, particularly on the North American continent, maintaining, however, its insularity from European politics. Rudimentary communication and transportation systems gave the United States time to consider and react to European affairs. Crises often dissipated by the time U.S. officials in Washington even heard about them.

Isolationism also did not mean that the United States had no contact with Europeans in Europe. The United States engaged in trade with all the major European powers under a liberal trade and monetary order sustained by Great Britain (1815–1917). Through example and incentives, Great Britain established free trade (reducing tariffs) and a stable monetary order (the gold standard). The political interests of states were subordinated to international economic stability and market considerations. Both the United States and Great Britain benefited extensively from free trade in terms of wealth and economic diversification.

U.S. isolation from European political affairs effectively ended early in the twentieth century with World War I. World War I is considered by many to be a senseless and irrational war because states fought for no identifiable geostrategic reason (Tuchman 1984). Rather, alliances and virulent nationalism drew states into "accidental war." After the war, President Woodrow Wilson stated that U.S. foreign policy would support democracy, anticolonialism, and self-determination internationally. Woodrow Wilson was the principal sponsor of the League of Nations and these values were incorporated in the League Charter.

Unfortunately for international stability and the League of Nations, the United States was unwilling to assume a liberal leadership role. Domestic politics and a resurgence of isolationist sentiment prompted U.S. officials to politically withdraw from European affairs. The U.S. Senate refused to ratify the League of Nations Charter and the League had no capable leadership. Great Britain was willing, yet unable to provide political leadership. Great Britain also could not bear the costs of sustaining the liberal international economic order as it had in the past. World War I nearly bankrupted Great Britain and weakened it politically, economically, and socially.

Absent effective leadership, states reverted to nationalistic, mercantilist policies. Capitalism for all intents and purposes collapsed, and the resulting Great Depression gave rise to the very illiberal policies of fascism and the New Deal. The world once again was at war in 1939. World War II ended in 1945 and the United States emerged from the war as the dominant state in terms of military and economic capabilities—in a position, politically and economically, to shape world order and to fashion a system in which it and other states could mutually benefit. The United States institutionalized liberal rules and norms in international politics through the creation of international organizations and a capitalist international economic order.

Liberalism is rooted in an intellectual tradition that is as rich and respected as realism. In the following section, we examine the liberal philosophical tradition. Then we outline the assumptions of liberalism as a theoretical approach to provide a different perspective regarding the nature of international organizations in a liberal world.

Like realism, liberalism has several variations that have both political and economic influences. And, like realism, liberalism generates compelling explanations about the dynamics of world politics.

PHILOSOPHIC ROOTS OF LIBERALISM

Hugo Grotius (1583–1645) is considered to be the father of international law. In *The Law of Prize and Booty* and *The Law of War and Peace*, Grotius identifies international norms and rules that states have agreed upon, either explicitly through treaties or implicitly through practice. He argues that states need to abide by their agreements in order to foster cooperative international relations. For Grotius, international relations includes economic as well as political transactions. The rules that emerged to govern those transactions shaped the way states interact with one another. Grotius's contribution to liberal international relations theory is his acknowledgment of the cooperation that occurs among states in an anarchical environment. Grotius also articulates how formal and informal rules governing international relations are in the self-interest of states.

John Locke's (1632–1704) *Second Treatise of Government* is considered the seminal work of liberal political thought and has had a significant, albeit indirect, influence on liberal international relations theory. John Locke focuses on the kind of government that is conducive to the happiness and well-being of its citizens. For Locke, individuals and individual happiness are the keys to a productive society. Human beings possess rights, rights that exist in nature and belong to individuals by virtue of their humanity. These natural rights include the right to life, liberty, and the pursuit of private property. They also include the right to political equality, equality under the law, and self-government.

Locke emphasizes the importance and value of the individual to society and prescribes a very limited role for the government. In the state of nature, human beings are essentially cooperative; however, the condition of scarcity compels individuals to act in a self-interested manner. In order to create a society, a government must protect private property and arbitrate disputes between individuals. With private property rights protected and legal mechanisms for settling disputes in place, individuals are free to realize their rights and potential to the fullest. For Locke, the best government is the government that "governs least." The best way to ensure good government is to allow individuals to participate in politics through voting and holding public office. Locke's more important contributions to liberal international relations theory are his view that human beings are essentially cooperative and the idea of limited government composed of, and influenced by, those governed.

Similarly, Adam Smith's (1723–1790) *The Wealth of Nations* addresses the essence of human beings and the role of government in society. According to Smith, human beings have a natural inclination to "truck, barter and exchange one thing for another." Human beings are essentially economic creatures driven by a quest to acquire and dispose of property. Society is born out of economic exchange between individuals. Smith argues that self-interest motivates individuals to action, yet this selfish behavior can have a surprising result—social harmony. Unlike Hobbes, who argues that selfish behavior makes life particularly nasty, Smith argues that the "market" can harness the selfish impulses of individuals and propel a society to progressively higher levels of development. How does the market mechanism do this? According to Smith, the market is governed as if by an "invisible hand" that regulates the behavior of individuals in a society. Self-interested individuals interacting with other self-interested individuals will create competition to generate the goods and services a society needs and wants, at a price it is willing to pay (Heilbroner 1986, 55). Goods and services are not produced out of kindness and goodwill. They are provided out of the self-interest of the producer. Competition ensures that no one provider will artificially raise prices to take advantage of consumers, because a competitor will offer the same good or service at a fair price. For Smith, this self-regulating market promotes the welfare of individuals and societies.

Smith recognizes that human nature is complex and that individuals could be driven by other passions, such as racism, nationalism, and religious devotion. Smith thought that these other passions could be held in check if the instinct for economic self-interest was developed. In other words, economic self-interest not only promoted social harmony but would also override other human passions that give rise to violent human conflict.

The writings of Adam Smith support Locke's idea of a limited government. The idea of society's being self-regulating because of the market's invisible hand suggests a limited role of the state in the market. Borrowing the term *laissez-faire* from the eighteenth-century French physiocrats, Smith argues that the government should not interfere in the market, lest it disrupt the market's natural tendencies toward equilibrium. Smith also contributes the idea that economic self-interest produces social harmony while passions such as racism and nationalism promote conflict and violence. Smith sees economics as being strongly associated with peace, and politics as associated with war. This separation of politics from economics represents a shift away from the mercantilist idea that economic activity should enhance the national treasury and serve the power interests of the state. For Smith and other liberals, the economic interests of individuals should determine the politics of the state. The "wealth of nations" results from the economic self-interest of individuals.

David Ricardo (1772–1823) builds on the work of Adam Smith and highlights the importance of international trade for states in his classic work, *The Principles of Political Economy and Taxation.* International trade is important to states because domestic economies are constrained by limited resources and conflicting interests while the international economy provides additional avenues for growth and expansion (Crane and Amawi 1997, 57). States benefit from international trade by exporting products in which they have a comparative advantage. Having a comparative advantage means that one state can produce a good or service at a lower cost than other states can. "The theory of comparative advantage holds that nations should produce and export those goods and services in which they hold a comparative advantage, and import those items that other nations can produce at a lower cost" (Balaam and Veseth 1996, 450). Through comparative advantage, global resources and welfare can be maximized.

The theory of comparative advantage means that states should specialize in providing a good or service to the export market that they can produce at a lower cost than other states. For example, the United States produces computer chips efficiently and at a much lower cost than other states. The United States also produces potato chips, but not as efficiently as Poland. Poland can produce computer chips, but at a much higher cost. The theory of comparative advantage would prescribe an international division of labor in which the United States would export computer chips and Poland would export potato chips. This division is the most efficient way to allocate resources. The principal beneficiaries, of course, would be individual consumers, who would have both computer chips and potato chips for the least possible cost.

Immanuel Kant (1742–1804) incorporates Locke's view of representative government and addresses the issue of individuals who are organized into territories. Kant argues in his classic *Perpetual Peace* that states need to form a federation whereby they can peacefully resolve their disputes. The formation of a world republic is part of the natural evolution of human society. Kant argues that the world republic should be composed of nation-states that are constitutional democracies. Peace and cooperation would be easier to achieve because the decision of whether or not to go to war would lie with the people. Kant's political philosophy is informed by the liberal writing of Smith and Ricardo in that he assumes that the economic self-interest of individuals contributes to peaceful relations among nation-states.

Jeremy Bentham (1748–1832) is commonly associated with a group of thinkers called the utilitarians. The utilitarians see individuals as rational creatures who are capable of engaging in cost-benefit analysis and deciding for themselves what their wants and needs are. Bentham differs from the other liberal writers of this time because he totally rejects the idea of natural law. Recall that Locke, Smith, Ricardo, and Kant appeal to "natural law" to support their theories of rights and government. The idea of natural law is that human beings and human society are governed by knowable laws of nature that need only to be discovered by man. For Bentham, law was man-made and must be judged on the basis of how it affects society. The utilitarian principle is that laws and institutions of a society should produce "the greatest good for the greatest number." Bentham reinforces the liberal ideas of limited, representative government and the market as an institution that generates a great deal of the wealth for a great many people.

Grotius, Locke, Smith, Ricardo, Kant, and Bentham have influenced, both directly and indirectly, the evolution of liberal international relations theory. For all of these thinkers, the relationship of politics and economics is a crucial one. Normatively speaking, economics should determine politics. Economic behavior is seen as the path to social harmony, or at the very least, as promoting cooperation. The state, which is the embodiment of politics, grows out of economic relations and should not interfere in the market. The market regulates itself and the behavior of the participants within it. Furthermore, the individual is of importance (not the state) because it is individuals that comprise the family, the firm, and the state itself. The liberal view shapes the expected behavior and policies of international organizations. In the following section, we'll look at the organizing assumptions of contemporary liberalism as a theoretical approach to international relations.

CONTEMPORARY LIBERALISM

The liberal theoretical approach to international relations is based on four assumptions. The first assumption is that both state and nonstate actors are important in international relations. The philosophic tradition of liberalism places a great deal of value on individuals and the social, economic, and political organizations to which they belong. As a result, liberals focus on households, firms, interest groups, governments, and international organizations. Substate actors such as individuals and interest groups can have important effects on international affairs, both directly and indirectly. Bill Gates, chairman of Microsoft, can shape global information networks by determining how and what kind of information is accessed. Interest groups can lobby governments for foreign policies that help them achieve some or all of their goals.

Liberals also see international and transnational actors as shaping the international landscape. International organizations include not only intergovernmental organizations (IGOs) but also nongovernmental organizations (NGOs) that can have both public and private functions. The activities of multinational corporations (MNCs), drug cartels, and terrorist organizations also influence international affairs. Contrary to the realist assumption that the state is the most important actor, liberals see nonstate actors as important because these actors have independent, as well as indirect, influences on the domestic and foreign policies of states.

The second assumption of the liberal theoretical approach holds that the state is not necessarily a unitary and rational actor. Governments are composed of individuals, bureaucratic agencies, and judicial and legislative bodies that can have differing and competing interests. As a result, what may be rational from the standpoint of a unitary state may not be rational from the standpoint of a government official, like the president or the secretary of state, or of an agency like the Department of Defense. While choices are still made on the basis of self-interest, what is considered "self" is determined by the level of analysis that affects the perception of rationality. This disaggregation of the state expands analyses of governmental decision-making and can explain why governments make the policy choices that they do.

In addition to being disaggregated, the state, as seen by liberals, is a much more fluid entity comprising competing interests that seek either to control the government or lobby the government to achieve their policy objectives. In other words, the state is not autonomous and it can be swayed by internal, as well as external, influences. The government may be controlled by any group (party) or coalition of groups (parties) at any given time. The difference between realists and liberals on this point centers on how to define the national interest. Realists see the national interest in terms of external considerations and the relative position of the United States vis à vis other states. Realists have criticized U.S. politics in the 1990s for being dominated by special interests; as a result, the national interest has been compromised with respect to other states. However, liberals argue that the national interest is defined by the equilibrium between all the competing interests within the United States. For example, according to the environmentalists, clean air is in the national interest. But the automobile industry argues that cars with combustion engines are in the national interest—their production employs people, promotes commerce, and makes it easier for everyone to travel. In liberal theory, these interests compete within the confines of the political process and are reconciled through compromise. The equilibrium of interests is the national interest.

The third assumption of liberalism is that the nature of international relations is a composite one—a combination of conflict and cooperation. This assumption stems from the liberal view of human nature as self-interested yet cooperative. Smith and Ricardo thought that self-interested economic behavior in a market led to social harmony. Most contemporary liberals are not this idealistic. However, modern liberals claim that self-interested market behavior creates wealth and leads to increased international transactions. These international transactions afford a situation known as complex interdependence whereby states and other actors within societies are interconnected through trade and finance. Complex interdependence provides incentives to state and nonstate actors to cooperate with each other because they rely on each other. Liberals acknowledge that mutual reliance is by no means symmetrical. Nevertheless, they see complex interdependence as fostering cooperation and reducing the likelihood of violent conflict. Complex interdependence is a defining characteristic of the international system—a characteristic that conditions the behavior of state and nonstate actors.

Many liberals argue that the proliferation of shared norms and values, brought about by the proliferation of representative, democratic governments, has also created a kind of moral interdependence. Societies organized around such democratic principles as individual rights, equality under the law, majority rule, and minority rights are predisposed to the peaceful settlement of disputes, collaboration, and compromise. Simply put, democratic societies identify with each other because of shared norms and values. Even when conflict persists, the conflict is not prone to violence because the decision to go to war does not rest solely in the hands of a single individual or small group. Decision makers in democratic societies are accountable to their citizens. Hence, democracies rarely make war on each other (Oneal and Russett 1997; Russett 1993; Nincic 1992). Coupled with the economic and political costs of unilateral action, this type of moral interdependence promotes international coordination and cooperation under existing international laws and organizations.

The fourth assumption of liberalism is that a variety of issues can come to dominate the international agenda. Unlike realists, who see security and military issues at the top of the agenda, liberals point to the fact that economic, social, and environmental issues are also important to governments and societies. Hence, Iraqi troop movements might be important one week, starving people in Somalia another week, and a financial crisis in Mexico or Thailand in yet another. Issue areas will involve multiple actors, from states to international organizations and nongovernmental organizations, and each will pursue its own strategies and goals (Keohane and Nye 1977, 37). For liberals, there is no hierarchy of international issues; consequently, international goals and interests are increasingly difficult to define.

LIBERALISM AND THE NATURE OF INTERNATIONAL ORGANIZATIONS

The liberal theoretical approach emphasizes several different kinds of international organizations—the IGO, the NGO, the MNC, and the regime. Hence, several different explanations regarding the origins and the essence of these organizations exist. Functionalism and institutionalism are two prominent liberal explanations regarding IGO and regime creation. Functionalism was once the dominant approach to liberal international organization theory, but its popularity among scholars has waned considerably in the last couple of decades because its predictions have not been borne out. According to Bennett (1991, 15), "The functionalist believes in the efficacy of a gradualist approach to world order with the attainment of political federation by installments." IGOs are created because of a basic need for them. The increase in transnational ties has led to integration and interdependence, which in turn has led many societies to share common problems. Many of these problems can be managed only through international cooperation, necessitating the creation of specialized international agencies with technical experts (Mitrany 1948, 1966; Haas 1964). IGOs are formed because, in effect, they "demand jurisdiction over preexisting national states" (Haas 1958, 16).

Functionalists recognize that state sovereignty is a well-entrenched principle in international relations. However, they argue that cooperation in narrow, nonpolitical (economic and social) issues areas leads to a "spillover" into larger, more politicized issues areas such as defense or monetary policy. Cooperation in economic and social spheres leads to confidence building, which promotes cooperation in more highly charged issues. IGOs socialize elites into recognizing that it is in their states' interest to join and participate in international organizations. As cooperative behavior becomes institutionalized, IGOs can evolve into supranational organizations such as the European Union (EU) or the World Trade Organization (WTO). The authority of the nation-state would be displaced incrementally by supranational institutions.

Institutionalism, which represents the most recent research in the liberal tradition on the study of international organization (IGOs and regimes), is a hybrid of realism, game theory, and functionalism. Robert Keohane's seminal work, *After Hegemony* (1984), examines how IGOs can assist egoistic state actors in overcoming collective action problems and encouraging cooperation under conditions of anarchy. Like realists, liberal institutionalists argue that a hegemonic power is necessary for the creation of IGOs and regimes. Like realists, institutionalists see the state as a unitary, rational actor interacting in a dangerous and uncertain world. Liberal institutionalists have been charged with being "realist by any other name" because of their adoption of realist precepts and assumptions (Mearsheimer 1995).

Unlike realists, however, institutionalists are more optimistic about the importance of international organization when a hegemon is in decline. Recall that realists who adhere to hegemonic stability theory argue that when a hegemon's power begins to wane, disorder and the decline of international organizations are the likely result. Liberal institutionalists argue that IGOs and regimes serve several purposes in addition to promoting the interests of the hegemon. IGOs and regimes reduce transaction and information costs to member states. They also regularize state behavior and promote transparency. Under conditions of complex interdependence, IGOs and regimes become valuable assets to states. They provide tangible benefits to members, who then become willing to share the cost of maintaining IGOs and regimes "after hegemony." This idea has been expressed in a game theoretic context using the concept of a *k group*. A *k group* consists of actors that would still benefit by providing for a public good (in this case, an IGO or regime) even if they have to bear the costs solely. A cost-benefit analysis of the payoffs between having an international organization or not having one suggests that the great, but nonhegemonic powers would find it rational and in their self-interest to maintain existing IGOs and regimes (Gowa 1988, 316).

Liberal institutionalists and realists both use game theory to explain the behavior of states, though institutionalists are more encouraging about the ability of international organizations to temper the ill effects of anarchy and the suboptimal outcomes it can yield for egoistic actors. By linking cooperation in one regime to cooperation in another, states become accustomed to using IGOs and regimes to achieve their goals and settle their disputes. This, coupled with the effects of complex interdependence, prompts states to abandon power-maximizing behavior and immediate self-interest for long-term stability.

The key to understanding the optimism of institutionalism and functionalism lies in their liberal identity. The international organizations we have discussed are liberal in nature. The world order the United States sought to institutionalize after World War II was based on economic and political liberalism. For many liberals, the key to U.S. hegemony is not so much economic or military as ideological. The United States possesses "soft" power, or the power of ideas (Nye 1990). The United States has been able to convince the world of the value of free trade and markets and has promoted the ideas of democratic and limited government. Antonio Gramsci (discussed in Chapter 4) identifies "ideas" as central to understanding hegemony. Hegemony is not simply based on material capabilities to coerce others. Hegemony is based on powerful and compelling ideas. Liberal ideas have become so pervasive internationally that they are widely accepted as economic and political "truths." Even though the United States has declined materialistically, the liberal world order it created will continue because it is based on time-tested and accepted ideas.

Institutionalists and functionalists both see IGOs and regimes as becoming something more than just the sum of their member states. Both see IGOs as important and influential actors in their own right, although they differ as to the degree of influence. Institutionalists do not see IGOs as displacing the nation-state. IGOs enable states to reach mutually beneficial outcomes in international relations (Schweller and Priess 1997, 3). States may be willing to cede some sovereignty to international organizations in some areas, such as trade, in exchange for the benefits provided by an autonomous organization. However, the state remains an important actor in international relations and still jealously guards most of its sovereign prerogatives.

In sum, the creation and nature of IGOs and regimes are explained by liberals in two ways. Institutionalists argue that hegemonic power is necessary for the creation of international organizations, but hegemony is not required for their continued maintenance. IGOs and regimes are collective goods that help promote the common interests and development of shared values. As a result, they are valuable to states and will be continued absent a hegemon. Hegemony is not required for functionalists. Issues and their complexity determine the need and creation of IGOs. Like-minded individuals and governments create organizations to manage complex problems.

MNCs are important international organizations for liberals because they see the private sphere as the locus of economic, social, and political innovation. MNCs are private, economic entities that are spawned by an expanding and increasingly efficient market. MNCs achieve global economies of scale whereby MNCs have control over, or access to, labor, production facilities, sales, and markets. For many liberals, MNCs are benign in nature. They are motivated by the profit motive, as are all individuals and firms participating in the market. The self-interest of shareholders drives MNCs toward greater and greater efficiencies and their activities propel international society to progressively higher levels of development. MNCs are the innovators of new technology and industrial organization. They create jobs and promote efficiency. More importantly, they bring high-quality goods and services to the world's consumers at a price they are willing to pay. MNCs are global citizens that respond to and serve the needs of an expanding market.

MNCs are also local and global citizens that serve their communities in more than just economic ways. They participate in partnerships with NGOs, universities, and individuals that contribute to governance and the development of knowledge, particularly in the area of environmental management and protection. For example, the Marine Stewardship Council (MSC) was created in 1999 as a result of a partnership between the World Wide Fund for Nature (WWF) and Unilever for the purpose of ensuring the long-term viability of fish stocks. In spite of the divergent organizational missions, the partnership helped both organizations develop "the shared perception of the added value of the partnership, over and above what each organization could achieve on its own" (Fowler and Heap 1998). This and other types of collaborative teams help "promote a more sustainable use of natural resources, improved economic opportunities for local communities and provide workable solutions for environmental problems (Kennedy, Lacher, Burton, Reis, Nations, Cesca, and Ramirez 1998, 32).

LIBERALISM AND THE ROLE OF INTERNATIONAL ORGANIZATIONS

Liberalism is more optimistic than realism about the contributions and independence of international organizations in international relations. Five interrelated roles can be discerned from the liberal approach. First, international organizations help states overcome collective action problems. Recall the Prisoners' Dilemma. Had the prisoners acted together (collectively) and kept silent, both would have achieved the optimal outcome, a light sentence. Yet, the uncertainty about what the other was going to do, plus uncertainty about what evidence the police had, provided incentives for both prisoners to cheat. The result was a suboptimal outcome for both players. Liberals, particularly institutionalists, argue that international organizations can change the rules of the game. With respect to the Prisoners' Dilemma, international organizations can function as figurative lawyers who advise their client(s). After all, the interests of the prisoners are not fundamentally opposed, especially in light of the consequences if both should confess. The prisoners could overcome their collective action problem if they had a lawyer or some kind of mediator/arbitrator.

Realists use the Prisoners' Dilemma to explain the security dilemma faced by states in an anarchical environment. The consequences associated with cooperation and defection are so dire for states because, in reality, security is no game. It means life or death for a great many people. Rational states really have no choice but to unilaterally pursue their own security interests, even if it means suboptimal outcomes for all states. Liberals point out that theory and practice can be quite different from each other. The pursuit of power and immediate self-interest have led to war, not to stability, as realists suggest. States that do not have significant military capability, like Sweden, Switzerland, Costa Rica, and Zimbabwe, have maintained their territorial integrity and avoided war. Alliances have worked to deter attacks on member states by credibly demonstrating that an attack on one member is an attack on all the members. For example, NATO is credited by institutionalists for preserving the peace in Europe during and after the Cold War (Duffield 1992, 1994a, b). NATO was instrumental in building confidence and trust among traditional enemies, arguably making it one of the most successful alliances in history. NATO also serves as the anchor for the EU, and its membership was urgently sought by Central European states such as Poland, Hungary, and the Czech Republic (and finally granted in 1999). For liberal institutionalists, NATO is the exemplar, the quintessential example of how egoistic states can overcome the most difficult of collective action problems—security. If each member state were seeking to obtain this goal unilaterally, it would bear enormous costs; moreover, such unilateral strategies would likely lead to suboptimal outcomes. By cooperating, each member state saves on cost and avoids the worst possible outcome—war.

States in successful alliances tend to have significant strategic, economic, and social ties. These ties inextricably bind the member states together to the extent that the security of one state is part and parcel of the security of other members of the alliance. The interdependence of an alliance builds over time, and its cohesion is closely associated with the deepening of economic integration. Alliance cohesion is as critical to the credibility of the deterrent as military capability. Alliances may possess significant military capabilities; however, if doubt exists that they will actually use those capabilities to defend an ally, then the utility of the deterrent is in question. Alliances with states that are tangibly intertwined, as are members of NATO, are more cohesive and therefore more credible.

Collective security organizations, like the UN Security Council, are similar to alliances in that an attack on one member is considered an attack on all. They differ in that collective security agreements entail universal membership and usually there is no presumptive aggressor (Goodby and O'Connor 1993). These variables considerably expand the number of possible outcomes and require states to look beyond their immediate self-interest. States must be willing to intervene in situations where they have no compelling strategic, military, or economic interests. Otherwise, collective security organizations run the risk of being just a cleverly disguised great-power concert.

Collective security organizations are considered less useful than alliances at maintaining peace. Membership in a collective security organization is diverse, or heterogeneous. Democracies, dictatorships, market, and command economies exist side by side, making it difficult to develop cohesion. Potential aggressors must be deterred by a credible threat of retaliation by the international community. It is one thing for the international community to respond to aggression in the Middle East where oil is involved. It is quite another to respond to aggression in sub-Saharan Africa where most members of the international community have little interest. Furthermore, in order for collective security to be successful, the permanent members of the Security Council and their close allies must not resort to unilateral uses of force. Liberals argue that, in spite of the obstacles to collective security, the post–Cold War era has witnessed dramatic steps toward a viable international collective security arrangement. They also point out that a great deal of cooperation fostered by international organizations has existed within the security realm, an area in which realists predict little or no cooperation outside of balance-of-power considerations.

Collective action problems exist in other issue areas ranging from the economy to the environment. The most difficult is the "free rider" problem. A free rider is an actor that benefits from the provision of a public good without contributing anything to providing that good. Public goods are "goods or services that, once provided, generate benefits that can be enjoyed by all simultaneously" (Balaam and Veseth 1996, 458). For example, liberals consider free trade a public good that is provided by the hegemon. The hegemon bears the costs of creating and maintaining the free trading system. In this case, a free rider is a state that benefits from the open markets of other states while at the same time keeping its markets closed to foreign competition. The hegemon usually carries a free rider because the gains associated with the free trading system outweigh the costs of the free rider. However, the balance of that equation shifts as the hegemon's capabilities decline. International organizations can help counter the free rider problem absent the hegemon by identifying unacceptable barriers to trade and providing a neutral forum for settling trade disputes. International organizations can, in a neutral manner, decide when it is permissible to discriminate against foreign goods. Under hegemony, a free rider gets away with free riding because a hegemon is willing to bear the costs. After hegemony, the free rider's position is increasingly untenable and international organizations provide a mechanism for discouraging such behavior.

A second role of international organizations is to promote economic prosperity and global welfare. Ideologically speaking, liberals argue that the world's goods, services, and resources should be distributed by the market. Liberals argue that the market yields the most efficient use of natural resources and the most efficient production of goods and services. Private ownership and private property rights are also important because private citizens and firms are more directly influenced by and can more easily adjust to market changes. Private citizens and firms are also more innovative and dynamic. Through the development of a global market based on comparative advantage, the welfare of the world can be maximized by improving the lot of individuals regardless of their nationality. International economic institutions, like the IMF and the WTO, exist to promote these goals.

International economic institutions have pursued several strategies in order to promote economic prosperity and global welfare. They have sought to reduce barriers to trade through multilateral negotiations. They have sought to eliminate protectionist measures by states, thereby forcing industries either to become efficient or lose out as casualties of the market. They have encouraged states to privatize industries and reduce their regulation of the market. They have development programs that encourage direct foreign investment by multinational corporations. They have provided funding for the creation of export industries that promote economic growth and development. They even help states adjust their economies to the new, global market realities. When international organizations promote global markets, trade, and investment, they are also promoting complex interdependence. Complex interdependence reduces the likelihood of war because the utility of military force in achieving national goals or settling disputes is greatly reduced.

A third role of international organizations is to help societies develop shared values and norms. Interdependence may reduce the chances of violent conflict; however, the problems associated with interdependence cannot be managed or solved unless societies have some common ground. International organizations foster certain values and help to establish certain norms that are conducive to the peaceful settlement of disputes, such as compromise, reciprocity, multilateralism, and the rule of law. International organizations promote democracy and democratic institutions. They promote and protect individual human rights. They promote values associated with a liberal international economic order based on neoclassical economic principles, such as private property rights and limited state involvement. But these values and norms are not universal, nor are they self-evident within or between societies, contrary to the writings of liberal writers. Some societies put the needs of the community over the needs of the individual. Some see the separation of church and state as a bad idea. For others, the state should eliminate private property or at least be responsible for caring for citizens "from cradle to grave," even if it means public ownership of industries or expensive welfare budgets.

For liberals, values and norms must compete in the "free marketplace of ideas" and evolve over time. Liberal values and norms have withstood the test of time, generating unprecedented levels of prosperity and individual freedom. Contemporary international organizations are agents of socialization for a political and economic order through which everyone can benefit. This liberal view contrasts slightly with the realist notion of international organizations of agents of socialization for an international order whereby one state or a group of states dominates lesser states in the international system.

A fourth role of international organizations is integrative and is performed principally by MNCs. MNCs are seen as a figurative needle and thread that binds societies together through the formation of a common global market. The activities of MNCs benefit societies because they bring jobs, industries, managerial skills, and technologies to societies. They are private economic organizations that transcend national boundaries and are responsible only to international stockholders. MNCs are a strong force for economic liberalism in the global economy (Goldstein 1996, 376). They command significant resources and have the ability to influence governments and IGOs. MNCs are interested in limited government involvement and the right to freely move capital to areas where it can be utilized more efficiently. MNCs are committed to capital mobility, and wherever they go they bring liberal ideology and a commitment to human rights with them.

A fifth role performed by international organizations in the liberal world is to provide assistance to the "victims of international politics." These victims include the abject poor, refugees, and those who have experienced environmental disaster, medical epidemics, and war. Liberals see these kinds of crises as being man-made. Choices are made by governments that have important consequences for its citizens. While environmental and medical emergencies may be influenced by nature, the policies and the reactions of governments play a decisive and often aggravating role. International organizations (IGOs and NGOs) seek to provide immediate relief to the victims of such "politics" and to find durable solutions.

In sum, international organizations are prominent features in the liberal landscape. International organizations help states overcome collective action problems and help promote economic prosperity and global welfare. In addition, international organizations foster shared norms and values among societies and further economic interdependence. Lastly, international organizations aid the victims of international politics. Rather than being marginal actors, international organizations are at the forefront of international governance.

LIBERALISM AND ITS CRITICS

The liberal theoretical approach to international relations and international organizations is widely criticized as ethnocentric (Viotti and Kauppi 1993; Strange 1983). The liberal world view is widely held by American and British scholars. Their arguments that the contemporary liberal order is beneficial to all is influenced by their own bias that their societal organization is superior to other kinds of organization. This bias is perpetuated in that international relations as a discipline is dominated by English-speakers from Canada, Great Britain, Australia, and the United States. The normative bias in liberal arguments is evident—democracy is a "better" form of government and capitalism is a "better" mode of production.

Ethnocentrism compromises the ability of liberal scholars to adequately assess and criticize the liberal order that they are describing. Take, for example, the idea that free trade is a public good. It is a mighty bold statement to say that free trade benefits all. Liberals claim that consumers benefit because free trade widens the range of consumer choice. However, consumer choice means very little if the consumer's job has been lost because foreign competition has driven the domestic employer out of business. Liberals also tend to focus on absolute rather than relative gains. In other words, they only ask whether societies are better off (in terms of prices and consumer choice) than they were before. Liberals do not consider relative gains, nor do they recognize that "development" is itself an ethnocentric concept. Why do liberals unconsciously assume that other societies want to be like the United States and the Western democracies?

A second criticism of the liberal approach is that "blame" for underdevelopment and poverty is placed squarely on the individual, firm, or government. Individuals are poor because they did not make the right choices in order to effectively participate in the market. They did not seek the right education or occupation that would provide them with an acceptable standard of living. Similarly, if societies are poor, it is because governments were corrupt or pursued irrational state policies that contributed to economic problems. Irrational state policies include subsidizing industries that do not have a comparative advantage, import substitution, state ownership of industries, and protectionism. Liberals rarely emphasize the fact that capitalism can create both winners and losers and that what determines a winner or loser has nothing to do with economic factors. Rather, it has to do with resources and existing power positions.

A third criticism of the liberal approach is its assumption that all interests are able to compete effectively in the political arena. Interest group theory holds up only if all interests have relatively equal opportunity and enough resources to influence government. If only big-money interests dominate the political process, then only their interests will be represented in the political process. Considerable evidence suggests that small, private-business interests are better able to influence governments than are large public-interest groups (Welch et al. 1997). After all, it is easier to stop legislation than it is to enact it. Private interest groups seek to reduce or impede government regulation. Public interest groups, such as environmental groups, seek government regulation of industry and consumers to protect the environment.

A fourth criticism of liberalism is its reliance on the market and economic considerations. Liberals argue that economics should determine politics. The state should not intervene in the market, absent a market failure. However, the market is driven by expansion and efficiency. Societies are compelled to adjust to market changes. Thus, in the United States, for example, the inefficient family farm is displaced by large corporate farms and high-paying manufacturing jobs are relocated to countries with lower wages and less rigorous environmental standards. And in Paris, the sidewalk cafe and boutique are giving way to McDonald's and T-shirt shops. Critics of liberalism argue that societies value more than efficiency. They cherish traditional institutions that reflect their moral, familial, national, and religious heritage as well. The global market fosters crass commercialism in which businesses must appeal to the lowest common denominator to reach the widest audience. It is, for instance, no accident that *Baywatch* is the most widely viewed TV program by the global audience.

Relatedly, liberals assume that the market is apolitical. That is, the market is driven solely by the laws of supply and demand, and the price mechanism. Irrational market behavior, such as price-fixing or racial/gender discrimination, is short-lived because it interferes with the efficiency of the market. According to liberals, it is irrational to hire a white male just because he is white when a black woman is better able to do the job. Companies that engage in discrimination become inefficient and will ultimately become casualties of the market. While the liberal logic is appealing, historical practice is different, suggesting one of two explanations—either the liberals are wrong or white men are better qualified and more productive than other races and women in terms of their ability to own and operate businesses and as employees. The latter explanation is unpalatable, especially in light of proven discriminatory practices on the part of firms operating in the presumably apolitical market.

The liberal response to racial or gender discrimination is that markets are the solution, not the problem. Discrimination may exist in the social and political realms; however, in the economic realm, markets erode discriminatory practices. All individuals are equally productive in theory and they make choices given their own personal circumstances. However, just assuming that all people are equal does not make them so in practice. By assuming all people are equal, liberals end up explaining that the status quo (dominance of white males) is a market equilibrium. Any differences between races and gender are the result of individual choice and residual discrimination from social and political realms.

Like realism, liberalism is plagued by tautological arguments. Liberals assume that markets lead to optimal outcomes; therefore, when suboptimal outcomes emerge, they must be caused by something other than the market. The suboptimal outcomes are the result of poor choices on the part of individuals, firms, and government. If the outcome is optimal, then the market was able to work its "magic." Assuming a conclusion rarely contributes to analysis. Liberals never seriously consider whether markets and capitalism cause international conflict and contribute to global inequality.

For liberals, the nature of international relations has fundamentally changed during the latter half of the twentieth century. The world has been tied together through economic, political, social, and moral interdependence, making effective international governance a necessity for nation-states. International organizations play an important and constructive role in international governance. Some liberals see international organizations as the pillars of a nascent new world order. Others see international organizations as assisting states in overcoming collective action problems. The liberal theoretical framework provides a mechanism for understanding the role of state and nonstate actors in the governance of international affairs and highlights the role of the market in promoting international change, economically, politically, and socially.

4

CRITICAL APPROACHES

C RITICAL APPROACHES TO INTERNATIONAL RELATIONS are useful for prompting reevaluation of commonly held views and beliefs. Marxism and feminism, which afford critiques of the mainstream approaches, offer alternative ways to assess the role of international organizations in world affairs. Marxism and feminism can be seen as critical reactions to the putative universality of realism and the ethnocentrism of liberalism. Like the mainstream approaches, critical approaches have philosophic origins and underlying assumptions that shape a particular kind of world view.

MARXISM

The Marxist approach to international relations makes several important contributions to understanding international relations and international organizations. First, and perhaps most important, Marxism provides a critique to the dominant approaches of realism and liberalism. Marxism challenges the realist assertion of the primacy of politics over economics and the liberal assertion that the expansion of the global market is beneficial to international peace and stability. Second, Marxism offers a comprehensive critique of capitalism as a mode of production. Marxist analyses of capitalism have identified issues that lead to genuine conflict within and between societies. Third, Marxism has articulated significantly different roles for international organizations. For Marxists, such organizations are neither great-power directorates nor relatively independent actors promoting the international public good; rather, they are tools of capitalism that undermine and exploit subordinate classes.

As an ideology, Marxism carries with it many negative connotations. Some people in the United States feel that American Marxists are traitors. Others see them as idealistic and misguided. Marxist-Leninist ideology is associated with brutal communist governments in the former Soviet Union, the former Eastern Bloc states, Cambodia, and China. Marxist ideology has also been at the heart of many social and political movements in the developing world, movements that were hostile to the United States and its interests. As a result, many tend to dismiss Marxist or Marxist-influenced explanations without considering whether or not they have any validity or provide any insight. Such a tendency is ill-advised because it narrows the scope of analysis. It is analogous to dismissing liberal ideas about representation and democracy because the United States practiced slavery and Thomas Jefferson and George Washington owned slaves. Ideas can have merit even if their practice is offensive.

Marxist analyses have generated insights and explanations that are useful in understanding contemporary international relations. Marxist insights regarding the drawbacks of global capitalism have been used by former presidential candidates Ross Perot and Patrick Buchanan, neither of whom is considered a Marxist. Environmental groups and labor unions accept Marxist explanations without necessarily embracing Marxist ideology. Many in the developing world have a world view that is a mixture of realism and Marxism. They are realists in that they are concerned about state sovereignty. After all, most developing states have experienced colonialism and have been formally independent only for the last couple of decades. Their relative weakness vis à vis the great powers has resulted in numerous interventions, and they understand the consequences of being a lesser power in an anarchical environment. Many in the developing world are also Marxist in that they are poor and economically disadvantaged. Their colonial history only reinforces their distrust of capitalism. In other words, many are on the short end of capitalism's stick. Their experience with capitalism is one of poverty, malnutrition, disease, and even violent death. Marxism enhances contemporary understandings of international relations and international organizations through its framework for understanding the relationship between economics and politics.

PHILOSOPHIC ROOTS OF MARXISM

Socrates (470–399 B.C.), the Athenian philosopher, may seem an unlikely contributor to Marxist thought; however, he has influenced many different kinds of theorists, not to mention lawyers, through his method of inquiry. Known as Socratic inquiry, this method is a process for discovering truth by juxtaposing two contradictory ideas. By pitting a thesis against its antithesis, we reveal a new truth—a synthesis. The synthesis then becomes the new thesis, which is pitted against its antithesis, whereupon the process starts all over again. For Socrates, progress and knowledge are promoted by using this method of questioning alleged truths.

Socrates gives Marxism and other theories a critical way to think about life. Progress is not always steady or even linear. It may occur in spurts, the result of a "two steps forward, three steps back" process. The first step in thinking critically is taking something that you believe to be true, say, "democracy allows most people to participate in politics," then opposing it with its antithesis, "democracy excludes most people from politics." Considerable evidence supports the antithesis. The history of U.S. suffrage suggests that participation was scarcely encouraged. The expansion of the electorate occurred over time, in the following order: exclusively adult white male property owners; adult white males; adult black males; adult black males de facto disenfranchised; adult white women; adult white and black men and women; eighteen-year-olds. In spite of the expansion of the electorate over the course of U.S. history, voting among eligible citizens has declined. A new truth, or synthesis, emerges: "Democracy as it is practiced in the United States deters otherwise eligible citizens from effectively participating in politics." This new truth is then juxtaposed with its antithesis and the process starts over. This democracy example illustrates Socratic inquiry in a simple fashion. Socratic inquiry represents a method of critical thinking that is often used in Marxist analyses of international relations.

Georg Wilhelm Friedrich Hegel (1779–1831) was one of the many theorists influenced by the Socratic method. In *The Philosophy of Right,* Hegel uses a dialectic, a process quite similar to Socratic inquiry, to pit competing ideas about social and political relations against each other. Hegel departs from the liberal, social contract thinkers of his time in that he sees human beings as essentially social rather than economic creatures (Cahn 1997, 734). For Hegel, human beings were not merely individualistic and solitary creatures who enter into society merely to "truck, barter and trade." Rather, the highest form of freedom for individuals is participating in a politically organized community, or the state (Cahn 1997, 734). Hence, he distinguishes between what he terms "civil society," where humans behave in an individualistic manner and interact in a contractual sphere, and the "state," the politically organized community that promotes the collective good. Hegel's work suggests that the individual can be truly free and happy only as a part of the political community. Therefore, the health of the state is important in order for individuals to become self-actualized. The central difference between liberal thought and Hegel's communitarian ideas is that liberals place value on the individual. If the individual is happy, then so is society. Hegel places value on the society so that the individual can be happy. Hegel's contributions to the Marxist approach to international relations are his use of the dialectic and his emphasis on the environment/context in which individuals and groups interact.

Karl Marx (1818–1883) is, obviously, an intellectual precursor to the Marxist theoretical approach. Marx's central work, *The Communist Manifesto,* was written with his collaborator, friend, and benefactor, Friedrich Engels. In that work, they argue that history and progress can be seen dialectically as societies shift from one mode of production to another. A mode of production is simply the way goods and services are provided for a society. Slavery, feudalism, capitalism, and socialism are examples of ways in which goods and services can be produced. According to Marx, society is shaped by a mode of production and is organized around classes, which are based on their relationship to the means of production. The means of production are the resources that are needed to provide goods and services. For example, under feudalism, the economy was, in large part, agriculturally based. The means of production were the land and the tools needed to work on and farm the land. Feudal society was based on two principal classes, the aristocracy and the serfs. The aristocracy consisted of the lords and their families and they owned the land. The serfs worked the land in exchange for protection, food, and a place to live.

Marx sees economics, not ideas, as the driving force of society and politics. Marx is known to have said, "I have taken Hegel and stood him on his head." Rather than seeing the clash of ideas as the driving force of progress as Hegel did, Marx sees class conflict and the contradictions inherent in different modes of production as propelling progress forward. Thinking dialectically, Marx's thesis is the antithesis to Hegel's thesis. Marx argues that each mode of production contains within itself the contradictions that will eventually lead to its collapse. Again, using feudalism as an example, we can see that its own contradictions undermined its dominance. These contradictions resulted from the clash between the social arrangements associated with feudalism coupled with technological advances. Emerging industrial technologies provided alternative ways for people to make a living and also created surpluses of goods. Under feudalism, land was passed down from father to the first-born son, so that estates could be kept intact. Second, third, and fourth sons usually had some money, but no inherited land. Once the father died, these sons often went off to the cities, investing in new technologies and starting new enterprises. Ironically, they became the foundation of a new class, the merchants. As these contractions became too great, feudalism collapsed; and in its wake a new, dominant mode of production emerged—capitalism.

After feudalism's collapse, capitalism emerges, and with it, the nature of society fundamentally changes. New classes arise. The bourgeoisie are capitalists who own the factories, hire workers, and control most of the money. The proletariat are wage workers and managers who sell their labor for a salary. Society reorganizes itself around this new mode of production, and social and political institutions reflect the underlying economic order. Just as aristocracy reflects the interests of a dominant class under feudalism, democracy reflects the interests and needs of the bourgeoisie. Legitimacy to govern is no longer based on the idea of heredity. Rather, the liberal ideas that all men are created equal and have the right to political participation form the foundation of legitimate governance under capitalism. Democracy is based on the rule of law—law that was made by the majority rule of consenting men (initially, white men who owned property). Liberalism undermines the political authority of the aristocracy and legitimizes the new political structures, which favor the interests of the bourgeoisie.

Marx predicts that capitalism will also collapse under the weight of its own contradictions. Marx identifies many contradictions of capitalism that would impoverish the workers to such an extent that they would rise up and seize the means of production. Three of these are discussed below. Note, however, that Marx did not invent these contradictions. They were real problems—the pressing issues in the political economy of his day—which were also addressed by the likes of Malthus, Mill, and Ricardo. With the exception of Malthus (who was nothing if not "dismal"), these liberals are considerably more optimistic than Marx about the ability of the market to deal with the problems faced by capitalism. Marx described these problems as contradictions leading to market failure, and showing, at the very least, that capitalism is unstable and prone to crises.

The first problem is the tendency of the market toward the concentration of capital. Capitalists operating under market forces are driven toward greater and greater efficiency in the production of the goods and services. Competition and efficiency demand that capitalists reduce the cost of producing goods and services for markets. Inefficient and uncompetitive enterprises are driven out of market, which leads to oligopoly and monopoly and the accumulation of wealth in the hands of the few. The consequences of this contradiction are serious for both workers and consumers. Efficient production ultimately translates into reducing labor costs because labor accounts for the lion's share of production costs. The masses are impoverished, owing to the resulting decline in wages and increased unemployment. When the market becomes dominated by a few firms (oligopoly) or one firm (monopoly), the remaining bourgeoisie can demand high prices. Once competition ceases to exist, so does capitalism.

A second contradiction of capitalism is the tendency toward overproduction. Liberals argue that the interaction of supply and demand, coupled with the price mechanism, prevents overproduction. Marx argues against this belief in the inherent equilibrium of the market, claiming that capitalism is prone to overproduction because greater efficiency allows capitalists to make more of the same good for the same or lesser cost. Demand for these goods also declines because the workers cannot easily afford them. As a result, the market is flooded with a surplus of goods and services.

A third contradiction is the falling rate of profit, which leads to oversavings on the part of capitalists. As capital accumulates, the rate of return on capital investments declines. Capitalists have less incentive to invest in productive enterprises and instead save their excess wealth. In other words, capitalist development is finite. Capital accumulation leads to a decline in investment returns until, finally, a point is reached when investment ceases. These contradictions lead to great disparities between rich and poor, the capitalists and the workers. The immiserization of the working class eventually leads to a socialist revolution, for the workers would have "nothing left to lose but their chains."

John A. Hobson (1858–1940), a British economist, indirectly provides an explanation as to why capitalism did not, in fact, collapse. His answer? Imperialism. Decidedly a non-Marxist, Hobson argues in *Imperialism* that overproduction, underconsumption, and oversavings force capitalists to seek new markets in order to sell their surplus goods and to find new outlets for investment. Hobson defines imperialism as "the endeavor of the great controllers of industry to broaden the channel for the flow of their surplus wealth by seeking foreign markets and foreign investments to take off the goods and capital they cannot sell or use at home" (Viotti and Kauppi 1993, 453). Hobson sees imperialism as a cause of war in that capitalist societies force their way into markets and even fight each other in order to gain access to new markets, cheap labor, and raw materials. Hobson might be considered a neomercantilist or economic nationalist in that he saw wars of imperial expansion as benefiting only certain segments of society (i.e., export capitalists, bankers) and not the nation as a whole.

Vladimir Ilyich Lenin (1870–1924) argues that the demise of capitalism, as predicted by Marx, was only postponed by imperialism. In *Imperialism: The Highest Stage of Capitalism,* Lenin argues that the contradictions of capitalism—overproduction, underconsumption, and oversavings—were temporarily resolved by the colonial expansion of capitalist states. "The acquisition of colonies had enabled the capitalist economies to dispose of their unconsumed goods, to acquire cheap resources and to vent their surplus capital" (Gilpin 1987, 38). Lenin argues that the expansion of capitalism through colonialism contributes to economic development internationally; however, that development is uneven. That is, capitalist powers develop unevenly, which leads to economic instability, political conflict, and war. Note that this explanation is quite similar to one type of realist explanation regarding the cause of war. Realists argue that uneven growth rates cause shifts in the balance of power and that can lead to war. However, Lenin emphasizes the underlying economic causes of conflict whereas realists stress the political causes.

Antonio Gramsci (1891–1937), an Italian Marxist, contributes to the Marxist approach through his criticism of "economism"—the idea that economic and technological advancements account for change while politics is merely a reflection of the underlying economic order. According to Marx, capitalism is advancing toward economic collapse as the contradiction between the forces and the relations of production become greater. Gramsci maintains that the notion of economism is a defect in Marxist theory because it encourages the working class to remain passive, just waiting for the inevitable capitalist crisis (Simon 1982, 11). Gramsci conceives of society as a series of relations between different groups and classes. To understand the power of the bourgeoisie in capitalist society, it is necessary to bring politics back into the analysis.

According to Gramsci, politics is "the entire complex of practical and theoretical activities with which the ruling class not only justifies and maintains its dominance, but manages to win the active consent of those over whom it rules" (Hoare and Smit 1971, 114). The ruling class develops "hegemony," a concept conceived by Gramsci. Hegemony "has to do with the way one social group influences other groups, making certain compromises with them in order to gain their consent of its leadership in society as a whole" (Sassoon 1982, 13). This concept of hegemony is different from the one of sheer domination employed by realists, liberals, and Marxists. Hegemony for Gramscian Marxists is the relation of consent to political and ideological leadership, not domination by force (Simon 1982, 11). This relation is based on compromise and incentive only to the extent of achieving deference. The core values of the ruling class, however, remain intact.

Gramsci provides another distinction between hegemony and dominance (Hoare and Smit 1971, 56–57). Domination results from the state's monopoly on the means of violence and its role as the final arbiter in all disputes. Hegemony, on the other hand, requires deference on the part of those who are led. Only weak states rely on force or domination to rule. Strong states rule through hegemony. A proletarian revolution would require an alternative hegemony that could displace the hegemonic relationship that already exists between the bourgeoisie and the masses.

Gramsci's contribution to Marxist thought (as well as to neoliberal and neorealist thinking) about international relations lies in the relevance of ideas to power. For Gramscian Marxists, the power of the bourgeoisie does not result solely from its control of the state and brute force. Any number of groups or coalition of groups can control the government. Power results from developing an ideology or hegemony where the interests of the dominant class or state are inextricably tied to the interests of subordinate classes, and workers buy into the system even though they are being exploited. The well-being of the firm is directly related to the well-being of the workers. Workers who question working conditions, seek to unionize, or try to improve wages are seen as threats not only by the bourgeoisie but also by other workers. Hence, labor leadership seeks reform within the system but refrains from trying to replace it. Social and political pressure is exerted on dissatisfied members of subordinate classes to conform to existing bourgeois norms and values. Violence is employed only as a last resort.

Socrates, Hegel, Marx, Hobson, Lenin, and Gramsci—all have influenced the Marxist approach to international relations. Socrates contributes dialectical reasoning. Hegel adds the idea of the context in which economic, social, and political relations take place. Marx provides an alternative view regarding class formation and identifies contradictions that threaten the stability of capitalism. Hobson and Lenin bring to the fore the economic causes and the political consequences of colonialism. Gramsci shows how ideas relate to power and the dominance of one class by another with their active consent. These influences are evident in the following section detailing the assumptions of the contemporary Marxist theoretical approach to understanding international politics and international organizations.

CONTEMPORARY MARXISM

The Marxist approach to international relations consists of many different perspectives. These perspectives are distinguished by their emphases on economically determined classes, the international division of labor, and economic forces as critical for understanding international relations. Like realism and liberalism, Marxism as a theoretical approach rests on several underlying assumptions. The first assumption is that global capitalism determines the position and behavior of actors in international affairs. For the Marxist, the defining characteristic of the international system is not the anarchy of realism or the interdependence of liberalism. Capitalism as a global mode of production is the systemic feature that explains the dynamics of international relations. The world capitalist economic system imposes constraints on actors and motivates their behavior. Private property, the profit motive, and the exigencies of the market affect economic actors and the societies in which they operate.

The assumption that capitalism as a global mode of production matters is not particularly divergent from realist and liberal systemic assumptions. The neorealist sees participation in the global economy as the key to great-power status. Having power enables states to pursue national security and interests under conditions of anarchy. The global economy currently happens to be capitalist. The liberal argues that interdependence results from interaction between private individuals in the market. The Marxist lens simply shifts the focus slightly and emphasizes global capitalism.

The second assumption of the Marxist approach is that the principal unit of analysis is economic class. Marxists see the actors in international relations as being defined by economic class. International relations are driven by economic production; therefore, the principal actors are distinguished by their role in the global production of goods and services. Two of the most prominent Marxist theories, dependency theory and modern world system theory, vary slightly regarding the role of class. Dependency theorists tend to take a traditional Marxist view on class and apply it to the international system (e.g., Packenham 1992; Valenzuela and Valenzuela 1978; Cardoso and Faletto 1979; Amin 1977; Evans 1979). These theorists seek to explain why economic development has not occurred in many Third World states, particularly those in Latin America. They argue that neocolonialism, capitalist expansion, and the creation of grossly asymmetrical interdependent relationships are responsible for under- and maldevelopment in the Third World.

Dependency theorists explain that underdevelopment in the Third World must be understood in historical context. The majority of Third World states were once colonies of the Western capitalist powers, serving both as captive markets and as sources of raw material and cheap labor. After decolonization, the international bourgeoisie continued to control these newly independent states through more subtle means. Whereas colonialism refers to territorial domination by force, neocolonialism refers to the nonterritorial, economic controls exercised by capitalist states over the developing world.

Neocolonialism represents a more sophisticated exploitation. The military conquest and the subjugation of a population are expensive endeavors. Colonial powers have to administer the affairs of the colonies, thus incurring costs. Recall Hobson's critique of imperialism, that it was a drain on state resources and benefited only those earning profits from international economic transactions. Under neocolonialism, newly formed Third World states possess sovereignty in legal principle; in practice, however, the colonial powers retain de facto control over the raw material, market, and labor. Within the Third World itself, the ruling class, composed largely of willing collaborators who helped administer the colonies, retained control after decolonization. Termed the *comprador class* by dependency theorists, this group of elites became a domestic bourgeoisie whose role was to aid in the exploitation of their own society by international and transnational capitalists (Viotti and Kauppi 1993, 458). The interests of the comprador class are tied to the interests of global capitalism, not to the development and progress of their own societies.

Dependency theorists analyze the impact of capitalism on developing states; hence it is fair to say that they consider states as important in international relations. Nevertheless, they see the state as a reflection of the dominant class interests, the domestic bourgeoisie. The state is subordinated to the bourgeois class that controls it. Seen in its best light, the state reproduces the necessary elements of capitalism (infrastructure, an educated workforce, and so on) and also enforces contracts and property rights. At worst, the state is the "executive committee of the bourgeoisie," which uses the state's coercive authority to further its own interests and exploit subordinate classes.

Modern world system theorists take a similar state-centric approach to international relations, viewing the system as one organized around nation-states. But they see these states as classes of states—each class being determined by a state's place in the international division of labor in a world capitalist system. Immanuel Wallerstein (1980) identifies three such classes, categorizing them as core, periphery, and semiperiphery. The core consists of industrialized states, which provide capital to the global economy, as well as highly skilled and well-paid labor. The periphery provides inexpensive, unskilled labor and raw materials. The semiperiphery represents the newly industrializing countries, which provide cheap, skilled, and semiskilled labor to the global economy. Put another way, the core represents the global bourgeoisie while the periphery and semiperiphery represent the global proletariat.

The systematic exploitation of the periphery by the core has occurred over the last five hundred years, although the character of the exploitation has changed significantly. From around 1500 until 1945, core exploitation of the periphery came in the form of (territorial) colonialism. After 1945 and until 1980, the pattern of exploitation shifted from territorial to economic means. Instead of forcibly extracting raw materials using cheap unskilled labor for use in the core, the core either leased the resources or purchased them cheaply on the open market. These resources were brought to the core for the production of highly valued manufactured goods. The manufactured goods were sold in the core and any surplus was exported to the periphery for sale.

This pattern of exploitation leads to bad terms of trade, meaning the ratio of the value of imports to the value of exports. Ideally, these values should be equal. But if the value of imports exceeds the value of exports, a state loses wealth because it must pay for imported goods with foreign currency—currency it can get only by borrowing or earning it through the export of its goods. Under bad terms of trade not enough wealth and capital can be accumulated to form the critical mass necessary for spurring sustained economic growth. Thus, bad terms of trade can be quite detrimental to development. Since the 1980s, the rapid globalization of production has changed the pattern of exploitation again. The periphery still provides raw materials and unskilled labor; however, the semiperiphery, which includes newly industrializing countries (NICs) such as Malaysia, Mexico, Brazil, and Hong Kong, has emerged as an intermediary in the production process. The semiperiphery serves two key purposes for global capitalism. First, it serves as a safety valve when wages become too high in the core. Second, it is the locus for manufacturing as the core economies shift to more service-oriented enterprises such as banking, insurance, and telecommunications.

The post-1980s pattern of capitalist exploitation has shifted economic analysis away from conceptualizing core/periphery/semiperiphery relations as state-based relationships—say, for example, the idea that France as a core state benefits from the economic exploitation of Algeria, a periphery state. Global production activities have increased the utility of using economic classes as a unit of analysis. Increasingly, workers throughout the core are experiencing either high unemployment or declining real wages. Core/periphery/semiperiphery relations can be characterized by an international bourgeoisie (which just happens to be French or British or American) that benefits at the expense of workers everywhere.

Modern world system theory and dependency theory both see class and the state as part and parcel of each other. Dependency theorists tend to view the state as a reflection of the dominant economic class. Modern world system theorists view the state and the nation-state system as necessary for capitalist accumulation. "A balance of power among a number of leading states inhibits the development of a single overarching political authority that could subvert international production and exchange" (Crane and Amawi 1997, 142). The capitalist accumulation process, of course, benefits the international bourgeoisie.

These Marxist views of the state contrast with the realist and liberal views of the state and the nature of other kinds of actors in international relations. Realists see the state as a unitary, rational actor seeking to maximize the national interest. Liberals tend to see the state as a disaggregated entity composed of a congeries of competing interests that results in the maximization of individual welfare. Marxists also see the state as a disaggregated entity composed of classes. In the Marxist world view, however, one class, the bourgeoisie, usually dominates the government.

A third assumption of the Marxist theoretical approach is that international relations are essentially conflictual. Exploitation breeds conflict within and between societies. Capitalism fosters violence as well as economic, social, and political inequality. For Marxists, as long as capitalism (or any other mode of production based on exploitation) dominates international economics, international conflict will continue. International conflict manifests itself in the form of interstate wars, terrorism, and intrastate violence such as government repression or civil war. In an era of global production and the interdependence it breeds, violence within a society often has international and global causes and implications.

A fourth, related assumption is that economic, not political or strategic, factors are most important to understanding international affairs. Issues that appear to be geostrategic and military in nature are rooted in capitalist accumulation and exploitation. After all, military capability and other elements of power are directly related to economic capability. Wars between great and lesser powers have occurred because of colonialism. In the post–colonial period, wars have occurred because of access to markets, labor, and resources. Hegemonic or great-power wars such as World Wars I and II were as much about how the world was going to produce things as about who would be the world leader. The Cold War was not the product of the Soviet Union's posing a serious military threat to the West. Rather, it was the result of the U.S. quest for an economic empire (Kolko and Kolko 1972). The Marxist theoretical framework provides an alternative mechanism for analyzing international relations. Its focus on global capitalism, economic classes, conflict, and economic motivations provides a different perspective regarding the nature of governance in the twentieth century.

MARXISM AND THE NATURE OF INTERNATIONAL ORGANIZATIONS

Like many liberals and realists, Marxists argue that international organizations are created through hegemony. However, traditional Marxists and Gramscian Marxists have diverging notions of hegemony, notions that lead them to different conclusions regarding the nature of international organizations. Traditional Marxists tend to equate hegemony with military and economic dominance. International organizations are created, then imposed on the rest of the world. International organizations reinforce and promote the capitalist mode of production whereby the dominant position of the core and the subordinate positions of the semiperiphery and periphery are institutionalized (see e.g., Bennis 1996).

International organizations are mechanisms of capitalist domination and exploitation. The international order established by the United States after World War II was a capitalist system in which the United States had a competitive advantage in industrial production. An international system based on liberal (capitalist) economic principles would allow American businesses to penetrate markets worldwide. For traditional Marxists, the root of U.S. hegemony was its ability to impose its capitalist vision. Political, economic, and social organizations reflect the underlying economic system. Contemporary international relations and organizations are shaped, informed, and reflective of contemporary world capitalism.

Gramscian-inspired Marxists differ from traditional Marxists and realists in that they have a broader conception of hegemony. Recall that Gramsci links ideas to power, claiming that hegemony is the relation of consent to political and ideological leadership (Simon 1982, 11). How does the ruling class (or class of states) get subordinate classes (or classes of states) to consent to their own domination and exploitation? The answer is, by linking the dominant class interests to the interests of subordinate classes. For example, the international order created by the United States was based on several principles—principles that developed U.S. hegemony in the Third World. First, the United States insisted on the end of colonialism and charged the UN with assisting in the decolonization process. Decolonization was based on the Wilsonian idea of "self-determination," the idea that each society has the right to decide for itself the type of government it wants as well as the right to chart its own course in international affairs. Self-determination is a very powerful idea, particularly to societies under the yoke of colonialism. U.S. leadership, then, represented their opportunity to become self-governing. However, decolonization also meant that U.S. corporations would finally have access to the markets, resources, and labor that had previously been denied by the Europeans. By tying U.S. interests to the interests of developing states, the United States was able to gain consent to its domination. International organizations like the UN facilitated this linking of interests and promoted U.S. leadership.

In other Gramscian Marxist perspectives, international organizations are seen as instrumental in the development of modern capitalism (see Murphy 1994, for example). International organizations are crucial for linking evolving capitalism to evolving nation-states. Thus, global governance by international organizations guides nation-states through the rough waters of global industrial change. International organizations facilitate and manage industrial change by conditioning the impact of states on changing markets and vice versa. These Marxists acknowledge contemporary international organizations as reflections of the underlying capitalist order, but they also attribute to international organizations a pivotal role in shaping the development of liberal ideology together with the development of capitalism.

Marxist, realist, and liberal explanations regarding the creation of international organizations are not wholly dissimilar, although their differences lead to different conclusions about the nature of international organizations. Many Marxists, realists, and liberals see hegemony as requisite for the creation of international organizations. Realists and traditional Marxists conceive of hegemony as military, political, and economic dominance. Liberal institutionalists and Gramscian Marxists view hegemony as domination, but also seek to understand why others would consent to domination. Liberal institutionalists argue that the hegemon gains deference to its leadership by providing public goods and making side payments. Gramscian Marxists argue that hegemony involves more than just buying off subordinate classes or lesser powers. It involves developing a coherent set of values that transcend class and national boundaries but never compromise the position of the dominant class.

The nature of international organizations, therefore, varies by theoretical approach. Realists see international organizations as no more than the sum of their member states. International organizations are largely intergovernmental, great-power directorates susceptible to great-power manipulation. The behavior of international organizations can be explained by the interests of the great powers and the underlying balance of power. For liberals, international organizations can be IGOs, NGOs, MNCs, and regimes. They can be relatively independent agents that help states overcome collective action problems and create an international environment conducive to economic growth. Marxists see international organizations as both public and private, consisting of state and nonstate actors. They conceive of these organizations as mechanisms of capitalist domination, both reflecting and legitimizing the underlying economic order. Each theoretical approach provides a slightly different focus, which leads to different explanations and understandings of international organizations.

MARXISM AND THE ROLE OF INTERNATIONAL ORGANIZATIONS

The Marxist theoretical approach suggests three interrelated roles for international organizations. For IGOs like the UN, they are political complements to capitalism. Financed and controlled by the capitalist states, they promote a capitalist agenda. The political institutions of the UN, such as the Security Council and the General Assembly, are hobbled by procedural rules that make them ineffective as organs of international governance. This enables capitalism to expand unchallenged. In an environment of interstate competition and rivalry, capitalists are unfettered by significant international restriction—they are free to seek new outlets for goods and new sources of raw materials and cheap labor. The principles of sovereignty and nonintervention allow the capitalist states to pick and choose when, where, and how the "international community" will act against a state. International intervention usually happens only when there is a compelling economic interest.

The only realm in which "supranationalism" is evident is the economic realm. Supranationalism simply means that international organizations exercise authority over states. IGOs such as the EU and the WTO possess the legal authority to override the policies of states that impede the free flow of goods and services across national boundaries. The interests of international and transnational capitalists are furthered at the expense of national capitalists and labor, whose interests are largely tied to national economies. Should a government seek to protect the latter's interests, the legal framework exists to nullify state policy.

The independent economic agencies of the UN, such as the IMF and the World Bank, impose capitalist features such as private property and wage labor on developing societies. These societies are forced to accept the market, rather than the state, as the mechanism for distributing wealth, resources, and values. As long as the market distributes wealth, resources, and values, the owners of the means of production will always benefit at the expense of wage earners. In the context of modern world system theory, the core will always benefit at the expense of the periphery. As long as the IMF and the World Bank continue to demand market reforms in exchange for development and stabilization loans, periphery states will see, at best, maldevelopment and, at worst, chronic underdevelopment.

The lending and development policies of the IMF and the World Bank are grounded in neoclassical economic thought. In other words, they are neoliberal or capitalist institutions. On the basis of comparative advantage, the liberal sees specialization as the key to maximizing global economic growth. However, in periphery states, the comparative advantage consists of providing raw materials and cheap unskilled labor to the global market, an "advantage" that cannot generate the same kind of wealth and income that comes from producing durable and highly valued manufactured goods. Producing potato chips is not as advantageous or lucrative as producing computer chips, and potato chip production does not generate the kind of income that enables the vast majority in the periphery to buy products containing computer chips. Periphery states will lose wealth and remain underdeveloped because they have chronic balance-of-payments problems resulting from their bad terms of trade.

A second, related role of international organizations is that of mechanism of domination. International organizations are tools that core states use to exploit and control the weak. Periphery societies are controlled politically because they are given a voice in organizations like the UN in which that voice carries very little weight. The decolonization process provided periphery states with the trappings of sovereignty. The newly formed states thus have the right to govern themselves but not the means. Their ruling classes are collaborators with the core states and their interests are tied to the core. The ruling class controls the government and that government is what is represented at the UN. Hence, many UN officials are the elites of periphery states. Their constituencies often include the ruling classes and are committed to capitalist values.

Self-determination is a principle that is recognized only when societies determine for themselves that they will embrace capitalism. Developing states that do not embrace capitalism or who threaten core economic interests are subject to intervention. The UN paid only lip service to the principle of nonintervention when the United States invaded the Dominican Republic, Grenada, and Panama while intervening covertly in Iran, Guatemala, Cuba, Chile, and Nicaragua. All of these states had one of two things in common. Their governments were guided by nationalist or populist sentiments and/or they sought to embrace a different mode of production—socialism or communism. Most of these governments were democratically elected, and those that were not had overthrown extremely brutal dictators or military regimes. Hobbled by its own rules and procedures, the UN did nothing.

Economically, international organizations have a more direct role in dominating weak societies. Private international banks have entangled developing states in a web of debt that permits their continued exploitation. The IMF and the World Bank provide just enough assistance to keep them from defaulting on their loans. Developing states are forced to borrow more just to pay on the interest. The result is a debt crisis (discussed in Chapter 8), which the majority of developing states now face. According to Marxists, this crisis is the inevitable consequence of global capitalism. Multilateral and international banks exercise a great deal of leverage and can force compliance with capitalist mandates.

For Marxists, the MNC is a classic example of an international organization as a tool of exploitation and a mechanism of domination that fosters underdevelopment. The drive for market efficiency leads MNCs to states that have lax environmental and labor standards. Many MNCs will use child and prison labor if it reduces costs. They will locate where labor is not represented by unions or any type of collective bargaining to order to keep their labor costs down. Where the liberal sees that the MNCs are providing jobs, the Marxists see that those self-same MNCs are exploiting global competition for jobs, driving down wages to subsistence levels or even below.

MNCs can also directly and indirectly challenge sovereignty. MNCs are exceptionally wealthy entities; thus, they can directly compromise a host state's sovereignty through bribery and even private armies. Moreover, most MNCs are headquartered in core states, where they possess all the rights and privileges of citizens. Hence, they can also challenge a host state's sovereignty by appealing to their home governments for intervention when their interests are threatened. International Telegraph and Telephone (IT&T) and United Fruit, for example, were integrally involved in U.S. intervention in Chile and Guatemala, respectively. And British Petroleum (BP), Shell, and a consortium of U.S. oil companies were linked to Cold War interventions in Iran and Egypt.

State sovereignty can also be compromised indirectly because the competition for capital gives MNCs significant leverage over governments. All states—core, periphery, and semiperiphery—seek to attract capital for development. This enables MNCs, effectively, to play governments off each other to get the best possible "location package." Such packages usually entail promises of infrastructure such as roads and utilities. More important, MNCs are able to negotiate significant tax concessions from local and national governments. These concessions usually entail allowing the MNC to operate tax-free for an extended period of time, sometimes indefinitely. The power to tax is the defining indicator of a sovereign government. When a government cannot or will not tax its subjects, its authority over them is considerably weakened. Of the two proverbial certainties—death and taxes—MNCs seem able to elude at least one.

Many observers have pointed out that the activities of MNCs are not necessarily beneficial to the home states (Biersteker 1978; Cohen 1986; Reich 1991). The credo of the 1950s, "What's good for General Motors is good for the U.S.A." is no longer true. What's good for General Motors is profits—profits that can be increased by locating in areas where labor is cheaper. For the United States, that means a loss of high-paying jobs and a reduction of the tax base. Entire communities are devastated and families are forced to pull up roots, moving to find jobs that pay a fraction of their previous wages or salaries. MNCs can also displace exports and domestic industries. Businesses that rely on domestic labor and resources cannot compete with MNCs operating with global economies of scale. National businesses are driven out of the market, causing unemployment and a further reduction of the tax base.

A third and closely related role of both private and public international organizations is as developers of hegemony. Traditional Marxists have tended to view hegemony as sheer domination. Hence, international organizations reflect, reinforce, and impose capitalism. However, coercive domination is not an effective means of control, at least in the long run. Effective control comes from the consent of the dominated. Gramscian Marxists see international organizations as important instruments for selling capitalism, an economic mode of production under which the vast majority of the world's people are impoverished, malnourished, and exploited. A tough sell? Not really—not when capitalism is coupled with the ideas of self-determination, human rights, and democracy and is, besides, the only game in town. The implementation of these ideas in the real world suggests that they take a back seat to market capitalism and are sacrificed if they interfere in any significant way with capitalist accumulation. Nevertheless, the ideas are important selling points.

The evolution of the market from local, to national, to international, and now to global suggests that hegemony must also evolve. The dialectical nature of this evolution suggests that new selling points must be developed, and that the dominant class must ensure that its interests become the interests of subordinate classes. Many observers have pointed to the increasing preeminence of the transnational capitalist class (e.g., van der Pijl 1984; Cox 1987; Gill 1991). Public international organizations (e.g., the UN, IMF, WTO, EU, and NATO) and private international organizations (e.g., the Trilateral Commission, the International Chamber of Commerce, and all MNCs) serve the dual purpose of fostering class consciousness (identity) among the transnational bourgeoisie and delegitimizing nationalist interests (labor and national capital) in both developed and underdeveloped societies.

Transnational capitalists are committed to the globalization of production and capital mobility (Gill 1991, 55). Global production requires the free flow of goods and services across national boundaries. Capital mobility requires the ability and the right to move capital from one national jurisdiction to another. The principal obstacles to achieving these transnational goals are governments seeking national goals, such as full employment and economic development at the expense of transnational interests. Hence, transnational interests are pitted against national interests—the antithesis of the Cold War experience when these interests were synonymous within the core states. Politics in Europe and the United States reflect this antithesis—whether or not to join the EU or NAFTA or the WTO, organizations that formalize the dominant position and interests of transnational capital. In the Gramscian tradition, transnational capital seeks to tie its interests to subordinate interests, namely national interests. That is, it is in the national interest of these states to join, even though clearly transnational capital will gain and national capital and labor will lose. The "new world order" is a world run by transnational capitalists who congregate in five-star hotels in the world's capitals, watch CNN

International, and read the *Economist*. They are connected by satellite TV, cellular phones, and computers. Private and public international organizations are part and parcel of this order. Politically, they reflect, reinforce, and impose capitalism. They can be subtle or overt mechanisms of domination. Finally, international organizations are important instruments for the development of hegemony.

THE CRITICS OF MARXISM

There is no shortage of criticism for the Marxist theoretical approach. First, Marxist predictions have been fairly inaccurate. Capitalism has not collapsed, and it has been able to reform itself. Former communist states are embracing the capitalist mode of production, and the global economy has grown considerably in the post–Cold War era. While real wages in the developed countries have declined, jobs and better wages have appeared in the developing world. In defense of the Marxists, creating jobs and hence wages in the developing world is no great accomplishment. It is one thing to say that jobs and low wages are better than no jobs and no wages. It is quite another to say that capitalism has improved the quality of life, especially on a global scale.

A second criticism is the tendency among many Marxist scholars to rely on economic factors to explain political behavior (Viotti and Kauppi 1993, 464–465). The idea that war and the foreign policies of states are principally driven by economics ignores the fact that war existed before capitalism. The foreign policy of states is indeed influenced by geostrategic security and other factors such as nationalism or religion. Marxists are hard pressed to explain how the intense violent conflict over such barren territory as the Gaza Strip or the West Bank is economically motivated. Similarly, it is difficult to explain Islamic fundamentalism as simply a function of class conflict.

The third criticism of the Marxist theoretical approach is its determinism. Subordinate classes and states are always going to be exploited. And most are not even aware they are being exploited because they have bought into the hegemony of the dominant class. If they are aware of the exploitation and seek to change their position, then direct pressure is applied. Marxists run the risk of making tautological arguments. Just as liberals see underdevelopment and poverty as the result of poor choices on the part of individuals and governments, Marxist see capitalism as the root of these problems. For liberals, the market is the solution, never the problem. For Marxists, capitalism is the problem, never the solution. Liberals blame the individual and Marxists blame the system. This makes the arguments of liberal and Marxists tautological because, in effect, they assume their conclusions.

In sum, Marxists posit different roles for international organizations in international relations and they have a very different notion of global governance. International organizations are tools of the dominant class that emerges with capitalism—the transnational bourgeoisie. They impose and reinforce the capitalist mode of production and facilitate capitalist exploitation. In terms of global welfare, capitalism generates enormous wealth for the few and poverty for the many. International organizations also serve as mechanisms for developing hegemony of transnational capitalists. Transnational capitalists, who are accountable only to their shareholders, are committed to the erosion of governmental regulation of the market and the mobility of capital. The consequences for the vast majority of individuals are continued exploitation, lower wages, and job insecurity.

FEMINISM

The feminist theoretical approach is relatively new to international relations. Its central purpose is to understand how "gender" affects international politics and our understanding of international processes. In this case, gender is defined as a social construction that indicates what it means to be masculine or feminine. Thus, gender is different from sex. While sex is the obvious anatomobiological difference between men and women, gender refers to societal norms and expectations regarding appropriate male and female behavior. For example, men are expected to engage in war fighting and women are not. Women are expected to care for children and men are expected to work outside the home. Gender roles might be rooted in biological differences, but they are not necessarily "natural." That is, just because only females can bear children, it does not follow that only females can care for children. The gender role of women as caregivers stems from their sex difference, but societal expectations are such that women are also expected to take care of the children. Gender analyses examine what it means to be male or female beyond the obvious anatomical differences. Feminist scholars argue that political, economic, and social relations are ordered around gender identities.

The use of gender as a lens provides important insights as to what is known about international relations and how it came to be known. In the 1980s, feminist scholarship emerged to challenge the hidden assumptions embedded in the traditional theoretical approaches of realism, liberalism, and Marxism. These approaches to international relations rest implicitly on universality. International conditions such as anarchy, interdependence, markets, and global capitalism are assumed to affect men and women in the same manner. These approaches assume that men and women will respond to these conditions in the same way and that the concepts and language used to describe and analyze international relations are gender-neutral. Feminists argue that gender is a useful category for examining global politics and criticizing mainstream approaches. Gender allows scholars to examine the impact of international relations on women and the role women play in those relations. Scholars also can examine gender as a "power relation." That is, they ask, "Why are women as a social category almost always underrepresented in relations of power?" (Pettman 1998, 488). Both the theory and the practice of international relations are "gendered," and that has consequences for men and women alike.

Feminism as a world view has been under attack by conservatives in the United States and elsewhere because it challenges status quo beliefs. Sometimes referred to as "femi-nazis" by such talk-radio commentators as Rush Limbaugh, feminists are excoriated for their staunch support of equal rights for women and the right of women to abort an unwanted pregnancy. Many conservatives see equal rights for women as destructive of the family, and abortion as the equivalent to a holocaust of children perpetrated by feminists. Feminists have also been stereotyped as crew-cut, man-hating "bull dykes." That way, it is easy to dismiss feminist insights. But such negative stereotypes or religious beliefs that run counter to feminist issues should not deter students from engaging those insights critically. Just as students can learn from Marxism without becoming Marxists, students can learn from feminism without becoming feminists. Feminism simply looks at the world through the lens of gender. What feminism discovers through this lens challenges traditional, status quo understandings, and that disturbs many conservatives in political as well as academic circles. But such disturbances are also, quite literally, thought-provoking. Not, all in all, a bad thing.

The international relations discipline has traditionally been populated by male scholars studying issues that have historically concerned men—war, politics, economics, and the like. Discussion of women's roles, contributions, and issues are rare, and tend to be trivialized because the female experience is not as valued as the male experience. Feminist international relations theory is controversial among scholars within the discipline and its analyses are widely viewed with skepticism. Is feminist theory marginalized because it represents the scholarship of women or is it just poor scholarship? Who gets to decide what is good scholarship? These questions will continue to be debated in academia for years to come. At the very least, the feminist approach to international relations has challenged realist, liberal, and Marxist theorists to reexamine their respective frameworks and revisit their conclusions (Keohane 1989; Niva 1998; Smith 1998).

Here we examine the contributions of feminist scholarship to understanding international relations and international organizations. The feminist approach enhances our understanding of the nature and behavior of international organizations in two meaningful ways. First, the lens of gender focuses on aspects of international relations and organizations that are often overlooked by the traditional approaches. Different questions are raised: How does war or the market affect women? How are women represented in international organizations? What impact do women have on policies of international organizations and vice versa?

Second, the feminist theoretical approach highlights the masculinity inherent in realism, liberalism, and Marxism and shows how that bias influences conventional explanations regarding the behavior of actors participating in international politics. Feminists maintain that international relations theory is, in fact, gender-biased and, as a result, so too are the usual analyses of international organizations. The feminist epistemological contribution lies in recognizing that what we know and how we know it is shaped by societal norms and expectations about what it means to be male or female.

FEMINIST INFLUENCES

No rich intellectual or historical tradition prefigures the feminist theoretical approach, at least in the conventional sense. Some argue that, historically, women were not scholarly writers or philosophers, so it is not surprising that they have contributed little to academic tradition, much less to feminism. No woman is considered a significant contributor to realism, liberalism, or Marxism because few, if any, women were scholars at the time. Feminist scholarship did not become prominent until the 1970s, as more women entered academia. This kind of explanation for the absence of women in international relations theory can be controversial because it assumes that feminism is strictly associated with the increase of women in academic roles. Feminists argue that while sex influences gender, it is gender (societal expectations) that explains why women have been excluded from scholarly analysis, either as academics or as analytic categories.

The feminist theoretical approach has been indirectly influenced by the international women's social movement (Rupp 1998). A social movement is a concerted effort among groups to achieve political, social, and economic change. In the United States, the women's movement has been closely related with the civil rights movement, which seeks equality of rights regardless of race, sex, creed, or culture. The civil rights movement began in the nineteenth century with efforts to abolish slavery. Slavery was a glaring contradiction to the Enlightenment philosophy, which had given rise to such liberal principles as "all men are created equal" and "all men were born with certain inalienable rights." Women began to appear on the political landscape, first as abolitionists, then as advocates of women's rights. Women in the United States finally gained the right to vote with the Nineteenth Amendment in 1920.

The early suffrage movements in the United States and Europe were facilitated by several international organizations. Such organizations included the International Council of Women founded in 1888, the International Women's Suffrage Alliance founded in 1904, and the International Women's League for Peace and Freedom founded in 1916. The early suffrage movements have influenced the feminist approach by highlighting the gender roles of women in Western societies during that period. The gender roles of women in large part relegated them to the home, the most private area of private life. The venture of women into the public sphere of politics by seeking the right to vote has contributed to societies' changing notion of gender. Women's right to vote was once thought of as a revolt against nature, whereupon women would grow beards and lose their babies (Welch et al. 1997, 174). Today, such fears are hardly taken seriously.

The women's movement and the civil rights movement did not end with the right to vote. An international women's movement has evolved and been facilitated by IGOs and NGOs geared toward improving the status of women globally. This movement is characterized by a series of struggles to gain equality of rights in fact as well as in law. Women in many developing countries do not even have the trappings of legal equality. In the developed world, women have formal equality, but are still denied equal access to schools, jobs, housing, and pay. The international women's movement affected the feminist theoretical approach in two ways. First, it enabled women to venture outside of their traditional gender roles, becoming lawyers, professors, and politicians. Second, the women's movement demonstrated how powerful social constructions are in shaping our understanding of the social, political, and economic worlds. Even after formal and legal barriers have been removed, women still do not receive equal pay for equal work. Women are still underrepresented in positions of economic and political power. Something other than legal impediment is at work to account for the differences in power between men and women. The feminist theoretical approach provides a different perspective by pointing out that we understand the world in gendered ways, and consequently, the female experience is either ignored or trivialized by history, political science, economics, and even the physical and biological sciences.

Feminist scholarship considers the ways in which gender has shaped our understanding of international relations. Consider the intellectual precursors to realism, liberalism, and Marxism. The gender lens magnifies the masculine nature of their contributions. Every one of the philosophers we discussed is a man speaking about men. These philosophers focus on the activities and the nature of men, which leads them to describe events in very masculine terms. The idea that Hobbes and Smith were theorizing about "human nature" is misleading. They were theorizing about the condition of men—masculine nature. Women, thought to be softer and more docile, were possessed of a more delicate and accommodating nature. The translation of historical writings into gender-neutral language does not eliminate their masculine bias. Rather, it essentially universalizes masculine behavior.

The philosophical roots of realism demonstrate how masculine behavior becomes universalized in theory. Thucydides focuses on the dialog between Athenian men and Melian men. Hobbes's Leviathan is clearly male, possessing very masculine characteristics. Machiavelli writes about a prince, not a princess. These great thinkers were men writing about men and the experiences of men. Contemporary realists use these insights to show how the "real" world is and how responsible leaders should behave.

Feminists point out that it is not the sex of the actors, it is their expected behavior. The social expectations created by the early realist thinkers are behaviors that are definitely masculine. International relations for the realist boils down to an ability to impose one's will physically and forcibly. Is imposing one's will physically and forcibly considered feminine behavior? No. To be feminine means having to take it, to be forced to accept the will of others. The masculine-feminine relationship is one of dominance and subordinance, of superiority and inferiority. Margaret Thatcher was able to impose her will militarily on the generals of the Argentine junta during the Falkland Islands War (1982). Margaret Thatcher, though female, was behaving in a masculine way and the generals, though male, were in a feminine position. Hobbes's Leviathan could be a woman, although she would be expected to behave in a violent, dominating, and threatening fashion. The realist world of international relations is a masculine world, even though women make up more than half of the world's population and more women are in positions of political power.

Liberal philosophers are equally masculine in their approach and their objects of study are principally men. Adam Smith argues that society is based on economic exchange. Social relationships are formed when men exchange goods and services with each other. Smith assumes that men emerge as fully formed and rational adults, ready to truck, barter, and trade. He ignores that other social relationship—the family. By ignoring the social relationships in the family, where women have influence, he is trivializing the feminine in economics. Smith's market, like the actors within it, is endowed with very masculine characteristics. The market is disciplined, logical, and unbiased; the actors are rational and self-interested. Being undisciplined, illogical, biased, irrational, and caring of others are feminine stereotypes and, as such, make up no part of Adam Smith's world.

Liberal political thinkers are uncomfortably quiet on the topic of women's rights, although John Stewart Mill did write on the status of women in *The Subjection of Women* (1858), in which he opposes the legal subordination of women (Cahn 1997, 929). Others are not so progressive. Kant argues that women should not be enfranchised because they are economic dependents and unequal to men. John Locke ignores women altogether, stating that men are entitled to their own private dominions where no government may interfere. This distinction between private and public is important because the private—the household—is where the women are.

Early Marxist influences also ignore women in their writings, although Marx and Engels did argue that the subjugation of women is property-based. Women were unequal because they could not own property; but once private property was eliminated, the inequalities between men and women would be rectified. For feminist Marxists, class analysis is insufficient for explaining gender inequalities or the kinds of work that are considered feminine. Marx emphasizes the condition of industrial workers, most of whom are men, and their exploitation by the bourgeoisie. Class analysis ignores unpaid "women's work" in the homes of the bourgeoisie and the proletariat.

Feminist theory is more compatible with Marxist theory because they both look at inequalities and superior-subordinate relationships. Both feminist theory and Marxist theory look beyond sheer domination and brute force to more subtle mechanisms of social, political, and economic control. They differ in that Marxists see class as defining history whereas feminists see gender.

The philosophical influences on the feminist theoretical approach to international relations are indirect. The feminist theoretical approach has been influenced by the women's movement, which has enabled more women to enter professions that allow them to speak authoritatively on issues. The approach has also evolved as a reaction to the masculine nature of realism, liberalism, and Marxism. This reaction offers substantially more than a critique of men for speaking about men and criticism of masculine issues. It involves identifying the hidden, gender-biased assumptions embedded in these approaches and providing an alternative for examining and explaining international relations and organizations.

CONTEMPORARY FEMINISM

The feminist theoretical approach to international relations does not speak with one voice. Just as realism has traditional, neo, and structural variations, feminism also has several variations. According to Ferber and Nelson (1993, 38–39), one strand of feminism emphasizes the exclusion of women from traditionally male activities and institutions while other strands emphasize the ways in which feminine activities and traits traditionally are devalued, trivialized, and associated with low reward or status. The former strand, or "traditional feminism," sees men and women as basically equal, attributing any inequality to gendered stereotypes. Thus the inclusion of women in traditionally masculine roles will erode gendered perceptions and beliefs. Among the latter varieties of feminism, there is the "neofeminism" strand, which valorizes feminine traits. These feminists, also known as essentialist feminists, tend to see the biological differences between men and women as accounting for many gender traits. Women are seen as more cooperative, sensitive, intuitive, and nurturing than men. However, these traits are denigrated, either through their exclusion from analysis or their dismissal as insignificant elements of international politics. Another strand of feminism, "postmodern feminism," emphasizes the gender-laden language and gendered concepts used to describe international relations. Adding gender or women as a category of study is not enough to dispel gender bias as they often appear as "victims" or as a residual category of the nonadult male. Hence, many feminists include the trials of women in the context of the ill-effects on women and children, which reinforces gender responsibilities and expectations regarding who is to be protected. Postmodern feminism challenges not only the substance of international relations but its methods of research as well.

These different strands of feminism also have liberal and Marxist variants. For example, traditional, liberal feminists focus on equality between the sexes and highlight exclusion of women from the political process. They see the empowerment of women as the key to improving the status of women. They differ from liberal neofeminists in that they do not think that men and women behave differently. For the liberal neofeminists, the inclusion of women will fundamentally change the political environment. Similarly, Marxist feminists challenge the idea that capitalism is beneficial for women either within or outside of their traditional gender roles (Bergeron 1999).

In spite of their differences, traditional, neo, and postmodern feminism strands and their theoretical variants are based on four interrelated assumptions. The first assumption is that gender matters. Gender can be biologically based, but the social meanings of gender are also important for understanding international relations. Gender as principal unit of analysis increases the purview of international relations issues. Wars are not just about troops, tanks, weapons, and battles. Wars include women engaging in traditionally male activities—as soldiers, guerrillas, heads of state, ambassadors, and reporters. Wars also include women operating in traditionally feminine roles—as mothers, nurses, prostitutes, and pacifists. Gender also refocuses on aspects of war that have not been systematically addressed, such as the close relationship between sex and violence, the role of rape in war, and the dire consequences of war for women and children.

In addition to expanding analysis, gender permits a reexamination of the language and concepts commonly used to describe international relations. Consider the realists' emphasis on the state or the liberals' emphasis on the individual. Both are considered rational. On the surface, this characteristic seems neutral enough, although scrutiny through the lens of gender shows that the state and the individual are quite masculine. "Rational" to realists and liberals means self-interested. Self-interested behavior for the realist is indicated by power or interest-maximizing behavior. For liberals, individuals engage in self-maximizing behavior in the market. This kind of behavior is contrasted with altruistic behavior, which is feminine in nature. According to realists, altruistic behavior can rarely take place, and according to liberals, it occurs only within the household. Liberals are able to bridge the gap between selfish behavior and the collective good by arguing, in a very rational way, that being selfish leads to social harmony.

A postmodern feminist interpretation might see debate between realists and liberals as a version of *quien es mas macho*. Both posit rationality, but offer competing versions of masculinity. The realists focus on military force and other elements of coercion. Liberals focus on economic prowess and the ability to offer positive and economic inducements. The debate between realists and liberals first manifested itself as a debate between realism and idealism. This debate has a gender bias in that realists somehow understood the "real" world while the idealists (liberals) maintained a utopian outlook. A postmodern feminist translation might argue that this is another way of saying that women can afford to be idealistic because they don't have to worry about the day-to-day realities that "real" men face. Realists trivialize liberal insights regardless of the merit of their arguments. Conversely, liberals have portrayed nationalism as irrational (feminine) and realism as something other than utilitarian. In other words, scholars are more than willing to use gendered language and methods to trivialize competitors from other paradigms.

A second assumption of the feminist theoretical approach is that the nature of international relations is essentially conflictual. Conflict results from the superior-subordinate nature of gender relationships. Biology may account for many differences between men and women (essential feminists), but the determination of whether "masculine" or "feminine" differences are superior or inferior is socially constructed. This assumption extends the analysis of international conflict to women in order to explain women in war, and how and why their experience differs from men. It also allows scholars to explain exploitation that extends beyond the market or economic class.

In addition to expanding analysis, the idea of gendered conflict allows for a re-examination of conflict in traditional international relations theory. These approaches focus on one of the following. Realists ascribe a central role to geostrategic conflict in which states are maximizing their self-interest. Liberals focus on individual and group conflict, but allow for the resolution of that conflict by democratic institutions and processes (market forces) that maximize the global welfare. Marxists shift the focus to class conflict, which emerges from market-based, capitalist economies. Feminists argue that conflict, as defined by these approaches, has a masculine bias in that it ignores women. Thus, conflict, while pervasive in other paradigms, is based on attributes other than gender.

A third assumption of the feminist theoretical approach is that international relations is characterized by patriarchy. Patriarchy, or male dominance, pervades almost every political, social, and economic organization and institution, whether domestic or international. These include government agencies, legislatures, courts, firms, universities, secondary schools, NGOs, IGOs, MNCs, and regimes. Feminists argue that male dominance has built into these organizations a bias toward masculine values and behaviors. The assumption of patriarchy "problematizes" the masculinity and the hegemony of men (e.g., Zalewski and Parpart 1998, 1). That is, the problems in international relations might be rooted in what is masculine about the world. Patriarchy is so prevalent within and between societies that it would be academically irresponsible not to explore the possible relationship between male dominance and social problems.

The fourth assumption of the feminist theoretical framework is that international issues are ranked in a gendered fashion. International issues traditionally considered feminine in nature—education, health, poverty, the environment, and justice—occupy low positions in the international agenda. Efforts to manage and find durable solutions to the problems associated with these issues are underfunded and subordinated to state or market interests.

In summary, the feminist theoretical approach to international relations rests on four assumptions. First, gender matters. Second, international relations are conflictual. Third, patriarchy is the principal feature of the international system. Fourth, the hierarchy of international issues is gendered, whereby "feminine" issues are marginalized. This framework provides a systematic critique of realism, liberalism, and Marxism as well as an alternative lens to understanding international relations and international organizations.

FEMINISM AND THEORIES OF INTERNATIONAL ORGANIZATIONS

The feminist theoretical approach uncovers the hidden masculine biases of realist, liberal, and Marxist interpretations of international organizations. The lens of gender focuses on the masculinities associated with conceptualizing the behavior and nature of international organizations. Realism, liberalism, and Marxism are similar in that they see international organizations in largely mechanical terms. International organizations are "tools," either to dominate other states or classes or to overcome collective action problems. The differences between the theoretical approaches can be interpreted through degrees of masculinity. Several scholars have pointed out that contemporary realism is extremely masculine in nature (Peterson 1992; Tickner 1988, Runyan and Peterson 1990). Realist concepts such as "state," "anarchy," and "high politics" all have masculine biases. For realists, the state is an entity that possesses sovereignty; that is, it has the final say within its territorial jurisdiction. The state determines what public policy will be, and no higher authority exists to review state decisions. The realist conception of the state as a unitary rational actor possessed of sovereignty smacks of the conventional (sexist) wisdom that a "man's home is his castle" and that "he is master of the house." No man has the right to tell another what he can do in his own home. Sovereignty also implies autonomy, another masculine attribute. Psychologically, men see themselves as separate from others, whereas women tend to see themselves as part of a collective (see Goldstein 1996, 111–112, for example). Relatedly, the idea of anarchy, or the absence of a higher authority, is quite masculine; it conjures up images of individuals interacting in a state of nature that reduces to survival of the fittest. Brute force is the final arbiter of disputes. This is why "high" politics focuses on geostrategic and military issues. These are male issues. "Low" politics consists of issues that are deemed feminine, like the environment, human rights, poverty, and education.

The masculine bias of realism leads to biased interpretation of international organizations in terms of which kinds of organizations are important in international relations and what their role should be. Realists argue that international organizations are little more than the sum of their member states. They are tools by which the great powers dominate lesser states. International organizations are subordinate to the state and dependent on the largesse of states. International organizations are feminized by realist theory in two ways. First, international organizations are objects to be used by states to further their interests in world politics. They have no significant independence. At best, they might function as the "wife" of the state, who exerts some influence in some areas but would not challenge the primacy of state sovereignty. Like the traditional wife, international organizations are dependent on states for their identity, direction, and income. Second, realists emphasize the IGO; NGOs (organizations in which women are more likely to participate) are excluded from realist analyses altogether. NGO activity in international relief and development efforts is trivialized by being relegated to the realm of low politics.

Liberalism has a different masculine bias, although it does allow for consideration of feminine issues. Liberals see the state as an aggregation of competing interests within a society. Assuming equality of resources (a questionable assumption), any group or coalition of groups can come to dominate the government. In this sense, women can have an important influence on government and public policy. Consequently, feminine issues (poverty, education, environment) can come to dominate the domestic and international agenda. Liberal institutionalism, a variation of liberalism, does conceive of the state as a unitary and rational actor, thus displaying the same masculine bias as realism—the autonomous state reacts rationally (self-interestedly), not in an intuitive or emotional manner.

Liberalism also emphasizes interdependence as an attribute of the international system. That is, states rely on each other mutually, although not necessarily in the same ways. Liberal international relations theory has feminine characteristics in that it accentuates the interconnectedness of societies and the idea that national security might best be obtained through collective, or multilateral, means rather than unilaterally.

In spite of the liberal emphasis on interconnectedness and equality, the central underpinning is masculine. The market is the key organizing concept, one that is masculine. Neoclassical economics, which provides liberalism with its understanding of the market, is based on mathematical models and proofs. According to Nelson (1996, 20–21):

> The idealized market is a place where rational, autonomous, anonymous agents with stable preferences interact for the purposes of exchange. The agents make their choices in accordance with the maximization of some objective function subject to resource constraints, and the outcome of their market interactions is the determination of an efficient allocation of goods along with a set of equilibrium prices. The prototypical market is one in which tangible goods or labor services are exchanged, with money facilitating transactions in which the agents are individual persons. The prototypical scholarly work in economics is an article that studies market behavior using sophisticated mathematics to formalize the model in the "theory" section, accompanied by econometrics analysis of data in an "empirical" section.

Liberals emphasize that the individual, household, or firm is operating in a market. In this sense, the liberal world is just as masculine as the realist's anarchic world. The debate between realism and liberalism is often gendered in that each tries to portray the other as feminine. For the liberal, the market is unbiased, governed by objective laws of supply and demand. The market becomes unpredictable (feminine) when it is disrupted by irrational (feminine) behavior that may be motivated by nationalism or religion. The state is feminized by liberalism, particularly if it governs too much. The state is fiscally irresponsible (feminine) and is incapable of carrying out complex tasks. States engage in irrational policies such as protectionism or economic nationalism that undermine the long-term national interests.

Realists portray liberals as idealistic (feminine) for insisting that economics can overcome most kinds of international conflict. Liberals are behaving irrationally if they conceive of national interest as anything other than narrow self-interest. The market can function only if a hegemon provides effective protection (masculine). Simply put, realists and liberals offer competing versions of masculinity while effectively denigrating the other as feminine (Ashworth and Swatuk 1998, 82–83).

Liberal understandings of international organizations provide such organizations with a positive and constructive role in international relations. International organizations offer a mechanism for states and other actors to settle their disputes peaceably. But the strategies for settling those disputes remain masculine, though not as masculine as physically assaulting an adversary. Liberals see the market and economic competition as a substitute for war and other forms of violent conflict. Put another way, men don't need to prove themselves on the battlefield if they can dominate the market and the boardroom. According to liberals, contemporary international organizations should seek to minimize the influence of the state in domestic and international markets. Liberals also place significant emphasis on the difference between public and private spheres. Normatively speaking, liberals believe that goods and services within a society and between societies should be provided and distributed by private or market mechanisms, not authoritatively by states or international organizations. For feminists, liberal international economic organizations, such as the WTO, IMF, or the World Bank, serve market interests and ignore the subordinate position of women and minorities in the so-called unbiased market. The market is seen as the solution to the problems faced by women and minorities and is rarely, if ever, seen as the problem.

The Marxist theoretical approach is the least masculine of the approaches discussed so far because it emphasizes exploitation and the consequences for collective society. Marxist and Hegelian approaches underscore societal development as critical to individual development. A society's mode of production shapes political and social arrangements. However, class analysis and capitalism cannot explain gender or racial discrimination. Marxist theory is very mechanical in that it argues that the subjugation of women and minorities will disappear when capitalism is eliminated. Marxist theory also focuses on dependency, a condition that creates a superior-subordinate relationship, rather than interdependency, which implies more benign and mutual relations. The superior-subordinate relationship between classes and classes of states is analogous to the superior-subordinate relationship between men and women, the masculine and the feminine. This kind of relationship leaves plenty of room for exploitation and abuse. It also leaves room for inattention and marginalization. Feminists see Marxist and realist theory as prevalent in developing states because they are in a subordinate (feminine) position, a position that is not very desirable. Marxist and realist theory prescribe certain kinds of state behavior that will eliminate the subordinate role or minimize its ill effects. The hidden assumption is that being dependent (feminine) is not desirable while being independent or autonomous is.

The Marxist view of international organizations as mechanisms of capitalist domination or as tools for developing transnational hegemony has a masculine bias because it assumes that the impact of international organizations is the same for men and women. Actions taken by, or on behalf of, international organizations disproportionately affect women, often adversely. Consider the effects of military force, economic sanctions, or structural adjustment programs, which burden women and children in different and perhaps more serious ways. When international organizations ignore women and trivialize gender issues, they reinforce their own patriarchal tendencies, legitimizing the subjugation of women.

The feminist theoretical approach enhances contemporary understandings of international organizations by pointing out the overt and hidden biases of realism, liberalism, and Marxism. The gender lens accentuates the subsumed masculinities associated with conceptualizing the behavior and the nature of international organizations. Feminism is more compatible with Marxism because both are critical approaches that challenge mainstream interpretations of international politics and organizations.

GENDERING INTERNATIONAL ORGANIZATIONS

The feminist theoretical approach genders international organizations in several ways. First, the feminist approach critically examines the role and contributions of women in IGOs (Heyzer et al. 1995; Whitworth 1994; Karl 1995; Winslow 1995; Staudt 1997, Goetz 1997). In terms of employment, women are largely excluded from traditional positions of power, making up less than 4 percent of the decision-making elite in the UN system (Peterson and Runyan 1993, 55). This includes UN ambassadors, top management, and senior staff. The United States, which prides itself on its record for the advancement of women, did not have its first female ambassador to the UN until 1980 when President Ronald Reagan appointed Jeanne Kirkpatrick.* Not surprisingly,

---

*Not all feminists regard the appointment of Jeanne Kirkpatrick as UN ambassador as a particular advance for women. The Reagan administration did little to hide its contempt of the UN and was more than willing to act unilaterally in international affairs. Moreover, Kirkpatrick's outspoken criticism of the UN and support for brutal dictatorships in Latin America denote masculinity, her female sex notwithstanding.

women constitute more than 85 percent of the UN clerical and support staff (Peterson and Runyan 1993, 55). After more than a decade of systematic review of UN hiring practices, some question still remains as to whether women workers in the UN have moved from "margin to mainstream" (D'Amico 1999, 19–40). The feminist theoretical approach highlights these kinds of gender inequities within IGOs.

Women who do occupy decision-making positions tend to lead agencies that are traditionally concerned with feminine issues. For example, women have headed the UN Fund for Population Activities and the UN Development Fund for Women (UNIFEM). Higher proportions of women are involved in agencies such as the World Health Organization (WHO) and the United Nations Children's Fund (UNICEF). Feminist scholarship also highlights the contributions of women operating within traditional gender roles and the accomplishments of "feminine" agencies within the UN system.

Second, feminist scholarship also spotlights the activities and strategies of NGOs (Connors 1996; Cook 1997; Penrose and Seaman 1996). These kinds of international organizations are involved with helping people (mostly women and children) at the grassroots level (Eldridge 1995; Aubrey 1997). Women are involved in social and revolutionary movements. They are active in NGOs that provide legal and medical assistance for issues that affect women and those that seek to promote change in extremely patriarchal societies. Such organizations tend to be more feminine in the sense that they are horizontally rather than hierarchically structured and are not governed by rigid rules of behavior. NGOs often work with IGOs to carry out the equivalent of international social or welfare policy. The contributions of NGOs are often ignored and are considered of less importance than the activities of IGOs.

NGOs are often the only groups willing to challenge state and IGO practices that have a significant impact on women. For example, Human Rights Watch released an extremely controversial report, "Hidden in the Home: Abuse of Domestic Workers with Special Visas in the United States," which charged that many diplomats and employees at the UN, World Bank, and the Organization of American States have abused the rights of their domestic workers by paying far less than minimum wage and even engaging in forced labor and physical abuse (Greenhouse 2001, A16). Human Rights Watch was willing to ask the tough questions when the U.S. government claimed that diplomats had special protections and IGO officials lamented the difficulties of taking action because "they are the employees of our employees (Greenhouse 2001, A16). NGOs are often the only voice for the most vulnerable in global society.

Third, the feminist theoretical approach examines the effects of patriarchy, or male dominance, in contemporary international organizations. Attitudes, policies, methods, and approaches that neglect women or treat them as insignificant contribute to gender inequities (Campbell and Stein 1992; Vuorela 1992; Staudt 1997; Alvarez 1997). World Bank and IMF officials who make decisions based on neoclassical economic theory and models are perpetuating gender inequalities because these models assume away gender and rely on methods that demand "hard" facts and documented evidence. For example, feminists and Marxists have charged that structural adjustment loans hurt women more than men. How does one measure "hurt"? World Bank and IMF officials measure structural adjustment effects in terms of lost jobs, declining wages, and economic stagnation, all of which particularly impact men. But the IMF and World Bank cannot track the effects of structural adjustment on women because they reside in the home or serve in the ranks of unpaid or unofficial labor. As a result, there is no "reliable" documentation that women are also hurt, in which case the World Bank and the IMF cannot conclude that their structural adjustment programs are "more" harmful to women. Feminists point out that the IMF is concerned about the market (masculine) effects and not the social (feminine) effects of structural adjustment. The market compels societies to adapt to its laws. Neoclassical economic thought, which currently dominates multilateral financial and development institutions, imposes a masculine economic world order. More women need to be in positions of power, and feminine approaches to politics and economics need to be incorporated into the activities and policies of international organizations. International organizations often pay lip service to gender equality issues, but budget priorities suggest that they are not willing to support those issues substantively and that "feminine" concerns largely rank at the bottom of the list.

The feminist approach is widely criticized as demonstrating poor scholarship, lacking both rigor and precision. The approach consists of traditional feminism, neofeminism, liberal feminism, socialist feminism, and postmodern feminism—variations that often contradict each other and raise questions about the utility of the feminist endeavor. Nevertheless, all feminists stress that gender is a useful category of analysis. The social expectations surrounding masculine and feminine behavior and identity influence how international organizations are studied. The feminist approach also accepts four interrelated assumptions: (1) Gender matters; (2) international relations is essentially conflictual; (3) patriarchy, or male dominance, is the principal feature of the international system; (4) the hierarchy of international issues is gendered, whereby "feminine" issues are marginalized. This framework provides a systematic critique of realism, liberalism, and Marxism as well as an alternative lens to understanding international relations and international organizations.

The feminist theoretical approach accentuates women's contributions in international organizations, both recognizing women in traditionally masculine roles and asserting the value of traditional, feminine gender roles as a worthy object of intellectual inquiry. International organizations are examined in terms of the role of women and in terms of gender equity. The feminist approach is optimistic about the role of international organizations in bringing "women's" issues into the forefront of domestic and international politics (see, for example, Whitworth 1994; Stienstra 1994). IGOs and NGOs, working in tandem with domestic groups, put political, economic, and social pressure on governments and other institutional structures (both private and public) to address hidden masculinist biases and to consider women's and feminist issues.

The feminist theoretical approach is controversial in academic and political circles because it expresses a set of concerns different from those that have traditionally dominated the field of international relations. It challenges not only traditional priorities but also the putatively "scientific" methodology that stresses narrow rules of evidence and excludes intuitive understandings of international relations. As a critical approach, it has prompted a reexamination of the presumably "universal" approaches of realism and liberalism.

5

INTERNATIONAL SECURITY

INTERNATIONAL WAR is among the most dire of the perennial problems that plague world affairs. Historically, war has ended the lives of hundreds of millions of people and left once thriving societies in ruins, subjugating and exploiting entire nations. With respect to the central issue of international security, then, it is legitimate to ask how and why international organizations respond to war and threats of war. Can international organizations prevent war? If so, how? And how do international organizations identify international aggression, diplomatically referred to as "breaches of the peace" or "threats to international peace and security"? Diplomatic euphemisms aside, the causes of war are numerous and intertwined. Societies fight for tangible reasons—territory and resources. They also fight for intangible reasons—ideology, nationalism, and religion. Yet the solutions to war are few and frustratingly elusive. A true balance of power might deter aggression; but if history is any indicator, a straight balance-of-power approach is flawed and prone to failure.

The causes of war have become increasingly complicated and its effects ruinous. Contemporary wars tend to have both internal and external sources, and sophisticated weapons are readily available to any party with money or credit enough to buy them. And though fighting itself may be confined within states, its consequences are felt elsewhere, often having international repercussions. International organizations and the attendant cooperation of member states offer some counter to the conditions and causes of war, providing the means to manage its ill effects as well as some promising mechanisms to prevent it.

In this chapter, we examine the role of the United Nations in making and keeping the peace. Specifically, we take a look at how the UN Security Council and other UN bodies carry out the important assignment of identifying and responding to threats to international peace and security. We outline the legal framework and the historical evolution of UN responses to the perennial problem of war, and we detail the origins of collective security, peacekeeping, and peacemaking. Then we apply the theoretical approaches of realism, liberalism, Marxism, and feminism to two actual cases—the Persian Gulf Crisis of 1991 and Srebrenica of 1995—in order to observe how each framework works in practice.

THE UNITED NATIONS

The UN was conceived in the fires of World War II and born in its ashes. In 1944, from August through October, representatives of the "big three" (U.S., UK, and USSR) fleshed out the framework for the UN at the Dumbarton Oaks Conference (Hilderbrand 1990). The UN's reason for being, its *raison d'être*, is identified in Article 1(1) of the Charter:

> To maintain international peace and security and to that end: to take effective collective measures for the prevention and removal of threats to the peace, and for the suppression of acts of aggression or breaches of the peace, and to bring about by peaceful means, and in conformity with the principles of justice and international law, adjustment or settlement of international disputes or situations which might lead to a breach of the peace.

The devastation of World War II, coupled with the advent of atomic weapons, brought about a renewed sense of urgency in preventing future wars. To bolster this mission, Article 2(4) of the Charter explicitly forbids member states from threatening or using force in their international relations. The exception to this prohibition is found in Article 51. Member states are permitted to use force only in cases of self-defense or for collective self-defense. The international peace and security interests of all member states could be served by effectively outlawing war as a legitimate option of international diplomacy.

Article 2(1) of the UN Charter recognizes the principle of state sovereignty and the territorially based state. Only states may be full members of the UN, and all states are equally sovereign in that their representatives (the government) have the final say within their own territories. Article 2(7) reinforces the principle of state sovereignty by limiting the jurisdiction of the UN: "Nothing contained in the present Charter shall authorize the United Nations to intervene in matters which are essentially within the domestic jurisdiction of any state or shall require the Members to submit such matters to settlement under the present Charter; but this principle shall not prejudice the application of enforcement measures under Chapter VII."

The architects of the UN sought to strike a balance between the status quo of territorially based, sovereign nation-states and the need for international governance and stability. Governments retained sovereignty domestically and agreed to the peaceful settlement of their disputes internationally. This balance is a precarious one. International peace is not necessarily an interest of all states at all times. From ancient Sumer to modern-day Sarajevo, violence has proven to be an effective form of leverage, and the threat of violence a useful tool for obtaining foreign policy goals. Historically, violence has been, in fact, the decisive mechanism of change and the final arbiter of international disputes. Thus, the UN Charter is revolutionary: It challenges long-established international practice by outlawing both the threat and the use of force and by creating a higher authority to maintain international peace as security. The UN Security Council is that higher authority.

THE SECURITY COUNCIL

Chapter V, Article 24, of the UN Charter gives the Security Council the responsibility for preventing and responding to war: "In order to ensure prompt and effective action by the United Nations, its Members confer on the Security Council primary responsibility for the maintenance of international peace and security, and agree that in carrying out its duties under this responsibility the Security Council acts on their behalf." As identified in Chapter V, the five permanent members of the Security Council are the United States, the United Kingdom, the Union of Soviet Socialist Republics (USSR), France, and the Republic of China. These states were the allied victors of World War II, and their great-power status enabled them to take on a special responsibility for providing international stability in the postwar period. As permanent members, the states retain a continuous seat from session to session; moreover, each possesses an absolute veto, meaning that each can nullify a decision without further discussion.* The veto provision was a controversial feature of the UN Charter as it violates the principle of the sovereign equality of states. That is, the permanent members are more sovereign than others: Their veto renders UN action against any permanent member impossible and keeps the UN from taking any other action without their consent. But many observers argue that the veto provision was simply necessary. It was there to prevent the UN from starting an enforcement action it could not finish or invoking the name of the UN to use force over a great power's objection, thereby quickly raising a local conflict into a global one (Riggs and Plano 1994, 57). In essence, the structure and the decision-making procedure of the Security Council are fully informed by a strong dose of political pragmatism.

Chapter V also mandates that the ten nonpermanent members of the Security Council be elected by the General Assembly, which is a plenary body. These ten nonpermanent members are elected for two-year terms and retiring members are not eligible for immediate reelection. The architects of the UN wanted the Security Council to represent the entire international community, not just the victors of World War II. By granting the General Assembly the power to elect the remaining members, they provided for a diverse membership in the Security Council, thereby ensuring that alternative viewpoints would be represented. The presidency of the Security Council rotates monthly among members alphabetically (English).

The task of the UN architects was to construct the Security Council as an organizational mechanism that would permit member states to act collectively to deter international aggression and provide a framework for a collective military response should deterrence happen to fail. However, they were faced with the stark reality that the first formalized experiment with collective security had failed dramatically under the League of Nations. Moreover, the principal lesson of World War II was fresh in their minds: Do not appease aggressors. The efforts of European leaders to pacify Adolf Hitler at the Munich Conference served only to embolden him. In his quest for an Aryan empire, Hitler went unchecked. Nor did any leader see fit to check Japanese aggression in China and Southeast Asia. Limited war was thus rewarded. In consequence, the international community had faced another world war close on the heels of the first one.

This time around, however, one important new factor was working in favor of collective security—the full cooperation of the United States. In fact, the United States, first under Franklin D. Roosevelt and then under Harry S. Truman, was taking a leadership role in the construction of the UN. Having emerged from the war predominant

---

*An absolute veto is the ability to nullify legislation or decisions without any further discussion. A qualified veto can also nullify legislation or decisions but can be overridden, usually with a qualified majority of voting members.

in military strength and economic power, the United States was willing to commit those resources to the UN, a commitment it never made to the League. Without U.S. participation, the League of Nations remained a fledgling organization, politically weak and hence ineffectual at problem-solving during the inter-war years. Arguably, that weakness was inherent in the League's Charter. Under the League of Nations Charter, for example, the Council could only make recommendations regarding the use of military and economic sanctions. In legal theory, these sanctions were mandatory; in practice, they were voluntary and discretionary. The League, as such, had no power to enforce its recommendations.

The UN Charter, on the other hand, contains much stronger provisions for peace enforcement. First, Chapter VII requires member states to abide by Security Council decisions and to contribute to UN enforcement in general. Second, and more specifically, Article 43 of Chapter VII requires member states to make armed forces available to the Security Council. Article 47 establishes a Military Staff Committee to advise and assist the Security Council in matters relating to military enforcement of Security Council decisions. Through these provisions collective security was institutionalized, at least on paper. Security Council decisions were legally binding. A UN security force and the Military Staff Committee were to be available for Security Council initiatives and to forcibly carry out decisions if necessary.

While the architects of the UN Charter were able to correct for the organizational shortcomings evident in the League's collective security arrangements, they could not change world politics. The Cold War, which pitted two of the most influential of the permanent members against each other, rendered UN collective security arrangements ineffective. The Military Staff Committee, consisting of the Chiefs of Staff of the permanent members, argued about the size and cost of the security force and how much each should contribute. The Military Staff Committee and the security force envisioned in Chapter VII died shortly after their inception. Other security initiatives designed to stabilize the immediate postwar environment also met an early demise. Early efforts to control the spread of atomic weapons were quickly gutted by suspicious enemies. The UN Atomic Energy Commission, the U.S.-sponsored Baruch Plan, and the USSR-sponsored Peace Offensive became little more than propaganda tools in the emerging Cold War. The veto provision led to near-complete paralysis of the Security Council in matters of international security. Thus collective security and arms control gave way to alliances, balance of power, and arms races.

Why did UN collective security falter so dramatically after its inception? According to Riggs and Plano, three factors—consensus, commitment, and organization—are necessary for collective security to work (1994, 100). The UN Charter provided member states with the organization, but consensus and commitment among the Security Council's permanent members were clearly absent. The lack of consensus was based not merely on practical questions—who contributes what and how much—but on fundamental differences as to how the world ought to be ordered. Perceptions of right and wrong are rarely negotiable. The United States and the USSR and their respective allies had essentially different world views, making any consensus fleeting at best.

Without a consensus, commitment is hard to establish. Member states must be willing to contribute to enforcement actions, even when those actions run contrary to their national interests. They must also be willing to refrain from using force unilaterally. Commitment makes efforts to change the status quo by violence unlawful and doomed to frustration through opposition in overwhelming force (Riggs and Plano 1994, 101; Martin 1952, 7). Unfortunately, the status quo is rarely just and tends to favor some over others. Most of the great social, political, and economic changes in world history have been born out of violence.

The lack of consensus and commitment extends beyond the permanent Security Council members. Developing states are less than satisfied with a status quo not of their making. Many such states have been victims of great-power colonialism and, as such, have been forced to fight for self-determination. In 1958, for example, France was permitted to carry on a brutal counter-guerrilla campaign against Algerian nationalists in what was once French Algeria. In the diplomatic world, many thought of that rebellion and the French response as a French internal affair not subject to international scrutiny.

The lack of consensus and commitment to collective security is less a problem in principle than a question as to what constitutes aggression. Were the attacks on the U.S. World Trade Center and Pentagon in 2001 aggression? A general agreement on this point is important because it is, presumably, an aggressive act that should trigger a collective response. In writing the UN Charter, its architects wanted to prevent another world war—a conflict like World War II, in which the character of aggression was fairly unambiguous. It was a basic land grab, involving the use of clearly identifiable, regular military forces. In that sense a state seeking to change its territorial boundaries by force would be an aggressor, in which case the UN could step in militarily to restore the status quo. In the postwar era, however, aggression became ambiguous, and the use of force more limited and nuanced. States did not try to conquer new territories. They used force to change governments or to help national liberation movements. Violent international conflict took several new forms, including proxy war, insurgencies, covert military operations, anticolonial rebellion, subversion, and terrorism. Violence was used by state and nonstate actors, each claiming a legitimate right to use force.

According to the UN Charter, the only permissible use of force is self-defense. Does this mean force cannot be used against colonial or racist regimes or governments committing genocide against their own people? Does this mean a state must wait to be attacked before it can act to prevent imminent hostilities? Does this mean a state must sit idly by while its citizens are *in extremis* abroad? These questions are troubling, in large part because aggression now appears to have many meanings, none of which is wholly clear. Consequently, international efforts to define aggression have met with little success. And if defining aggression is difficult, then so is determining an appropriate collective response. In effect, the UN is largely silent on these thorny problems. After all, Article 2(7) prohibits the UN from intervening in matters that are essentially within the domestic jurisdiction of states. Sometimes, supraviolence is not the answer to violence.

The complexity of the political landscape in the postwar environment doomed the UN experiment with collective security. The UN Security Council did authorize a military response to the North Korean invasion of South Korea in 1950; however, that response was possible only because the USSR was boycotting the Council to protest the denial of a seat to the newly formed communist Chinese government. When the USSR returned, it used its veto to block any more Security Council decisions.

The Cold War record of the UN Security Council in providing for collective security is, by most accounts, quite poor. However, the UN's *raison d'être* was not completely abandoned. The prevention of violent conflict involves more than just a credible threat of a collective violent response. Breaches of the peace can be prevented through airing of grievances, diplomatic negotiations, mediation, arbitration, confidence building, and other forms of nonviolent conflict resolution. The Security Council, the General Assembly, and the Secretary-General have improvised to approximate the UN's central mission in spite of political exigencies that prevented successful collective security.

THE GENERAL ASSEMBLY

The General Assembly's influence in the realm of international security stems from two Charter provisions—the authority to make recommendations regarding international security issues (Articles 10 and 11) and control of the UN budget (Article 17). During the Cold War, the General Assembly stood as a voice against aggression by condemning illegal uses of force through resolutions. Such resolutions fell far short of the expectations generated by the ideals of collective security and peace enforcement because the General Assembly had neither the authority nor the resources to do anything about breaches of the peace. Nevertheless, they expressed the conscience of the community and served as a reminder of the main purpose of the UN. The General Assembly also supported "peacekeeping" by establishing it as a budget priority. Peacekeeping, discussed in more detail below, developed as an alternative to collective security and has been an important feature of international conflict resolution.

The General Assembly's first foray into international security came on November 3, 1950, with the "Uniting for Peace" resolution (UNGA RES 377):

> If the Security Council, because of lack of unanimity of the permanent members, fails to exercise its primary responsibility for the maintenance of international peace and security in any case there appears to be a threat to peace, breach of peace, or act of aggression, the General Assembly shall consider the matter immediately with the view of making appropriate recommendations to Members for collective measures including in the case of a breach of the peace or acts of aggression the use of armed force when necessary, to maintain or restore international peace and security.

This U.S.-sponsored resolution expanded the mandate of the UN General Assembly by giving it a more active role in international security matters when the Security Council was too paralyzed by politics to act. It even allowed for the UN General Assembly to be called into emergency session at the request of seven Security Council members. While originally designed to circumvent the Soviet veto, this resolution has been used by the General Assembly nine times, several of which were in response to armed aggression by France, Great Britain, and the Soviet Union (Howard 1990). No armed response has ever been recommended, although the General Assembly did express the majority sentiment of the international community. Members were reminded of their commitment not to threaten or use force in their international relations. Postwar relations would not be business as usual and aggressive war would not go unchallenged, even if it could not be challenged forcibly.

THE SECRETARY-GENERAL

The role of the Secretary-General in international security is complicated and difficult to understand without understanding this position in the overall UN organization. The Secretary-General is the chief UN diplomat and is the head of the Secretariat. The

Secretariat is the professional bureaucracy that administers UN programs and executes UN policies. The Secretary-General is selected for a five-year, renewable term through an elaborate process whereby the Security Council makes a recommendation to the General Assembly, which must then approve the nominee with a two-thirds majority. The selection process is highly politicized because any recommendation is subject to the Security Council permanent member veto. Furthermore, the candidate must be acceptable to two-thirds of the members of the General Assembly. Hence, it is not surprising that the selection of the Secretary-General is an arduous and difficult process shot through with conflicting interests and rivalries.

Once in office, the Secretary-General must perform a balancing act, representing the UN on the one hand and responding to member states on the other. The Secretary-General's role as head of the Secretariat means that he is the chief bureaucrat. He must foster neutral competence in the international civil service so the UN can develop a reputation of professionalism, expertise, credibility, and impartiality. This entails developing bureaucratic loyalties that extend beyond national loyalties. At the same time, the Secretary-General must answer to member states. The United States, for example, succeeded in derailing the reelection of former Secretary-General Boutros Boutros-Ghali because it was dissatisfied with perceived UN excesses and Boutros-Ghali's penchant for expanding peacekeeping missions without state authorization.

The Secretary-General plays a key role in identifying threats to international peace and security and attempting to resolve violent conflicts. However, the UN Charter is not specific about the Secretary-General's role in the maintenance of international peace and security. Article 99 states that the Secretary-General "may bring to the attention of the Security Council" matters that threaten international peace and security, but this provision has rarely been used. The Secretary-General's role is subtler than that. He exercises considerable influence over fact-finding activities and he is responsible for carrying out UN policy with regard to international security. In short, "it's all in the execution," meaning that the way in which a policy is implemented profoundly shapes the policy itself, not to mention its outcome. The Secretary-General, together with the appropriate Secretariat agencies, is responsible for evolving and developing what has emerged as the alternative to collective security.

PEACEKEEPING

Peacekeeping was not envisioned by the architects of the UN Charter. Former Secretary-General Dag Hammarskjöld once joked that peacekeeping was permitted under "Chapter Six and a half" (Goldstein 1996, 279). He was referring to the tacit compromise between the UN's role in diplomatic efforts at conflict resolution as outlined in Chapter VI and its role in collective security as it evolved. As collective security arrangements proved increasingly unworkable, the UN's role in nonviolent conflict resolution gained in prominence.

Defining precisely what peacekeeping is presents a difficulty because peacekeeping operations have been developed, implemented, and modified as particular responses to particular situations (Weiss, Forsythe, and Coate 1994, 48). However, two conditions are essential: The consent of the principal parties involved and a temporary cease-fire. No UN personnel are deployed until these conditions are in place. The first full-fledged UN peacekeeping operation occurred during the Suez Crisis in 1956, when Egyptian President Gamal Nasser announced that he was nationalizing the Suez Canal, which was jointly owned by Great Britain and France, two former colonial powers in the region. After several months of intense and hostile negotiations, Israel invaded Egypt (with the tacit consent of Great Britain and France). French and British forces invaded a few days later, purportedly to protect the canal. The United States and the USSR called for an immediate cease-fire, as did the General Assembly. Then the General Assembly created the UN Emergency Force (UNEF), which was deployed to operate the Suez Canal and provide stability during the stand-down of hostilities. UNEF consisted of approximately 6,000 lightly armed peacekeepers from ten countries. In order to build confidence within the highly charged political atmosphere, UNEF excluded forces from the permanent members of the Security Council. Later, the mission of UNEF shifted to overseeing the withdrawal of foreign troops and establishing a buffer zone between the Egyptian and the Israeli troops. UNEF was finally withdrawn in 1967. Hostilities resumed shortly thereafter, with the 1967 Arab–Israeli War.

The UN's first experience with peacekeeping generated several important lessons (Taylor 1998, 280). First, it established that peacekeeping operations should be as neutral as possible, using force only if peacekeeping forces are attacked. Second, peacekeeping forces must be deployed with the consent of the host state. Third, the Secretary-General should control peacekeeping forces to bolster the neutrality of the mission. Peacekeeping clearly involves a different dynamic than collective security. With peacekeeping, no aggressor is identified or acted against. The parties involved are not assessed blame. This approach permits parties to disengage from violent conflict without losing face, thereby facilitating more peaceable conflict resolution.

The UN conducted nineteen peacekeeping missions between 1947 and 1989. This figure includes observer missions that monitor cease-fire agreements or election procedures. Peacekeeping can be costly, and such missions have met with varying degrees of success. Most agree, however, that they have saved countless lives, which can have no price tag. Since 1989, UN peacekeeping operations have expanded considerably. The UN has authorized dozens of missions in more than twenty countries including Tajikistan, India, Haiti, Bosnia, Kosovo, and Mozambique. The end of the Cold War marks the beginning of a second generation of peacekeeping that extends beyond observer missions and lightly armed multinational contingents. According to Mackinlay and Chopra (1997, 175–197) peacekeeping has evolved to include preventive peacekeeping, supervising ceasefires between irregular forces, assisting in the maintenance of law and order, protecting the delivery of humanitarian assistance, guaranteeing rights of passage, and enforcing sanctions and Security Council decisions. The end of the Cold War provided the international community with an opportunity for greater cooperation in peacekeeping, and as events began to unfold in the Middle East in 1990, the international community was also able to revisit the idea of collective security.

CASE STUDY 1: THE PERSIAN GULF CRISIS

The idea of collective security experienced a rebirth during the Iraq–Kuwait crisis of 1990. In August of that year, Iraq invaded Kuwait, quickly occupying and annexing that tiny, oil-rich kingdom. Several factors made this crisis unique among those generated since World War II. First, the Iraq invasion was a textbook land grab, a kind of aggression not witnessed since World War II. The Korean War could be interpreted as a civil war or a war of national liberation. Other invasions involving force had occurred, but they were for reasons other than the occupation and annexation of territories legally belonging to another sovereign state. In this case, however, the Iraqi use of force clearly violated Article 2(4), the key UN provision designed to thwart efforts to change territorial boundaries by force. This kind of "naked" aggression drew condemnation from around the world. Second, the Iraqi aggression occurred during a period of transition in world politics. The USSR was becoming less obstructionist and was seeking a different role for itself in international affairs under Soviet President Mikhail Gorbachev. The warming of East–West relations and the clear-cut nature of the Iraqi aggression enabled the collective security arrangements of the UN to function in the manner originally intended.

On the date of the Iraqi invasion, the UN Security Council met in emergency session; it condemned the invasion as an unlawful use of force and demanded an immediate withdrawal of Iraqi forces. Iraqi forces quickly entrenched themselves in Kuwait, fortifying their positions along the Saudi Arabian border. The United States immediately moved rapid-deployment combat forces into the region to help defend Saudi Arabia and its strategic oil fields. The forces deployed were not sufficient to repel an Iraqi onslaught, but they did make the Iraqi leaders think about the possibility of engaging U.S. forces in combat. The United States informed the UN that it was deploying its military in accordance with Article 51 of the Charter, permitting the use of force of collective self-defense. Moreover, both the Kuwaiti government and the Saudi Arabian government had requested U.S. military assistance.

On August 6, 1990, the Security Council passed Resolution 661 calling for mandatory economic sanctions against Iraq. The sanctions were comprehensive although humanitarian and medical supplies were exempted. UN members, bound under Chapter VII of the UN Charter to abide by Security Council decisions, were obligated to honor this Resolution. In the past, however, such economic sanctions had not always been enforced; and in this case, supplies and arms continued to flow to Iraq, especially from Jordan and Turkey. On August 25, 1990, the Security Council authorized the use of force if necessary to implement the economic sanctions—this, to ensure the isolation of Iraq and to remind members of their UN obligations.

While the UN was applying diplomatic pressure on Iraq, the United States was putting together a "multinational" force dubbed Desert Shield. Although composed largely of U.S. army, air, and naval forces, Desert Shield also included military units from the Arab League, Great Britain, and France. On November 29, 1990, the Security Council passed Resolution 678, authorizing "all means necessary" to extract Iraq from Kuwait and setting a deadline of January 15, 1991, for the Iraqi withdrawal. On January 16, 1991, Operation Desert Storm, a U.S.-led, UN-sanctioned military response, was launched to force Iraqi troops from Kuwait. The Iraqi invasion was effectively reversed on March 16, 1991, when Iraq, having been driven from Kuwaiti territory, agreed to a cease-fire.

What factors precipitated the Persian Gulf Crisis? Was the UN role constructive, scripting a leading role for the UN on the stage of world politics? Who was affected by the UN action, and how? Was the Gulf Crisis an important precedent for collective security? The answers to these questions depend on your theoretical orientation or your world view. Understanding the role of the Security Council in the Gulf crisis is conditioned by the tools that analyze it. We must recognize, however, that the UN Security Council is an IGO and that decisions are made by representatives of the governments that belong to it (Weiss, Forsythe, and Coate 1994). Hence, interpreting the actions of the Security Council is a matter of interpreting the motivations of the states involved. The realist, the liberal, the Marxist, and the feminist approaches differ in their conceptions of the state and in their identification of factors that motivate the behavior of governments. These differences, in turn, generate different explanations about how international organizations behave, whose interest they serve, and how their policies affect societies.

A REALIST CUT

Realists see international organizations like the UN as tools or extensions of great powers. They are usually created by a hegemon or formed through the cooperation of great powers. According to realist theory, international organizations must serve the interests of the great powers or be bypassed in favor of unilateral action if great-power consensus cannot be reached. The Persian Gulf Crisis exemplifies why power politics will always take precedence over, and shape the actions of, international organizations. Realists argue that the Persian Gulf crisis is a classic lesson in power calculation and miscalculation, proving that might does indeed make right in world politics.

For realists, the Persian Gulf Crisis was the consequence of a very risky Iraqi gamble, one that Iraq lost and continues to pay for today. Iraq has always been a strategic power in the Middle East, playing a balancing role between the East and the West during the Cold War. A virtual client of both the USSR and France, Iraq has historically played a central role in Middle Eastern politics. As an oil producer and a long-time adversary of Iran, Iraq's strategic value was not lost either on the United States or the USSR, both of whom have provided arms and assistance to Iraq.

The mainstream U.S. media have largely interpreted Iraq's invasion of Kuwait as the folly of a madman. But, from a strategic point of view, it was a gamble that could have paid off handsomely for Iraq. Consider the decision to invade from Iraq's position. In the twentieth century, Iraq has been a second-rate power at best. First as a colony, then as an independent state, Iraq was overshadowed by the Cold War. Iraq's patron, the USSR, was cutting back on its international commitments. Worse, Iraq's devastating war of attrition with Iran had drained its treasury and left its army demoralized. Meantime, right next door, was Kuwait, an unpopular neighbor with impressive oil reserves, a lot of money, and no defenses worthy of the name. Many in the Arab world viewed Kuwait as an arrogant puppet of the United States. During the Iran–Iraq war, Kuwait had reflagged its oil tankers with the U.S. flag and repeatedly exceeded its OPEC quotas, lowering the price of oil in global markets. A successful takeover of Kuwait would make Iraq the power in the Middle East controlling the largest standing army in the region together with more than a third of the world's oil supply. A quick military action would present the world with a fait accompli, which few states could do anything about. And once entrenched, Iraq could be extracted from Kuwait only under very difficult conditions and at extreme cost. The only state capable of such a task was the United States, whose forces in the region were negligible. (Note: Some sources have indicated that the United States had signaled to Iraq that it would not respond militarily to an Iraqi offensive against Kuwait [Salinger 1995].) By Saddam Hussein's calculations, then, a successful military action would raise Iraq to great-power status with one quick, relatively cost-free stroke.

But the UN, and particularly the Security Council, had its own calculations. Its role and behavior can be explained by the interests of the status quo great powers. The Security Council did not ignore the Iraqi invasion; it reacted because it directly threatened the interests of many of the permanent members. If Iraq's aggression were not reversed, there would be a permanent shift in the balance of power in the Middle East, and perhaps the world. Iraq was perceived as dangerous because its population was Muslim, its leaders nationalist, and its agenda aggressive.

Clearly, Middle Eastern oil is crucial to the military and economic security of Europe and the United States. The Carter Doctrine designates access to Middle Eastern oil as a key strategic interest of the United States, an interest in which the United States would militarily intervene. Iraq never threatened to deny oil to the West, but its control over such a significant portion of the world supplies was an unacceptable risk. Iraq could manipulate oil prices or impose a boycott during times of conflict.

Mere dependence on oil is not sufficient reason for the great powers to intervene militarily. Iraq was challenging the status quo order. First, it challenged U.S. leadership. U.S. hegemony has depended, to a large extent, on its ability to provide the world with access to oil at relatively low prices. Iraq threatened that ability. The shift in the balance of power would destabilize the Middle East and weaken U.S. leadership capability. Hence, U.S. interests were more directly engaged than those of other powers dependent on Middle Eastern oil.

Second, no existing state has ceased to exist because of military conquest since World War II. In the postwar era, governments have come and gone through military force and states have been dismembered; but no state has disappeared completely through external violence. Yet Iraq was trying to accomplish just that. And Iraq's aggression was so naked that it was unacceptable, even to those that would otherwise be sympathetic to its position. Saddam Hussein did not even go through the pretext of getting some high-ranking Kuwaiti official to "invite" an Iraqi intervention, as the United States did in Grenada and Panama and as the USSR did in Afghanistan.

Was the UN useful? Absolutely. Would the United States have acted without the UN? Absolutely. The UN was useful only by virtue of a rare congruence of interests among the great powers and the permanent members of the Security Council. The USSR, much preoccupied with internal difficulties, was increasingly interested in rapprochement with the West. Although Iraq was an informal ally of the USSR, the USSR was not going to risk Western aid, nor would it court a possible military confrontation with the United States. Similarly, China was seeking to repair its international reputation after Tiananmen Square, so that country would maintain silent. Moreover, its usual diplomatic style is to abstain in voting situations in which it has no direct interest.

Realists see international organizations as arenas that reflect the existing balance of power (Mearsheimer 1994). At the time of the Gulf Crisis, the West, led by the United States, was able to exercise its power within and outside of the UN, bringing significant force to bear against Iraq. But despite the "global community" and "new world order" rhetoric, the military action against Iraq was far from unanimous. Both France and the USSR were reluctant to authorize military force and hesitated up to, and perhaps beyond, the January 15 deadline. They argued that the sanctions had not had enough time to work and that more time was needed to compel Iraq's withdrawal. Several nonpermanent members of the Security Council also expressed reservations about the use of force. India, Cuba, China, and Yemen either abstained or voted against economic and/or military sanctions. Yemen was punished for its abstentions by the United States, which cut off a planned aid package (Weston 1991, 524).

Key states that did not belong to the Security Council also needed persuading, and/or positive inducements to support "collective security" action. The United States forgave billions of dollars in loans to Egypt and promised to provide significant military hardware to Saudi Arabia. Israel received then-state-of-the-art Patriot missile systems in exchange for their noninvolvement in the conflict in spite of direct Iraqi provocations and SCUD missile attacks. Germany and Japan were pressed to finance the largely American use of force, monies that went directly into the U.S. treasury. The so-called united world response to the Iraqi aggression was manufactured through the application of U.S. and Western European economic and military capabilities. The UN was largely a U.S. creation and the United States used it masterfully to meet its national security interests. The fact that these interests did not conflict significantly with those of other permanent members of the Security Council yielded a unique convergence—the first since 1950. It is also unlikely that such a configuration of interests, circumstances, and events will align again.

The United States and its allies could have acted legitimately without the UN. Article 51 of the Charter permits collective self-defense and the Kuwaiti government was desperately seeking the assistance of anyone who would help. Certainly, events could have unfolded differently; however, the lack of Security Council approval would not necessarily have deterred the United States from acting. After all, the United States was still mopping up from its 1989 invasion of Panama when Iraq first set its sights on Kuwait. If the lack of UN support did not discourage the United States from unilaterally using force in Panama, it certainly could not deter it from using force in a strategically vital area against a foe that represented a direct challenge to its hegemony. And, as a precedent, the Gulf Crisis has not constrained the United States from employing unilateral force in other areas, such as the strikes against Afghanistan and Sudan in 1998. The UN failed to investigate or even challenge the United States on these, at best, questionable uses of force.

The United States manipulated the UN to serve its interests in the Gulf Crisis and continues to do so. While Operations Desert Shield and Desert Storm were conducted under the auspices of the UN, it was U.S. military capabilities that enforced the economic sanctions and conducted military operations. The UN had no control over the kind of force that was employed, nor could it limit the amount of military force that was used. On several occasions, Secretary-General Javier Perez de Cuéllar disagreed with the United States as to which of the Security Council resolutions authorized military force (Crozier 1991, 40). The United States prevailed, and its position was solidified with Resolution 678, which authorized "all means necessary"—a diplomatic euphemism for war—to restore the sovereignty and the territorial integrity of Kuwait.

The Security Council could only authorize the use of force; it had no military forces it could deploy itself. As long as the UN must rely on the armed forces of member states, then only member states that have a compelling interest are likely to volunteer to participate in enforcement action. Thus, in crisis situations the UN response will always be politicized, reflecting the interests and power calculations of leading member states. In other words, either the UN will behave in a manner consistent with the interests of the great powers or it will be marginalized. If great-power interests happen to be congruent, the UN can play a leading role because it will represent those interests. But if great-power interests conflict, the UN will be marginalized and states will act unilaterally or in concert with its allies.

The UN and its agencies were not significant actors in their own right during the Gulf crisis. Rather, they were just a few of the many tools in the statesmen's toolbox. The UN provided legitimacy to the largest deployment and use of force since World War II. Yet, it was the United States that provided the military capability, controlled the use of the military, and made all of the command decisions. Several observers have indicated that UN approval has enabled the United States to escape condemnation for the excessive loss of Iraqi life and the destruction of Iraqi infrastructures. The extensive levels of destruction, along with the high civilian casualty rates, raise important questions as to whether the UN response was proportional and whether all nonforcible means had been exhausted before military force was applied (Weiss, Forsythe, and Coate 1994, 70; Weston 1991; Gardam 1993).

The UN had little or no independent influence on the calculations and the interests of states. The UN collective security system did not deter Iraq from invading Kuwait. The UN could not have done anything about the invasion without the consensus (acquiescence) of the permanent members of the Security Council. Even with the consensus of the permanent members, the UN had to rely upon the military capabilities of the United States. The UN served as little more than window dressing to the U.S. exercise of political and military power. At the very best, it facilitated great-power collusion at a rare moment of great-power consensus. At worst, the Persian Gulf Crisis has created a "mirage of global collective security" and instilled "delusions of grandeur" in UN effectiveness (Carpenter 1997).

A LIBERAL CUT

The liberal theoretical approach provides a different perspective regarding the role of UN agencies in the Persian Gulf Crisis. It emphasizes the role of shared values and norms, as well as the contributions of individuals. Most liberals recognize that power and politics remain important features within international organizations (see, for example, Weiss, Forsythe, Coate, 1994; Keohane and Martin 1995; Claude 1993). Yet, the principal impediment to UN collective security was the ideological polarization of the Cold War and the U.S.–USSR rivalry (Bennett and Lepgold 1993; Flynn and Scheffer 1990). With the end of the Cold War, a "new world order" based on the rule of law and peaceful relations can be established. According to George Bush's Address to the Joint Session of Congress on September 11, 1990, the Persian Gulf Crisis offered the UN a rare opportunity for

> a new era—freer from the threat of terror, stronger in the pursuit of justice, and more secure in the quest for peace—an era in which the nations of the World, East and West, North and South, can prosper and live in harmony. A hundred generations have searched for this elusive path to peace, while a thousand wars raged across the span of human endeavor. Today that new world is struggling to be born, a world quite different from the one we've known: a world where the rule of law supplants the rule of the jungle; a world in which nations recognize the shared responsibilities for freedom and justice; a world where the strong respect the rights of the weak.

These words are not mere rhetoric. They reflect attainable goals, goals that are widely held within the international community. While the UN approach to the Gulf

Crisis was flawed, it represents an important landmark in contemporary international relations. For liberal institutionalists, the UN played an instrumental role in the Gulf Crisis for several reasons. First, it provided states and their leadership with a framework for action. Recall that in addition to consensus and commitment, collective security requires "organization" to implement decisions once they are made. The Security Council participated in and oversaw the creation and the implementation of Desert Shield and later Desert Storm. While arm-twisting and side-payments were part of the policymaking process, such tactics are common, even central, in most democratic institutions. The Security Council represents a diverse cross-section of nation-states, all of whom had input into the decision-making process.

Second, the UN served the pragmatic interests of governments. Consider the United States. Its economic and security interests were directly engaged and it probably would have acted unilaterally. However, it would have been a wholly different kind of war if the UN had not facilitated and enforced the embargo of Iraq. Had Iraq continued to receive military supplies and been able to sell its oil, the fight could have been much longer and considerably nastier. In many respects, UN involvement controlled the conflict. This regional conflict did not escalate into a global conflict because UN forums promoted common goals and a common agenda. UN diplomatic efforts were also instrumental in allowing the United States and its allies to deploy their forces, and may even have deterred Iraq from moving against Saudi Arabia. UN negotiators played a very important and independent role in securing the release of Western hostages which, according to many, Iraq would use as "human shields" to deter the United States from attacking. Thus the UN reduces many uncertainties associated with crisis situations and the use of force.

Third, the Security Council facilitated both great- and non–great-power cooperation and collaboration. Great-power cooperation is often difficult to achieve because of the complexity and the intensity of interests. The Security Council provided a framework whereby member states could articulate their national interest and their conception of the collective interest. The international collective good is determined in large part by the compromise of competing interests of groups within international society. The Security Council was a very important mechanism for developing common goals out of a vast array of interests.

The Security Council also helped shield the leadership of the permanent members from internal dissent. The leaders of the member states were able to appeal to their international obligations and the international legitimacy of the UN to support their actions. France and French companies had vested economic interests in Iraq. French oil companies held Iraqi oil leases, which were quite lucrative. The USSR may have been seeking warmer relations with the West, but it could not easily abandon its strategically located client. Domestic constituents within the USSR, such as the military and the KGB, pressured the Soviet leadership to support their de facto ally in the Middle East (Crozier 1991, 40). Iraq also owed the USSR billions of dollars in loans. Even the United States, which was leading the world response, had difficulties internally. The Congress narrowly passed a resolution supporting the president's use of force in the region. The vote in the Senate was 52–47. The Security Council enabled the leadership to appeal to international commitments and the idea of collective security to sell the war at home.

The staff, rules, and procedures of UN agencies were effective at helping states define their common interests during the Gulf Crisis. Participation in international organizations encourages decision makers to consider the interests of others when determining their own national interests (Lyons 1995). The Gulf Crisis also illustrates that more was at work than a mere congruence of state interests. Individual leaders also played an important role in making the collective security efforts possible. Both George Bush and Mikhail Gorbachev preferred multilateral negotiations and approaches to bilateral ones. Their precedent has been followed by world leaders since. Both Bill Clinton and Boris Yeltsin conducted the bulk of their foreign relations through the UN. European leaders such as John Major, François Mitterrand, and Helmut Kohl, accustomed to multilateralism with the European Union, also fostered the spirit of cooperation. Tony Blair and Jacques Chirac have continued the precedent. When decision makers share common values, then governments change.

International cooperation during the Gulf Crisis was not a fluke. It was possible because of the commonly held belief in the rule of law. Furthermore, societies are increasingly tied together and interdependent, a fact whose reality the Gulf Crisis and its aftermath brought home. Security Council actions in Somalia, Haiti, and the former Yugoslavia (Bosnia and Kosovo) demonstrate that international cooperation is possible even when "aggression" is difficult to define, when the costs of intervention are high, and when great-power interests are not directly engaged. In fact, Security Council actions in Somalia, Haiti, and the former Yugoslavia have greatly expanded its purview because it has linked situations occurring wholly and materially within the domestic jurisdiction of a sovereign state to international peace and security.

The Security Council demonstrates how international cooperation can continue "after hegemony." While the United States had the military capability, it could not finance the Gulf War on its own, as it had done forty years earlier in the Korean War. The financial contributions of Germany and Japan were instrumental in making the collective effort possible. In more theoretical terms, other states become more willing to bear the costs of maintaining international organizations and their operations, absent a hegemon.

A MARXIST CUT

The Gulf Crisis from a Marxist perspective highlights the legacy of imperialism and the influence of world capitalism. The crisis must be understood in the historical context of colonialism and the policies of the core, capitalist states toward the entire region in the postcolonial era. The role of international organizations has been to foster, promote, and legitimize the aggressive policies of the leading capitalist states. International organizations under capitalism reflect the underlying economic order. The interests of the dominant classes, the national and international bourgeoisie, are furthered by facilitating the expansion of the market and the reduction of state intervention and regulation. The UN role in the Persian Gulf Crisis is a rare example of political intervention on the part of the Security Council—an intervention that benefited the U.S. military-industrial complex, multinational oil companies, and the tiny capitalist creation "Kuwait, Inc."

The nation-states of the Middle East are largely colonial constructions. The territorial boundaries of virtually all the Middle Eastern states were drawn by French and British diplomats after the end of World War I. During the Great War, Russia, Britain, and France negotiated the Sykes-Picot Agreement, which carved up the Arab

world, including areas of North Africa and the Middle East. Great Britain, the leading colonial power, received territory that encompassed much of present-day Israel,
Jordan, Iraq, and Kuwait in the form of a mandate. The British then partitioned this
territory into nation-states, with the idea that they would one day be self-governing.
While these states were to be technically independent, their borders were artificially
created to serve the strategic and economic interests of Great Britain. Political authority was handed over to the native ruling class, the very same people who had collaborated with both Ottoman and British colonial officials. This ruling class was given
control over national industries, and a special relationship was created between the
local and British authorities. Their economic and political interests remained tied to
their colonial benefactors. The division of the Middle East into nation-states really
meant that they were colonies in almost every way, except in name. Hence the era of
neocolonialism was born.

The Iraq–Kuwait border dispute began with the creation of that border in 1922
by Sir Percy Zechariah Cox (Nemeth 1990). Iraqi and Saudi Arabian officials claimed
Kuwait as a historical province and Kuwaiti officials claimed that Kuwait was semi-independent under the Ottomans and therefore should become an independent state.
Cox settled the dispute by arbitrarily drawing borders defining Iraq, Kuwait, and Saudi
Arabia. Saudi Arabia and Iraq formally became independent while Kuwait became a
British protectorate until its independence in 1961. Iraq refused to recognize Kuwait
after Kuwait declared independence from Great Britain. Iraq again stated its historic
claim to the territory and sent troops to the Kuwaiti border, but was forced to acknowledge Kuwaiti sovereignty in 1963 after the British and the Arab League (discussed in Chapter 6) deployed troops in Kuwait to deter any Iraqi military action. All
of this occurred before Saddam Hussein emerged on the political landscape.

The formal creation of Kuwait and its artificial boundaries exemplifies how the
traditional colonial powers can continue to control strategic areas without a direct imposition of colonial rule. The colonial powers "came up with a proposal whereby these
same areas would be ceded to them by the League of Nations as their 'mandates' under
the fiction that these territories were being prepared for self-rule" (Ahmad 1991, 31).
The colonial powers carved up the Middle East and structured their mandates in a
manner that suited their interests. Kuwait retained the Port of Uqair, which provided
strategic access to the Persian Gulf. While oil had not yet been discovered in Kuwait,
it was widely believed that the territory was oil-rich. The colonial powers ensured that
no rival power could rise out of the Middle East by drawing unnatural borders and fostering economic division between oil-rich and oil-poor Arabs. By creating a variety of
oil-producers, market forces would keep the price of oil low and political manipulation
would keep the supply flush.

Just as the League of Nations served the interests of the colonial powers by establishing mandates, so too did the UN serve the interests of the newly dominant capitalist
state, the United States. When the UN was established, another new world order was
implemented. This order was based on the end of formal colonialism, self-determination, democracy, free trade, and free markets. Through free trade and free market
agreements, American and European oil companies controlled almost all of the Arab
and Iranian oil by 1954 (Keohane 1984, 151–159). The UN imposed the West's will on
Arab countries from the beginning. The creation of Israel in 1948 signaled the permanent U.S. presence through a strategically located client. While Cold War tensions

prevented further UN political action, UN conservatism did little to correct the injustices of colonialism. Its very orientation is to maintain a status quo, which is unjust and exploitive of most of the world's population. The UN did nothing while the capitalist powers attacked developing states, both politically and militarily, when they sought to chart their own courses or deviated from capitalism. The nationalist regimes of Mossadegh, Nasser, Allende, Arbenz Guzmán, and Castro were systematically undermined because of their nationalist, leftist orientation.

The UN's actions in the Gulf Crisis set several disturbing precedents. First, the initial UN collective security action in the post–Cold War era was used to liberate an antidemocratic, oil-rich kingdom with strong historical ties to the capitalist West. Kuwait Inc., as Kuwait is known both to critics and admirers, is one of the first transnational corporate nation-states. Its national income comes from two main sources: the Kuwaiti Oil Company, which was once a joint venture between Gulf Oil Corporation and British Petroleum, and the Kuwait Investment Office (KIO), which manages an international investment portfolio worth more than $120 billion. After the invasion by Iraq, KIO operations continued almost uninterrupted from its headquarters in London, the capital of its former colonial benefactor (Phillips 1990, 32). Revenues from the KIO are thought to outpace oil revenues, which means Kuwait's economy continued to grow even after Iraq seized its oil fields and refineries.

The Kuwaiti government-in-exile set up operations in the five-star Sheraton Hotel in Taif, Saudi Arabia. Kuwaiti officials, most of whom were members of the royal family, occupied luxurious suites equipped with cable TV, CNN-International, and Internet access. Very few in the Arab world had much sympathy either for the rulers or the citizens of Kuwait. According to the 1990 Statistical Survey (Europa World Year Book 1990), non-Kuwaiti residents (1,463,954) greatly outnumbered Kuwaiti citizens (550,181). Kuwait society was divided into rigid and distinct classes where non-Kuwaitis comprised more than 80 percent of the workforce and occupied lower-paying and lower-status jobs. Palestinian workers in Kuwait supported the Iraqi invasion, sensing that Hussein was the lesser of two evils. Hussein may be a brutal despot, but his continued popularity in the Arab world is due to his willingness to stand up to the West and to represent Arab unity and anti-imperialism (Ahmad 1991; Al-Radi 1995).

Second, the collective security operation, which was sanctioned by the UN and carried out by U.S. military forces, was financed in large part by Kuwait and Saudi Arabia. While much is made of the contributions of West Germany and Japan, their contributions accounted for only a third of the reimbursement to the United States. Kuwait and Saudi Arabia paid the remaining two-thirds (Clark 1995). Collective security under the UN might be for only those that can pay for it. As for democratic ideals, the Security Council made the world safe for monarchy, not democracy as was ideally envisioned by President Woodrow Wilson in 1917.

Third, and perhaps more disturbing for many developing states, was the passage of Security Council Resolution 688, establishing safe-haven zones for Kurds in northern Iraq. This resolution links human rights violations in Iraq to international peace and security. In other words, it allows for "humanitarian" intervention, whereby the sovereignty of a state may be militarily overridden by the UN to correct for perceived human rights violations. Developing states are well aware that it is their sovereignty that will likely be overridden in such cases (Pease and Forsythe 1993). The UN is certainly not going to intervene in British affairs regarding Northern Ireland or in Spanish affairs regarding the Basque region. Furthermore, given that the military forces of member states are used instead of UN forces, any state not aligned with the United States or Europe will fear UN intervention (Alvarez 1995, 8). This humanitarian exception to Article 2(7) of the UN Charter may lead to intervention for economic and political reasons unrelated to human rights under the guise of humanitarian concerns. Not surprisingly, China abstained, while India, Cuba, and Yemen voted against Resolution 688.

UN organization and procedures are not going to change the status quo in any significant way. The Gulf Crisis represents the North–South conflict (Snow 1993). This conflict manifested itself in the 1970s with an effort on the part of developing states to establish a New International Economic Order (NIEO). The NIEO centered on how international income and resources should be distributed. Many in the developing world sought to increase their political and economic autonomy by endorsing measures that emphasized the authoritative allocation of income and resources, rather than through market mechanisms (Krasner 1985). Marxists emphasize that the market is not as unbiased as liberals claim. The market favors the powerful at the expense of the vanquished and the exploited. Violence is often the only way to change the distribution of resources. The Kuwait–Iraq dispute pits rich against poor, and it is not surprising that the UN supports the rich.

The Marxist approach also highlights who stands to benefit the most from the UN action in the Gulf Crisis. The "follow the money" compass points squarely at the U.S. military-industrial complex and U.S. oil companies. Defense contractors received billions of dollars in domestic and international orders, and U.S. oil companies obtained new contracts from Kuwait and their newly liberated oil. The alleged assassination plot against former President Bush was uncovered by the Kuwaitis during a visit by Bush and former Secretary of State James Baker, who were in Kuwait to negotiate contracts for a consortium of Texas oil refineries after they had left public office.

A FEMINIST CUT

The feminist theoretical approach highlights the gender bias of the UN Security Council and the consequences for women and children. The first glaring fact regarding UN collective security during the Gulf Crisis is the almost complete absence of female decision makers. The only woman in any significant decision-making capacity was Prime Minister Margaret Thatcher of Great Britain, and she was removed by her own political party in November of 1990. All the chief executives of the member states and their permanent representatives to the Security Council were male. The Secretary-General was male. Traditional, liberal feminists point out that women were virtually excluded from the decision-making process in Iraq, in the United States, and the UN.

Neofeminists, who argue that biological differences between men and women account for differences in behavior, point out that male dominance conditions the policies of states and hierarchically structured IGOs. That is, the UN is more likely to sanction the use of coercive means and violence because that is the way men settle their differences. Similarly, Iraqi men used force against Kuwaiti men to settle their disputes. Unfortunately, it is the women and children who must suffer the consequences. Feminists note that the policies adopted by the UN toward Iraq had a greater impact on women and children than they did on the Iraqi leadership and Iraqi soldiers.

The UN economic embargo is a case in point. UN Security Council Resolution 661 imposes a complete economic embargo except for immediate humanitarian supplies. These economic sanctions impacted the most vulnerable in Iraqi society, women and children. Women often bear the brunt of the sanctions because they sacrifice their rations of food for the other members (usually male) of their families. The effect of economic sanctions, whether intended or not, has dramatically raised the child mortality rate and caused severe malnutrition among women and children in Iraq (Ascherio et al. 1992). The United Nations Children's Fund (UNICEF 1998) found that 90,000 deaths yearly in Iraq were due to sanctions and 5,000 children *a month* were dying as a result of sanctions. Sanctions have lead to a breakdown of water and sanitation, inadequate nutrition, and nonexistent health care. The continued use of sanctions prompted the head of UNICEF and the head of the "oil-for-food" program to resign from their offices.

Once the UN/U.S. war with Iraq began, it was again the women and children who suffered. The war began with air and missile strikes on areas populated heavily with Iraqi civilians. UN/U.S. forces unleashed an impressive barrage of firepower from the safety of planes and ships hundreds of miles away. The men, the soldiers, the war-makers on both sides, were protected by the latest military hardware and technology while the women and children were left exposed. The ground war that would pit man against man did not begin until several weeks later, after the civilian centers and infrastructures necessary to sustain human life, like electricity, water, and sewage systems, had been destroyed. The Iraqi prisoners of war (POWs) received more protection and assistance from the International Committee for the Red Cross (ICRC) and UN than did Iraqi women and children.

The priorities of the UN are masculine in that military force, violations of sovereignty, and territorial integrity are most important to UN members, which conditions their methods (Enloe 1993). The UN Security Council sought to pressure the Iraqi leadership by imposing sanctions that hurt those who could do nothing about Iraqi policy. However, assassinating or militarily removing Saddam Hussein is impermissible. Charging him with war crimes is an unacceptable precedent. As a result, the leadership stays the same and the Iraqi women and children continue to suffer. The interests of the sovereign state and the rules that govern how states and men behave with each other are more important than the lives of women and children. Meanwhile, even though there were women soldiers in the U.S./UN Gulf forces, they were forced to keep a lower profile than their male counterparts so as not to offend their Saudi hosts.

Women have comprised the principal opposition of the UN/U.S. war against Iraq and continue to oppose UN sanctions and military strikes. Women's groups are part and parcel of the peace movement that opposes all nuclear proliferation and militarism. Women participate in such all-female NGOs as Minnesota's Women Against Military Madness and the Aldermaston Women's Peace Camp (UK) as well as in such mixed NGOs as the War Resisters International. Women make up an international network of tens of thousands of peace advocates that extends from Australia to Turkey. Yet, their activities are marginalized by governments, the UN, and the media because of their more feminine orientation toward peace. They are characterized as naive, idealistic, or misguided individuals that have little understanding of the realities of international politics.

Steve Niva (1998) provides an interesting postmodern feminist interpretation of the Gulf Crisis as a "remasculation" of the United States. The United States has suffered from an identity crisis since the 1970s, having lost the Vietnam War, experienced a crippling oil crisis, and had its wishes repeatedly ignored within UN agencies. Presidents Reagan and Bush attempted to diminish the Vietnam Syndrome with minor military interventions in Grenada (1983) and Panama (1989), respectively. Hollywood did its part, too, with Sylvester Stallone and Arnold Schwarzenegger playing macho soldier roles, single-handedly defeating the Soviets, the Arabs, or both. Yet, the Vietnam Syndrome was not easily shaken. The Vietnam War and the resulting American decline in international and diplomatic affairs raised serious questions about U.S. capability and about its will to lead. In other words, it raised questions of U.S. manhood. The Gulf Crisis remasculated the United States because it was able to defeat Iraq, control Middle Eastern oil, and dominate the UN.

The feminist theoretical approach emphasizes women and gendered roles in the Gulf Crisis. The lens of gender focuses on the conspicuous absence of women from the UN decision-making process and their unique experience under UN policies. Feminists highlight the masculinity of the use of armed forces and the construction of international politics during the Gulf War. The activities of women, operating in their traditional gender roles as pacifists and nurturers, are highlighted and valorized.

THE SECURITY COUNCIL AND IRAQ AFTER THE GULF WAR

Iraq continues to challenge the authority of the Security Council by denying access to UN arms inspectors and being generally uncooperative. The Security Council has periodically responded with air strikes against military targets by British and American forces, but clearly the coalition against Iraq has begun to splinter. In November of 1997, the crisis in the Gulf threatened to deteriorate into violence again as Iraq thwarted UN inspectors and demanded the removal of U.S. members of the inspection teams. The international response has been quite mixed. In spite of overwhelming evidence that Iraq is hiding weapons of mass destruction, few members of the international community want an enforcement action. The difference of opinion stems from differing world views about the political, economic, and social forces at work in the Gulf Crisis. Realist thought can easily be discerned. According to Thailand's *Daily News*, "To be fair, Iraq, as a sovereign nation, has as much a right as ten or so other mostly big nations who develop nuclear, chemical and biological weapons" (U.S. Information Agency 1997a, 12). Sri Lanka's *Sunday Times* questions whether UNSCOM is the tool of the United States: "The question that UN Secretary-General Kofi Annan cannot dodge is how quickly and effectively he can rescue the United Nations from the United States. . . . Countries like China, Russia, India, and Japan represent more plainly 'We, the people' more truly than the United States. Right now, however, the Sheriff in the White House, playing globocop in a unipolar world, has picked his posse" (U.S. Information Agency 1997a, 12). Revelations of intelligence sharing between UNSCOM and the CIA have done little to assuage concerns about UNSCOM as an extension of the United States.

The liberal world view of the crisis is also represented in the world's media. According to Nigeria's *Guardian*, "Dialogue, diplomacy, and restraint have prevailed over the option of war offered by the friction in Baghdad. This is a celebration of the resolution of a potentially volatile situation and the triumph of the ideals of the UN" (U.S. Information Agency 1997a, 13). Germany's *Die Welt* states, "Ending the delaying tactics with the UN inspectors would be the quickest way to end the sanctions. That this is not happening is almost proof enough of secret and dangerous arsenals in Baghdad and a reason to continue the inspections" (U.S. Information Agency 1997a, 12). Great Britain's *Guardian* claims, "The choices that still have to be made . . . will help decide not only what kind of country Iraq, potentially an immensely powerful state, will be in the future, but what kind of place the Middle East will be, and the kind of world in which we are all going to live in the next century" (U.S. Information Agency 1997a, 7).

The Marxist world view is also represented. According to Pakistan's *Nation*, "During the previous Gulf War, America and her allies had staged a gory drama, the parallel of which is hard to find in recent history. These so-called custodians of human values had let loose hell on the Iraqi people, the disastrous effects of which are still felt by the Iraqi people in the form of various sanctions imposed on them. As a result of this horrendous war, oil wealth and the entire Middle East region has virtually fallen in the hands of America and Arab countries have been virtually reduced to the status of surrogates" (U.S. Information Agency 1997a, 12–13).

The feminist perspective, however, is conspicuously absent from the world media. Feminists would applaud any media coverage of the suffering of the Iraqi people and the way in which UN sanctions have negatively affected the lives of women and children. The mainstream media has been largely silent on the issue and the dissemination of information comes from "minor" UN agencies and NGOs that are on the ground working with the most vulnerable in Iraqi society. The international media reaction to UN airstrikes and sanctions shows that competing world views exist. In 2001, the Iraqi situation continues at a stalemate. UN inspectors have not been in Iraq since 1998, sanctions are still in place, and the United States and UK periodically carry out airstrikes against Iraqi installations. On February 16, 2001, U.S. airstrikes against Iraq angered many in the Muslim world. The Organization of Islamic Conference (OIC) condemned the raids and questioned their timing (*Washington Report on Middle Eastern Affairs* 2001, 38). The Secretary-General of the OIC, Dr. Abdul-Wahid Belkziz of Morocco, stated that the United States had once again overstepped UN Security Council authority and poisoned the move toward Iraqi reconciliation with the UN. Moreover, the raids were unjustified and a violation of international law. Clearly different world views exist and they complicate, yet expand, our understanding of international organizations and their roles in world politics. The following case study regarding the UN safe area of Srebrenica examines the UN response to another threat to international peace and security—the dissolution of Yugoslavia.

CASE STUDY 2: SREBRENICA 1995

In July 1995, Bosnian Serb forces seized the UN safe area of Srebrenica and systematically exterminated over 7,000 Bosnian Muslim men and boys. Muslim women and children were terrorized, raped, and expelled. On November 15, 1999, the Secretary-General issued a report, "The Fall of Srebrenica" (A/54/549), which details the events and the UN responses that led up to tragic events in Srebrenica. The following account is drawn from this report.

In 1991, the break-up of the former Socialist Federal Republic of Yugoslavia came to dominate the international agenda. The Yugoslav Federation was, at one time, a multinational state that consisted of six republics—Serbia, Slovenia, Croatia, Bosnia-Herzegovina (Bosnia), Macedonia, and Montenegro. These republics were largely based on nationality; however, each had sizable minorities from the other republics. The end of the Cold War provided the republics with an opportunity to secede from the Serb-dominated Federation, which resulted in wide-scale violence between the break-away republics and the Yugoslav Federal Army (JNA). After separate declarations of independence and subsequent international recognition of former republics of Slovenia, Croatia, and Macedonia, the next to leave the Yugoslav Federation was Bosnia in 1992. However, unlike the other republics, no single nationality had a majority in Bosnia. Rather, Muslims were the largest group, comprising about 40 percent of the population, with ethnic Serbs and Croats largely making up the remainder.

The fighting that ensued between the other break-away republics and the JNA was relatively short-lived compared to the battle over territory and control in Bosnia. Both Croatia and Serbia (with the Serbs using the JNA) moved to "protect" their nationals in Bosnia by sending troops and establishing paramilitary forces. In other words, the armed conflict had both an international and internal dimension. Foreign troops were sent to Bosnia but they were also working in concert with their ethnic nationals who were citizens of Bosnia. Their goal was to take the adjacent territory belonging to Bosnia—territory that was largely dominated by Croat and Serb nationals. This left the minorities in these areas in peril, as large numbers of Serbs and Muslims resided in territory desired by Croatia and Croats, and Muslims lived in the areas desired by Serbia.

The UN responded to the initial crisis in the former Yugoslavia by taking a number of steps. First, when the fighting broke out between Croatia and the JNA, the UN Security Council passed resolution 713 (1991) which stated that "all states shall, for the purposes of establishing peace and stability in Yugoslavia, immediately implement a general and complete embargo on all deliveries of weapons and military equipment to Yugoslavia until the Security Council decides otherwise." Many observers argued that the embargo would favor the Serbs as they dominated the JNA and the Yugoslav defense industries (UNGA, A/54/549 1999, 8). Second, the Secretary-General requested the creation of a small peacekeeping force to help implement a ceasefire between Croatia and the Yugoslav Federation. The Security Council obliged with resolution 743 (1992) creating the UN Protection Force (UNPROFOR). UNPROFOR's mandate was expanded a few months later to include Bosnia Herzegovina with Security Council resolution 758 (1992). Third, the United Nations High Commissioner for Refugees (UNHCR) was dispatched to Bosnia to deliver food, medical, and housing assistance. UNHCR activities were severely hampered by the JNA and the Bosnian Serb Army (BSA) as they attempted to use the humanitarian assistance as a bargaining chip and, if necessary, use its denial as a weapon of war. Fourth, the UN tried to negotiate a political solution to the crisis by working with the European Union, the Organization on Security and Cooperation in Europe (OSCE), and the Organization of Islamic Conference (OIC). A political solution was elusive as Serbs and Croats controlled large sections of Bosnia and had ethnically cleansed many of the towns in these areas. None of the strategies proposed by the UN were acceptable to all of the parties at any one time. The fighting intensified and the humanitarian situation became far more dire.

Srebrenica is a small city in eastern Bosnia near the Serbian border. In 1992, it, along with dozens of other cities in Bosnia, was under siege and experiencing a humanitarian crisis. This crisis was precipitated by widespread violence and ethnic cleansing by all parties, although by most accounts, the Serbs were particularly brutal and effective at it. At the beginning of the Bosnian conflict Srebrenica's population of about

40,000 was approximately 75 percent Muslim and 25 percent Serb. In March 1992, Serb paramilitaries took control of Srebrenica and began expelling Muslims from their homes. By May 1992, the Bosnian Muslims militarily retook the city and drove the Serbs out. These Muslim forces were able to retain control of Srebrenica and the outlying areas but were unable to territorially hook up with Bosnian government forces to the west and south. As a result, Srebrenica quickly became a Muslim enclave surrounded by Bosnian Serbs.

The spiraling violence and the deteriorating humanitarian situation in and around Srebrenica between March 1992 and 1993 raised serious concern from the UN but very little in the way of consensus. One proposal that was considered and then later adopted was the creation of "safe areas." Initially the permanent members of the Security Council were not supportive. According to the Secretary-General (UNGA, A/54/549, 1999, 8), the first consideration of the idea of a safe haven came with a carefully worded paragraph in Security Council resolution 787 (November 1992) inviting the "Secretary-General, in consultation with the United Nations High Commissioner for Refugees and other relevant international humanitarian agencies, to study the possibility of and the requirements for the promotion of safe areas for humanitarian purposes." In order for the safe areas to become viable, several conditions would need to be met. First, the UN would need the consent of the parties involved. Second, the safe areas would need to be demilitarized. Third, UNPROFOR would need to be beefed up with troops and hardware to provide security for the safe areas. The various UN agencies were debating the feasibility of safe havens for months when events on the ground forced a UN decision. In April 1993, Serb paramilitaries stated that they would launch an offensive against Srebrenica unless the city was surrendered and the Muslims evacuated. The Security Council responded with resolution 819 (1993) declaring Srebrenica a safe area and demanded an immediate cessation to hostilities. Yet the Security Council sent contradictory messages as UNPROFOR was informed that resolution 819 created no military obligation to actually protect the safe haven (UNGA, A/54/549, 1999, 20).

UNPROFOR, outnumbered and out-gunned by the Serbs, decided to pursue the demilitarization of Srebrenica. UNPROFOR convinced the Bosnian Muslims to hand over their weapons in return for a ceasefire and UNPROFOR protection. The demilitarization agreement was signed by the Bosnian Muslims and the Bosnian Serbs on April 18, 1993. UNPROFOR moved into Srebrenica and disarmed the Muslims. The Serbs, unfortunately, continued to shell Muslim-held territory, including the safe areas. The Security Council passed Resolution 836 (1993) weakly authorizing UNPROFOR to militarily protect the safe haven when "acting in self-defense." It also authorized member states, acting alone or with regional organizations, to use air power to support UNPROFOR (UNGA, A/54/549, 1999, 24). Serb shelling continued almost unabated. NATO and UNPROFOR articulated a plan for the operational capability to use airpower against the Serbs, causing the Serbs to withdraw from a few key strategic positions.

With the new cooperative attitude of the Serbs, UN peace talks resumed. The peace proposal that emerged called for the union of three ethnic republics, which would involve the swapping of Serb-held territory around Sarajevo (the Bosnian capital) for the Muslim enclave of Srebrenica. The Bosnian Muslims objected to the plan and fighting resumed. On February 5, 1994, a crowded Sarajevo market was shelled, killing sixty-eight and injuring hundreds. UNPROFOR and NATO responded by developing an exclusion zone around the safe area of Sarajevo. In March 1994, Bosnian Serbs began an offensive against the safe area of Gora. After several days of issuing warnings against the advancing Serbs, NATO responded with air strikes on Serb artillery positions. Bosnian Serb military commander, General Ratko Mladic, warned that UN personnel would be killed if the NATO airstrikes did not stop. After another round of Serb artillery and brief NATO airstrikes, the Serbs took 150 UN personnel hostage. The Serbs continued their assault on Gora. In April, another ceasefire agreement was reached after another NATO ultimatum. This ceasefire agreement provided for the release of UN personnel, the demilitarization of Gora, and the free movement of UNPROFOR and humanitarian organizations.

In October 1994, Serb forces began an offensive against the safe area of Bihac, which ended in December of the same year. Events similar to those in Gora played themselves out in Bihac. The Serbs were warned to cease their military assault or face airstrikes. After airstrikes, new exclusion zones were created. Increasingly, the Secretary-General called for more rigorous strikes against the Serb militias, strikes that were opposed by UNPROFOR on the ground. UNPROFOR remained outnumbered and out-gunned and feared retaliation by Serb forces. The Security Council and NATO remained indecisive.

After a "cessation of hostilities agreement" was reached in January 1995, the parties enjoyed a brief respite from the violence. However, once again, the agreement was short-lived as Croat forces began an offensive against Serbs in southwest Bosnia. In Srebrenica, the UNPROFOR force, largely made up of Canadians, was replaced with a Dutch contingent. The Dutch peacekeepers had political difficulties with the Bosnian Muslim commanders and their access to the exclusion zones was restricted. When the Dutch ignored the restrictions, 100 peacekeepers were taken hostage for four days by Bosnian Muslim forces. By April 1995, a general state of warfare existed throughout Bosnia (A/54/549, 1999, 47). Sarajevo once again garnered international attention as fighting on all sides erupted in the heart of Bosnia. NATO responded with air strikes and the Serbs responded with mortar fire. An air-burst weapon over the town of Tuzla killed 71 people and injured 200. Serbs were suspected in the attack as they had threatened to retaliate against Muslim safe areas. In late May, hundreds of UN personnel, including French peacekeepers in Sarajevo, were taken hostage. Many more had their activities severely restricted. Several UN peacekeepers and aid workers were killed.

The fall of Srebrenica began on July 6, 1995, and effectively ended on July 11, 1995. The Serb military offensive consisted of heavy artillery and mortar fire on the outskirts of Srebrenica, with troops closing in. Muslim commanders in Srebrenica requested the return of the weapons they had surrendered under the 1993 demilitarization agreement so they could defend themselves; however, the UNPROFOR commander denied their request. As the Serb offensive intensified and UNPROFOR positions were directly targeted, the UNPROFOR commander made a request for NATO airpower. That request was denied. On July 8, Serb forces overran an UNPROFOR observation post and surrounded two others. An UNPROFOR peacekeeper from the Netherlands was killed by Bosnian Muslim forces. On July 9, five more UNPROFOR observation posts were attacked. The Serbs were warned by the UN that airstrikes were imminent unless they stopped their offensive on Srebrenica. The Serb offensive continued, but the air strikes were deferred as there was some confusion as to who was actually firing on UNPROFOR positions (A/54/549, 1999, 66). On July 11, UNPROFOR in Srebrenica again requested airstrikes and, according to the Dutch peacekeepers, they fully expected airstrikes within a half-hour of their request. The expected airstrikes did not come. The Bosnian Serb forces advanced. UNPROFOR stood aside. Srebrenica fell. By July 20, the Serbs had summarily executed over 7,000 Muslim men and boys. Serb forces also raped, tortured, and deported the remaining Muslims.

What factors precipitated the Bosnian Crisis and the massacre at Srebrenica? Was the UN role constructive? What determined UN action? Who was affected by UN action and how? Once again, the answer to these questions depends on your world view.

A REALIST CUT

The tragedy of Srebrenica has been played out a thousand times before in history. It shows that power, especially military power, is ultimately the final arbiter of disputes. Any party that relies on others for their physical security is likely to find themselves in extreme peril unless the national interests of the powerful are directly engaged. International organizations and agreements are meaningless in the face of indecisive members and determined adversaries. The UN can only be effective in international security matters when there is great power consensus and that consensus was clearly absent in the Balkans Crisis. Consider the positions of some of the Security Council members and other involved parties. One group of countries, (Bosnia-Herzegovina, Turkey, and Pakistan) wanted rigorous UN enforcement action under Chapter VII and were willing to contribute troops to the effort. Pakistan, a nonpermanent member of the Security Council and the Non-Aligned Movement, expressed the concern of many that the safe areas could not be adequately guaranteed and more decisive action was necessary. When it became apparent that the Serbs were going to militarily challenge the UN and rigorous enforcement was not going to happen, Pakistan sponsored a draft resolution that would lift the arms embargo against the Muslims. Cape Verde, Djibouti, Morocco, Pakistan, the United States, and Venezuela voted in favor of the resolution and Brazil, China, France, Hungary, Japan, New Zealand, Russia, Spain, and the UK abstained (A/54/549, 1999, 27). The resolution, therefore, did not pass. UN indecisiveness was criticized by the Organization of Islamic Conference which stated if the Security Council was unable to take action to protect the Muslims then they should at least be allowed to defend themselves. (A/54/549, 1999, 28).

Powerful members of the Security Council, the United States, the UK, and France, were reluctant to use direct military power against the Bosnian Serbs as the Serbs were informal allies of Russia. The extensive use of military power, especially under the auspices of NATO, could be provocative and destabilizing. The Europeans were also concerned about Iran's involvement in arms trafficking to the Bosnian Muslims and the creation of a Muslim state in the heart of Europe. Siding against the Serbs might give Islamic militants an opportunity to control the Bosnian government. NATO was also divided. The United States did not want to get involved, Germany was sympathetic to the Croats, and France (not a full member of NATO at the time) was sympathetic to Serbs. Furthermore, NATO members were preoccupied with preventing the loss of any members of their armed forces or their peacekeepers. From a Serb perspective, UNPROFOR was primarily interested in protecting itself. Airstrikes, if they came, happened only when UNPROFOR itself was threatened.

Yasuchi Akashi, the Special Representative of the Secretary-General, stated that "with a consensus absent on the Council, lacking a strategy, and burdened by an unclear mandate, UNPROFOR was forced to chart its own course. There was only limited support for a "robust" enforcement policy by UNPROFOR. UNPROFOR thus chose to pursue a policy of relatively passive enforcement, the lowest common denominator on which all Council members more or less agreed" (A/54/549, 1999, 17). The Serbs merely made a rational calculation to take territory strategic to its goal of joining Bosnian Serb territory with adjacent Serbia. After all, the U.S. position at the peace talks was that an ethnically pure Serb Srebrenica would make a lasting peace easier to reach. Why not present the "international community" with a *fait accompli*? The Secretary-General acknowledged as much by stating, "We were, with hindsight, wrong to declare repeatedly and publicly that we did not want to use air power against the Serbs except as a last resort, and to accept the shelling of the safe areas as a daily occurrence. We believed there was no choice under the Security Council resolutions but to deploy more and more peacekeepers into harm's way. The Serbs knew this, and they timed their attack on Srebrenica well" (A/54/549, 1999, 107).

In the "Victims of Bosnian Realpolitik," *The Economist* (July 22, 1995, 47) argues "there is more than one interpretation of the recent events in Bosnia. . . . Since war in Bosnia began, it has seemed likely to end either when one side has achieved overwhelming military superiority or when there was a balance of military and territorial advantage. Though the recent Serb advances make it look as if they are going for total victory, the real outcome of the fall of the enclaves may be to bring the balance of forces closer, following some kind of settlement to be negotiated in the brutal endgame of Bosnian Realpolitik." In other words, peace in Bosnia could be achieved only when the military situation on the ground is balanced. That peace agreement was negotiated in November 1995 at Wright-Patterson Air Force Base in Dayton, Ohio. The price for the Dayton Accords was the prestige of the UN, an organization that ignored military realities, and the thousands of Bosnians that placed their fates in the hands of that organization.

A LIBERAL CUT

Making and keeping the peace in the post–Cold War World is a complicated and difficult task that defies a pat, fixed formula. The disintegration of the former Yugoslavia presented the international community with a series of never-before-experienced challenges. The UN responded with an arms embargo, humanitarian assistance, and a lightly armed peacekeeping force. Srebrenica is a tragedy, but it must be understood as part of the collective learning experience of the international community. While mistakes were made, the UN has taken steps to learn from those mistakes. With regard to the Bosnian Crisis, the Security Council structures were unable to help members overcome their collective indecision. However, the UN was successful in providing humanitarian assistance in this very dangerous situation and it at least tried to protect innocent civilians. The carnage and suffering of *all* parties in Bosnia would likely have been far worse had the UN not intervened. The UN has examined and reexamined its actions and institutional weaknesses. It has accepted its share of responsibility. It has objectively assessed the roles of the Bosnian Serbs, Croats and Muslims, as well those of Serbia and Croatia. The UN has maintained the record of evidence, regardless of how unpleasant or embarrassing that record is for the institution or its members.

According to the Secretary-General, the errors of the Security Council stemmed "from a single and no doubt well-intentioned effort: we tried to keep the peace and apply the rules of peacekeeping when there was no peace to keep" (A/54/549, 1999, 108). The Security Council members were engaged in a collective version of "wishful thinking" that peacekeeping, as it was practiced in the past, could be applied to a situation of war. This placed UNPROFOR in an untenable position of having to protect safe areas without the military capability to do so. In spite of this, UNPROFOR "was able to assist in the humanitarian process, and to mitigate some—but, as Srebrenica tragically underscored, by no means all—the suffering inflicted by the war" (A/54/549, 1999, 108).

The UN's response of creating safe areas and demilitarizing the inhabitants was not a sufficient reaction to ethnic cleansing and genocide. In fact and in hindsight, it was the wrong decision, as the safe areas were neither safe from Serb assault nor could the Bosnian Muslims defend themselves. At the same time, the Bosnian Muslims forces must shoulder a little of the responsibility for the violence in Bosnia. Muslims did not completely demilitarize and, in isolated incidents, used safe havens as bases to try to draw NATO into their war with the Serbs. In spite of wrongdoing by all the parties, the parties were not "moral equivalents" and the Serbs must bear the most responsibility for the deaths and suffering.

The UN has learned several lessons from the case of Srebrenica as articulated by the Secretary-General (A/54/549, 1999, 110–111). First, peacekeeping operations should not be used as a substitute for political consensus. The idea of placing a peacekeeping force in Bosnia emerged because the Security Council could not reach a consensus regarding what to do with this active military conflict. Hence, the peacekeepers were placed in a war-fighting situation without the necessary resources to carry out even limited peacekeeping tasks. Second, safe areas must either be completely demilitarized with the consent of the belligerents involved or be fully protected by a credible military deterrent. Third, do not appease belligerents. Fourth, the Security Council must be willing to use force early in a conflict, especially when there is a "deliberate and systematic attempt to terrorize, expel or murder an entire people" (A/54/549, 1999, 111).

For liberals, UN actions leading up to Srebrenica were well-intentioned, yet misguided by the factors mentioned above. This does not mean the international community cannot see the positive or learn from its mistakes. The UN began the process of reflection and analysis. The UN bears witness and some responsibility. It has created the International Criminal Tribunal for the former Yugoslavia (discussed in Chapter 10) to prosecute those responsible for atrocities in Bosnia: Serb, Croat, and Muslim alike. More importantly, the UN has come to realize that it must make moral judgments when faced with genocide.

A MARXIST CUT

For Marxists, the Srebrenica case is an example of how ineffective UN agencies are outside of the economic realm. Absent a compelling economic interest or a threat to important natural resources, the West, using the UN and NATO, sought only to contain the Bosnian conflict to prevent it from destabilizing the region. The reason the UN even paid as much attention as it did was because the violence and carnage occurred in Europe rather than in the developing South. Had this crisis unfolded in Africa or Asia, the UN response would have been even more anemic. One has only to look at what the UN did not do in Sudan where *2 million* people have died in that civil war, or in Angola where *1.5 million* people have died, or Rwanda where 800,000 people died in a few short months in 1994. The UN knew full well the nature and the scope of genocide in Rwanda by the time the Bosnian Crisis was peaking (May–July 1995) and still it did nothing to protect civilians. The OIC offered the UN a force of 10,000 to keep the peace in Bosnia and the Islamic community's offer was declined (*New York Times* February 11, 1994, A6). The mistakes of Srebrenica might be excused had that not come on the heels of other such massive tragedies. UN peacemaking and peace enforcement comes only when the West's economic interests are at stake. Rather than seeing Bosnia as part of the same global pattern of internal disintegration due to poverty and inequality, it was viewed as a nuisance. It was a painful reminder that the liberal new world order has some serious flaws.

While UN inaction is seen by many as part of the problem, the Srebrenica crisis also set a couple of troubling precedents. First, the Security Council resolution 836 authorizing the use of military force was fuzzy and it opened the door to NATO becoming a military arm of the Security Council. NATO has de facto replaced the UN Military Staff Committee, raising a whole host of new concerns about the nature of peacekeeping and peace enforcement. Will the West now use the UN and NATO to legitimize its interventionist policies? Western intervention is motivated by a variety of reasons; however, rarely is the deciding factor humanitarian. What will be the role of Russia and China? As is discussed in Chapter 6, NATO would soon move militarily without UN authorization in another Balkan crisis—Kosovo. Second, the ideal of a "neutral" UN has come under fire. While the UN has always been biased in favor of Western interests, it has tried to maintain a pretense of neutrality. After Srebrenica, the UN determined it was important for the institution to take sides. The Secretary-General's report, "The Fall of Srebrenica" broke new ground "by effectively condemning the organization's tendency to try to remain neutral in a civil conflict" (Crossette, November 16, 1999, A6). This opens a "Pandora's Box" for the UN and those groups seeking to change the inequitable status quo. Given the UN's liberal bias toward the West and the United States, those seeking meaningful, rather than cosmetic, change, or to challenge capitalist priorities, are likely to find themselves on the wrong side of the UN.

Srebrenica and the Bosnian Crisis also show that there is money to be made in civil conflict. In spite of the arms embargo, none of the parties found themselves particularly short of weapons. All sides, including the Bosnian Muslims, received money and arms shipments from their friends around the world. In fact, as the Security Council was maintaining the arms embargo, the United States gave the go-ahead for Iran and Malaysia to pay for $800 million worth of arms to be delivered to the Bosnian Muslims via Turkey (Hedges, November 8, 1996, A1; Beelman 1996; Timmerman 1996). The so-called Iranian pipeline was run out of the U.S. embassy in Croatia. All told, arms imports by the various factions from 1992–1995 were estimated at $2 billion a year (Klare 1996). The Muslims in Srebrenica were one of the few groups not armed at this stage of the Bosnian crisis.

A FEMINIST CUT

The feminist perspective highlights the role of gender in the Bosnian conflict. First, feminists criticize the UN Security Council and UNPROFOR. From the outset, it was clear that UNPROFOR, which at the time consisted of men who were supposed to be doing the protecting, was primarily interested in protecting itself. Instead, what little resources were allocated to Bosnia and to the protection of safe areas went to ensuring the safety of UN peacekeepers. Muslim women were raped systematically as Serb forces advanced on safe areas and the UN did nothing. More than 200,000 people died in Bosnia-Herzegovina, most of whom were civilians. However, it was the torture and deaths of 7,000 men and boys in Srebrenica that turned the tide for the UN. These men were murdered, in part, because they were or could become soldiers. Plausibly, the Serbs could argue the usual "military necessity" defense, a defense that is often used when civilian centers are targeted. These men were, after all, the ones who had to be disarmed by UNPROFOR in 1993. What was horrifying for Security Council members, subconsciously, was that these men could be slaughtered like sheep. These men were vulnerable and dependent, a dependency created by the UN itself. In Srebrenica, men became the victims and that is what prompted UN outrage. Put in a postmodern light, the UN feminized the Muslim males and that was its greatest crime.

Liberal feminists point out that every key UN decision maker and UNPROFOR commander or officer of importance, save for Madeleine Albright, was male. The U.S. ambassador to the UN is an important figure; however, the institutional expectations of the UN were shaped by androcentric policy that focused on issues important to men at the time—sovereignty, military strategy, and control over the situation on the ground. Madeleine Albright might be able to bring human rights and the plight of women into the discussion, but the UN response is conditioned by how men understand these issues and how they usually respond to problems. An indirect effect of Srebrenica was to highlight the extent of the suffering of Muslim women who not only lost their fathers, husbands, and sons, but who were also raped as part of a Serb ethnic cleansing program. Liberal feminists note that the UN has responded to these shortcomings by including more women in NATO-led peacekeeping in Bosnia after Srebrenica. On October 31, 2000, the Security Council issued its first resolution recommending that women take the lead in peacekeeping missions. According to the *International Herald Tribune* (November 1, 2000, 7), Secretary-General Kofi Annan was urged to use women as chief envoys to pursue peace talks and to head peacekeeping missions. The resolution also asked the Secretary-General to provide peacekeepers with special training to protect women, to support local women's peace initiatives, and to prepare a study on the impact of war on women and girls and the "gender dimensions of peace processes and conflict resolutions."

Neo-feminists point out that the "oldest profession" is alive and well in Bosnia and the war has been good for this illegal business. The UN was criticized rightfully for not deploying a peacekeeping force of sufficient size to handle the job. At the same time, the deployment of a large military force is accompanied by other problems. The Dayton Peace Accord in 1995 led to a NATO-led peacekeeping force of 21,000 peacekeepers and 10,000 police officers. This has led to a dramatic expansion of the sex industry in Bosnia. A former UN police officer, Kathryn Bolkovac, claimed she was fired because she reported that UN officials forged documents for trafficked women and tipped sex club owners of impending raids (Kole and Cerkez-Robinson 2001, 5A). While many sex workers voluntarily participate in the industry, many others are forced. David Lamb, a former Philadelphia police officer on duty in Bosnia, stated that he was told routinely not to look too deeply and when he tried to investigate UN personnel, he was stonewalled. "It was just incredible to see the resistance we got from mission headquarters. There was a game being played, and investigators were being intimidated. I was trying to root out the corruption but I couldn't get any support" (Kole and Cerkez-Robinson 2001, 5A). The UN continues to try to keep the less than bright side of UN peacekeeping operations from public scrutiny.

SECURITY COUNCIL REFORMS

The criticisms of the UN and the Security Council during the Gulf War and the breakup of the former Yugoslavia have given rise to a variety of reform efforts, none of which has yet been realized. These reform efforts are important because they attempt to make the UN more credible as an inclusive global institution (see, for example, Kennedy and Russett 1995; Alger 1996; Bedjaoui 1994). One major reform effort under consideration at the UN is to change the membership of the UN Security Council. In 1965, the UN Charter was amended to expand the Council from nine to fifteen members. The expansion was necessary because the overall size of the UN had increased by virtue of the decolonization process and the formation of new states (*UN Chronicle* 1997, 31). Many newly independent states, acutely aware of the consequences of war and other forms of international aggression, sought a greater voice in the decision-making process relating to international security. With the Gulf War, the end of the Cold War, and the establishment of even more states seeking UN membership, the question of Security Council composition and procedures assumes renewed importance.

Expanding both the permanent and nonpermanent membership of the Security Council is under consideration. The president of the General Assembly has recommended expanding the Security Council membership to twenty-four, adding five more permanent seats and four nonpermanent seats (GA/9228 [Press Release] 1997). However, concerns about making the Council unwieldy render such further expansion somewhat doubtful.

One proposed reform is to change the composition of the permanent members to make the Security Council more "representative," but the best way to do that depends on your world view. Some argue that permanent membership ought to be based on capability. The waning UK and France should be removed while Germany and Japan should be added. Others argue that geography is important. Europe is overrepresented while the Indian and South American continents have no representation. Still others argue that economic status is important, hence China is not an adequate representative of the developing world and India or Brazil should perhaps have a veto. Observers are quick to point out that changing the composition of the Security Council's permanent membership without expanding it is politically impractical. The UK, France, and China are not likely to relinquish the veto power under any circumstances. Better representation based on geography or economic status might lead to the same kind of paralysis experienced during the Cold War, except that the world would be divided between North and South rather than between East and West.

Another reform that could strengthen the credibility of the Security Council is to change the veto power of the permanent members. The UN could do away with the veto altogether and make decisions based on majoritarian principles, or it could institute a procedure whereby a veto could be overridden by a significant majority of both the permanent and nonpermanent members. This reform would make the Security Council truly supranational, although such a reform would be meaningless unless the UN revived the Military Staff Committee and established an international military force. None of these options, however, is likely to sit well with nationalist interests within member states. Numerous mixtures of all these reforms have also been proposed; however, none has been adopted.

CONCLUSION

In this chapter, we have briefly outlined the UN's role in maintaining international peace and security, tracing the activities of the UN Security Council and highlighting the functions of the UN General Assembly and UN Secretary-General in international security matters. We have seen that the UN and its organs do not exist in a vacuum; rather, they are influenced by a variety of actors, forces, and international dynamics. The case studies of the Gulf Crisis and Srebrenica illustrate what the different theoretical approaches have to say about which actors and forces are determinative of UN behavior and what the consequences are to societies. Each theoretical lens enhances our understanding of the UN and the nature of governance in the new world order. For realists, the UN is a mechanism of great-power collusion that is either manipulated by the United States or ignored. International governance takes place through hegemony or a great-power concert in which powerful states pursue and protect their interests. For liberals, more is at work than simple balance-of-power calculations. The UN provides an important mechanism that fosters international cooperation, not just great-power collusion. The international community was represented, and members had input into the decision-making process. The UN minimized much of the uncertainties associated with the use of military force by facilitating the arms embargo and negotiating the release of foreign hostages. The UN provided humanitarian assistance and represented the rule of law based on the consent of increasingly interdependent member states. While all is not perfect, the UN makes a positive and important difference in the lives of many.

The critical international relations approaches challenge the mainstream approaches. Marxism highlights the colonial and imperial legacy of the Middle East and the division of labor internationally and within societies. The UN reinforces and legitimizes a status quo in which the vast majority of the world's people are impoverished and subordinated to the will of the capitalist powers. Feminists emphasize the lack of women in the UN decision-making process and the impact of UN policies on women. They criticize masculinist approaches and show how the UN response in the Gulf and Bosnian crises can be understood in terms of patriarchy and masculine behavior. The mainstream and critical approaches provide for an improved understanding of international governance, in terms of class and gender, as it relates to international peace and security.

6

REGIONAL SECURITY

T HE HISTORY OF UN COLLECTIVE SECURITY consists of just two operations—the Korean Conflict and the Persian Gulf War. In the former, action was possible only because the USSR was boycotting the Security Council, while the latter came during an extraordinary period of transition. The failure of UN collective security during the Cold War and after can be attributed, in part, to ideological divisions and to the diversity of government types in the UN and on the Security Council. Absent an effective UN collective security arrangement, governments have created regional alliances and organizations to augment their power and to deter potential aggressors. Article 51 of the UN Charter permits collective self-defense and Chapter VIII permits regional arrangements. As the world divided politically and ideologically during the Cold War, several military alliances formed: the Rio Pact (1947), the North Atlantic Treaty Organization (NATO 1949), the ANZUS (Australia, New Zealand, and the U.S.) Treaty (1951), the U.S.–Japanese Security Treaty (1951), and the Warsaw Pact (1955). NATO is perhaps the best known and arguably the most successful multilateral military alliance in contemporary world politics. This security alliance, which unambiguously links the security interests of North America to Western Europe, is anchored by U.S. conventional and nuclear capabilities. NATO became the prototypical alternative to UN collective security during the Cold War, and may even form the basis of collective security after the Cold War. In this chapter we briefly review the history and the organizational structure of NATO. We'll examine NATO's Cold War roles and the transformation of NATO in the post–Cold War era. The theoretical lenses are then focused on the case of NATO expansion to highlight the differing perspectives regarding the future roles of NATO in global governance.

Also in this chapter we will examine a multipurpose regional IGO, the Arab League, in terms of its structure and its role in Middle East security. Recall that one of the reasons the UN Charter permits regional organizations is because regional and local solutions are often preferable to global approaches. The Arab League was created in 1945 and has played a complicated role in Middle Eastern politics and the decolonization process. Our theoretical lenses are trained on the 2000 Palestinian Uprising to explain the behavior and actions of the Arab League and other international organizations in reaction to this very serious threat to regional security. Students are reminded that there is no clean and neat way to completely separate regional security from international security. The organizational roles of the UN and regional organizations often overlap, making assessments of the independent role of regional organizations difficult.

POST–WORLD WAR II SECURITY ALLIANCES

After World War II, security alliances formed in rapid succession. Most of these postwar military alliances were created by one of the superpowers—the United States or the USSR. The United States in particular formed a ring of alliances that extended its reach globally as part of its overall strategy of containing the Soviet Union. The Rio Pact, created in 1947, is the first U.S.-based alliance of the postwar era. Formally known as the Inter-American Treaty of Reciprocal Assistance, the Rio Pact declares that an armed attack against any American state is an attack on all American states. Members are obligated to come to the aid of an ally, using both forcible and nonforcible measures if necessary. The Rio Pact also permits armed force against aggression that does not take the form of an armed attack. This provision is controversial because it is understood to mean that members of the Rio Pact could counter "aggression" militarily even if that aggression were nonviolent (Cockcroft 1996, 41). Critics argue that this renders the definition of aggression very elastic. It could include, for example, something as benign as the formation of a communist party in Chile. Allowing military force to counter aggression of a nonviolent nature also invites U.S. intervention in the internal affairs of Latin American states. "The Rio Pact sidestepped the United Nations and provided a legally binding 'self-defense' approach for future U.S. covert and overt interventions against reformist democracies in the name of combating Communist aggression" (Cockcroft 1996, 41). The United States and its Latin American allies were determined that communism would not gain a foothold in the Western Hemisphere and formed the Rio Pact to achieve that aim.

The second alliance to form was NATO in 1949, followed closely by a U.S. military pact with Australia and New Zealand (ANZUS) in 1951. The ANZUS treaty provides the regional security architecture for Australia and New Zealand. It commits the parties to mutual security and calls for extensive joint training opportunities. The United States also negotiated a bilateral security agreement with Japan in 1951. The U.S.–Japanese Security Treaty formally leases military bases to the United States and allows the U.S. naval fleet docking rights. Both ANZUS and the U.S.–Japanese Security Treaty ensure a stabilizing and active U.S. presence in the region. But of all the alliances created after World War II by the United States, the NATO alliance has been seen as the most important and most successful in keeping the regional peace.

NATO: HISTORY, MEMBERSHIP, AND STRUCTURE

NATO was created on April 4, 1949, and its stated purpose was to safeguard the security and freedom of its members. While the NATO Charter does not explicitly identify the USSR as the target of the alliance, it was implicit in the politics of the day. At the time, the USSR was solidifying its control over Eastern Europe, establishing client governments in Poland, Czechoslovakia, Romania, and Hungary. Winston Churchill had warned just a few years earlier in his famous "Iron Curtain" speech that Europe was being physically divided between East and West and that the USSR threatened the security of the entire European continent. The USSR not only posed a significant threat to the territorial integrity of western European states, but it also represented an ideological alternative to the war-ravaged and poverty-stricken populations of Europe. NATO was designed to provide immediate security to Western Europe in the face of that territorial and ideological threat.

The original members of NATO were Belgium, Canada, Denmark, France, Iceland, Italy, Luxembourg, the Netherlands, Norway, Portugal, the United Kingdom, and the United States. Then, in 1952, Greece and Turkey joined the alliance. Greece and Turkey had received significant amounts of U.S. military assistance to fight communist insurgencies and were in the process of stabilizing politically and economically. Both of these states were symbolic targets of the Truman Doctrine, which stated that the United States would oppose communism and support governments that were fighting communism domestically. The inclusion of Turkey and Greece in NATO would prove to be problematic, as the two continued to clash politically and militarily over Cyprus. West Germany and Spain joined NATO in 1955 and 1982, respectively, rounding out NATO's Cold War membership.

Many saw the inclusion of West Germany as a provocative act on NATO's part because of Germany's history of aggression against the USSR. The USSR had lost an estimated 40 million people during the two world wars. Moreover, the USSR had suffered Western interference when the United States and France intervened militarily during its civil war in 1919—the internal conflict that followed Russia's withdrawal from World War I after the Russian Revolution of 1917. The formation of NATO itself—and then its inclusion of West Germany in 1955—thus confirmed well-established (and well-founded) Soviet fears of Western intervention in its affairs. The USSR and the Eastern Bloc states formed their own alliances, the Warsaw Treaty Organization and the Warsaw Pact, shortly after the announcement of West German membership in NATO.

The Warsaw Treaty Organization and the Warsaw Pact are often thought of as the same organization, but the two are different, at least technically: The Warsaw Pact was patterned after NATO, and included the Central Asian Republics as well as the European states. The Warsaw Treaty Organization was restricted to the European states and was a purely defensive alliance. The following is from Article 14 of the Warsaw Treaty:

> In the event of an armed attack in Europe on one or more of the States Parties to the Treaty, each State party to the Treaty shall, in accordance with Article 51 of the United Nations Charter, afford the State or States so attacked immediate assistance, individually and in agreement with the other States Parties to the Treaty, by all the means it considers necessary, including the use of armed force. (Cited in *Force Comparison* 1987, 7)

The sixteen allied members of NATO have been able to avoid war with the USSR, the Warsaw Pact, and each other for the last fifty years. Many credit NATO with this remarkable feat. It was able to stabilize the European continent after centuries of violent conflict and build a lasting peace between such historical adversaries as France and Germany. In spite of its longevity, however, the alliance was not without internal dissent. Several incidents have threatened to disrupt NATO's unity. In 1956, for example, the United States parted company with its allies, France and the UK, during the Suez Crisis. The United States refused to support the tripartite invasion of Egypt by France, the UK, and Israel after the nationalization of the Suez Canal. The United States sided with the USSR, condemning the invasion and demanding the immediate withdrawal of all foreign forces from Egypt. The Cuban Missile Crisis in 1961 also strained NATO relations, in part because of the Soviet demand for the removal of Jupiter nuclear missiles from Turkey in exchange for the removal of Soviet missiles from Cuba. Had that deal been formally struck, the U.S. commitment to the NATO alliance would have been seriously in doubt. Furthermore, NATO European allies feared that an attack on Cuba would prompt a retaliatory attack by the Soviets in Turkey or Berlin, creating a formal test of the alliance. In 1964, Great Britain, Turkey, and Greece almost came to blows over the fate of Cyprus. The UN established a peacekeeping force (UNFICYP) to help mediate the conflict between Greek Cypriots and Turkish Cypriots, but negotiators have had little success. In 1974, Turkey invaded Cyprus, generating a political crisis at the UN and NATO. Consequently, Greece withdrew its military forces from NATO out of disgust with NATO indecision regarding an ally's aggression. Greece did not rejoin the alliance until 1980. Relations between Turkey and Greece remain tense and are exacerbated by the Bosnian Crisis and the Kosovo Crisis.

In 1966, France withdrew from NATO's integrated military command and demanded the prompt withdrawal of all foreign troops from French soil. NATO Supreme Allied Headquarters was forced to move from Paris to its present location in Brussels, Belgium. Although France continued to participate in the political functions of NATO, the expulsion of American and NATO military forces signaled serious divisions between the United States and France. France questioned the U.S. commitment to European security and challenged U.S. leadership in Western Europe. France did not fully rejoin NATO until 1997.

During the 1980s, several NATO allies expressed serious alarm and vigorous dissent when the United States unilaterally reinterpreted the Anti-Ballistic Missile (ABM) Treaty (1972) to allow for the Strategic Defense Initiative (SDI), waggishly dubbed Star Wars, a space-based weapons system (Garthoff 1987). The ABM treaty sought to create nuclear stability by instituting Mutual Assured Destruction (MAD) as strategic doctrine. The treaty placed strict restrictions on defensive weapons systems, thereby ensuring that both the United States and the USSR would have second-strike capability. But SDI was of dubious legality because it would require testing outside of a laboratory, which the ABM treaty explicitly prohibits. Key NATO allies perceived the U.S. action on SDI as unnecessary, bellicose, and belligerent (Forsythe 1990, 15). Not only was NATO's leader acting without consulting its allies, but also its action represented a major shift in strategic nuclear doctrine, possibly giving the United States a destabilizing first-strike capability. These political strains notwithstanding, NATO remained intact and focused on its principal goal—containing the Soviet Union both geographically and ideologically. NATO's longevity is due in part to its organizational structure. NATO provides the institutional framework whereby member states can coordinate their military activities and participate in joint training exercises (see Figure 6.1 on page 132). Furthermore, NATO promotes transparency and long-range strategic planning, which build confidence among members.

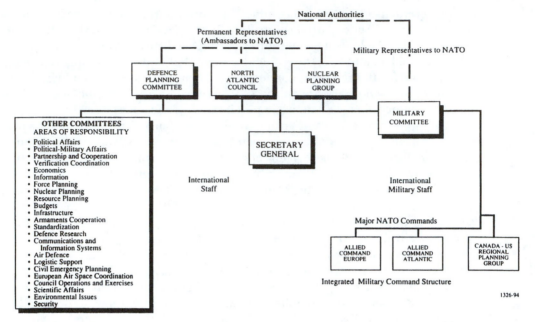

FIGURE 6.1   NATO's CIVIL AND MILITARY STRUCTURE

Source: Courtesy of NATO Public Information.

Like all military alliances, NATO is an IGO with limited membership. It consists of several complex organs, which carry out both political and military functions.* The North Atlantic Council (NAC) provides the highest levels of political leadership for NATO. The NAC is normally staffed by the permanent representatives of member states; however, it is also attended by foreign ministers or heads of state on special occasions. Through the NAC, members can consult and make decisions regarding security issues. Decisions are reached on the basis of unanimity, and each member state retains sovereignty over its own military forces and command decisions. The NAC is the body responsible for articulating NATO's new directions after the Cold War and for approving out-of-area operations.

The Defense Planning Committee and the Nuclear Planning Group are responsible for developing conventional and nuclear collective defense strategies, respectively. The Nuclear Planning Group is also a consultative body that advises on the role of nuclear forces in defense policies. Both of these committees are senior committees, meaning that they are attended either by the permanent representatives or the defense ministers of member states. Both committees work in conjunction with and report to the NAC. The Defense Planning Committee and the Nuclear Planning Group essentially function as specialized subcommittees of the NAC.

The Secretary-General is the senior diplomat representing the NATO organization. The Secretary-General facilitates external and internal relations between member states and with other international organizations, including both IGOs and NGOs.

---

*The description and functions of NATO organs are drawn from the NATO Handbook (1995).

This individual is responsible for directing decision making and may use his "good offices" to settle disputes among member states or disagreements between decision-making bodies. This role of the Secretary-General cannot be underestimated, given the competing interests of NATO members. The Secretary-General also heads the International Staff, which is NATO's bureaucracy. The International Staff executes the organization's policies and provides logistical and technical support to NATO offices.

The Military Committee is the highest military authority within the NATO organization. Consisting of the Chiefs of Staff of member-states, these military officers are responsible for recommending to political authorities strategies and requirements for the successful defense of member states. The Military Committee is also responsible for drafting exercise plans and developing military operations. The Military Committee is under the direct authority of the NAC. More specifically, the Military Committee works very closely with the Defense Planning Committee and the Nuclear Planning Group. The Military Committee provides the planning committees with the necessary expertise to make the long-range strategic plans.

The Integrated Military Structure provides the organizational framework for defending the territory of member countries against threats to their security or stability. It includes subordinate military commands covering the whole of the North Atlantic area. It provides the basis for joint exercising of military forces and the collaboration in fields such as communication and information systems, air defense, logistic support for military forces, and the standardization and the interoperability of procedures and equipment (NATO Handbook 1995, 98–99).

The Integrated Military Structure consists of the Integrated Command, which includes the Allied Command Europe and the Allied Command Atlantic. Headed by the "supreme allied commander," who has always been a U.S. military officer, the Integrated Military Structure is subordinate to the political authority of NATO. The subordination of the military to civilian leadership is consistent with NATO values. Civilian control of the armed forces is a prerequisite for NATO membership, and the norm is institutionalized in NATO's organizational structure and chain of command.

NATO is a complex security alliance that enables sovereign states to retain control over their armed forces while providing for a coordinated integrated defense strategy. Historically, NATO has been anchored by U.S. military power. During the Cold War, the United States maintained a system of bases in West Germany, Turkey, Italy, Great Britain, and Greece. These bases retained both conventional and nuclear capabilities to deter a Soviet attack. Today, NATO member states remain under the U.S. nuclear umbrella while both Britain and France maintain independent nuclear deterrents. The United States continues to have a conventional and nuclear presence in Europe, although its forces have been significantly reduced in accordance with its arms-control agreements with Russia.

Is NATO a success? It is very difficult to judge. One could argue that NATO checked Soviet expansion into Western Europe; however, that presumes that the Soviets had designs on Western Europe. The difficulty in measuring the effectiveness of an alliance as a deterrent is that we do not know for sure what an aggressor might have done. The fact is, deterrent value can be measured only by failure—an enemy attack. Furthermore, the ability of NATO member states to fight together has never been really tested. From its inception until today, many question whether the United States would risk a thermonuclear war and court its own destruction over a NATO ally.

Theoretically, the effectiveness of an alliance is related to two factors: alliance cohesion and alliance goals. Alliance cohesion refers to the factors that contribute to alliance solidarity (Kegly and Raymond 1990). Such factors might include a common enemy, longevity, cultural or historical ties, similar government type, or civilian control. High alliance cohesion results from institutionalized cooperation among like-minded governments. Goals can also affect an alliance. The simpler the goals, the easier they are to effect. Alliances that seek to maintain a territorial status quo are likely to be more successful than those that are more aggressive and ambitious. Put another way, alliances that are defensive in nature are more likely to be successful than those that seek to use military force to achieve other kinds of political goals. In the case of NATO, the member states are more or less democratic and are in close geographic proximity. During the Cold War, they faced a common enemy. Cohesion was high and the goals were simple—contain the Soviet Union and the Eastern Bloc. But despite the apparent gravity of the Soviet threat, cooperation by NATO members was not an easy feat.

The principal challenge that NATO faces in the post–Cold War era is defining its purpose absent a Soviet threat. Alliances can be fluid, as membership and goals tend to change as world politics change. For example, after the defeat of Nazi Germany in 1945, the U.S.–USSR alliance dissolved and the two became adversaries. Absent their common enemy, ideological differences replaced their wartime cooperation with postwar conflict. Similarly, Japan and Germany, once mortal foes, are now among the staunchest of U.S. allies. With the breakup of the former Soviet Union, NATO's original mission has become more or less obsolete; thus, NATO must change or become an anachronism.

NATO's member states maintain that the alliance is still needed because threats to European security remain. According to former NATO Secretary-General Willy Claes, "Islamic fundamentalism is at least as dangerous as communism was. Please do not underestimate it" (Klare 1995, 22). NATO planners are developing a "southern" defense to counter threats posed by fundamentalist regimes and by rogue states from Africa and the Middle East. And Europe still has concerns regarding its Eastern flank. The Balkans are experiencing exceptionally violent turmoil, which could easily spill over into neighboring states. Russia, which retains considerable military power, may seek to reassemble its former empire. NATO remains central to the security architecture of Europe.

NATO has responded to the post–Cold War challenges in four substantive ways. First, it is seeking a closer integration of NATO structures with Europe's political institutions, including the European Union (EU), the Organization for Economic Cooperation and Development (OECD), the Western European Union (WEU), and the Organization for Security and Cooperation in Europe (OSCE). These ties are necessary to counter the declining military presence of the United States and to assist with NATO burden-sharing among the European allies. The U.S. cuts in NATO spending have led to an increase in Europe's shares as well as a redistribution of those costs among European members. Second, NATO has beefed up its Southern Command headquarters in Naples in order to monitor military and political developments in the Balkans, North Africa, and the Middle East (Klare 1995, 23). Third, NATO has created new programs, such as the Partnership for Peace, in order to promote confidence and goodwill between its former adversaries of the Eastern Bloc. The new "partners" will not be extended the solemn security guarantee, but will be allowed to participate in joint conferences and exercises. Fourth, NATO has decided to expand the alliance to new members.

The first three initiatives are largely uncontroversial. The decision-making process within the NATO organization was streamlined, and new lines of communication were opened with existing international organizations and the emerging supranational institutions of Europe. A formal process of economic and political integration has been under way since international economic cooperation was made a prerequisite for assistance under the Marshall Plan. This ambitious plan, formally known as the European Recovery Programme in Europe, was designed to help rebuild war-torn economies (thereby making the Soviet alternative less attractive) through the creation of open markets and subsidies to key industries. Oversight of the Marshall Plan was carried out by the Organization for European Cooperation, the precursor to the OECD.

While Europe has had considerable success with some degree of economic integration, it has had difficulty with political integration and developing a common European defense policy. Efforts to establish the European Defence Community in the 1950s failed, and the WEU became the principal vehicle for solely European cooperation in defense-related areas. The WEU has been criticized as an "alliance on paper" because, absent U.S. military capability, it lacked the teeth to give it credibility. France and Germany experimented with a joint military force; however, this force was more symbol than substance. With the end of the Cold War and the scaled-back U.S. military presence, greater integration of NATO with Europe's political and economic institutions is a logical first step in adapting to the new strategic and political environment.

NATO has also proposed numerous confidence-building conferences with Russia and the erstwhile Eastern Bloc states—former members of the Warsaw Pact (which formally disbanded in 1991)—whose political and territorial reorganizations (e.g., the breakup of the Soviet Union and Czechoslovakia) created instability in the central corridor of Europe. These conferences were designed to plan for political change, to promote transparency, and to ease the tensions associated with uncertain political environments. The development of a "southern" strategy was politically popular owing to the sense of insecurity in Europe generated by the Gulf Crisis and the subsequent increase in immigration from North Africa and the Middle East.

The integration of NATO into the larger political architecture of Europe, the creation of confidence-building programs such as the Partnership for Peace, and the "southern" strategy are mild initiatives compared to the decision to extend full NATO membership to several central European states. Some cynics see the former initiatives as a way to make the latter more palatable to critics who come from across the political spectrum. The expansion of NATO raises serious questions regarding the alliance's purposes, goals, and credibility. It also provides a unique case study of the dynamics of international and alliance politics.

CASE STUDY 3: NATO EXPANSION

Several dramatic events from 1989 to 1991 marked the end of the Cold War in Europe: Communist governments across Central and Eastern Europe collapsed, the Berlin Wall was toppled, and the Warsaw Pact was disbanded. The USSR signaled that it would not intervene and turned inward to manage its own political and economic problems. The Union of Soviet Socialist Republics itself disintegrated in the summer of 1991.

The Baltic states (Latvia, Lithuania, and Estonia) were the first to become independent, followed by eleven of the other republics, including Ukraine, Georgia, and Belarus. The Russian republic retained most of the Soviet military and assumed the USSR's international obligations, including its Security Council seat.

Perhaps the most remarkable event was the reunification of Germany on October 3, 1990, after more than forty years of partition. The new Germany was immediately extended full membership in NATO, raising the possibility that other former Eastern Bloc states might also join NATO. Russian insiders argue that during German reunification talks in Moscow, U.S. and Soviet officials struck a bargain: The USSR would not oppose the union of East and West Germany and, in return, the United States would not expand NATO (Reynolds 1998). Presumably, this bargain paved the way to a peaceful unification of Germany with Russia's blessing. According to American and British officials, however, the debate on NATO expansion has never been about whether to expand, but when and how (Hurd 1994, 2).

Since the end of the Cold War, NATO members have explored a variety of plans to expand NATO eastward. Thus, in July of 1997, at their Madrid Summit, NATO officials announced that they would extend invitations to Poland, Hungary, and the Czech Republic—a promise that was fulfilled in 1999. And analysts predict that Slovenia and Romania will be invited to join next, in spite of the precarious state of democracy in Romania and the lack of a military in Slovenia (The Stanley Foundation 1997, 9). Is NATO expansion a good idea? Who stands to win and who stands to lose from expansion? How does NATO expansion affect political, economic, and social relations in Europe?

A REALIST CUT

Many realists tend to oppose NATO expansion for four interrelated reasons. First, they argue that the *raison d'être* for NATO no longer exists; thus expansion serves only to facilitate NATO's inevitable decline. States form alliances in response to a common enemy or threat (Walt 1987; Stuart and Tow 1990). The usefulness of an alliance declines when the common enemy or threat no longer exists. The collapse of the USSR and the Russian adoption of democratic and market reforms suggest that Soviet and communist expansionism are artifacts of the past. NATO expansion weakens an already waning organization. Furthermore, the absence of a major war in Europe was the result of the bipolar balance of power between the United States and the USSR, not NATO (Mearsheimer 1995). The multipolar power configuration will force changes in NATO that will make it unrecognizable as a military alliance.

Second, from the perspective of U.S. realists, the expansion of NATO stretches U.S. security commitments so far that they are not credible; hence, they are dangerous. The United States could find itself engaged in conflict with a still powerful Russia over places in which it has no compelling national interest. The political and economic future for Russia is far from certain. An ultranationalist Russia may wish to reassert itself in its traditional sphere of influence, prompting a military confrontation with NATO. If the United States chooses to respond militarily, it runs the risk of nuclear war. And if it stands by while an ally is attacked, then the credibility of NATO would irretrievably shatter, thereby threatening the stability of all of Europe. NATO expansion serves only to antagonize Russia, strengthen Russia's nationalist sentiment, and destabilize its political and economic reforms. Relations with Russia should have priority over those with minor powers in Central and Eastern Europe.

Third, rational states do not commit themselves and their resources to rhetorical, "fuzzy" goals. NATO's post–Cold War goals are purportedly the same as its Cold War goals—to protect the territorial integrity and the political stability of its members. However, during the Cold War, those goals were clear—contain the USSR and counter Soviet-led communism. After the Cold War, the threat itself lost its unidimensionality, and goals became complex. Existing members may not face immediate territorial threats, but they face indirect threats, such as illegal immigration, terrorism, and drug trafficking. Increasing NATO membership renders the organization unwieldy and makes consensus difficult (Butcher 1998). Realists, then, stress that states should limit their international commitments to tangible, achievable objectives.

NATO membership commits the allies to defending each other's territorial integrity and political stability. But threats to territorial integrity and political stability are just as likely to come from within, inflamed by ethnic and religious conflict. Security in the central corridor of Europe involves too many unknowns to be addressed successfully by a traditional alliance. NATO involvement could easily turn a local conflict into a regional or even a global one. Alliances have been known to escalate conflicts rather than contain them (Siverson and Tennefoss 1984).

Fourth, the expansion of NATO effectively transforms it from a traditional alliance to a collective security arrangement. According to U.S. officials, NATO membership is open to anyone and NATO targets no particular state (Christopher 1997; Albright 1997). If this is true, then NATO is exposed to all the problems associated with collective security. NATO members must therefore grapple with an assortment of definitions for "aggression," including the vexation of deciding whether a conflict is internal or external. NATO decision making is further complicated by the UN. The UN Security Council has turned to NATO to carry out its decisions in the former Yugoslavia. NATO forces and Russian forces are part of the UN stabilization force in Bosnia (UNPROFOR). While the Security Council consists of NATO members (the United States, the UK, and France), the dual chain of command and different priorities muddle the decision-making process. NATO may identify a threat to European security, but Security Council dissension may veto strategies or actions altogether. The crisis in Kosovo was a case in point. In June 1998, NATO allies sought to curb Serb violence against ethnic Albanians in Kosovo and carried out an exercise in neighboring Macedonia—Operation Determined Falcon—to demonstrate NATO resolve. Yet Russia (still angry about the NATO expansion) and China (worried about Taiwan and Tibet) warned that Kosovo was an internal Yugoslav affair and threatened to veto any UN authorization. NATO was faced with acting without UN approval or backing down. The former option conceivably would make NATO an aggressor; the latter weakens NATO's credibility.

Realists argue that NATO expansion serves no immediate self-interest and threatens its viability as an alliance. States should reevaluate their military and security commitments in light of the post–Cold War reality. According to an editorial in *De Standaard*, an independent Catholic newspaper in Belgium, "Principally, Europeans should think of the consequences. One way or another, Russia will get a say in NATO decisions, which means that the Atlantic Alliance—enlarged . . . to 25 members—will be under the pressure of an American-Russian axis. At the extreme, this could mean that NATO has became NARO: North American Russian Organization" (U.S. Information Agency 1997c, 7). The balance of power in Europe is shifting; it is becoming multipolar rather than bipolar, and the United States is disengaging militarily from the continent. These factors contribute to NATO's growing irrelevance as a military alliance.

NATO may even need to be downsized, not expanded (Joffe 1995). The argument that NATO is being transformed into a political association of peace-loving states is just rhetoric. "The Czechs, Hungarians, and Poles knew they were applying to an alliance created to oppose Russia, and that's why they wanted to get in. Bill Clinton may think there is a new NATO, but the Central Europeans admit privately that they are joining the old one" (Nelan 1998, 1). All of the invitees have experienced Russian power in recent history and are not eager to experience it again. Yet realists point out that the Central Europeans are exchanging one form of dominance for another. As Russia's official government newspaper *Rossiyskaya Gazeta* warns, "Watch out: You may lose your chastity playing games with the West" (U.S. Information Agency 1997c, 7).

The confusion over NATO's new mission has raised serious doubts about its effectiveness as a military alliance and as a political institution. Expansion weakens alliance credibility. During the Cold War, allies wondered if the United States would risk itself in the event of a Soviet attack. Will the United States risk nuclear war over places most Americans cannot find on a map? The transformation of NATO into a political institution also raises the quandary of attempting to find military solutions for essentially political problems in Central Europe. For realists, NATO's attempts to be an alliance and a political institution make it ineffective at both. The political and financial costs of expansion simply cannot be justified. Germany's *Frankfurter Rundschau* asks "whether the enlargement does not resemble lemmings marching toward the sea instead of a far-seeing policy in favor of a European security structure" (U.S. Information Agency 1997c, 7).

A LIBERAL CUT

Liberals argue that NATO expansion provides the best opportunity for stability in post–Cold War Europe. NATO's success in keeping the peace must be understood in the context of the overall political environment of Western Europe. According to Secretary of State Madeleine Albright (1997, 21), NATO's principal goal was to contain the USSR, but it also provided the confidence and security shattered economies needed to rebuild themselves. It helped France and Germany become reconciled, making European integration possible. With other institutions, it brought Italy, then Germany, and eventually Spain back into the family of European democracies. It denationalized allied defense policies and stabilized relations between Greece and Turkey—all without firing a shot. In Secretary Albright's view, NATO can do for Central Europe in the post–Cold War era what it did for Western Europe during the Cold War.

Several strands of liberal thought can be discerned in Secretary Albright's words. First, liberals argue that political stability is required for market economies to take hold. The transition from a command economy to a market economy is a difficult process, requiring enormous resource commitments to currency stability and infrastructure development. Political stability within and between the Central European states is a prerequisite for domestic and foreign investment. Extending security guarantees goes a long way toward easing the fears of external threats and allows states to focus on domestic reforms.

Second, economic integration is fostered by expanding markets, creating a complex web of social and political as well as economic ties. The increase in transnational ties reinforces security in Europe because the cost of violence becomes too high. The initial costs associated with NATO expansion are an investment in the future. Defense issues are denationalized and member states see their interests as lying with the collective. "This denationalization of security policy tempers the natural rivalry and the competition for military primacy that might otherwise occur among the major European powers, and it helps to preclude any intra-European use of military posturing for political influence" (Duffield 1994b, 763).

Third, the requirements of NATO membership promote the peaceful settlement of disputes. In many respects, NATO can serve as a midwife to democratic institutionalization. States are required to have democratic institutions that foster norms of compromise, cooperation, and nonviolence. NATO expansion can help rehabilitate former totalitarian states and promote and protect human rights within those societies. NATO can keep very serious conflicts, like those between Greece and Turkey, from becoming violent or spilling over into neighboring countries.

Fourth, NATO is part of a vast array of actors comprising the security regime in Europe (Duffield 1994b). This regime includes IGOs such as the EU, OSCE, WEU, and the Council of Europe. NGOs such as the North Atlantic Assembly (NAA), the Atlantic Treaty Association (ATA), and the Interallied Confederation of Reserve Officers (CIOR) are also part of this regime. NATO has contributed to stability in Europe because it promoted transparency and confidence between members and fostered the development of common norms. This elaborate security regime enables all the members of Europe to participate in shaping the future, whether or not they join NATO (Christopher 1997).

NATO expansion can help promote economic and political reforms within new member states. The states make the initial commitment to democratic and market reforms. The extension of security guarantees provides the stable international environment for the institutionalization of democracy, human rights, and free markets. Internationally, cooperative norms such as the peaceful settlement of disputes and compromise serve to stabilize interstate relations and promote transnational political, social, and economic ties. The security framework works in tandem with expanding markets, so they reinforce each other. The result is an incremental process through which European states can be integrated economically and, to varying degrees, politically.

NATO is changing to adapt to an interdependent world and is the lynchpin to European and North American security. According to British Foreign Secretary Malcolm Rifkin in the *Times*, "To make the whole of Europe as peaceful and secure as Western Europe, we need to extend NATO's assurances and habits of trust. NATO is on course to do this through its enlargement, by establishing new arrangements with Russia and Ukraine, and by strengthening cooperation with all of our partners to the east. If we can involve all Europe in Europe's security, we can entrench freedom and trust for us all" (U.S. Information Agency 1997c, 7). Liberals see the costs of NATO expansion as an investment in the future: Commitments of resources to NATO now decrease the likelihood of an even more costly European war later. The continued engagement of the United States ensures that Europe and the United States remain military partners and not military competitors. It also limits the chances of a competitive and dangerous arms race.

NATO expansion is necessary to project stability eastward to the fledgling democracies. Dariusz Rosati, Poland's foreign affairs minister, states in *Le Figaro*: "NATO's expansion means, in fact, expanding the area of stability and democracy, thus expanding peace. It would seem that those opposed to NATO's expansion are forgetting this" (U.S. Information Agency 1997c, 6). NATO is a tool for preventing conflict and a mechanism for managing European transition. NATO's intentions are neither sinister nor threatening. Rather, NATO reassures members by integrating political and military security.

A Marxist Cut

Marxist critiques of NATO expansion center on the original reasons for NATO—the Russian question, the German question, and issues relating to economic integration in Europe. For Marxists, the formation of NATO after World War II is better understood as the establishment of a capitalist economic empire in Europe, not as the result of a power vacuum in Europe (van der Pijl 1984; Kolko and Kolko 1972). The United States and its World War II allies were not peaceful democracies so bewildered by the Soviet Union's Eastern European policies that they were forced to create NATO to defend themselves. Rather, the United States and its allies wanted to impose a liberal world order where they and their firms would dominate "free" markets. At the time, the Soviet Union was the only state with capability to stand in their way. NATO was created to stabilize capitalism in Western Europe and to threaten the USSR and its allies. The USSR was perceived as a threat to those markets and the capitalist way of life because it represented a viable alternative to the war and poverty caused by capitalist competition.

After the Cold War, NATO's priorities remain the same—stabilize markets from civil unrest and contain external threats to those markets. The only difference is that the main external threats to expanding markets are nationalism and fundamentalism rather than communism. Russia still represents the principal external threat because of its military capabilities coupled with its nonliberal tendencies. Governments in Russia have tended to be very authoritarian. Russia was a monarchy under the czars and totalitarian under the communists. The Yeltsin government was a de facto dictatorship, although its power was arguably rivaled by exceptionally violent criminal syndicates. Strong governments and Mafia-style organizations can threaten open markets and market reforms. Russia must be isolated until free market reforms are institutionalized and hence less likely to be reversed.

Russian officials at the highest levels have opposed the expansion of NATO because they see it as an aggressive act that threatens their security. Russia has been invaded twice during the twentieth century by German forces (not to mention Napoleon's invasion in the nineteenth century) and is legitimately alarmed by NATO's encroachment. According to an editorial in the centrist *Novaya Gazeta*, "Discussions on NATO have revealed the sad truth—Russia has no allies in this world anymore. And it may soon have many enemies" (U.S. Information Agency 1997c, 2). While the West has indicated that NATO expansion is an open-ended process that does not exclude membership for Russia, exclusion of Russia is almost guaranteed. In Russia, NATO is an institution associated with threats and intimidation. Russia could no more join NATO now than it could participate in the Marshall Plan after World War II. The Marshall Plan was antithetical to the USSR, and the new NATO is antithetical to the New Russia. NATO may want Russia integrated into Europe, but it wants that integration to take place on Western terms, regardless of its ethnic and cultural differences.

NATO expansion also serves the economic and political interests of Germany. Many observers have pointed out that NATO plays an important role in controlling Germany militarily (Joffe 1995; Duffield 1994a). However, most observers fail to recognize that the German government and German firms are the largest investors in Central and Eastern Europe. NATO expansion provides a mechanism for Germany to guarantee its investments and to exercise political influence without raising international concern. The world does not necessarily fear German territorial expansion; however, its influence is extended through international organizations such as the EU and NATO, which, in turn, facilitates its economic dominance. Germany is leading the push for NATO expansion because it has the most at stake in Central Europe.

Western Europe and the United States have also expressed an interest in extending NATO to the Central Asian republics. NATO's Secretary-General Javier Solana toured several Central Asian republics in 1997, again raising concerns about NATO motives. The vast oil and natural gas reserves of the Central Asian republics are of particular interest to the West, which wants to reduce its dependence on Middle Eastern oil. According to the reformist weekly *Moskovskiye Novosti,* "NATO's partnership with Central Asia has to do with the West's economic as well as military interests, and with time may become an instrument of influence" (U.S. Information Agency 1997c, 2). Then-Secretary-General Solana's visit was the first step in extending Western control over Central Asia energy reserves. The U.S. and British military forces are now stationed in many Central Asian states as part of the U.S. fight against the al Qaeda terrorist network and global terrorism.

The Russian and the German questions are related to the overall thrust of NATO expansion—making Central and Eastern Europe safe for capitalism. Current NATO members are far more interested in markets than in democratic reforms. According to Marxists, market reforms create financial instability, unemployment, and inequality. In the transition to capitalism, governments are required to cut back on social welfare programs, leaving the working class to bear the brunt of reforms. Moreover, in spite of democratic reforms, many leaders in Central Europe retain dictatorial powers relating to the economy. This power is necessary to enforce painful reforms and to quell internal dissent. NATO provides these governments with a stable international environment. More importantly, it assures both public and private investors that their money is safe.

Of course, the military-industrial complex also benefits from NATO expansion. The U.S. Congressional Budget Office has estimated that it will cost approximately $61 billion to bring the military capability of Poland, Hungary, the Czech Republic, and Slovakia up to baseline NATO standards; moreover, it will cost an additional $64 billion to prepare bases for NATO use or a permanent NATO presence (Zimmerman 1996, 14). These aspiring members will have to buy Western arms and technology from Western firms with Western military assistance. The modernization of the militaries of the newest NATO members is also likely to spur a very profitable arms race with non-NATO members. Nonmembers will be forced to upgrade their militaries in order to balance the threat posed by NATO.

NATO expansion is more closely related to economic considerations than it is to security, and Western officials all but admit it. The candidates for NATO membership have no immediate security threats. Rather, these states are the ones most economically poised to become members of the EU. They hold the lion's share of Western economic investments. And they have instituted market reforms, provided political and civil rights on paper, and attracted direct foreign investment. Now they are being rewarded with NATO membership. NATO will help stabilize these emerging markets as they experience the internal unrest caused by the inevitable financial crisis and the cyclical booms and busts associated with capitalism.

A Feminist Cut

Feminist views on NATO transformation and expansion are quite diverse, sometimes even opposed. Most traditional liberal feminists applaud the idea of an alliance over unilateral security policies. Alliances emphasize the collective while unilateral policies center on self and autonomy. The idea that the security of one is directly related to the security of others reflects the feminine experience and feminine priorities. Liberal feminists also applaud decision making based on cooperation and consensus. Collective security and the development of cooperative behavioral norms have been trivialized by realists as idealistic and naive. Liberal feminists argue that this masculine world view denigrates connectedness and collective action as inconsequential and promotes competitive and aggressive international behavior.

Feminists of all stripes recognize that alliances also involve military institutions. While some militaries are more progressive than others, these institutions epitomize what it means to be masculine. Hence, many essentialist feminists oppose NATO as a masculine structure; thus, they oppose its expansion. Militaries are authoritative and hierarchical; moreover their culture degrades and dehumanizes women. Drill instructors degrade new [male] recruits during basic training by calling them women, girls, or faggots. The military, as an institution, uses language and encourages behavior that emasculates the enemy.

Liberal feminists, on the other hand, are more optimistic about the possibilities of progressive change within military establishments and NATO. Liberal feminists point out that women have made many contributions to NATO as members of the armed forces. Many NATO countries use the talents of women in their militaries, especially in administrative and medical areas (Harris 1997, 25–26). The U.S. military relies on nearly 200,000 women in uniform, and women troops from several nations are on the ground as part of NATO forces in Bosnia. Liberal feminists also stress that NATO still has a long way to go to successfully integrate women into NATO's mission. Most of these women are in noncombat positions, which keep women from being promoted to the highest ranks of the military establishment. They tend to perform support and logistical functions, which are not rewarded as highly as combat positions. Some NATO countries such as Turkey, Italy, Spain, and Greece either have no women in the military or have but a token female presence.

NATO has no guidelines for members regarding the integration of women in the armed forces. Each member is allowed to staff its own military as it sees fit. NATO could do a lot more to improve the status of military women in member states. Currently, NATO has a Committee on Women, which serves as a consultative body concerning women in uniform and assists members with integration initiatives. However, committee recommendations are not binding, and the inclusion of women in the armed forces remains a low priority.

NATO as a political organization is characterized by the virtual absence of women in key decision-making positions. Women comprise more than 80 percent of the secretarial and support staff. Women serve as protocol and public relations officers. The high-ranking political and bureaucratic staff is still very much a man's club. As a result, the status of women in the armed forces is not a consideration for NATO membership, nor is it factored into NATO expansion plans.

NATO expansion has direct, and not always positive, effects on women in host communities. The development of bases, whether domestic or foreign, creates a peculiar kind of economic dynamic that supports the base. Women in host communities are usually employed by the base in traditional women's jobs; they serve as secretaries, receptionists, and housekeepers. Often, sex-industries spring up around the base, offering prostitution, live sex acts, and pornography. NATO's tolerance of sex discrimination and lack of military standards as they relate to women reinforces the marginalization and the objectification of women in host communities. Liberal feminists see potential for NATO as a vehicle for improving the status of women in the military and the civilian world; however, significant reforms are needed within NATO itself.

Essentialist neofeminists see NATO as an inherently masculine, military institution and they oppose what it stands for: violence. NATO is a patriarchal organization that harnesses the most technologically advanced and sophisticated weapons with masculine dominance. NATO expansion threatens to project violence eastward for no tangible security reason. While joining NATO may be voluntary, it is voluntary only on the part of statesmen. No member of NATO has ever placed its membership in the alliance on a national ballot where women can have a direct influence on policy. If anti-American sentiment in Europe is any indicator, NATO would likely be disbanded if it came up for a popular vote. Essentialist feminists highlight the superior-subordinate relationships between alliance members. One major power usually dominates smaller powers. One of the superpowers has always anchored the post–World War II alliances. Host countries are thrust in harm's way in the interest of the dominant power. As such, they are placed in a feminine position, dependent on the dominant power for security, identity, and well-being. Yet, essentialists also argue that alliances are perpetuated or undone by the communities in which alliance bases are located (Enloe 1990, 67). NATO bases have been challenged by peace and women's movements in European countries because the bases threatened international peace. In spite of their facade of normalcy, these bases represented domination and destruction. Greenham Common, a U.S. base that once held both intermediate-range cruise and nuclear missiles, was peacefully besieged by British women between 1981 and 1988 (Cook and Kirk 1983). This technically Royal Air Force Base was in fact controlled by the United States and U.S. troops were stationed there. The British protestors saw the U.S. deployment of intermediate-range cruise missiles as a threat to their nation's security and a provocative military act. In spite of being portrayed as freaks and lesbians by the mainstream media, the Greenham Common women drew national and international attention to the subservient position of Great Britain to the overall strategic plan of the United States. Essentialist feminists argue that women can draw upon their strengths as mothers, nurturers, and peacemakers to oppose the expansion of NATO military installations.

NATO AFTER THE BALKANS

The violent conflict in the Balkans represents a watershed episode for security in Europe and perhaps the world. The UN peacekeeping and peacemaking missions—UNIFOR, UNPROFOR, UNSFOR, etc.—are really NATO "in drag." NATO military forces, having donned their blue UN helmets, implement Security Council decisions by force if necessary. Does this represent the transformation of NATO from an alliance to a true collective security arrangement? It is important to recall that while both collective security and alliances are based on the principle that an attack on one is an attack on all, they are not the same thing. Collective security arrangements have universal membership and are designed to deter international aggression. Alliances have restricted membership and usually involve a presumptive aggressor. Alliances tend to be more manageable and less cumbersome than collective security because membership and goals are limited.

The future of NATO as an "on call" UN force has several problems. First, neither Russia nor China is part of NATO. China and Russia are suspicious that the West will use the UN and NATO as tools to legitimize their own aggression or intervene in the internal affairs of sovereign states. Kosovo is an example of the West's using NATO to intervene in the affairs of Yugoslavia. Kosovo is a republic of Yugoslavia and falls within its domestic jurisdiction. NATO militarily intervened in 1999 without Security Council authorization. Its massive air campaign against Serbia generated international outrage and created a refugee crisis that made conditions worse for the Kosavar Albanians on the ground, and destabilized neighboring Albania and Macedonia. The jury is still out on whether UN and NATO intervention has led to a more stable situation in the Balkans. With the Kosovo precedent, what is to stop NATO from intervening in Africa or the Middle East without UN approval?

Second, the politics of NATO burden-sharing are such that the expense of out-of-area operations could divide the alliance. The United States is unwilling to continue to shoulder the lion's share of NATO's regular costs, much less take on additional military commitments. The peacekeeping mission in Bosnia alone costs more than $1 billion a year. The U.S. government has had a difficult time selling the peacekeeping operation to the public and the U.S. Congress. The mission placed U.S. troops in harm's way, directly in the middle of conflict in which it has no immediate security interests. Now NATO peacekeeping has expanded to include Kosovo and an expanded presence in Macedonia.

Third, the conversion of NATO from a military to a political organization may mean that NATO does not have the capability to conduct collective security operations. The U.S. military presence in Europe has been drastically reduced. A significant portion of U.S. forces that were once stationed in Europe are now located in the Persian Gulf. None of the allies has increased its military contribution to compensate for the U.S. cutback. All of these factors work against using NATO as the collective security arm of the UN.

The continued existence of NATO into the twenty-first century seems likely—in what capacity, however, is unclear. NATO members have emphasized the political functions of NATO rather than its military functions. However, the military cutbacks have weakened NATO's overall capability. Politically, NATO faltered in Bosnia, as disputes between allies led to paralysis and indecision. Tens of thousands of lives were lost in Bosnia before the Dayton Accords were signed in 1995, and the carnage repeated itself, albeit on a lesser scale, in Kosovo and Macedonia. NATO's fate will likely be determined by the outcome of the Balkan conflict. NATO may yet play a leading role in European economic and political integration—or it may eventually become moribund, a mere "alliance on paper" and a shell of its former self.

THE ARAB LEAGUE

The Arab League, known formally as the League of Arab States, is a pivotal organization in Arab and Middle Eastern affairs. Created in 1945, the Arab League is designed
to foster international cooperation among Arab-speaking states, promote Arab solidarity, and provide a collective security arrangement for the region. It consists of twen-
ty-three members from North Africa and the Middle East, including the Palestine
Liberation Organization (PLO). Its permanent headquarters is in Cairo, Egypt, although it was temporarily (from 1979 to 1989) moved to Tunis, Tunisia, after Egypt's
membership was suspended as a result of its peace treaty with Israel. As an IGO for developing non-Western states, the Arab League has historically been committed to anticolonialism, Arab nationalism, and Pan-Arabism. It has received renewed attention
in recent years because of its role in the Persian Gulf War and the Israeli–Palestinian
Crisis, but it has always been active in the volatile politics of the strategic Middle East.

The Arab League has been presented with a series of political challenges, beginning
with the creation of Israel in 1948 and continuing with the Iraqi and Israeli–Palestinian
crises of today. In between, the League has attempted to address the Suez Crisis (1956),
several Arab–Israeli wars, the Lebanese civil war, and the Iran–Iraq war. In addition to these
challenges, the Arab League has been tested by regional terrorism, religious fundamentalism, and glaring disparities between the oil-rich and oil-poor Arabs. The monumental problems faced by the League have led to its paralysis in times of crisis; however,
its immobility at critical junctures belies its institutional complexity. The institutional
composition of the Arab League includes political, military, and economic forums.

THE COUNCIL

The League is headed by the Council, which is a plenary body of all Arab League members. Each member of the Council has one vote and decisions are made on the basis
of unanimity. The Council meets twice a year and occasionally functions as a summit
body for Arab heads of state. The unanimity rule reflects both the true intergovernmental nature of the Arab League and its emphasis on the sovereign equality of members. The companion principle of nonintervention is included in Article 8 of the Arab
League Charter to represent its opposition to western imperialism and its commitment
to the self-determination of Arab peoples.

The Council's powers and functions are extensive. It may consider any issue at the
request of two members and pass resolutions on those issues. The Council is responsible for approving budgets and for routine League initiatives. It is also responsible for
mediating disputes between Arab League members and between its members and
other countries or international organizations. The Arab League Council is similar to
the UN Security Council in that it is responsible for the maintenance of peace and security. It differs in that any member of the Arab League can disapprove of a Council
action. The Council is also charged with coordinating its activities with other IGOs, especially with the UN and the Organization for African Unity (OAU).

THE JOINT DEFENSE COUNCIL

The Joint Defense Council (JDC) was created by the Treaty of Joint Defense and Economic Cooperation in 1950 and it reports directly to the Council. The JDC is responsible for formulating common defense policy and for creating and implementing military

plans (Taylor 1984, 184). It is composed of the foreign and the defense ministers of member states and their task is to oversee Arab security. The JDC meets at least once a year in regular session and meets continuously during emergency sessions. The actual development of collective defense strategies is done by the Permanent Military Commission, which is also responsible for the day-to-day military affairs of the Arab League.

THE ECONOMIC COUNCIL

The Economic Council was also created by the Treaty of Joint Defense and Economic Cooperation and it reports directly to the Council. The Economic Council is responsible for promoting economic cooperation and development among Arab League members and is attended by the highest level economic officials. The Economic Council is also responsible for mobilizing resources for regional security action (Taylor 1984, 183). The Council meets annually, and its decisions are made on the basis of a simple majority. The resources for the Arab League are generally contributed by the oil-rich kingdoms of Saudi Arabia, Kuwait, the United Arab Emirates, and Qatar. Far more populous and impoverished, Algeria, Libya, Egypt, Jordan, Syria, Lebanon, and Iraq account for less than 35 percent of total contributions.

THE GENERAL SECRETARIAT

The Arab League bureaucracy is quite elaborate. It is composed of a Secretary-General, Assistant Secretaries-General, and departmental staffs. "The Secretariat has departments dealing with political, economic, legal, cultural, press, and publicity, administrative and financial, social and Palestinian matters. There is also an Institute of Arab Studies, an Institute of Arab Manuscripts, a Refugee Boycott Office, and an Anti-Narcotics Office" (Bennett 1995, 247). The Secretariat is responsible for developing proposals for the League, administering League business, and carrying out League decisions.

Case Study 4 focuses on the 2000 Palestinian Uprising to explain and describe the role of the Arab League and other organizations in regional security. Using our theoretical lenses we can see that the Arab League is a collection of diverse sovereign states with competing interests that often hampered its ability to act decisively during the Israeli–Palestinian Crisis. The Arab League is also a valued partner in the community of international organizations and provides a voice and a political vehicle to a large number of people who share values and culture. At the same time, the Arab League represents a contradiction to the liberal world order in that this order is supposed to be accepting of alternative values and views but at the same time is dismissive of organizations whose values and approaches are non-liberal. The Arab League is clearly biased against Israel and it often allows religious considerations to determine its directions. In many respects, the Arab League represents a premodern version of masculinity whereby men control all the decision making and have made the crisis worse with their posturing and promises without any good-faith attempt to reach a negotiated peace settlement.

CASE STUDY 4: PALESTINIAN UPRISING 2000

In September 2000, Ariel Sharon, a prominent member of the conservative Likud party in Israel, visited the Temple Mount in Jerusalem. The Temple Mount, a place sacred to Judaism, is the surrounding area of the Al-Aqsa Mosque. Recall from Chapter 2, the arson of the Al Aqsa Mosque while under Israeli control prompted the formation of the

OIC to protect Islam's holy sites. Sharon's visit sparked violent demonstrations among Palestinians who saw it as an affront to Islam and their desire for autonomy. Furthermore, Ariel Sharon had led the 1982 Israeli military assaults on the Sabra and Shatila Refugee Camps in Lebanon in which thousands of Palestinians were killed. Demonstrations have continued in Gaza, the West Bank, and Jerusalem almost unabated since then. Terrorist attacks against Israel have also increased dramatically.

Israel has responded to the Palestinian uprising, or intifada, with military repression, targeted assassinations, selective occupation, and economic pressure. Then–Prime Minister Ehud Barak, along with the U.S. President Bill Clinton, continued peace negotiations even though the situation continued to deteriorate. However, Ehud Barak lost the public's and the Knesset's (parliament) support and Ariel Sharon was elected prime minister in February 2001. With a disengaged United States under the new George W. Bush administration and the hawkish Sharon at the helm in Israel, the cycle of violence spiraled upward to unprecedented levels.

The Arab League first responded to the Palestinian uprising at a two-day summit in October 2000. Nine key points emerged (*APS Diplomat Recorder* October 28, 2000). First, Arab League members were called upon to review and reduce their relations with Israel. Second, the intifada was praised. "The Summit salutes the Intifada of the Palestinian people in the occupied Palestinian territories. . . . The Arab Leaders blame Israel for bringing the region back to an atmosphere of tension and violence through its practices and aggression and its siege of the Palestinian children." Third, League members pledged more than $1 billion dollars to support the intifada. About $800 million will finance the preservation of Arab identity in East Jerusalem (the Al Aqsa fund) and $200 million will assist the families of the martyrs of the Intifada (the Jerusalem Intifada fund). The League also called upon members to open Arab markets to Palestinian goods and services and to exempt them from taxes and duties. Fourth, the League demanded that the UN Security Council establish an international criminal court to try Israeli war criminals, "based on the example of the courts set up by the Council to try war criminals in Rwanda and Yugoslavia." Fifth, the UN was called upon to protect the Palestinian people from Israeli occupation. Sixth, the League called for the establishment of an impartial international committee to investigate the reasons and responsibility for the deterioration of order in the occupied territories. This committee would be created under the auspices of the UN and the UN Human Rights Commission. Seventh, the League articulated three conditions of Middle East peace— a sovereign Palestinian state with Jerusalem as its capital, the return of all Arab occupied land, and the release of Arab prisoners. Eighth, the League pledged to pursue multilateral approaches to peace. Ninth, the League decided to hold regular summits, with the next summit to be held in Amman, Jordan, in March 2001.

In March 2001, the Arab League met again to follow up on the October 2000 summit points and to assess recent developments of the Palestinian uprising. Although more than $1 billion had been promised to assist the intifada, less than a quarter of the money had been delivered (*APS Diplomatic Recorder* March 17, 2001). The money that had been donated was deposited into the Islamic Development Bank in an investment fund because no guidelines or rules had been set for using the money. The Palestinian Authority was on the verge of bankruptcy and the Arab League decided to give the Palestinian Authority $40 million a month to avoid the disintegration of the Arafat government. The Arab League used the March 2001 summit also to express dismay at a U.S. veto of the UN Security Council Resolution that would have created an observer force in the West Bank and Gaza (*MEED, Middle East Economic Digest* April 6, 2001, 3). The Arab League once again called for trials of Israeli "war criminals."

The intifada continues at the time of this writing. Since the March 2001 summit, serious attacks against civilians and officials have occurred. These attacks have been carried out by Hezbollah, Hamas, the Muslim Brotherhood, Israeli settlers, Israeli Defense Forces, and the Mossad. The September 11, 2001, attacks on the United States have added caution and fuel to this very dangerous situation. On the one hand, retaliatory action on the part of the United States threatens to ignite Muslim discontent and encourages Israel to find a military, rather than a political, solution to the intifada. On the other, an engaged United States in the peace process might bring about a sovereign Palestinian state, an outcome greatly desired by the Arab League. How do we explain, describe, and analyze the response of international organizations to the Palestinian Intifada? Middle Eastern politics has been dominated by the seemingly perpetual Israeli–Palestinian crisis and political indecision among Arab League members. What factors determined Arab League actions? How does the Arab League response affect individuals and groups within the Middle East? Has the Arab League played a constructive role in the Israeli–Palestinian crisis? Are other types of international organizations important to study in this crisis?

A REALIST CUT

The Arab League represents a diverse group of states that has rarely spoken with one voice. The Arab League, like the UN, suffers from having very broad and ambitious goals without adequate tools to achieve them (Maksoud 1995, 582). During the Cold War, League members were divided into three camps—Pro–United States, Pro–Soviet Union, and Non-Aligned. As a result, the League's policies were largely reactive to the policy goals of the superpowers. The Cold War polarization often left the League paralyzed even regarding the Israeli–Palestinian issue. Toward the end of the Cold War, the Arab League divided into "Rejectionist," "Moderate Rejectionist" and "Accommodationist" camps based on each members' willingness to co-exist with the state of Israel and their relationship with the United States and the West (Zacher 1979, 168–169). Arab governments that have been either "Rejectionist" or "Moderate Rejectionist" include Syria, Iraq, Yemen, Algeria, Somalia, Sudan. "Accommodationist" states have included Egypt, Saudi Arabia, Kuwait, Oman, United Arab Emirates, and Jordan. What is noteworthy is that the wealthiest Arab League members tend to be accommodationist as their wealth comes from their oil dealings and investments with the West. Their national interests clearly lie with the interests of the Western powers. The United States provides security to the Persian Gulf states and exploits the cleavages between large and small Arab states, as well as oil-rich and oil-poor states. While Arab League members may be pro-Palestinian in this conflict, their national interests lie with the United States, Israel's strongest ally and largest benefactor. As a result, any Arab League response to the Palestinian–Israeli crisis will be anemic at best.

Arab League members are also competitive with each other. Syria and Egypt are deeply suspicious of each other. Lebanon and Jordan have large numbers of Palestinian refugees that have destabilized their governments. Palestinians make up a large proportion of the "guest workforce" in the oil-rich, population-poor kingdoms of Saudi Arabia, Kuwait, Oman, and the United Arab Emirates. Iraq has tried to expand territorially into Iran and Kuwait. Non–Arab League member, Iran, sponsors Hezbollah, which operates out of Lebanon but carries out attacks against Israel. There is growing concern among Arab members about the influence and popularity of Iran among Palestinians, in Lebanon and the Middle East in general. In January 2001, Iran organized a conference in Beirut to establish a new organization to promote the Palestinian cause and to liberate Jerusalem (Paz 2001). This organization is described as "an alternative to all the official Arab bodies that deal with the issue of Jerusalem" (Paz 2001). Moderate Arab states see Iran and its militant version of Shia Islam as a destabilizing force in the Middle East. Palestinian support of Iraq's Saddam Hussein and Iran's militant Shiite regime have done little to curry favor with wealthy Saudi Arabia and Kuwait. Therefore, it is not surprising that the $1 billion promised has not materialized and that the Arab League Summit in March 2001 was much more subdued than the October 2000 summit. The Palestinian cause again took a backseat to national interests and geo-strategic concerns of the Arab League's wealthiest and most powerful members and the far more powerful interests of the United States.

A LIBERAL CUT

The Arab League has been an important institution of regional cooperation in the volatile Middle East. While it suffers from the same institutional weakness of the UN and other types of collective security arrangements, the League has attempted to address the problems associated with the Israeli–Palestinian crisis in a constructive manner. First, the League is the principal financial backer of the Palestinian Authority, which functions as the governing body in Palestinian controlled areas. Without the Palestinian Authority, the Palestinian territories could disintegrate into chaos. The Arab League is one of the strongest political and monetary supporters of the Palestinian people and their goal of a Palestinian state.

Second, the Arab League functions as a forum for debate where members with diverse backgrounds can air their concerns and grievances. Since its inception, the Arab League has weathered external and internal strife and remained a voice for Arab unity and anticolonialism. Even states with the best intentions will disagree and the League can generate understanding and opportunity even if the debate is often vitriolic (Satloff 2001). Arab states, working through the League, can achieve compromise on the very delicate issue of the Palestinians' uprising. The March 2001 summit called for the "resumption of negotiations and all tracks from where they stopped" and, rather than calling for more violence, the League asked the Palestinians to be vigilant, determined, and committed (Satloff 2001, 2). In short, the League can be an important voice for peace.

Third, the Arab League works closely with the UN and NGOs to provide humanitarian assistance to the Palestinian people. Millions of Palestinians have been displaced by the conflict and have been under the care of the United Nations Relief and Works Agency for Palestine Refugees (UNRWA). The Arab League members are among the largest contributors to UNRWA and the League Secretariat administers a variety of programs that benefit Palestinian refugees in Lebanon, Jordan, and Syria.

Fourth, the League is respectful of other peace efforts and avoids measures that may undermine them. For example, when League members were called upon to review and reduce their relations with Israel, the resolution exempted Egypt, the Palestinian Authority, and Jordan who had reached peace agreements with Israel in 1979,

1993, and 1994, respectively (*APS Diplomat Recorder* 2000). The League clearly did not want to compromise past peace agreements and sought to use those agreements as a platform for future negotiations.

The Arab League's contributions to Middle East security does not shield it from criticism, however. Its political and organizational weaknesses must be addressed if it is to be effective at finding a durable solution to the Israeli–Palestinian issue. The League needs to have a more balanced approach to the crisis. Statements at the March 2001 Summit from Syrian Leader Bashar al-Assad, "Israelis are worse than the Nazis," and Iraq's Saddam Hussein, "May God damn the Jews," do little to further the cause of peace in the region (Satloff 2001, 2). Its anti-Israeli bias make it a poor candidate for brokering a lasting peace with Israel. Similarly, the Arab League calls for a UN war crimes tribunal to try only Israeli officials overlooks the fact that crimes have been committed by many parties in the region. All parties must be held accountable if such a tribunal were to have any legitimacy. Finally, the UN intervention called for by the Arab League would likely be condemned as a neo-colonial adventure if it did not result in a Palestinian state with Jerusalem as its capital. The UN is "damned if it does and damned if it doesn't." The Arab League cannot have it both ways.

The Arab League created the Palestine Liberation Organization in 1965 and has supported the Palestinian Authority since 1993, hence its real influence lies with its ability to get the Palestinians to the negotiating table. The Arab League can be a strong partner in the peace process if it pursues strategies that involve nonviolent means of conflict resolution. Its historical commitment to anticolonialism and a sovereign Palestinian state can help level the playing field for the Palestinians. However, the League must be willing to compromise on the issue of Jerusalem, a place sacred to all the major religions, not just Islam, and accept the permanent existence of the state of Israel. Until the Arab League embraces the values of the peaceful settlement of disputes and compromise, its actions often exacerbate the situation rather than solve it.

A MARXIST CUT

The Palestinian uprising and the Arab League response must be understood in the context of European imperialism and U.S. neo-imperialism in the Middle East. Recall from Chapter 5 that the Sykes-Picot Agreement (1917) gave Great Britain and France much of the territory in the Middle East and North Africa as "mandates." The territory known as Palestine became an international zone. Shortly after the Sykes-Picot Agreement was reached, the British issued the Balfour Declaration, which said the following:

> His Majesty's Government view with favor the establishment in Palestine of a National Home for the Jewish People and will use their best endeavors to facilitate the achievement of the object, it being clearly understood that nothing shall be done which may prejudice the civil and religious rights of the existing non-Jewish communities in Palestine, or the rights and political status enjoyed by Jews in any other country (cited in Anderson, Seibert and Wagner 1998, 69).

This declaration was designed to gain Jewish support for the Allies during WWI, without alienating the Arabs (Anderson, Seibert, and Wagner 1998, 69). It also indicated that the British sought to exercise political influence in the internationalized zone, which it managed until 1947. Between 1917–1947, large numbers of European Jews emigrated to Palestine, demanding the right for Jewish self-determination. The immigration was encouraged by the United States and many European powers as a result of the Nazi genocide in Europe. During the same time, Arab Palestinians sought to exercise their right to self-determination. The result was essentially a civil war in Palestine.

In 1947, the UN took over from the British and called for the establishment of two independent states in the territory of Palestine by July 1948. The Palestinians and several Arab countries rejected the plan as a colonial attempt to gain a foothold in the strategic Middle East. (Anderson, Seibert, and Wagner 1998, 84). The Arabs launched military strikes against Zionist forces but were ultimately defeated. The state of Israel was established in 1948 and was quickly recognized by the United States and European powers. Israel became a member of the UN in 1949. Since the creation of Israel, Arabs and Israelis have gone to war four times, in 1948, in 1956 (the Suez Crisis), in 1967 (the Six-Day War), and in 1973 (The Ramadan or Yom Kippur War). Each time, either Europe or the United States sided with Israel, effectively ending each conflict with an Arab defeat.

The experience of Palestine shows how the Western colonial powers disregard the history and the rights of indigenous peoples to further their own interests. The United States used the UN, which it created, financed, and controlled, to establish an "outpost of Western hegemony" (Anderson, Seibert, and Wagner 1998, 68). The Arab League could not respond in a meaningful way because League members were played off each other by their colonial benefactors. The West created a system of political competition and jealousy among the Arab states. The Arab League has always played a subordinate role because the "accommodationist" faction within the League is corrupt and easily manipulated by the West. The leaders of these accommodationist states recognize the distance between themselves and their populations regarding their pro-Western stance and use payoffs and repression to stay in power. The money to do this comes from the West. The ruling elites of the accommodationist states are, in effect, in league with the West and not the Arabs. The victims are the Palestinians, the working class of the Middle East.

Arab League politics have been dominated by two issues that are decidedly non-liberal: OPEC and Islam. The former represents manipulation of the world capitalist economy's lifeblood and the latter represents a synthesis of religion and government. The goals of pan-Arabism and Arab unity, which could be fostered by OPEC and Islam, are undermined by the competitive nation-state system created by the colonial powers. While liberal ideology is supposedly open to different ideas and viewpoints, the West has actively opposed both issues by using its wealth to buy off Arab political and religious elites. Even members of the Palestine Authority have sent their families and fortunes abroad (Shahin 2001). With the leadership of the Arab in the pockets of the West, the masses, including the vast majority of Palestinians, remain vulnerable to violence and exploitation by the West and the accommodationist elites. They also are susceptible to the draw of Islamic fundamentalism and the likes of Osama bin Laden.

A FEMINIST CUT

The Arab League is a masculine institution characterized by the almost complete exclusion of women from the decision-making process. The only prominent woman represented in the Arab League is Hanan Ashwari, a Christian Palestinian who serves as a spokesperson for the organization. Hanan Ashwari, who also served as the spokesperson for the Palestinian delegation at Middle East peace talks, has been vocal in highlighting the feminine experience under Israeli occupation. According to Ashwari, women tend to suffer more from Israeli occupation because deportations and detentions separate the family unit and reduce the family's income (*Off Our Backs* 1992). The economic warfare practiced by the Israelis make it difficult for women to meet their basic human needs or the needs of their families. Ashwari became the spokesperson for the League in July 2001 and she is seen as a bridge between the Arabs and the West. She has challenged the Western bias of the international press and condemned the September 11 attacks on the United States. She has also kept the spotlight on Israeli policies, while at the same time arguing that the Arab world needs civilized speech and language in order to communicate more effectively with the West (*Washington Report on Middle East Affairs* 2001, 41).

Many feminists also stress the role of NGOs in the struggle for a Palestinian state (e.g., Gluck 1995; Ahmed 1984; Peteet 1991). Numerous NGOs have been founded that have furthered the cause of Palestinian nationalism and promoted the status of Palestinian women. These NGOs include Palestinian Women's Union, which organized literacy, sewing, first aid and nursing courses, and founded orphanages, hospitals, and schools, and the General Union of Palestinian Women, which raised feminist issues such as the conditions of working women and the reform of family law (Gluck 1995, 5). Women from around the world have taken up the cause of Palestinians. Women In Black (WIB) was created by Palestinian and Israeli women in 1988 after the first Palestinian intifada to protest the Israeli occupation of the West Bank and Gaza Strip. WIB is now a worldwide movement to protest racism, the arms industry, and violence against women (Hanley 2001). On June 8, 2001, WIB held simultaneous silent vigils in 145 cities to express solidarity with the Palestinians in the occupied territory and to protest violence against unarmed civilians on all sides (Hanley 2001). Critics of peace organizations such as WIB argue that such groups are naive and do little to affect change on the ground; however, peaceful demonstrations provide the grassroots basis of civil disobedience and call attention to the plight of those who have no voice. NGOs provide a vehicle for women who have been largely excluded from the activities of IGOs such as the Arab League.

The IGO that has had an important impact on the lives of Palestinians, both men and women, is UNRWA and its Microfinance Program. The program began in 1994 and has provided over 18,000 loans to 12,000 individuals, half of whom are women from the poorest sectors of Palestinian society (*UN Chronicle* 2000). This program has reduced poverty, created employment, and helps women obtain self-sufficiency. Since the first intifada in the 1980s, women have come to play the role of breadwinner in Palestinian society, as many men were either imprisoned or deported (Usher 1993). With the Microfinance Program, women have been able to take control of their lives and make independent financial decisions. The 2000 uprising and the Israeli restrictions on the movement of Palestinian laborers have made these women crucial to the survival of the Palestinian community.

Palestinian women from the Shatila refugee camp have also tried to make the Israeli military account for its alleged crimes. In 2001, the three Palestinian women represented by Lebanese lawyer Shibli Mallet went to Brussels, Belgium, to accuse Prime Minister Ariel Sharon of crimes against humanity. Earlier that year, a Belgium court had convicted two Catholic nuns from Rwanda for genocide and crimes against humanity for their complicity in the Rwanda genocide. The Palestinian women sought to bring

Sharon to trial for his role as commander of the Israeli Defense Forces during the Shatila and Sabra Refugee camp massacres. Belgium has agreed to hear the case and Sharon has appointed a legal team to represent him (Shahin 2001). Contrast the efforts of these women with the rhetoric of the Arab League. The Arab League has attempted to shame the UN into creating a war crimes tribunal, which it knows the UN will not do. These women have accomplished more by going to a national court willing to hear their claim because justice, not political gain, was their aim. While the case is still pending, their success has brought international attention to the alleged crimes of the Israeli military.

THE ISRAELI–PALESTINIAN CRISIS AFTER SEPTEMBER 11

The Palestinian uprising has taken on a new, and perhaps a more dangerous, dimension since the September 11 attacks on the United States. Television coverage of Palestinians rejoicing in the street after the attacks have angered Americans and made the United States less sympathetic to the Palestinian cause. This cause has been adopted by Osama Bin Laden and has been a rallying point for Arabs and Muslims around the world. The reaction of the Arab and Muslim press shows the disconnect between the West and the Islamic world regarding the causes and the significance of the attacks. According to Abdulmu'em Al-Shirawi in the semi-official Arabic language paper *Al-Ayam* in Bahrain:

> I wish that our Arab and Islamic regimes, who dance to the beat of America's drums, would tell us who this war is against. I pray to God and ask him not to give them a role in this big American lie. . . . The statements of the American Cowboy, who does not have political experience, are clear and do not need an explanation or interpretation, starting with his stupid announcement that it will be a "crusade," then saying he wants bin Laden "dead or alive" and ending with his statement that the war against bin Laden and the Taliban is just the beginning of a long war which will include all those who will be categorized as "terrorist," according to the "Americaneili"—I mean "American-Israeli"—definition of terrorism. The goal is clear and it was reinforced when Netanyahu was asked to appear before the Congress to explain to them what is terrorism and who are the terrorists. (U.S. Department of State, September 27, 2001)

According to an editorial in Morocco's *Bayane Al Youm*:

> From the first glance at the U.S. list of terrorists organizations, it becomes clear that all organizations are Arab and Muslims. . . . Why were not Ariel Sharon, Ehud Barak, Benjamin Netanyahu and the list is long of Israeli leaders whose hands are stained with the blood of Palestinian children and women included on the list? (U.S. Department of State, September 27, 2001)

Qatar's Issa Al-Isaac wrote in the semi-independent *Al-Sharq*:

> Israel is trying to label all Palestinian and Islamic resistance groups as terrorist organizations. Now more than ever we need a clear definition of terrorism. Organizations who are resisting against (foreign) occupation should not be included on the American list of terrorist targets. We urge the U.S. not to fall into Israel's trap. The U.S. should not fight Israel's war against the Palestinians under the cover of fighting terrorism. The daily murder of innocent Palestinians is no different from killing innocent Americans in New York and Washington. (U.S. Department of State, September 27, 2001)

Arab and Muslim media reaction also suggests divergent views within the Islamic community. According to Kuwait's *Al-Qabas*:

> Although bin Laden opposed the presence of American forces in Saudi Arabia, he never told us how he planned to evict the Iraqi oppressors who occupied Kuwait killing, looting and raping. This is something we have never seen the American and foreign "occupiers" do. . . . This is the difference between the American "occupiers" and bin Laden, who horrified the world with bombing in Africa, Khobar, Aden, and now finally Washington and New York. (U.S. Department of State, September 27, 2001)

According to Saudi Arabia's moderate *Okaz*:

> Certainly, the responsible and insightful dialogue, understanding and substantial bilateral discussions between King Fahd and President George Bush on September 25 was a clear example of the process of coordination to activate the bases of mutual cooperation which have existed between the Kingdom and the United States for more than half a century. (U.S. Department of State, September 27, 2001)

The political sentiment reflected in these Arab and Muslim newspapers suggest that Arab League and Middle East politics is likely to remain divisive and volatile. Whether this divisiveness and volatility is due to competitive nation-states, a lack of shared values, class conflict, or gender depends on your theoretical lens.

7

TRADE

Oₙₑ OF THE OLDEST AND MOST CONTROVERSIAL FEATURES of international relations is trade—the seemingly simple act of exchanging goods and services between societies. On the one hand, international trade yields mutual benefits: It increases the diversity and quality of consumer goods and services, it facilitates the diffusion of technology, it provides jobs, and it promotes efficiency. On the other hand, trade can also destroy national industries, displace workers, and threaten national culture and identity. Thus international trade has been, and continues to be, a force that engenders both cooperation and conflict between societies.

The controversies generated by trade make it one of the leading issues in contemporary international affairs as the mass demonstrations in Seattle, Washington, and Prague indicate. In this chapter, we look at some of those controversies, reviewing the historical development of trade and the current rules governing international trading policies and practices. We examine the World Trade Organization (WTO) in terms of its organization and its role in handling contemporary trade issues. Then we investigate the case of the U.S. Clean Air Act in order to understand, from four different perspectives, the influence of the WTO on increasingly interdependent societies. In the second case study, we explore how other international organizations, namely multinational corporations (MNCs) and nongovernmental organizations (NGOs), involved with trade, approach the controversial issue of trade in genetically modified (GM) foods and organisms. The case studies illustrate how economic issues are also political issues and are better understood in the context of the political framework that gives them meaning and significance.

THE HISTORY OF INTERNATIONAL TRADE

Trade and trade issues predate the modern nation-state. The ancient and medieval worlds knew trade issues. Thucydides stressed the strategic importance of trading routes between the city-states of Sparta and Athens and the kingdom of Macedonia. Aristotle struggled with the contradictory effects of trade on ancient Greek society. The Roman Empire depended for its lifeblood on trade throughout the ancient world, from Brittania to conquered Greece and Egypt. And the Roman Catholic Church engaged in transnational exchanges around the world, dealing with a variety of cultures. The Crusades, for example, quickened the flow of goods from East to West and back.

The history of significant trade between nation-states began in the sixteenth century during what is called the mercantilist period. The monarchs of the emerging Western European states used trade as a tool for enhancing national wealth and power. States sought to achieve a "favorable" balance of trade whereby their trade surpluses (exports greater than imports) translated into growing national treasuries. The basic purpose of trade was to accumulate wealth. States engaged in "predatory" practices, seeking to establish monopolies in foreign markets and establishing colonies that could serve both as captive markets and as reservoirs of cheap resources and labor. States could enrich themselves by controlling their trading industries and stockpiling gold.

In the latter part of the eighteenth century and the early nineteenth century, the influential writings of Adam Smith (1723–1790) and David Ricardo (1772–1823) became popular among the emerging class of merchants and entrepreneurs. Smith argued for the government to take a laissez-faire approach to the economy, including international trade. Ricardo, through his theory of comparative advantage, argued that mercantilist trading practices actually hurt states because they promoted inefficient industries. International market forces, not monarchs or parliaments, should determine what industries a state should specialize in. A trade surplus cannot be maintained because it causes inflation at home, making domestically produced goods less attractive in foreign markets.

These liberal economic thinkers formed the ideological foundation for British hegemony and for the rules of nineteenth-century trade. Trade was characterized by multilateralism, low tariffs, and the limited use of quotas. After 1846, international trade expanded considerably with the repeal of the British Corn Laws, a unilateral reduction of agricultural tariffs. This action was reciprocated internationally, so that trade in both natural resources and manufactured products grew. Technological innovations and the industrial revolution increased the number and the diversity of traded goods. It should be noted, however, that trade was not always voluntary. European states possessed colonies in Africa, India, Southeast Asia, and Latin America; and they had coerced trade agreements with other societies like China and Japan. While international trade brought wealth to many in Europe and the United States, it also brought violence and domination to others.

The expansion of trade continued until it was disrupted by World War I in 1914. World War I spurred aggressive economic competitiveness among nations that were not fighting each other. Governments, influenced by the ideas of Alexander Hamilton and Friedrich List, adopted nationalist policies to protect and expand the industrial sectors of their economies. Later, the Great Depression caused states to be even more protectionist as governments scrambled to shield domestic industry from predatory trade. In 1930, for example, the United States enacted the Smoot-Hawley Act, which levied tariffs of more than 50 percent on imports, in response to the protectionist measures of other trading states. U.S. trading partners responded in kind, and international trade came to a virtual standstill. Then, after German and Japanese aggression brought about World War II, international trade remained distorted and limited.

In hindsight, U.S. officials, most of whom had a liberal world view, argued that economic nationalism and the predatory "beggar thy neighbor" policies of the early twentieth century precipitated both world wars and the intervening depression. In other words, politics and the immediate needs of states had triumphed over economics and private individual initiatives. They also recognized that Roosevelt's New Deal programs had generated positive effects on the domestic economy and raised citizens' expectations. Thus, after World War II, the challenge for U.S. leadership in the international economy was a big one—how to establish a liberal international economic order in a world of nations ravaged by war and hampered by underdevelopment.

The United States met the postwar challenge by establishing the Bretton Woods System, named after the New Hampshire town where much of the postwar planning took place. The architects of the Bretton Woods System, most notably British economist John Maynard Keynes (1883–1946), sought to strike a balance between the interests of states and the need for international economic stability. Characterized as the compromise of embedded liberalism, the Bretton Woods System required governments to commit to liberal economic principles, with the recognition that states have legitimate economic interests, including full employment, low inflation, and steady economic growth (Ruggie 1982). To that end, states retain the right to regulate the domestic economy but must agree to participate in various forms of multilateral policy negotiation and coordination.

The Bretton Woods System was based on three pillars: economic development, monetary stability, and trade. The first two pillars were anchored by the World Bank and the International Monetary Fund (IMF), respectively (discussed in more detail in Chapter 8). The third pillar of Bretton Woods, trade, began with a series of negotiations that resulted in the General Agreement on Tariffs and Trade (GATT). In 1946, the Economic and Social Council of the UN (ECOSOC) convened a conference to consider the nature of the postwar trading order. The GATT was designed to be an interim measure until the proposed International Trade Organization (ITO) got off the ground. However, the ITO Charter, which was hammered out during the 1948 UN Conference on Trade and Employment in Havana, was not ratified by the U.S. Senate. The requisite two-thirds majority could not be achieved, as both the left and the right criticized the lack of protection for U.S. workers and national industries. Many in the Senate also expressed concern about U.S. sovereignty because the United States did not have a veto over ITO decisions. The ITO treaty was withdrawn by Truman in 1950; thus the GATT became, by default, the post–World War II institutional framework for international trade.

The principal goal of GATT was to jumpstart international trade through tariff reduction, with the imposition of reciprocity, nondiscrimination, and multilateralism. These goals were accomplished through a series of "rounds" in which trade negotiators would seek a reduction in tariffs for one country, then apply it to others. The central tool in this process is most-favored-nation status (MFN). MFN means that member states must treat all fellow member states the same. If a state grants a trade concession to one member, it must provide that same concession to all members. The United States and other member states have used MFN under GATT to liberalize trade and also to encourage good behavior internationally.

GATT was an institution designed for market economies, so most communist countries have taken no part in GATT negotiations. The market economies have succeeded in reducing tariffs on industrial and manufactured goods through a series of negotiations—notably, the Kennedy Round (1962–1967), the Tokyo Round

(1973–1979), and the Uruguay Round (1986–1993). The latter GATT rounds involved talks on previously taboo areas. These areas included trade in agricultural products and trade in services such as banking and telecommunications.

In addition, new forms of trade protectionism, known as nontariff barriers (NTBs), have had to be addressed. NTBs are more difficult to identify and harder to negotiate because they include such traditional state policy tools as taxes, subsidies, and regulation. Governments legislate and regulate for the "public good," and their actions can inhibit the free flow of goods—and now services—across national borders. By exercising traditional policy tools, states have created new, more sophisticated forms of protectionism.

NTBs can include subsidies, which may be direct or indirect. Governments can, for example, simply write checks, making payments directly to firms. Or they can hand out tax breaks or provide needed services, thus subsidizing firms indirectly. Whether direct or indirect, such subsidies afford firms protection from international competition. With governmental assistance, they do not have to compete on the same level as foreign firms. Consider Boeing, Inc. Boeing receives billions of dollars a year in defense contracts for its products—aircraft ranging from high-performance fighter jets to huge transport and freight planes. These defense contracts permit Boeing to develop aeronautical innovations paid for by taxpayer dollars, innovations that also have commercial applications for civilian aircraft. Thus Boeing has a considerable advantage over foreign producers seeking to compete in the civilian aircraft market. Can we say, then, that defense contracts constitute a nontariff barrier to trade?

Another kind of NTB is the voluntary export restriction (VER). VERs are bilaterally negotiated agreements whereby exporters agree to limit the number of goods they send to the other country. In the 1980s, for example, the Reagan administration pursued VERs with Japan to reduce the number of Japanese autos exported to the United States. Japanese officials have claimed that such restrictions were far from "voluntary," and that they were in fact but mirror images of the quotas that had been all but eliminated under the GATT. Japan agreed to the VERs, not on its own initiative but because U.S. officials threatened to limit Japanese access to U.S. markets.

Governmental regulation can also serve as NTBs. Governments can mandate that products meet certain safety and environmental standards, which tends to exclude foreign competition. Some states even have an industrial policy that utilizes governmental regulation and subsidies to give preferential treatment to certain industries, which helps them compete abroad. These firms do not have to worry about going out of business because they are part of a nation's long-term industrial plan. They can "dump" products, selling them below cost, and corner international markets. NTBs have been the source of considerable difficulty under GATT, in part because of its ad hoc procedures. Decided on a case-by-case basis, the process of determining whether a specific government action is an impermissible NTB or a legitimate state policy is highly politicized.

Latter-day rounds of GATT have demonstrated that contemporary trade negotiations have entered into a new phase of contentiousness. Traditionally, agricultural products and agricultural industries have been matters of national security: A state unable to feed itself is vulnerable to an enemy embargo. Moreover, in many countries, the family farm is a repository of cultural heritage and a symbol of national identity. And, in some states, like France and Japan, agricultural interests exert enormous domestic political pressure and are disproportionately represented in legislatures. For these reasons, agricultural industries have been protected through tariffs and are heavily subsidized.

Trade in financial, commercial, and technological services is also politically contentious. In many countries, important financial and commercial institutions such as banks, insurance companies, and utilities are either owned or extensively regulated by the state. Arguably, these services are so critical to the economic health and the physical well-being of societies that they cannot be trusted to foreign-owned providers. Disagreements regarding the liberalization of such services have paralyzed negotiations—so much so that it has been difficult even to place the issue on the agenda.

According to free-trade advocates, the protection of agricultural industries and services has made them inefficient and uncompetitive. In their view, many farms in the United States were so heavily subsidized that they ceased to be businesses and became welfare recipients. Accordingly, agricultural subsidies were cut extensively in the United States, and to a lesser degree in Europe, in the 1980s. The reduction of subsidies led to the demise of many family farms, and agricultural industries were compelled to reorganize after being exposed to market forces. This reorganization had extensive social and political consequences. Farmers staged protests across Europe, and EU subsidy reform slowed to a crawl. In the United States, music groups held concerts to raise money for Farm Aid, a nonprofit organization created to help struggling and displaced farmers. In spite of domestic support for small farmers in the United States, protective measures were reduced and many went out of business. Their place was taken by large corporate farms—agribusinesses that could efficiently produce large volume for domestic consumption and overseas markets.

THE WORLD TRADE ORGANIZATION (WTO)

The difficulties in liberalizing the agricultural and service sectors, together with the increasing use of NTBs, prompted GATT members to form the WTO. The GATT was considered to be inadequate for several reasons. First, the GATT was fundamentally a provisional international agreement. When it became clear that the ITO would never get off the ground, negotiators were forced to develop ad hoc procedures for settling disputes. This made the dispute process chaotic, complicated, and inconsistent. Second, the GATT's jurisdiction was quite limited. Technically, only tariffs and quotas on manufactured and industrial goods fell under the purview of GATT. However, with the globalization of production, further liberalization and the removal of NTBs increased in urgency. Third, GATT as an organization had questionable legal status; it needed to become both more impartial and more authoritative to tackle the volatile issues of contemporary trade. Often deprecated as the "General Agreement of Talk and Talk," the GATT had no mechanisms for authoritatively and systematically resolving disputes. Thus, as the last order of business during the Uruguay Round, GATT members voted the World Trade Organization into existence.

On January 1, 1995, the WTO officially became operational. Headquartered in Geneva, Switzerland, the WTO consists of 132 members. It incorporates previous GATT agreements, but its mandate has been expanded to include agriculture, services, and intellectual property rights. The WTO also has the authority to review state policies affecting trade and to authorize sanctions against errant states. Funding for the WTO is based on each member's share of the total trade among WTO members.

The WTO has had some success. In the first year of its existence, the WTO was able to get its members to commit to liberalization talks on financial and telecommunications services. In 1997, sixty-eight states agreed to "wide-ranging liberalization measures" for basic telecommunications while seventy states agreed to open their financial services sectors, thereby accounting for "95 percent of trade in banking, insurance, securities and financial information" (WTO 1999).

The WTO has also been exercising its authority to settle trade disputes, particularly as they relate to NTBs. This aspect was particularly controversial because the WTO is permitted to review the regulations and the tax codes of members to determine if their intent or overall effect is trade protection. This is troublesome for states, accustomed to the final say in policy within their own territories. The WTO attempts to balance state interests and the interest of free trade (represented by economists and trade experts) such that both can be represented and neither always assumes dominance over the other.

The WTO touts itself as a member-driven, consensus-based IGO.* That is, the WTO tries to reach decisions through consensus. When consensus is not possible, its voting procedures demand either a two-thirds or three-fourths majority rule, each state having one vote. The WTO is organized around four levels. At the top is the Ministerial Conference, which is attended by all member states. The Ministerial Conference must meet at least once every two years and is responsible for the long-term strategic planning of the organization. While the WTO encourages consensus, four situations are likely to trigger a vote of WTO members. First, a vote may be required for interpretation of existing multilateral trade agreements. Second, a vote may be necessary to waive an obligation assumed under trading agreements. Third, amendments to existing multilateral agreements require ministerial approval. Finally, the admission of new members to the organization must be approved by WTO members. Since its inception, no WTO decision or ruling has required a vote of the Ministerial Conference.

The day-to-day operations of the WTO are handled by the remaining tiers. Below the Ministerial Conference is the General Council. The General Council consists of overlapping bodies, including the Dispute Settlement Body and the Trade Policy Review Body. These very important organs oversee dispute settlement procedures and scrutinize members' trading practices. The third level of organizations consists of councils that oversee broad areas of trade. These include the Goods Council, the Services Council, and the Trade-Related Aspects of Intellectual Property (TRIPS) Council. The fourth level breaks these areas down even further into specific aspects, such as "access" or "technical barriers." All the members of the WTO belong to these organs; however, much of the work is done in committees.

The WTO is supported by a small bureaucracy (500 people) called the Secretariat. The Secretariat leadership consists of the Secretary-General, currently Renato Ruggiero, and four Deputy Directors-General. The Secretariat is staffed by trade experts and economists who review the trade policy of members and provide the General Council with expertise, training, and technical support. The Secretariat, which provides the "expert panels" that adjudicate unresolved disputes, is part and parcel of the appeal process. The function of the Secretariat is to denationalize multilateral trade negotiations by providing neutral analyses. Its neutral competence is designed to take the politics out of trade.

---

*The description of the organization and decision-making procedures of the WTO is taken from its Web page: <www.wto.org>.

Depoliticizing and denationalizing trade is a formidable task. Politics is about determining who gets what, when, how, and why. Trade involves the global distribution of resources and wealth, and governments are reluctant to allow markets or international organizations to divide "the global pie." States practice protectionism for many, interrelated reasons—reasons that may have little to do with efficiency or comparative advantage. They may, for instance, seek to protect certain industries or restrict trade in certain technologies for reasons of national security. Industries involved in producing military hardware or sophisticated war-fighting technologies are critical to a state's security. Thus, when Chrysler threatened to go bankrupt in the late 1970s, the U.S. government responded with a no-interest loan of $100 million. The prospect of tens of thousands of Americans out of work was daunting enough. But it can be argued that Chrysler's production of tanks and troop carriers made it indispensable to the security of the United States.

States may also protect industries that hold the most promise for future economic growth and prosperity. In the 1980s, the United States extended trade protection to American computer chip manufacturers. Comparative advantage may have dictated the production of another product, say, potato chips; but U.S. firms were going to produce computer chips, whether or not it was efficient to do so. Computer chips were the industry of the future and American firms were going to be part of that infant industry, regardless of its initial profitability.

Governments may also practice protectionism to give mature industries time to adjust to new competitors or evolving market realities. The Reagan administration made extensive use of VERs to limit the number of Japanese auto exports to the United States. Japanese automakers had garnered a significant share of the U.S. market, contributing to layoffs and unrest in the ranks of American labor, not to mention cries of "foul" among American managers and shareholders. This normally free-trade administration provided the mature U.S. automobile industry with the time to restructure and retool in order to become competitive domestically and internationally.

Democratic societies are likely to protect industries because the nature of their politics demands it. In pluralistic societies (such as the United States and Canada), interest-group pressure can establish protection for certain sectors and industries in an ad hoc fashion. But European states and Japan, each to varying degrees, tend to formulate some kind of industrial policy, which is a concerted plan to develop the economy and manage international trade. Industrial policy tends to favor certain groups over others in terms of subsidies and tax breaks. Critics of industrial policy claim that it promotes cronyism and the "good old boy" network. Defenders counter that pluralism, as it is practiced in the United States and Canada, amounts to much the same thing, except that it is protection to the highest bidder. Either way, the end effect is government protection of industries, which inhibits free trade.

Most governments use protectionist measures to promote domestic well-being. In the nineteenth century, tariffs and duties were the principal sources of revenue for national governments. Now, tariffs are almost gone and most governments obtain their revenue through income taxes. Governments cannot collect taxes if people are not working; laid-off workers and firms that have gone out of business have no income to tax. However, protectionism can encourage unproductive and inefficient industries—industries that will eventually fail with or without government intervention. The WTO has a tough road ahead: A further liberalization of trade will be difficult because it involves a further erosion of the traditional prerogatives of states. Government leaders are obviously committed to the principles of free trade; otherwise, they would not have created an organization devoted to perpetuating and enforcing them. Yet, national concerns and national rivalries threaten the expansion of free trade.

MULTINATIONAL CORPORATIONS (MNCS)

MNCs are a potent force behind free trade. The reduction of tariffs, quotas, and NTBs is important to MNCs because it lowers the costs of production and allows them to distribute their product globally. Multinational banks and telecommunications firms are very interested in the liberalization of services because they are poised to enter markets that were previously closed to them. Intellectual property rights, which can range from movies, music, computer hardware, and computer software, to pharmaceuticals and genetics, are also important because MNCs have invested significant resources in their research and development. MNCs are concerned about the pirating of their products by competitors. If a technology or a technique or a product can be easily copied, MNCs stand to lose billions in profits. Without state enforcement of their intellectual property rights, MNCs are reluctant to make the initial investments in research and development.

The activities of MNCs are, of course, controversial, accounting, in some part, for the controversies attending trade as an international issue. Furthermore, MNCs have changed considerably since they first became an integral part of the trading scene. Early MNCs were largely European- or American-owned firms that were involved in extracting raw materials, including oil and ores. They were headquartered in advanced industrialized countries and their subsidiaries were located in colonies and former colonies. The subsidiaries exported raw materials to the West where they were turned into a variety of manufactured goods by both national and multinational firms. The manufactured goods were then exported to the developing world for sale. Developing states experienced chronically bad terms of trade because exports of relatively cheap raw materials could not balance out the far more expensive manufactured imports.

MNCs changed their direct foreign investment strategy when they ventured into manufacturing outside their home countries. MNCs now engage in horizontal investment whereby they manufacture the same goods everywhere. This allows them to bypass protectionism in host countries (Gilpin 1987, 254). Host countries gained the advantage of goods produced within their territory; however, their domestic industries were displaced and their infant industries were unable to compete with the more seasoned and advanced industries. Home countries, too, suffered disadvantages; manufacturing jobs were lost and industries waned as MNCs adjusted and expanded into new markets.

During the 1980s, MNCs shifted to a vertical investment strategy, in which outputs of some factories serve as inputs for others (Gilpin 1987, 255). The production process is broken down into its component parts and distributed around the world. The purchase of a manufactured product is now a global transaction, from concept to design and manufacture, and then to the showroom floor (or Internet site). For example, a multinational automobile company producing a car for U.S. markets might have the automobile designed in Germany, the electronics assembled in Korea, the brakes made in Mexico, and the tires made in Ohio. The product is then assembled in stages at different plants before it is turned out to market. Profits for the sale of that automobile are distributed to shareholders from around the world. In short, MNCs have developed global economies of scale and have become truly multinational in nature. While MNCs are still mainly headquartered in the West, they have shareholders globally. Their primary allegiance is to their shareholders, and not necessarily to the countries in which they are located.

The WTO is currently holding talks with officials mainly from advanced industrialized countries regarding a Multilateral Investment Agreement (MIA). The MIA would greatly restrict the ability of governments at all levels (national, state or provincial, and local) to regulate the activities of MNCs. The MIA would restrict the government's ability to give preferential treatment to local firms or to require the use of local services, workers, and products. The MIA also would give MNCs standing to sue governments. The MIA is still in early stages of negotiations; however, its emphasis is clearly comprehensive. Government regulation of MNCs and their activities can be interpreted as inhibiting free trade and, therefore, impermissible under WTO rules.

Free trade, the WTO, and MNCs have many opponents. Free trade is not always seen as a universal good. It creates winners and losers, and the benefits of trade are often grossly unequal in terms of distribution. Entire groups within and between societies are marginalized. Many argue that the WTO magnifies and intensifies the differences between winners and losers, claiming that the winners come out on top not by virtue of extraordinary market savvy or some revolutionary innovation, but because they are powerful enough to create the rules that inevitably favor them. Some predict that the WTO and MNCs will dismantle the capitalist welfare state because it is too interventionist. Free traders want governments that are laissez-faire, regardless of what the people in democratic societies may want, all for the sake of efficiency and corporate profits.

The arguments of both the opponents and the proponents of the WTO and free trade are shaped by their world views, and each emphasizes different aspects of trade. In the following case study of the WTO and the U.S. Clean Air Act, we look at the pros and the cons of free trade.

CASE STUDY 5: THE U.S. CLEAN AIR ACT

In 1996, the first grievance was filed with the newly created WTO. This grievance, lodged by Brazil and Venezuela against the United States, claimed that certain provisions of the 1990 U.S. Clean Air Act discriminated against their gasoline exports to the United States. Under Environmental Protection Agency (EPA) regulations, gasoline companies must produce the same quality of gasoline that they produced in 1990 (Crow 1996, 37). That is, the Agency pegged the amount of pollutants released into the atmosphere to 1990 levels in an effort to stabilize that amount. Accordingly, each company was assigned a different baseline level because each company produced different kinds and quality of gasoline during the baseline year. Determining the 1990 baseline quality of domestic producers was relatively easy and readily verifiable; however, determining the baselines of gasoline imported from foreign sources was not. As a result, the EPA assigned foreign producers a special baseline—one that was the "average" of all the domestic producers in 1990.

In their complaint, Brazil and Venezuela argued that the EPA regulation discriminated against their exports and was an impermissible barrier to trade. They claimed that the environmental standards set for their companies were unfairly high and that their firms should receive the same treatment as U.S. domestic producers. In other words, the Brazilian and Venezuelan firms ought to have an individual, not an average, 1990 baseline. In response, the United States argued that its domestic producers would face unfair competition. The foreign imports would be cheaper because the imports were of a lesser quality, falling far below the U.S. average (*Oil and Gas Journal* 1996, 21). The WTO convened a panel of experts to review the grievance and ruled, in January 1996, that the EPA regulations did in fact discriminate against imported gasoline. The United States appealed the decision, but the ruling was upheld by the WTO appellate body in April 1996.

The Clean Air Act case was an important test of the WTO as a governance institution. The grievance filed by Brazil and Venezuela marked the first time WTO procedures were used to authoritatively resolve disputes, and it involved its most powerful member, the United States. As James Baccus, a U.S. representative to the WTO appellate body, said, "Without the U.S., the WTO would weaken and wither away. It would become a commercial 'League of Nations' incapable of enforcing the rules of trade. The emerging rule of law in world trade would be replaced by a ruinous reign of commercial chaos, confusion and collapse" (cited in Crow 1996, 37). Nevertheless, the WTO told the strongest country in the world that one of its environmental regulations was an unfair barrier to international trade; moreover, the United States abided by the WTO ruling. The EPA has since revised its rules to permit foreign producers to petition the EPA for individual baselines for gasoline exported to the United States.

What lessons are to be learned from this case? What issues and actors are important for understanding international trade? Did the WTO and the countries involved make the right decisions? How do their decisions affect individuals and groups within and between societies?

A REALIST CUT

Traditional realists and economic nationalists see the WTO ruling as an unacceptable erosion of state sovereignty. They fear that the WTO will undermine governments, compromising their ability to regulate the domestic economy. The capacity of WTO officials to review government policies and to declare them "impermissible" effectively means that the WTO has the final say regarding policy and regulation. This interpretation of WTO sovereignty over the U.S. government is rather extreme; the United States can, in fact, withdraw from the WTO or simply ignore its decisions. Criticisms of the WTO as a threat to sovereign prerogatives make good press for conservative politicians, but do not translate into any measurable loss of sovereignty. As Clayton Yeutter, the trade representative during the Reagan administration, said, "The sovereignty argument is pointless, for every trade agreement we've signed in the past 200 years has in some way infringed on our sovereignty" (cited in Crow 1996, 37).

Neorealists see in the WTO a useful tool, one the United States can use to achieve its immediate and long-term trading goals. Recall that neorealists and neomercantilists are all for free trade and markets when it suits national interests. Participation in markets is seen as the path to great-power status. Free trade or markets, however, should not prevail if the national security is threatened. An EPA regulation implementing the Clean Air Act is hardly a pressing national security interest of the United States. In fact, the EPA regulation itself compromised U.S. energy security because it limited the number of suppliers of petroleum products (*Oil and Gas Journal* 1996, 21). While crude oil supplies are important for national security, so are reformulated gasoline sources. Increasing the number of suppliers, both domestic and foreign, has always been the goal of the United States. U.S. domestic firms are not seriously threatened by foreign competition, so no governmental protection is necessary (Buckley 1996, 70).

In deciding to abide by the WTO ruling, the United States made a shrewd political move. The WTO nullifies a law that sets environmental standards too high for domestic and foreign producers of gasoline alike. Meantime, the United States publicly sacrifices its sovereignty for the "collective good," thereby setting the precedent for WTO authority internationally. The United States gains additional suppliers of reformulated gasoline while simultaneously strengthening the organization it has long wanted to create. A robust WTO is necessary to root out and eliminate trade discrimination, the vast majority of which is against U.S. products and services (Buckley 1996, 70).

Thus, the United States sacrifices little and gains a lot. National governments want organizations like the WTO to support their policies, share the blame for unpopular measures, and increase their access to markets and resources (Bayne 1997). The WTO decision in the Clean Air Act case fits the bill. Since this case, the WTO has often ruled in favor of the United States against some of its more intractable trading partners. For example, the United States received a favorable ruling against the EU in an important computer networking case (Sanger 1998, C1). The WTO will also be extremely useful to the United States in trade negotiations with Japan (Lincoln 1997). For neorealists, the issue turns less on sovereignty and more on security. The central question, then, is how an international organization can facilitate the long-term economic and security goals of the United States. The United States can certainly ignore any WTO decision that genuinely threatens its security—and WTO officials know it. Therefore, they are not likely to issue any such decision.

A LIBERAL CUT

The WTO ruling in the Clean Air Act case demonstrates the constructive role that a liberal supranational institution can have on the settlement of trade disputes. The United States, having quarreled with Brazil and Venezuela about the legitimacy of the EPA regulations for several years, had achieved no breakthroughs in the ongoing negotiations. In 1994, the EPA had proposed new regulations that would have allowed foreign producers to petition the EPA for an individual baseline, provided supporting data were supplied (Crow 1996, 37). The U.S. Congress rejected this proposal, despite EPA claims that most foreign gasoline was likely to be on par with domestic gasoline. According to Jeffrey Schott of the Institute of International Economics, the "U.S. implicitly admitted the violation and attempted to negotiate a settlement with Venezuela" (cited in Crow 1996, 37). The WTO confirmed what many trade experts already knew—the regulation unfairly and unnecessarily discriminated against Venezuelan and Brazilian exports.

The Clean Air Act case was a technical, complicated trade issue, not the broad environmental issue portrayed in the media. The preamble of the WTO recognizes the importance of environmental protection and concerns. The WTO incorporates the GATT exception to discriminatory measures used to meet valid societal goals such as environmental protection. The panel of trade experts determined that the regulation was not crucial to environmental protection and served only to exclude imports. The continued existence of the regulation is more likely the result of congressional parochialism and bureaucratic inertia.

The WTO remains concerned about the environment and has created a committee to consider the impact of free trade on the environment. It must also be recognized that trade protectionism can be quite sophisticated, often well hidden in politically popular policies. Unilateral environmental regulations are important and legitimate prerogatives of states; however, they may not be used to discriminate against foreign imports when no environmental benefit can be demonstrated.

The principal goal of the WTO is to liberalize trade, which can be compatible with environmental protection (Steinberg 1997). According to liberals, free trade generates the resources necessary for environmental protection, leads to environmental technologies, and forces the efficient use of natural resources through competition (Nissen 1997). The link between wealth and high environmental standards has been clearly established: Wealthy societies can afford stringent environmental regulations. Trade liberalization encourages multilateral efforts to protect the environment, raising the environmental standards in the developing world.

For liberals, the Clean Air Act case was an NTB case—one that the WTO helped to denationalize and depoliticize by using scientific data and trade experts to distinguish between permissible state policy and illegal protectionism. Trade and environmental protection must be allowed to reach a global balance or equilibrium. The issues of trade and the environment encompass a multitude of groups with competing national and international interests. Liberals see the market as the best mechanism for balancing all these interests at a price individuals from all nations are willing to pay.

A MARXIST CUT

For Marxists, the Clean Air Act case demonstrates that environmental protection and free trade are rarely compatible. The WTO prefers businesses over people and threatens other laws designed to protect the environment and consumers (Khor 1996). Businesses, free markets, and free trade are privileged at the cost of consumers, workers, and the environment (Laarman 1996). Worse, the WTO has overridden the wishes of the American people: "Industry pounded the Clean Air Act at every stage of the lawmaking process: in congressional hearings, in congressional drafting of the legislation, in the EPA's protracted rule-making process, in threatened lawsuits. Venezuela was well represented too, by the elite Washington, D.C., law firm of Arnold and Porter" (*Multinational Monitor* 1996, 5). When those efforts failed, the WTO finished the assault.

Marxists assert that the domestic and foreign components of the oil industry are the chief beneficiaries of the WTO ruling—a notion confirmed by the industry's own leading journal: "[T]he EPA may find itself so distracted by the politics of foreign baselines that it loses its taste for even stricter regulation of U.S. gas" (*Oil and Gas Journal* 1996, 21). Existing and future environmental regulations must, perforce, take a back seat to the expansion of trade. The WTO rejected the argument that the EPA regulation was designed to achieve the valid goal of limiting the amount of pollutants in the air. As a result, substandard gasoline may now be imported to the United States while the EPA is deterred from raising gasoline standards.

The WTO decision is problematic for two reasons. First, the WTO emphasizes markets and trade as a solution to social and environmental problems and does not consider that they might be part of the problem. The cause of environmental problems lies in the use of natural resources to produce goods for ever-expanding markets. Lip service to "sustainable development" notwithstanding, the WTO Committee on Trade and the Environment is more concerned with the effect of environmental protection upon free trade than with the impact of trade upon the environment (Williams 1996). Within the WTO framework, there is no provision to coordinate multilateral environmental and trade negotiations. Thus many multilateral environmental treaties can either be nullified by the WTO or marginalized in the wake of fast-track trade negotiations. Even liberals recognize that the WTO does not distinguish between national and international environmental protection measures, and that WTO procedures must be amended to ensure environmental protection both nationally and internationally (Helm 1996; Hudnall 1996; Steinberg 1997; Nissen 1997; Schoenbaum 1997).

Second, the WTO is shrouded in secrecy (Weissman 1994). WTO hearings are closed to the public and documents are classified. The public and NGOs have little input in the decision-making process. MNCs, on the other hand, are amply represented by their governments, whose officials participate in the WTO. These companies help to elect public officials in each country; furthermore, they happen to be the countries' largest employers. Also, MNCs fund research, raising concerns about a corporate bias in scientific studies on environmental effects. Many of the scientists conducting these studies have been employed by the very industries suspected of causing the alleged environmental damage (Castleman and Lemen 1998, 28). The "neutrality" of the WTO, putatively based in impartial science and economics, really advances the interests of international business at the expense of national industries, the environment, and labor.

The incompatibility of environmental protection and free trade is demonstrated by the "race to the bottom" phenomenon (Brecher and Costello 1994). Societies around the world are reducing labor and environmental protections in order to attract foreign direct investment and to keep firms from relocating abroad. The WTO's mission is to lower trade barriers to promote international competition. It also creates competition among governments to attract businesses to locate within their territory and to employ their citizens. Environmental and labor regulations are being attacked both domestically and internationally. The result is an overall reduction in the protection of people globally. Since the WTO ruling in the Clean Air Act case, environmental regulations protecting dolphins and sea turtles have been ruled as impermissible barriers to trade (*New York Times* 1998, A18).

A FEMINIST CUT

Feminists argue that the central problem with the WTO is its assumption that trade liberalization and WTO policies have gender-neutral effects. Feminists maintain that trade liberalization has differential effects on women and men, particularly as it relates to their wages, employment, and social burden (Wide 1998). The lowering of wages and the displacement of workers affect women in the workplace and in the home (see Chapter 8). The lowering of trade barriers encourages firms to exploit cheap sources of labor, which, because of the wage differential, are mostly women in the developing world. Feminists also decry the absence of women in key policy-making positions within the WTO and the exclusion of women as subjects of study in trade analyses.

The Clean Air Act case exemplifies how the environment and other social causes are marginalized by the pursuit of free trade. While the nullification of one regulation does not have a direct effect on all women, it shows that WTO trivializes issues that tend to be important to women. If environmental regulations are vulnerable in the most advanced and industrialized economies, then environmental protection in less developed countries (LDCs) becomes less likely. Women's experiences in the developing world are different from men's (and from Western women's) because they are directly tied to the environment for their survival. Environmental degradation lowers the quality of life for women and children.

The discourse attending the Clean Air Act case accents the masculine bias of the WTO's liberal orientation. Postmodern feminists point out that a superior-subordinate relationship obtains between the issues of free trade and the environment. Free trade is given priority "because liberal conceptions of progress have fostered a split between man and nature where nature is to be dominated (Ashworth and Swatuk 1998, 87). Natural resources are to be exploited, and "science" and "development" will save the world from the consequences of environmental degradation. The treatment of trade and the environment as separate, technical issues is a very masculine way of understanding the world (Shiva 1989). By breaking down trade and environmental regulation into their smallest components, WTO experts have, in effect, "missed the forest for the trees." Every environmental regulation distorts trade in some manner.

CHALLENGES FOR THE WTO

The WTO is a fledgling organization created in a posthegemonic era. The United States has declined in terms of its leadership capabilities, but its liberal ideology has no immediate rival. The WTO faces an uncertain political and economic future. The Clean Air Act case foreshadows environmental protection as one of the principal challenges for the WTO. Some scholars argue that international organizations guided by a "global ecological Keynesianism" can sustain capitalism and free trade (Murphy 1994). However, if recent WTO decisions are any indication of future decisions, the environment will continue to take a backseat to trade liberalization and the expansion of markets. As we will discuss in Chapter 10, some liberals argue that markets are the best way to protect the environment.

In 1997, the WTO and its member states reached a historic deal regarding the liberalization of financial sectors. The international response to the WTO-sponsored agreement was mixed and can be broken down by world view. Realist or economic nationalist sentiments were evident. According to Russia's reformist *Izvestia*: The "agreement in Geneva will create problems for Russia and other countries that are in the process of joining the WTO, since, being no party to the talks, they will have to accept the levels of liberalization established in Geneva" (U.S. Information Agency 1997d, 2). Malaysia, too, questioned the pace of liberalization. According to the government-influenced *Business Times*:

> Malaysia needs to be comfortable with the march [toward liberalization] too; just as the United States took more than 50 years to grow into a global and economic titan, Malaysia and other developing countries also need to be stable and strong enough to face the challenges of liberalization. Involving the people without solid preparations would be tantamount to economic suicide. (U.S. Information Agency 1997d, 5)

Even countries that have traditionally been guided by liberal ideals are worried about growing protectionism in the advanced industrialized countries. Sweden's conservative *Svenska Dagbladet* states:

> Protectionist currents have, on the contrary, grown stronger lately and most clearly this can be noticed in the United States, where President Clinton lost his 'fast track authority' about a month ago. The development in the United States is not unique. Also within the EU there is a constant struggle between the supporters of free trade and the protectionists. (U.S. Information Agency 1997d, 5–6)

Realists point out that the incentives to free-ride on the trade liberalization are great, given uncertain political and economic futures.

Liberals applauded the agreement as a success for global governance. According to India's *Indian Express*:

> The financial services agreement is the third feather in the World Trade Organization's cap this year, after the information technology and telecoms agreements. Given the Asian crisis, any financial services pact is an achievement. . . . Anti free trade voices have been particularly sharp in America of late. In the end, it was at once a true compromise. (U.S. Information Agency 1997d, 6)

This sentiment is shared by *The Australian*:

> As the Asian currencies have fallen to new lows in recent days, the World Trade Organization pact signals a welcome renewal of the region's commitment to freer and fairer trade. . . . It reassures investors in Asia that the region's governments are serious about more transparency and certainty for overseas investors, while recognizing that policies which protect domestic industry at the expense of competition are likely to exacerbate their national economic problems." (U.S. Information Agency 1997d, 4)

Predictably, the Marxist world view is not nearly as optimistic as the liberal world view. According to Hong Kong's *South China Morning Post*:

> It is striking how the delight over last weekend's 102-nation pact to liberalize financial services has come from the Americans and Europeans. It is they who stand to benefit the most from the World Trade Organization accord to open up markets all over the world for powerful multinationals to dominate. . . . U.S. Trade Representative Charlene Barshefsky could scarcely contain her jubilation, talking of it in terms of a trade deal rather than a genuine attempt at liberalization, and frankly admitting that it would provide tremendous opportunities for American firms. (U.S. Information Agency 1997d, 4)

The liberalization of financial services allows foreign firms unprecedented access to domestic banking and insurance industries. Such access can destabilize developing countries and threaten national firms.

In August 2000, a United Nations–appointed study team reported that the WTO was a "nightmare" for developing countries and should be brought under UN scrutiny (*Reuters* 2000, 13). The UN Subcommission on the Promotion and Protection of Human Rights concluded that rules are "grossly unfair and even prejudiced" and "reflect an agenda that serves only to promote the dominant corporatist interests (*Earth Island Journal* 2001, 16). This UN report, along with other types of international criticism, has raised questions regarding the legitimacy and the promise of the WTO.

The WTO has also come under fire from its own members. In October 2000, the smaller members called for a change in the WTO dispute system. Led by Japan, the smaller countries argued that "the U.S. and the EU are using the dispute settlement rules in ways that suit them and not abiding by the rules for everyone else" (Olsen 2000, 9). Under existing rules the plaintiff party determines whether the defendant country is in compliance with the WTO ruling. This allows large states, with large economies, more leverage because the compliance decision can used as a negotiating tool. If a state is found in violation of WTO rules, that complaining party is allowed to impose trade sanctions against the offending party. Those sanctions are supposed to be lifted when the complaining party is satisfied of compliance. In practice, this has allowed large economies, like the United States and the EU, to use a determination of compliance (regardless of whether or not the practice has actually stopped) to get concessions from the defendant state in any kind of negotiating situation. This means that the United States and EU, if they are in conflict, can reach a compliance agreement to satisfy each other but not actually comply with WTO rules. Because the economies are valuable to each other they can use compliance as carrot or stick in their relations. Conversely, the smaller states lack the clout to force compliance from the larger economies. The larger economies simply acknowledge the WTO ruling and accept sanctions without actually complying. Put another way, the large economies know sanctions against them hurt the small states more, which reduces the bargaining power of small states. The Japanese-led coalition wants to change the rules so that the WTO determines whether or not a state is in compliance with WTO rules, and not the plaintiff state. To date, the United States and the EU have resisted this particular reform.

The process of liberalization that is taking place under the auspices of the WTO tends to be divorced from issues of social justice. The disparity of wealth and other forms of economic and social inequity cause instability and conflict between rich and poor. How the WTO "experts" define the issues of social justice and the causes of inequities will be important in managing internal and international conflict. How WTO officials define issues will depend on their world view, which, at this point, is plainly liberal. In the following case study, we examine the contentious trade issue of Genetically Modified (GM) foods. What is GM food? Is GM food safe? Do states have the right to regulate the trade of GM foods and organisms? Is such regulation impermissible protectionism? What is the role of international organizations in this trade debate?

CASE STUDY 6: GENETICALLY MODIFIED FOODS AND ORGANISMS

Genetically Modified (GM) foods and organisms are products that have had their DNA and other genetic materials manipulated by scientists. Unlike hybrid plants, which involves the joining of related plants and organisms, GM products have the desired gene from one organism—a bacterium, plant, or animal, implanted into the DNA of another organism (Maynard 2000). Consider a GM soybean. "A soy DNA is spliced with petunia DNA to produce a plant engineered to survive otherwise toxic doses of herbicide" (Maynard 2000). This would mean that weeds could easily be killed among the standing soybean crops. This process of genetic engineering is also called "transgenesis" or "transgenetic" manipulation. This process allows scientists to create crops that are disease- and insect- resistant or that are high in minerals or vitamins. This, in turn, leads to higher crop yields and less pesticide and herbicide use. The most common GM foods include corn, soybeans, potatoes, and tomatoes, and their derivatives like corn flour or tomato sauce.

As a trade issue, GM products have several points of contention. The first point of contention focuses on the intellectual property rights of GM products. Can firms patent a tomato or potato line once it has been genetically manipulated? This has significant implications because if GM foods and organisms become mainstream within the food supply, MNCs could own the intellectual property of the food basics. At the same time, MNCs such as Monsanto and DuPont have invested vast resources into the development of GM products and want a return on their investment. A second point relates to the safety of GM products. Do these products pose a hazard to humans, plant or animal life, and the environment? Critics of GM products say safety tests have not been adequate to insure public health or environmental protection. Third, how should trade in GM products be regulated? Given the promise and the potential threat of GM foods, governments have had to navigate a political minefield to craft trade policies that balance domestic concerns with the requirements of a liberal trading order. Trade policies have been categorized as "Promotional," "Permissive," "Precautionary," and "Preventive" depending on the degree to which governments attract or deter GM products (Paarlberg 2001, 27).

GM products are a source of friction between the United States and EU and between the United States and developing countries. These countries disagree regarding the benefits and risks associated with GM foods and these disagreements have manifested themselves in a full-fledged trade dispute. The WTO has not formally addressed the issue; however, a case, filed by Thailand in 2000, is now pending (*Agra Europe* 2000). In January 2000, 130 states met in Montreal to hammer out an agreement on biosafety rules, called the Biosafety Protocol. This treaty, which pitted the United States against everyone else, allows states to bar imports of genetically modified seeds, microbes, animals, and crops that they deem may harm the environment (Pollack 2000, A1). Critics of the treaty claim it contains too many loopholes; however, it does recognize that GM products are distinct and need to be regulated separately from other products (Pollack 2000, A6). While the central aim of the treaty is to protect the environment of unintended consequences of genetic engineering, the United States has argued that such protection can also be used to discriminate against U.S. agricultural exports and MNCs. The controversy surrounding GM products has not gone away as the EU has continued to reject GM exports from the United States. How do we understand and make sense of this issue?

A REALIST CUT

The issue of GM foods and organisms relates to national security in two interrelated ways. The first has to do with the safety of the GM products. States must ensure the safety of GM foods for human consumption and for the environment. Governments should not rely on the assurances of MNCs, which supposedly have conducted exhaustive tests, or on international agreements for safety guarantees. International agreements by their very nature are watered down compromises and not an adequate form of protection. The increase of "bio-threats" make it incumbent upon governments to ensure food safety themselves. Second, the state must achieve food security. That is, the state must ensure that the country has enough food to sustain itself. If GM products can deliver on their promises, then countries, especially the poor ones that have chronic food shortages, should embrace the technology. Government should avoid becoming dependent on foreign MNCs for the bulk of their food supply and should be willing to challenge patents and intellectual property rights. In other words, they should accept intellectual property rights on paper, but not actually enforce them. Their farmers and national industries should take full advantage of the new technology if it is proven safe.

The experience of European states serves as an example of how states put their national interest in restricting GM foods and organisms ahead of European unity and good trade relations with the United States. Their experience with "mad cow" disease, bacteria-contaminated meat, benzine in soft drinks, hoof-and-mouth disease, and dioxin in poultry, pork, and beef has called into question the efficacy of EU in assuring health and consumer protection. As a result, the screening of GM products for biosafety is done at the national level (Paarlberg 2001, 23). In 1999, France banned a type of GM maize because a sufficient risk assessment had not been conducted (*Agra Europe* 1999). The EU has since issued a moratorium on approving genetically modified organisms at the behest of EU governments until EU regulations are updated to satisfy public concerns. Until European governments have reviewed the safety of GM foods, they will only allow the import of those proven safe. Good relations with the United States depends on much more than the trade of a few GM seeds and crops. The recent terrorist attacks on the United States have put this particular trade issue on the back burner. While U.S. firms and farmers have lost nearly $1 billion in exports, the war on terrorism has made a U.S. complaint to the WTO a remote possibility. According to Carol Forman, member of Bush's agricultural trade policy advisory committee, "We have every reason to get along with the European Union right now. They are our biggest supporters in a life-and-death struggle" (Lambrecht 2001, A8). States need to make calculated decisions based on their national interest and their bargaining position at the time.

Similarly, many developing countries have resisted GM products by refusing to buy GM seeds and planting them. Countries like Kenya, India, and Brazil have very precautionist policies because of the safety concerns; however, their dependence on food assistance from donor countries like the United States leaves little choice in terms of what to accept in humanitarian aid. China, on the other hand, has embraced GM technology and has engaged in large-scale planting. U.S. firms, however, remain concerned about their intellectual property rights.

A Liberal Cut

Genetically modified foods and organisms represent a technological innovation that could revolutionize food production on a global scale and better the lives of millions of people. In addition to higher crop yields and less use of pesticides and herbicides, GM foods hold a great deal of promise, which includes frost-tolerant sugar cane, rice engineered with vitamin A to prevent blindness in the people of developing countries, milk with reduced lactose for lactose intolerant people, nuts and other products that do not cause allergies, cereals with enhanced fiber content, oil with increased essential fatty acids, and fruit with increased vitamin and mineral content (Maynard 2000, 22). Such innovations are important if we are going to able to feed nearly 9.1 billion people, the Earth's expected population in 2050.

Genetic modification techniques also have nonfood applications. Genetically modified crops can be used to produce modified oils, chemicals for the pharmaceutical industry, and biodegradable plastics (Halford 2001). Human testing has already begun on edible plant vaccines against diarrhea, E. coli, and Hepatitis B, which could be extremely beneficial to countries that do not have access to clean syringes and needles (Halford 2001).

Neoclassical liberals argue that "hysteria" surrounding GM food is unfounded. Firms that specialize in GM foods and organisms have strong incentives not to bring to market products that are harmful. Companies like DuPont and Monsanto spend millions of dollars on research and development to ensure the safety of their products. It would be irrational for them to place products on the market that could harm their customers, destroy their reputations, and anger their shareholders. If the self-interest of MNCs is not enough, these firms must also jump through governmental hoops to prove their products are safe. In the United States, GM food and organisms are tested according to U.S. Department of Agriculture (USDA) and the Environmental Protection Agency guidelines. One of the most prestigious organizations, the National Research Council, has systematically analyzed the data and found that environmental concerns, such as whether GM crops spliced with a pesticidal trait might impact nontarget species, are real. However, the impact is likely to be smaller than the impact of using chemical pesticides, the traditional way of protecting crops (*Journal of Environmental Health* 2000). European and EU complaints regarding GM crops and their subsequent restriction amounts to protectionism, which will make their farmers even more inefficient than they already are. Europe, leading the developing countries, is using national passions and unfounded fears regarding safety to discriminate against higher quality products. They may protect farmers in the short term but the consequence is the stunting of Europe's GM industries that will make them even more uncompetitive in the long term (*The Economist* 1998b).

Other liberals do not see the controversy surrounding GM food and organisms as a necessarily bad thing. NGOs, women's groups, MNCs, and the scientific community have put forth their views in the free market place of ideas, which has led to the development of knowledge regarding GM food and organisms. Almost all of the scientific evidence suggests that GM food is safe; however, these groups have brought to the forefront potential problems, such as new allergies and unintended environmental consequences. It has contributed to the growing partnerships between otherwise adversarial groups. For example, the top economic advisor to DuPont is Paul Gilding, the former head of Greenpeace (Friedman 1999, A31). In 2000, more than fifty MNCs have joined a UN environmental pact that obligates them to take steps toward improving the environment. The UN has suggested that GM foods be available to poor countries to alleviate poverty and malnutrition as the benefits outweigh the risks (Schrope 2001, 109). The competition of interests between all the involved parties can lead to an equilibrium of interest in which all needs are addressed.

NGOs have lobbied governments and IGOs extensively to at least give consumers a choice of whether to consume GM foods and organisms. The bulk of these lobbying efforts have been geared toward labeling of GM products. These efforts have been more successful outside the United States because current U.S. regulations do not distinguish between GM food and other types of food. Firms are concerned that the public is misinformed about the risks and the benefits of GM foods and organisms and labeling the foods would make them unsellable. This is supported by the EU market research agency, Eurobarometer, when it found that ill-informed skepticism was fueling the public's aversion to GM food (*Agra Europe*, April 28, 2000). The better approach is to provide the public with as much information as possible without implementing unnecessary regulations. This can be accomplished through international cooperation. The EU and the UN have agreed to set up an international biosafety information exchange center with a Web site open to the public (*European Report* 2000, 504). "The center will collect legislative, legal, and scientific data on genetically modified organisms (GMO) and how they are marketed and compile a list of the GMOs that are authorized or banned in each country. It will be run by independent experts, research scientists, lawyers, representatives of industrial concerns and nongovernmental organizations (*European Report* 2000, 504). International organizations can bring a variety of resources—diplomatic, technical, and financial—to bear on problems to the satisfaction of most of the interested parties.

A MARXIST CUT

The controversy surrounding GM food and organisms illustrates the power of MNCs to manipulate scientific studies, government agencies, and international organizations. First, many of the scientific studies of GM food have been funded by the MNCs themselves. Monsanto, DuPont, and Cargill have spent millions of dollars researching the safety of their products and, not surprisingly, have found that their products are safe. Scientists and researchers are well aware of which "scientific" results lead to more funding and research grants. Serious questions remain about the adequacy of the testing, the validity of the conclusions, and therefore the safety of GM products (Callahan 2000; *Greenpeace* 1999; Warwick 2000; Klotter 2001). Government agencies do not provide an effective check. Government agencies such as the USDA, the FDA, and the EPA implement regulations that favor and are tailored to the needs of business. These firms have contributed millions of dollars to elect officials who will serve their interests. These officials in return pass laws that favor the GM firms. Agencies in the United States proceed on the premise that products are safe until proven hazardous. Risk tests are only done on GM foods that have a history of causing allergies or illness (Pires-O'Brien 2000). If government agencies are effective at restricting these GM products of questionable safety, then MNCs can turn to international organizations. The EU is already moving to force its members to lift its ban on GM products and the UN is advocating the use of GM foods in developing countries. It is only a matter of time before the WTO weighs in on the issues and it is a sure bet that they will deem the safety regulations of member states as an impermissible nontariff barrier to trade. MNCs are able to coopt personnel of governments, IGOs, and many NGOs.

One of the more troubling aspects of GM foods and organisms is the insistence of MNCs and their home governments on the acquisition and enforcement of intellectual property rights. This amounts to the privatization of nature, as MNCs tinker with the genetic makeup of plants and animals and then claim ownership of the genetic material. Increasingly, every aspect of life right down to the DNA is reduced to private property. Resources belonging to everyone are few as MNCs are insisting that governments and the WTO grant and enforce their property rights. This amounts to the "highjacking of the global food supply" and "biopiracy" (Shiva 1997; 1999).

The liberal promise of GM food as a means of alleviating world hunger and malnutrition is also problematic. Currently, there is enough food to meet the nutritional needs of every man, woman, and child on the planet. The dire Malthusian predictions of population growth outpacing food production have not come true because of innovations in agriculture. Yet, today millions of people die from starvation because they do not have access to food. Today, millions of tons of food spoil because the market is oversaturated. The market distributes food resources only to those that can afford to buy them. The supply of food is not why people are starving, it is the way food is distributed. None of the MNCs that produce GM food has ever suggested that food prices might actually decline so that they might be affordable to the world's poor. In fact, the agricultural industry is one of the world's most subsidized industries because, if left to market forces, food prices would collapse. MNCs that produce GM foods and organisms only seek to revolutionize agriculture production to favor their techniques and products; however, they provide no real discernable benefits to the world's population.

MNCs also create a corporate dependence. These firms purchase seed companies and co-ops that sell seeds to local farmers. Farmers are bound by the intellectual property rights of the MNC which means they cannot engage in the time-honored practice of taking the seeds from a harvested crop for the following planting seasons (Grogan and Long 2000, 42). MNCs cannot monitor every farmer from Nicaragua to Nigeria, so they have used GM techniques to create sterile seeds. Termed "terminator" technology, biotech MNCs have developed the ability to engineer sterility into the second generation seeds, which could affect the livelihoods of the 1.4 billion people who rely on farm-saved seeds (Warwick 2000, 50; Paarlberg 2001, 99–100). Farmers would be forced to buy new seeds every year. Another strategy of MNCs is to surround the farmer with interlocking technologies which forces the farmer to buy products from the firm. A firm that sells disease resistant GM seeds may also sell compatible herbicide. Or they may sell an "upgrade" such as a chemical that may improve yields or processability (Warwick 2000, 51). Unless the rights of farmers are protected or the GM technology regulated, MNCs could control the world's food production. This amounts to "biocolonialism."

A FEMINIST CUT

The gender dimensions of the issue of GM foods and organisms are interrelated and threefold. First, it is through NGOs that women have had the greatest voice regarding their concerns about GM products. NGOs such as the Canadian-based Rural Advancement Foundation International or the National Federation of Women's Institutes have been vocal and active opponents of GM technology and have pressured governments to take their concerns seriously. Women, through NGOs, have mobilized to take on the MNCs and their home governments and have been successful in enacting restrictive policies, especially in Europe and India. Other NGOs that have large female participation include The Campaign, Greenpeace, RAGE, Mothers for Natural Law, and the Bioengineering Action Network.

Second, women have been the principal opposition to GM foods. Public opinion polls in the United States and Europe show that women are far more skeptical than men regarding the safety of GM foods. In one ABC television poll, 62 percent of women thought GM foods were unsafe compared to 40 percent of men (Langer 2001). More importantly, 65 percent of women said they are less likely to buy GM products; men only

49 percent (Langer 2001). What accounts for this gender gap? Women's traditional gender roles involve feeding the family unit. This entails subsistence farming in many areas of the developing world and, in the developed countries, women are the primary shoppers. It has been women's groups domestically and internationally that have demanded the right of replicate seeds and the labeling of GM food and organisms. Women seek to have choice about what they feed to their families and, given the uncertain safety of GM foods, they are even willing to pay more for unaltered food (*Pulse* 2000). Women are also more likely to oppose GM food on ethical grounds. Women tend to be more uncomfortable with tinkering with nature and are more wary of the unknown and unforeseen effects of the genetic modification of plants and animals.

Third, the discourse of the debate regarding GM foods emanating from MNCs, governments, and IGOs is quite gendered. Critics of GM foods and organisms are dismissed as hysterical, irrational, and anti-science. Opponents of the labeling of GM foods claim that the public is uninformed regarding the benefits and hazards of GM foods, and labeling will hurt sales and serve no safety purpose. After all, the AMA and the FDA have found that there was "no scientific justification for special labeling of GM foods" (Langer 2001). Examined through a postmodern feminist lens, this translates into saying that women are uninformed and irrational regarding GM foods, so it is up to the FDA and other organizations to protect women from themselves. In other words, women, who do the shopping, are not to be trusted with making consumer choices regarding food. Similarly, any government or IGO that questions the safety or the usefulness of GM foods is feminized as silly and irrational. International organizations, like many NGOs or UN agencies, that highlight the intrusion of culture, power, dominance, or wealth on the practice of science are trivialized and marginalized. In short, hidden gender assumptions are at play in the contentious issue of GM foods and organisms.

CONCLUSION

The debates surrounding the U.S. Clean Air Act and genetically modified foods and organisms demonstrate that trade issues will remain politically charged throughout the twenty-first century. As a result, the WTO, NGOs, and MNCs will be at the center of controversy. As Chapters 8 and 9 demonstrate, trade issues are inextricably tied to economic development and environmental protection. None of these broad issue areas can be divorced from the theoretical frameworks that give meaning and interpretation to the debates.

8

DEVELOPMENT

ECONOMIC DEVELOPMENT represents one of the principal challenges of twenty-first century international relations. Chronic poverty, malnutrition, and disease characterize most of the developing world and are creeping into segments of the developed world. Economic stagnation and rampant inflation cripple economies, causing high levels of debt, unemployment, and underemployment. The economic disparities between rich and poor continue to widen at an accelerated pace. The disparities between rich and poor are contributory causes of war both within and between nations. In the view of many, stable economic development is the best strategy for avoiding violent conflict and averting political upheaval in the future. Unfortunately, no consensus exists as to the causes of poverty or the meaning of development. As a result, development issues remain extremely controversial in international forums.

In this chapter, we examine the controversies surrounding the issues of poverty and development. We look at the international organizations that are involved in economic development and the alleviation of poverty. The Mexican peso crisis and the Indonesian economic meltdown serve as the case studies to illustrate how development issues are directly related to international economic stability. These case studies also show how differing world views expand our understanding of the complexities of international development.

WHAT IS DEVELOPMENT?

The conceptual confusion attending the meaning of "development" emanates from competing world views. Thomas (1998) characterizes the debate as a struggle between the "orthodox" and the "critical." The orthodox approach largely follows the mainstream tradition, interpreting development in the Western, liberal manner. Measured quantitatively with economic statistics, development implies increases in gross domestic product (GDP) per capita over time, and rising levels of industrialization (Sen 1996). It involves the transformation of traditional societies, which are agrarian and subsistence-based, into modern societies founded on wage labor, cash, and consumerism (Rostow 1971). Markets are the preferred solution to poverty and underdevelopment because they have proven to be the most efficient way to promote diversification, industrialization, and production. Markets also efficiently distribute resources and generate significant levels of wealth. The status of the poor within societies will rise as the economy expands.

In the orthodox view, chronic underdevelopment and poverty are the results of irrational state policies and regulations. States that practice extensive protectionism or seek to develop export industries in which they have no comparative advantage encourage inefficient industries. Such industries are doomed to fail because they cannot compete once they are exposed to international competition. The state cannot protect domestic industries indefinitely. Economic development can occur only if states integrate into a global economy based on free trade, specialization, and an international division of labor (Gilpin 1987, 266). Governments that interfere with the price mechanism or seek to bureaucratically "plan" economic development sacrifice efficiency, growth, and wealth for good intentions that cannot be realized.

The obstacles to development include population growth, corruption, and excessive government spending. The poorest developing states have high population growth rates, which undermine their economies' sustainability. Corruption compounds the problem. Venal government officials literally steal millions in foreign assistance for personal gain while forcing MNCs to pay millions in kickbacks and bribes, thus deterring foreign investment. Excessive government spending to subsidize transportation, energy, or prices of manufactured goods creates huge government deficits and massive debt. Many developing states are mired in a cycle of poverty and debt that undermines long-term, stable, sustained economic growth. Development can be accomplished only by introducing significant market reforms and reducing state intervention in the market.

The critical approach is, in a word, critical: It attacks the orthodox view of development because it is ethnocentric and because it is inadequate at measuring the quality of life. Consider the orthodox indicators of development—GDP per capita and levels of industrialization—which take only market exchanges into account. They do not measure barter transactions, nor do they take into account such forms of unpaid labor as the work of women in the home or children on the farm. GDP per capita ignores informal sectors of the economy not exposed to market forces. Western conceptions of development include only the growth and the expansion of the market. They assume that the expansion of the market translates into a higher standard of living for individuals.

The critical approach brings a different, more flexible conception of development to its analyses. Development, to critical theorists, is the ability of people to meet their material and nonmaterial needs through their own efforts (Thomas 1998, 453). This allows different societies to set their own standards for progress and frees them from meeting the Western standard, a standard that judges all societies by the extent to which they resemble the West. Development is measured by different criteria—the fulfillment of basic human needs, the condition of the natural environment, and the extent to which the marginalized are politically empowered (Thomas 1998, 453). These criteria are gauges of the quality of life, not measures of each person's share of the GDP.

GDP and levels of industrialization ignore many quality-of-life issues important in the developing world. They do not measure the extent to which people have access to adequate nutrition or sanitation, nor do they measure the differences between the rich and poor within developing societies. GDP statistics do not show that the gap between rich and poor continues to widen. GDP statistics are also misleading. For example, the value of a forest is not included in GDP calculations until it is cut down and sold as lumber. GDP does, however, include the value of medical services for treating cancer caused by pollution and chemical contamination. Given the disparities between rich and poor in terms of income and quality of life, GDP figures reflect the enrichment of elites in developing countries, but they are silent on the costs to the vast majority of citizens. The orthodox measures are useful only to Western economists trained to understand the world in terms of abstract mathematical models—models they believe to be universal despite their irrelevance to reality in the developing world.

The orthodox approach to development also ignores the colonial history of many developing countries and the patterns of exploitation by former colonial powers. The historical experience of Africa, Asia, and Latin America is significantly different from that of Europe and the United States. According to Frank (1979), underdevelopment of the periphery is a consequence of expanding capitalism. Capitalism in the West flourished because the West had captive resources, labor, and markets. The periphery continues to be exploited through neocolonialism. Developing countries are relegated to subordinate positions in the international division of labor. The developing world continues to provide inexpensive raw materials and labor to the global economy. This subordinate position leads to chronic balance-of-payments difficulties as developing states import expensive manufactured goods. Wealth flows from the periphery into the core.

The critical approach to development focuses on the relative gains between and within societies. In other words, they maintain that the distribution of benefits is important for understanding development. Critical theorists question the orthodox view that everyone benefits from free trade. In periphery societies, millions of people are displaced by governments seeking to develop export industries in specific raw materials. Land that once fed families is now used to produce cash crops to be sold in world markets. Only the elites, who sell cash crops, benefit from exports while the vast majority of the population becomes poorer. Coca-Cola and Adidas sweat pants may now be available at the lowest possible cost; but adequate housing, health care, and educational opportunities are scarce.

Regardless of which view of development you embrace, the development picture of many countries is bleak. One-quarter of the world's population lives on less than $1 a day (Pearlstein 2000, 17). More than 3 billion of the world's 5 billion people live on $2 a day (Kahn 2000, 1). According to the United Nations Human Development Report, the richest fifth of the world's people consumes 86 percent of all the world's goods and services while the poorest fifth consumes 1.3 percent (Crossette 1998). The average African household today consumes 20 percent less than it did twenty-five years ago (Crossette 1998). Of the 4.4 billion people living in developing countries, three-fifths lack access to safe sewers, a third do not have access to clean water, a quarter do not have adequate housing, and a fifth have no access to modern health services (Crossette 1998). The ability of developing countries to increase their GDP and enable their citizens to meet their basic human needs is impaired by the massive debt they have acquired in the last forty years.

DEBT

Between the orthodox and critical views, development issues are extremely contentious; however, the two approaches do have some common ground. Both agree that the principal obstacle to development is external debt. External debt is money that is owed to foreigners and repayable in foreign currency. The external debt of the developing world is estimated to be more than $700 billion, and the servicing of that debt accounts for more than 20 percent of their exports. How did the poorest nations acquire such a large debt? And what are the best ways to handle that debt without compromising economic growth? It is here that the orthodox and critical views part ways: They differ on the origins of debt and hence on strategies for solving the debt crisis.

The orthodox view of development tends to focus on the endogenous, or internal, causes of Third World debt. Excessive government spending and domestic consumer demands led to the explosion of external debt. Governments provided social welfare, health, and educational programs even though they did not have the tax base to support such programs. Third World governments borrowed from abroad instead. They also borrowed money to subsidize the prices of energy and domestic manufactured goods—goods their citizens could ill afford. In addition, Third World governments spent excessively on their militaries. Seeking to modernize their militaries, they spent billions of borrowed dollars to acquire the latest, most sophisticated military hardware. To compound the problem, pervasive government corruption meant that billions of dollars were stolen by the very officials who were supposed to guide the development of their own countries. Many development loans were channeled to inefficient businesses—businesses that had little chance of succeeding in competitive international markets. In sum, developing states simply borrowed more than they could afford, mismanaged a large portion of it, spent a lot of it frivolously, and lived well beyond their means.

Critical approaches to development emphasize the exogenous, or external, causes of Third World debt. Critical theorists argue that the debt of developing states was the result of exogenous factors beyond the control of government officials. Third World external debt began to accumulate when neoliberal economists at the IMF and the World Bank advised developing states to borrow the capital they needed to achieve economic takeoff. However, the international economy was prone to chronic instability during the 1970s, making it extremely difficult for states to plan economic growth. Developing states were forced to borrow heavily from both Western governments and private Western banks, not for economic ventures, but just to survive. Furthermore, much of the bilateral "development" assistance from the West came in the form of "military credit," whereby developing countries received loans solely for the purchase of military hardware. In effect, such loans served as indirect subsidies to Western defense industries, but failed to strengthen Third World economies.

The Third World debt first ballooned after OPEC—the Organization of Petroleum Exporting Countries—quadrupled oil prices in 1973–1974. This action, which triggered the embargo of the United States by OPEC, had its origins in a political dispute between the United States and Arab oil producers, who were angry about U.S. support of Israel during the Arab–Israeli conflict. But the effects of the sharp rise in price were worldwide. Non–oil-producing states were forced to borrow heavily from private and public sources in order to meet their legitimate energy needs. Whereas the West experienced economic stagnation and inflation, developing states suffered more acutely because their economies were not as diversified. Their exports dropped precipitately as no one was buying raw materials for manufacturing. Their fragile economic base was compromised even further when another round of oil price rises in 1978–1979 led to the virtual collapse of their export markets.

During this period, private international banks encountered significant pressure to lend as "petrodollars" began to pour into their accounts. Bankers, eager to put together attractive loan packages to Third World governments, negotiated low but adjustable interest rates. Unfortunately, these loan packages lost their attractiveness as U.S. interest rates rose into double digits, approaching 20 percent by 1979. As a result, developing states were forced to borrow even more at those higher rates just to pay the interest on previous loans. They also had to export more in order to earn the foreign currency to make loan payments. Commodities markets became flooded, lowering prices, then driving them down further. The situation was exacerbated by a full-fledged economic recession in the United States during the early 1980s. The resulting global economic contraction forced the leading Third World debtors, such as Mexico and Brazil, to seek relief from the spiral of external debt service.

The orthodox and critical views of development and debt management are reflected in the international organizations involved in promoting economic development. Public international financial institutions like the World Bank, the IMF, and the regional development banks take a traditional, orthodox approach to international development, as does the WTO. MNCs are also quite orthodox in their outlook. UN bodies directly involved with poverty alleviation and development, such as the UN Conference on Trade and Development (UNCTAD), the UN Industrial Development Organization (UNIDO), and the UN Development Program (UNDP), are more critical in their orientation. Many NGOs, such as Third World Network, Consumers International, and the Asia Indigenous Women's Network, have also adopted a more critical view of development and advocate alternative development strategies. Such strategies include microlending, which was first pioneered by the Grameen Bank of Bangladesh. In the following section, we discuss the World Bank Group, the IMF, UNCTAD, and UNDP in terms of their organizational structures, their roles, and their development approaches.

THE WORLD BANK GROUP

The World Bank Group consists of four distinct but interrelated parts—the International Bank for Reconstruction and Development (IBRD), the International Finance Corporation (IFC), the International Development Association (IDA), and the Multilateral Investment Guarantee Agency (MIGA). The IBRD was created as the development "pillar" under the Bretton Woods system. It is an independent agency within the UN system and is responsible for UN multilateral lending. Originally, the IBRD focused its lending almost exclusively on the reconstruction of Europe. It did not start lending extensively to the developing world until the late 1950s. Multilateral public lending was designed to supplement private loans in order to jumpstart both domestic and foreign investment in Europe and later the Third World. With productive investment, capital would flow to the areas where it is most needed and where the returns on investments are greater.

The International Bank for Reconstruction and Development remains the conservative base of the World Bank Group; it makes traditional loans, although at somewhat lower interest rates than those of commercial banks. The IBRD lends almost exclusively to governments and makes its lending decisions on the basis of a weighted voting scheme that reflects the proportion of member states' contributions. In other words, the IBRD is shareholder-owned. Its resources come from states and from capital markets through private borrowing. Its lending policies are determined by the board of governors. Over time the IBRD has vacillated, shifting from a conservative lending institution to a development agency (Mikesell 1972). The IBRD has sought to alleviate Third World poverty by making loans to governments for projects that contribute to a state's earning and productive capacities (Sanford 1988).

In 1956, the first affiliate of the World Bank, the International Finance Corporation, was created to encourage private investment in developing states (Bennett 1995, 313). The IFC provides "seed money" to attract investment capital from a variety of domestic and foreign sources. The IFC also makes loans and direct equity investments in private companies to stimulate private enterprise and private investment (Riggs and Plano 1994, 288). In 1989, the IFC established the International Securities Group (ISG) to advise companies from the Third World how to issue stocks, for example, and how to get listed on the major stock exchanges (Riggs and Plano 1994, 188). By attracting domestic and foreign investors in the Third World industries and companies, developing countries can accumulate the "critical mass" necessary for sustained economic growth and development.

The International Development Association was created in 1960 to serve the investment needs of the poorest Third World nations. Many developing states are so mired in poverty and burdened by debt that, even under the best of circumstances, they could never meet the conservative lending criteria of the IBRD. Thus, the IDA, the second affiliate of the World Bank, provides "soft" loans—loans whose repayment periods are extensive, ranging from thirty to fifty years, and whose interest rates are very low, ranging between 1 and 3 percent. Some loans may be interest-free, in which case the countries are usually assessed a small administrative fee. In order to qualify for IDA loans, countries must meet income guidelines, measured by GDP per capita. These guidelines are adjusted periodically. In 1997, countries could qualify for IDA loans if their GDP per capita was less than $925. The IDA provides development loans to the poorest of poor in order to generate economic growth in areas otherwise marginalized in the global economy.

In 1988, the Multilateral Investment Guarantee Agency was created as the third affiliate of the World Bank. Although MIGA's goal is similar to that of its affiliate counterparts—encourage domestic and foreign investment in developing economies—it is not a lending agency. Rather, MIGA insures private investment against loss. Specifically, it insures against losses that result from political risk, such as war, civil strife, or expropriation (Riggs and Plano 1994, 289). Thus, MIGA helps private investors spread the risk of investing in politically and economically unstable areas. The guarantee of investments encourages private investors to take a look at otherwise shaky ventures.

The World Bank's Articles of Agreement commit the bank to economic and political neutrality. The World Bank and its affiliates are supposed to make loan determinations on the basis of sound principles of international finance, not a state's political or economic orientation. According to Article 4(10) of the Articles of Agreement:

> The Bank and its officers shall not interfere in the political affairs of any member; nor shall they be influenced in their decisions by the political character of the member or

members concerned. Only economic considerations shall be relevant to their decision, and these considerations shall be weighed impartially in order to achieve the purposes stated in Article I.

In spite of this commitment to political and economic neutrality, the World Bank has been politicized. It serves the political interests of its donors (Ascher 1990, 115–140). The United States, which is the largest contributor to the World Bank, has used its voting share to block loans to politically undesirable states and reward allies. The Bank engaged in significant lending to repressive regimes in the Philippines, Argentina, and Haiti, enabling these regimes to continue their abusive practices. The Bank is also accused of engaging in destabilizing "nonlending." In Chile, for example, it cut off loans to the newly elected Allende government (Brown 1992; Swedburg 1986). Donor efforts to manipulate the Bank's lending and lending policies have drawn international criticism from both orthodox and critical circles.

The World Bank Group is headed by a Board of Governors, one governor for each member state. The Board of Governors, which meets at least once a year, provides long-term strategy for the Bank. Decisions are based on a weighted voting system that is roughly proportional to their share of Bank contributions (which is based on their share of capital and trade). A Board of Directors runs the day-to-day operations of the Bank. It consists of twenty-one directors, who are elected by the Board of Governors. Each director wields the vote of the country that elects him or her (see, e.g., <www.worldbank.org>). The Board of Directors elects the president of the World Bank, who represents the Bank politically and provides leadership and direction.

The World Bank Group is administered by a bureaucracy that strives to distance itself from political control. Under the leadership of former World Bank President Robert McNamara, the World Bank developed considerable autonomy by creating a complex project review process and by boosting the volume of Bank lending. The project review process emphasizes perfection in project proposals. Proposals are "ultrasophisticated—large in scale, elaborate in design, and highly technical" (Ascher 1990, 127). The executive directors, through whom donor states exercise direct influence, are basically presented with polished, finished proposals, which they almost always approve. The World Bank staff helps countries prioritize economic plans and prepare project proposals. The staff is able to exert influence by manipulating what goes before the directors. "The very sophistication of the models on which they [the projects] are based limits the opportunities for criticism, especially from the directors, thus promoting the Bank's autonomy" (Ascher 1990, 127).

The World Bank has also been able to increase the volume of its lending through two measures. First, the World Bank has successfully encouraged contributions from other states, including the oil producers. Second, the Bank has successfully raised money through international capital markets. The increase in the volume of Bank lending has diluted the voting share of some of the larger donors. Changing levels of donations among the larger donors has engendered recurring disagreements as to what particular voting shares should be. In 1986, for instance, Japan sought to increase its voting share in the IDA. The top three contributors to the IDA—the United States, Japan, and West Germany—contributed 25, 18.7, and 11.5 percent, respectively. However, the United States has 20.10 percent of the voting power to Japan's 4.99 percent and Germany's 4.97 percent (*The Economist* 1986, 83). Periodic adjustments in the voting formula are made because of the shifts in contribution levels.

World Bank lending is rarely done in isolation. In fact, it is part of a vast array of co-sponsored projects and programs. Most of the World Bank's loans are used in conjunction or are coordinated with the regional development banks or UN agencies. The World Bank's principal partner in development assistance is the third pillar of the Bretton Woods System, the IMF. The World Bank and the IMF distribute the lion's share of the available multilateral development assistance.

THE INTERNATIONAL MONETARY FUND (IMF)

The International Monetary Fund was also created at the 1944 Bretton Woods conference and was charged with providing for a stable international monetary order. To that end, the IMF coordinates international currency exchange, the balance of international payments, and national accounts (Goldstein 1996, 363). Money is a crucial lynchpin to any economy. It facilitates the efficient exchange of goods and services. However, a stable monetary order is difficult to construct and maintain. A stable monetary order rests on three important factors: liquidity, adjustment, and confidence (Gilpin 1987). Liquidity refers to the amount of currency needed to conduct transactions. Adjustment refers to the mechanism through which national accounts are settled. Confidence refers to a widely held subjective belief that the currency is, and will continue to be, worth what the government says it's worth.

The IMF under the Bretton Woods system provided for a stable monetary order by making the U.S. dollar the key currency, then tying the dollar to a fixed value of gold. One ounce of gold was equivalent to $35. The currencies of the world were then fixed to the dollar. Liquidity was provided by U.S. deficit spending at home and abroad. International markets were flooded with U.S. dollars, which were used to exchange currencies. Adjustment in national accounts was done internally by the IMF and the central banks. When states joined the IMF, their central banks deposited with the IMF a certain amount of their currency and a certain amount of gold and dollars. (Today, countries deposit a certain amount of hard currency.) States could then use these reserves or borrow from the IMF to settle their national accounts. Recall that a state's financial position is related in large part to its balance of trade in goods and services and direct foreign investment. The IMF settled the differences in balance of payments accounts through changes in hard currency reserves. Confidence was provided by U.S. gold reserves.

The Bretton Woods monetary system was based on the idea of "embedded liberalism." Under embedded liberalism, states have a great deal of autonomy with respect to their currency and national accounts. States were permitted, with IMF approval, to readjust their currency exchange rates to help with long-term balance of payments difficulties. States could also borrow money from the IMF to meet their short-term balance of payments deficits. In other words, the IMF is the central bank of the world's central banks. The IMF did much to stabilize the international monetary system during the reconstruction of Europe and Japan.

This pillar of the Bretton Woods system collapsed in 1971 when the United States unilaterally delinked the dollar from gold. The U.S. dollar had become extremely overvalued owing to the deficit spending the U.S. government used to finance the Cold War, the Vietnam War, and Great Society programs. Delinked from gold, the dollar was devalued by more than 10 percent. Consequently, the values of the core currencies were exposed to market forces in a "managed float." That is, the values of major currencies are determined by market-driven flexible exchange rates, but governments can inter-vene to stabilize key currencies experiencing volatility. The IMF now serves as the forum for intergovernmental consultation regarding the management of market-determined exchange rates.

In structure, the IMF is very much like the World Bank (see Figure 8.1), having a Board of Governors and a Board of Directors, over which a managing director pre-sides. Voting is weighted, based on each member's quota. It is administered by a pro-fessional bureaucracy that scrutinizes loan applications based on conservative lending principles. Since the collapse of the monetary pillar of Bretton Woods, the IMF has become increasingly involved with Third World development and the transition of the former Eastern Bloc and Soviet successor states from command to market economies. The currencies of these countries are exceptionally unstable, and the IMF and World Bank have worked together to create comprehensive aid packages designed to pro-vide immediate stability and to stimulate economic growth and long-term develop-ment. In many respects, the IMF has become the "lender of last resort," giving loans to otherwise insolvent governments.

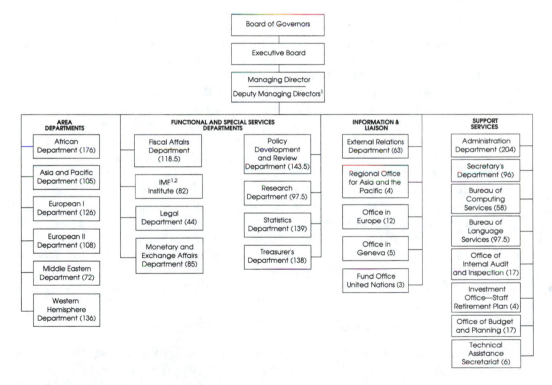

Note: Organization as of April 30, 1998. Parentheses indicate number of budgeted regular staff.
[1]The Institute supports the Joint Vienna Institute, a training center in Vienna, Austria.
[2]Beginning in May 1998, the IMF-Singapore Regional Training Institute, a new regional training center, was established and will receive support from the IMF Institute.

FIGURE 8.1   INTERNATIONAL MONETARY FUND CHART OF ORGANIZATION

Source: Courtesy of the International Monetary Fund.

In the late 1980s, the lending practices of the IMF and the World Bank shifted considerably in response to the Third World debt crisis and the chronic instability of economies in developing states. In the mid-1980s, the debt crisis in the developing world had became so acute that several of the world's largest debtors—Mexico, Brazil, and Argentina—threatened to default on many of their loans. The "normal" capital flows were reversed, with the South sending more capital to the North. The IMF and World Bank, together with private lending institutions, thus engaged in a series of debt restructuring initiatives (even, in rare cases, debt forgiveness) in order to stabilize currencies and economies.

IMF and World Bank loans to developing countries, termed structural adjustment loans, now come "with strings attached." That is, they are conditioned on the recipient state's implementing conventional [orthodox] market reforms (Danaher 1994, 3):

selling state enterprises to the private sector
raising producer prices for agricultural goods
devaluing local currencies to their world market value
reducing government deficits
encouraging free trade
attracting foreign capital

These reforms, which are designed to introduce market forces into the economies of developing states, reflect the orthodox view of development. The orthodox view of development parallels liberalism as a world view in that both see the market as the solution to underdevelopment while ascribing to state intervention and protectionism a causal or exacerbatory role in underdevelopment. Given that trade, development, and currency stability are intertwined, market reforms appear to be essential. Unless these market reforms are made, the IMF and World Bank are, in their view, "just throwing good money after bad." However, structural adjustment loans, and their attendant strings, are controversial because they drastically reduce the role of the government in managing the economy. So controversial are their actions, IMF and the World Bank meetings have been targets of mass, violent demonstrations in Washington, D.C., and Prague in 2000. Ministers, bankers, and other participants needed armed escorts, and police established a two-mile perimeter around the meeting places to keep demonstrators from disrupting the meetings. Now, the IMF and the World Bank must consider security when planning their meetings and have found it difficult to find cities to host the meetings because of the damage caused by the demonstrations.

THE UN CONFERENCE ON TRADE AND DEVELOPMENT (UNCTAD)

Critical responses to orthodox approaches have found a voice in UNCTAD. Created in 1964 by a General Assembly resolution, UNCTAD serves under the auspices of the ECOSOC. UNCTAD emerged as a forum for developing states dissatisfied with their terms of trade, their growing poverty, and Western restrictions on commodities. Ironically, the first UNCTAD was organized by the seventy-seven less-developed nations, known as the Group of 77 or G-77, to pressure the developed countries into further trade liberalization, particularly with respect to commodities and agricultural exports. Led by Raul Prebisch, the former head of the Economic Commission on Latin America (ECLA), UNCTAD 1 argued that reducing tariffs on manufactured products served the interests of the North while ignoring those of the South because developing states' exports (raw materials and commodities) remained subject to steep tariffs. Furthermore, the prices of commodity products were very unstable and any sustained growth in the South would require stable commodity prices. UNCTAD pointed out that the international division of labor relegated the developing states to the relatively unprofitable production of raw materials. As a result, wealth flowed from the South to the North. To counter the net flow of capital to the North, UNCTAD called on the developed states to transfer at least 1 percent of their GNP to developing countries in the form of multilateral development assistance.

The demands of developing states fell largely on deaf ears. The developed countries were strongly opposed to any measures that involved the authoritative, rather than the market, distribution of resources (Krasner 1985). But the Group of 77, a title that now refers to more than 125 developing countries, was able to institutionalize UNCTAD by making it a permanent UN body that reports directly to the General Assembly. The G-77 exercised its majority in the General Assembly to give UNCTAD a larger voice in international trade issues. Located in Geneva, Switzerland, UNCTAD is served by a small Secretariat, and the Conference as a whole meets at least once every three years. The Trade and Development Board meets annually to address the issues of developing states in global trade. UNCTAD is funded through the voluntary contributions of member states and all members of the UN may belong to UNCTAD. Needless to say, contributions from developed nations have been quite small.

UNCTAD has had several plenary meetings: UNCTAD 2 (1968), UNCTAD 3 (1972), UNCTAD 4 (1976), UNCTAD 5 (1979), UNCTAD 6 (1983), UNCTAD 7 (1987), UNCTAD 8 (1992), and UNCTAD 9 (1996). All these meetings have reemphasized the developing world's view that their position in the international division of labor, a position that was coerced and imposed by the North, is the cause of their underdevelopment. In the 1970s, the conflict between North and South manifested itself in an effort on the part of Third World states to establish a "new international economic order" (NIEO). Third World states sought to authoritatively raise the prices of raw materials and agricultural products. Emboldened by the success of OPEC during the 1970s, many Third World countries attempted to form commodity cartels to "artificially" raise the price of commodities on open markets. These efforts met with little success because most commodities, unlike oil, have a large number of producers and are easily substituted or stockpiled. Agreements among producers are difficult to reach, making the commodity vulnerable to "cartel-busting" strategies.

The NIEO called for Third World states to have more say in the IMF and the World Bank, asking, for example, that they be granted additional Special Drawing Rights (SDRs). SDRs, which the IMF created after the United States delinked the dollar from gold, resemble a world currency; they are based on the average of all the major currencies to replace the dollar-gold standard. Special access to SDRs would permit developing states to correct for trade imbalances and balance-of-payments difficulties without having to induce a recession through austerity measures. Developing states did not want to rely on the IMF's weighted voting system, which the developed states controlled, in order to get stabilization loans. In 1974, the G-77 successfully used its majority in the General Assembly to pass the Charter of Economic

Rights and Duties of States (UNGA Resolution 3281), which called for equal participation in international financial institutions and a more equitable distribution of wealth.

The G-77 was more successful in gaining trade concessions from the West. The
NIEO also called for a Generalized System of Preferences (GSP) whereby developing
states could export to developing states duty-free. This amounted to developed states'
granting most-favored-nation status to developing states without requiring the usual
norm of reciprocity. This strategy would allow developing states to improve their balance of trade without threatening fledging industries.

UNCTAD's influence in shaping development issues has waned a great deal since
the collapse of the Soviet Union. With the end of the Cold War and the transition of
the former Eastern Bloc and Soviet successor states into market democracies has come
the end of an ideological alternative to capitalism. During the Cold War, developing
states were in a better bargaining position because they could play West against East.
The United States and its allies were generous with military and development assistance as part of their joint efforts to contain communism in the Third World. Absent
the communist threat, the developed world has little reason to listen to the concerns
of the developing world. Furthermore, the transition of the former communist states
means that more states are seeking a slice of the global development pie. Given finite
resources and lacking a viable economic alternative, developing states are forced to
play by the rules created by the advanced industrialized states.

UNCTAD still maintains that developing states are caught in a perpetual cycle of
poverty and underdevelopment because of their disadvantaged position in the international division of labor. Their export income is derived from low-profit primary products, rendering them vulnerable to economic expansions and contractions in the global
economy. Global economic recession induced by the U.S. recession in the 1980s hit developing states extremely hard, deepening their already serious debt. During the 1980s
and early 1990s the UN shifted its focus from development activities to relief as violent
conflict and economic collapse led to large humanitarian crises. Cracks began to appear within the developing world as their economic situations continued to worsen.
Some states sought reconciliation with the North while others advocated "delinking"
from the international economy. UNCTAD was also politically opposed by the developed states as they cut their voluntary contributions to UNCTAD, opting to fund the
UN Development Program (UNDP) instead.

UNCTAD has been criticized for its confrontational approach to economic development. UNCTAD lays the blame for malnutrition, underdevelopment, and poverty in the South squarely at the feet of the North. UNCTAD 9 (1996), which was held
in Midrand, South Africa, placed special emphasis on poverty as the principal threat
to international instability. In the opening address, South African President Nelson
Mandela stated that "Without relief of the poverty which pervades much of the world,
our democracy and human rights will for many be a formality, and always in jeopardy"
(UNCTAD 9, 1996). The tone of UNCTAD 9 was more conciliatory, calling for "greater
international cooperation" in addressing globalization and marginalization. UNCTAD
10 (2000) held in Bangkok, Thailand, addressed the issue of social justice in a globalized world. UNCTAD sought to expand the discussion of globalization beyond the unification of markets to the idea of shared knowledge for security and development.
Most members of UNCTAD, however, remained pessimistic about the prospects for
alleviating poverty in the developing world under the existing world system.

THE UN DEVELOPMENT PROGRAM (UNDP)

The UNDP was created in 1965 when the General Assembly merged two UN development programs: the Expanded Program of Technical Assistance (EPTA) and the Special United Nations Fund for Economic Development (SUNFED). UNDP is funded through voluntary contributions of members. It coordinates development projects with other UN specialized agencies and the World Bank and the IMF. UNDP emphasizes technology transfers and aids developing states with technical development assistance. UNDP operations are more palatable to the developed states because they do not stray far from the orthodox view of development and liberal approaches to achieving economic growth. Yet, even the UNDP has criticized orthodox development efforts, especially structural adjustment loans. According to Budhoo (1994, 20–23), the UNDP estimates that 1.2 billion people now live in absolute poverty—twice as many as when structural adjustment loans were first instituted. In 1992, the UNDP reported that the disparity between the world's richest fifth and the poorest fifth was a ratio of 150:1, which is the result of inequities built into structural adjustment programs.

UNDP coordinates projects with the UN Children's Fund (UNICEF), the World Food Program (WFP), the World Health Organization (WHO), and many NGOs such as World Vision and Oxfam. These groups are "on the ground" and thus are witnesses to the human suffering and the social consequences of structural adjustment. The UN development bureaucracy advocates a bottom-up approach to development rather than a top-down approach. In this sense, they lean toward the more critical view of development: They see development as the ability to meet basic human needs—clean water, good sanitation, and adequate housing and foodstuffs—rather than a simple increase in a nation's GDP per capita. A local, bottom-up approach to development reaches more people than do the macrolending policies of the IMF or the World Bank.

The orthodox and critical views of development correspond with the theoretical approaches used in this text. Liberals adhere to orthodox views regarding development and hence advocate market-oriented prescriptions. Realists tend to see development in an orthodox light, but oppose liberal prescriptions, particularly those that remove the state from key sectors of the economy. Orthodox approaches can undermine the power of the state, and that is unacceptable for many nationalists in the developing world.

Developing states have fought brutal nationalist wars against colonial powers and have experienced great-power intervention during the Cold War. Third World states are wary of political, economic, and social initiatives that impinge on their sovereign prerogatives. Hence, many developing countries combine realism with Marxist views of exploitation. Many developing countries see liberal strategies as protecting the rich at the expense of the poor. Liberal approaches tend to blame the state or individuals and do not consider the global context and the international division of labor that fosters underdevelopment. Marxists argue that absent a change in the capitalist mode of production, developing states should shield themselves from market forces as periodic crises in markets cause global instability. Governments should promote domestic industries and grassroots efforts to allow people to help themselves. Most feminists, save for liberal feminists, also have a critical view of development because orthodox views ignore the differential impacts of development programs on women. In our case study of the Mexican peso crisis, we intertwine the orthodox and critical views of development with the theoretical approaches of realism, liberalism, Marxism, and feminism in order to understand the origins of the crisis and to evaluate international efforts to manage the crisis.

CASE STUDY 7: THE MEXICAN PESO CRISIS

On December 19, 1994, the Mexican government unilaterally devalued the Mexican peso. The Mexican government argued that the peso, which was pegged to the U.S. dollar at a fixed exchange rate, had been overvalued, stifling economic growth. Mexico's exports had become unaffordable in foreign markets while foreign imports remained quite affordable in Mexican markets. The trade deficit, particularly with the United States, was undermining domestic expansion. But when the Mexican government devalued the peso by 20 percent to curb excessive imports, it did so without consulting either business or labor (Lustig 1995, 46).

The peso devaluation caused a panic in Mexican financial sectors as skittish foreign investors abruptly withdrew from Mexican markets. The run on Mexico's foreign currency reserves forced the government to allow the peso to float freely against the dollar. The peso float had the unfortunate consequence of spurring speculation, causing an additional decline in the peso's value and the loss of $8 billion in foreign currency (Ramirez 1996, 129). The panic soon spread to neighboring markets in Latin America. While these markets and their currencies were not particularly overvalued, foreign investors retreated to traditionally safer markets. The value of the U.S. dollar also declined dramatically against other hard currencies.

Several political factors were also at work and are suspected of intensifying the peso crisis (Wiarda 1995). First, Mexico appeared to be, for the first time in more than three decades, politically unstable. While other Latin American countries had experienced high levels of political violence and turmoil, Mexico's PRI party had authoritatively dominated the Mexican political scene for years. Prior to the peso devaluation, however, the Zapatista revolt in Chiapas had shaken the Mexican government and shocked the world. Second, two political candidates were assassinated. And third, the brother of former Mexican President Carlos Salinas de Gotari was charged with murder. Mexico had begun to look like the stereotypical "banana republic," scaring investors back to traditional safe havens in the West.

To keep the Mexican government from going bankrupt, the United States, Japan, and Europe, together with the IMF and World Bank, put together a $50 billion stabilization package. And, in accordance with past practice, that stabilization package came with strings attached. First, the United States, which contributed $20 billion to the recovery effort, insisted on almost immediate repayment. The U.S. Congress was reluctant to bail out Mexico, so President Clinton was forced to dip into Federal Reserve funds normally used to protect the dollar against speculative runs. The United States demanded that revenues from PEMEX, Mexico's state-owned oil company, be directly deposited into the Federal Reserve. PEMEX is one of the largest earners of foreign currency for Mexico.

The IMF required the usual structural adjustments. The structural adjustment programs introduced during the 1980s had failed to reduce Mexico's external debt or to significantly curb government spending. According to Ramirez (1996), the IMF package involved austerity measures that included a 10 percent cut in all government expenditures, an immediate 35 percent increase in petroleum prices, an immediate 20 percent increase in electricity prices, a value-added tax of 10–15 percent, and a sharp reduction on the availability of money and credit. The IMF claimed that these measures would reduce Mexican consumption and increase savings, which in turn would restore investor confidence in the Mexican market. The total stabilization package induced an economic recession for about a year, after which economic growth rebounded (*The Economist* 1998a, 8).

What precipitated the peso crisis and how does it affect Mexico's development? How should the IMF and World Bank have handled the crisis? What are the effects of World Bank and IMF policies in Mexico? Who stands to benefit and who stands to lose from World Bank and IMF intervention? The realist, liberal, Marxist, and feminist theoretical approaches generate different answers to these questions, highlighting different development issues and dynamics.

A REALIST CUT

The variants of realism differ slightly regarding the wisdom of the Mexican bailout. Traditional realists see the Mexican peso crisis as a classic example of why the market should ultimately serve the state and why interdependence is not necessarily a good thing for sovereign states. In 1994, just a year before the peso crisis, the United States, Canada, and Mexico formed the North American Free Trade Agreement (NAFTA), which created a common market among the three members, reducing many remaining tariffs and other barriers to trade. The ultimate goal of NAFTA is to establish a free trade area covering the entire Western Hemisphere. Many nationalists in the United States, Canada, and Mexico adamantly oppose NAFTA because the agreement reduces state autonomy, erodes national borders, and undermines national industries. Furthermore, NAFTA makes it easier to transmit economic and political ills from one member to another. The peso crisis illustrates this point. The peso crisis weakened both the Canadian and the U.S. dollars. The United States had no choice but to bail out its ailing neighbor because U.S. leaders had unwisely tied its fate to an economically and politically unstable Mexico.

Neorealists see expanding markets as a potential source of wealth and power, but insist that states cannot be ruled by them. Markets and individuals do not, as in the liberal view, behave rationally; rather, markets and investors often react irrationally, spurred by rumor and driven by unwarranted panic. Most observers see the peso crisis in just such a light (Wiarda 1995; Roett 1997). It was this kind of behavior—an irrational response—that nearly brought down the Mexican state and threatened the U.S. economy. The market must serve the interests of the state, not the other way around. States must be concerned about the long-term health of the country, not the immediate short-term interests of skittish foreign investors that want governments to subsidize their risks.

A realist analysis of Mexico's position criticizes the liberal choices made by the Mexican government over the years (Vasquez 1997). Mexico's economic woes are the result of its attempts to follow a liberal model of economic development. This model fosters asymmetrical interdependence relationships with the United States, giving the United States undue influence over Mexican affairs. The peso crisis is just another phase in the long history of Mexican chronic instability, which is caused by its proximity to the United States and its effort to develop along the same path.

The peso crisis is directly related to the debt crisis that traps Mexico in a vicious cycle of interest payments on loans so large that repayment is inconceivable. According to the IMF and the World Bank, Mexico must increase its exports in order to earn foreign currency, which it needs to pay its external debt. However, much of Mexico's external debt is the direct result of U.S. political choices in the Middle East in 1973. The IMF and the World Bank perpetuate the cycle of dependence by providing structural adjustment loans. Yet, structural adjustments have not been proven to provide long-term economic stability and growth (Kudlow 1994, 46). The United States has used Mexico's debt and the peso crisis to secure access to Mexican oil and Mexican markets through the IMF. The IMF imposes unfair costs on the Mexican people. According to Mexico's nationalist *Excelsior,* "The reduction of public spending and the financial and monetary contraction will eventually lead to a collapse of the productive sector, which will accelerate the already alarming levels of unemployment. . . . The adjustments . . . push the nation to the brink of social tolerance" (U.S. Information Agency 1995b, 2). The pain of structural adjustment should be borne by American investors and not the Mexican people.

Realists also criticize the choices made by the U.S. government. The U.S. government's decision to liberalize the financial sector and deregulate U.S. banking has put the entire American financial system in peril. The lending practices of banks were such that many banks made loans for which they never expected repayment (Isaak 1995, 185). Knowing that states do not go out of business, banks figured they could lend money without risk and were quite loose with their financing. Gambling on sovereign borrowing, they thought they could not lose because they would continue to earn interest over an indefinite loan period, making money even if they lost the principal.

Mexico was clearly taking advantage of this situation. Following the advice of the Cambridge School of Economics, Mexico borrowed as much money as the West would lend (Isaak 1995, 186). The Cambridge advisors, who were leftist in bent, argued that Mexico could increase its leverage with the United States if it became heavily indebted to U.S. banks. "As economist John Maynard Keynes observed, if you owe your bank a hundred pounds, you have a problem; but if you owe your bank a million pounds, the bank has a problem" (Isaak 1995, 186). The devaluation of the peso and the resulting peso crisis forced the United States to bail out Mexico because it would have caused the financial collapse of several U.S. banking and investment institutions. The U.S. government and the IMF are indirectly insuring U.S. investment in Mexico by enabling investors to make speculative ventures with very little risk.

Realists are also critical of the IMF and the World Bank for the secrecy attending their proceedings, decision making, and assets. During the initial stages of the Mexican peso crisis, the IMF claimed that it lacked the resources to adequately address Mexico's immediate financial needs. Yet, a few days later, it announced that it was negotiating a $15 billion aid package to boost the Russian ruble, even though the Russian government had done little to stabilize the ruble itself (*The Economist* 1995a, 1). The Russian government continued to spend excessively and was fighting a very costly war in Chechnya. Mexico was a far better candidate than Russia for IMF assistance, yet the IMF could not find the resources for Mexico whose currency crisis had occurred first.

Many realists see NAFTA and the Mexican peso fiasco as part and parcel of the globalization process—a process that has undermined U.S. and Mexican national industries and jobs. Former presidential candidate Ross Perot described NAFTA as that "great sucking sound," which was the sound of U.S. jobs and businesses going down the drain, presumably to Mexico. NAFTA opponents argued that U.S. manufacturing jobs would move to Mexico to exploit the cheap labor market and lower environmental standards. These firms could then out-compete firms that stayed in the United States, abiding by U.S. labor and environmental law. NAFTA advocates argued that the loss of those jobs would be replaced by a corresponding growth of jobs related to the increase in exports. Unfortunately for the pro-NAFTA argument, the U.S. trade surplus with Mexico vanished almost overnight when the peso was devalued. The devalued peso made U.S. goods in Mexico prohibitively expensive, drastically slowing U.S. exports. The net loss of U.S. exports means the net loss of U.S. jobs. NAFTA and economic globalization have compromised long-term growth both in Mexico and in the United States.

A LIBERAL CUT

The extreme libertarian position on the IMF/World Bank bailout of the Mexican peso mirrors the realist position, except that libertarians object on economic rather than political grounds. The IMF and the World Bank are interventionists in the market. IMF/World Bank bailouts underwrite investors and bond holders. The IMF is not a defender of free markets. Rather, it socializes personal investment risks (Hawke 1995, 110). The IMF/World Bank packages disrupt the relationship between reward and risk and hence encourage foolish investment. The market should determine which businesses and banks succeed and fail. Instead, Third World bureaucrats mismanage the economy by creating an artificial financial environment to attract foreign investments (Herbener 1995). If multinational banks and investment firms make bad decisions, they should pay the consequences, as should their individual shareholders—the ones who raked in big, double-digit returns in the first place. North American society would continue to thrive if states would allow for market corrections; in fact, it would be better off.

A less extreme liberal position sees the IMF and the World Bank as instrumental in averting economic crises. The peso crisis posed significant risks to the world financial system because it threatened the stability of the dollar and emerging markets. According to the *Excelsior,* "The anticipated credit will deactivate a dangerous if not major time bomb: It will prevent Mexico from declaring a debt moratorium, which could have sparked a great global financial crisis, in which the first to drop dead of bankruptcy would be the emerging markets" (U.S. Information Agency 1995b, 2). The IMF should not bail out every country that mismanages its economy (*Economist* 1995b). However, as the lender of last resort, it can stabilize economies and encourage market reforms. The IMF and the World Bank can help monitor capital flows in emerging markets and improve on early warning.

The IMF and the World Bank did not create the debt crisis, nor are they responsible for the peso devaluation. These institutions help developing states achieve economic growth and help restore their creditworthiness. Developing states have run into economic difficulties because they have not allowed market forces into previously protected areas. The trouble with the peso stems from the fact that its exchange rate is pegged to the dollar (Meigs 1997). The exchange rate of the peso was fixed to the dollar by the Mexican government. This fixed rate was designed to encourage foreign investments by those concerned about exchange rate instability. The Mexican government even issued Tesobonos, bonds that insured investors against devaluation. A major draw-back of the fixed exchange rate is that the peso could not be adjusted when the demand for Mexican capital assets rose (Meigs 1997). A flexible exchange rate, in which the value of the peso is largely determined by market forces, automatically adjusts for changes in capital flows.

A fixed exchange rate is fine for "soft" currencies as long as the government is re-sponsible and disciplined. Most observers expected the Mexican government to "cor-rect" the exchange rate of the peso in early 1994 because its overvaluation was curbing growth potential (Lustig 1995). In 1993, IMF officials told Mexico that the peso was over-valued and was creating a trade imbalance large enough to threaten long-term eco-nomic health (Kudlow 1994). But the Mexican government did not want to raise interest rates (to induce savings) or devalue the peso, as both would be politically un-popular at home: Mexican businesses would find it difficult to afford loans and Mexi-can citizens would find foreign goods suddenly out of reach. Political considerations outweighed sound economic policies. The issuing of Tesobonos further undermined confidence in the peso and the Mexican government, making it clear the government lacked the liquidity to meet its international obligations. Poor political choices ulti-mately undermined economic confidence in an economy with a lot of promise.

The IMF and World Bank, through their policy-based loans, are the best mecha-nisms for handling economic crises and instituting market-based reforms. They also help governments make good economic choices. Austerity programs are necessary for societies that have been living well beyond their means. While initially quite painful for citizens, such programs compel adjustment; and the long-term benefit of adjustment is stable, healthy economic growth. Economic adjustments are like Band-Aids. You have to get them off, but you have a choice: Should you rip the adhesive strip off all at once, in one quick motion, or do you ease it off slowly? The former hurts a lot, but not for long; the latter hurts a little, but the pain goes on. Either way, however, adjustment is inevitable.

Some liberals argue for a gradual implementation of neoliberal policies and re-forms. They argue that austerity stifles long-term economic growth and employment in Mexico because deflationary measures decrease the rate of capital accumulation (Ramirez 1996). The IMF and World Bank, on the other hand, advocate the quick ap-proach through their structural adjustment loans. Gradual reforms are less likely to take hold because they introduce confusion and chaos in the economy and hence are un-likely to significantly alter government and consumer behavior.

The IMF and World Bank loans also prevent contagion, or the so-called tequila ef-fect. During the initial stages of the peso crises, other Latin American markets also ex-perienced investor panic. The aid packages went a long way toward providing investor confidence and controlling the panic spillover into other emerging markets. The IMF and the World Bank promote interstate cooperation to help societies manage the ill effects of interdependence.

Recall that liberal institutionalists argue that international organizations help states overcome collective action problems. Through the creation of international regimes, economic growth and prosperity in an anarchic world can be achieved. The growth in global finance has been made possible only through concerted efforts of states, facilitated by their respective central banks and the IMF (Kapstein 1996). This global finance regime gives states the central responsibility for the supervision of banks, which enables governments to manage financial crises like the Mexican peso crisis. President Bill Clinton has commended the G-7 (the seven wealthiest nations) and the IMF for their instrumental role in addressing the Mexican crisis. The advanced industrialized countries agreed at the 1995 Halifax conference to establish an early warning system that called for early and full disclosure in monetary and financial information, and for tougher reporting standards. This will allow markets to "react more quickly and nations will be pressed to implement sound policies in a timely manner" (U.S. Department of State Dispatch 1995, 4). This cooperation would not be possible without the institutional cooperation and independence of the central banks and the IMF.

Finally, liberals defend NAFTA, arguing that the peso crisis occurred in spite of, not because of, NAFTA. NAFTA, they claim, levels the playing field. Tariffs between the United States and Mexico were at an all-time low when NAFTA was finally approved. The NAFTA agreement simply recognizes and regularizes the market that already exists between Mexico, the United States, and Canada. Had NAFTA been defeated in 1993, the peso would have collapsed, whereupon immigration to the United States would have increased dramatically (Wright 1995). NAFTA helped defuse the peso crisis because it ensured an engaged United States with an interest in its third-largest export market. NAFTA and the IMF offer the best defense against the crony capitalism that leads to political corruption of the market.

A MARXIST CUT

Marxists understand the Mexican peso crisis through class analyses. Traditional Marxists see the peso crisis as the result of the chronic instability of capitalism and residual colonialism. The wealthy business class seeks to pass the cost of instability onto the working class through the coercion of the state and international organizations. The IMF and World Bank are agents of capitalism, although Marxists differ as to whose specific interests they serve. Those that take a state-centric approach see the World Bank and the IMF as agents of the core states, which exploit the resources and the labor of the periphery and the semiperiphery. The debt crisis of the 1980s was largely the result of money's being foisted upon periphery/semiperiphery states by core banks with the approval of core countries (see, for example, Gilpin 1987, 323). Yet, the creditor nations, which are the largest shareholders in the IMF and the World Bank, would not accept any responsibility for the debt crisis and insisted on full repayment (Kahler 1985; *Economist* 1991).

The creditor nations and the IMF have decided to take a case-by-case approach to debt relief rather than a comprehensive approach. This strategy has allowed the debt crisis to fester, allowing otherwise insolvent banks to continue to exploit the developing world. The IMF and the World Bank, which are supposed to be politically and economically neutral, make it a condition of their financial support that debtors should continue to service their bank debt. This strengthens the bargaining position of core banks. "The IMF and the Bank, it seems, used both their muscle and their money to rescue banks from embarrassment; living standards and the prospects for growth in the debtor countries appeared to rank low among their priorities. This interpretation undoubtedly exaggerates the institutions' freedom to act. But it has a disturbing core of truth—as many insiders would privately admit" (*Economist* 1991, S23).

It is not surprising, then, that the IMF would bail out private investors from the United States when the peso crashed. The United States used its influence in the IMF to ensure that the investments of U.S. capitalists were protected at the expense of tax-payers, the bulk of whom are of the working class. According to India's *Telegraph*, "The peso rescue package . . . exposed Mexico to the most criminal neo-colonial plunder by U.S. business. . . . The dictates of the new world order and the IMF–World Bank–WTO are pauperizing the masses more and more" (U.S. Information Agency 1995b, 8).

Traditional Marxist analyses highlight the effects of IMF and World Bank condi-tionality on the working class. The structural adjustment programs produce a very grim reality for most Mexicans—reduced wages, reduced social services, increased energy prices, and higher prices for consumer goods (Heredia and Purcell 1996, 274). Most Mexicans have their wages and savings in pesos while their elites maintain their fortunes in hard currencies safely deposited and insured in multinational banks. The austerity programs implemented in the 1980s for debt relief did not help the Mexican econo-my. While these programs were in effect, the standard of living of most Mexicans fell and the disparity between rich and poor widened. "Since 1982, privatization and dereg-ulation have contributed to a steep concentration of income and wealth. In what ana-lysts term a 'trickle up' process, there has been in Mexico a massive transfer of resources from the salaried population to the owners of capital and from public to (a few) pri-vate hands" (Heredia and Purcell 1996, 282–283). Poverty and underdevelopment sim-ply have not diminished, even with government cutbacks, NAFTA, and increased privatization. Poverty has actually worsened and social justice remains nonexistent. The working and the middle classes have borne the brunt of structural adjustment and will pay the costs of the peso crisis. "The international rules of the game give labor and capital asymmetrical treatment. Whereas capital can always find a safe-haven coun-try, labor cannot freely enter other countries" (Lustig 1995, 85).

The peso crisis serves to further impoverish Mexican workers. Their wages buy only a fraction of what they used to buy. On the other hand, Mexican-based exporters and the owners of maquiladoras benefit because of reduced wages and increased ex-ports to the United States (Koechlin 1995). With fewer jobs and higher interest rates, workers in Mexico will have difficulties meeting their basic human needs. A Chase-Manhattan memo acknowledges this fact, but disregards its implications, expressing concerns that President Zedillo might respond to mass demonstrations by "yielding to worker demands which [would] further aggravate the economic situation" (cited in Cockburn and Silverstein 1995, 66). Chase-Manhattan is interested in stability and in-vestor confidence, which means that the interests of workers must be suppressed. The use of wage repression policies as an international debt mechanism is a common fea-ture of structural adjustment and contributes significantly to worker poverty (Adel-man and Taylor 1989).

U.S. workers are also bearing the costs of the Mexican bailout. U.S. taxpayers are subsidizing the peso and Mexican debt, bailing out the Wall Street speculators who have far more money and resources. The U.S. government and the IMF do not criti-cize capitalists for their risky investments. Instead, investment houses are rescued by the people who can least afford it. And while the workers are saving capitalists from their own "risks," U.S. corporations have increased investments in Mexico. After the deval-uation of the peso, the United States maintained a trade deficit with Mexico, largely because U.S. multinationals were displacing U.S. exports. The result was a net loss of jobs for the United States. Although jobs were created in the United States, many of those jobs were part-time, service-sector jobs with no benefits. Good-paying manufacturing jobs headed south, where wages are low and labor is not organized. Both Mexican and U.S. workers received the short end of the stick with NAFTA and the IMF bailout of the Mexican peso. Not surprisingly, record profits of U.S.-owned factories in Mexico have been reported since the peso bailout.

According to Gramscian-inspired Marxists, the Mexican peso crisis exemplifies the growing dominance of the transnational capitalist class. In their view, international organizations like the IMF, the World Bank, and the WTO serve to perpetuate neoclassical, liberal economic theory. This theory legitimizes the dominant position of transnational capital, portraying capitalists as risk-takers whose shrewd investments justify their enormous rewards. Neoclassical theory also undermines national interests that are both business- and labor-related. States and unions interfere with the market and are responsible for disrupting economic growth: A boom economy is the result of savvy entrepreneurial effort while a slumping economy is the result of excessive labor demands or ill-advised government policies.

The IMF and World Bank bailout of the Mexican peso benefited foreign investors who stood to lose fortunes. The U.S. government and the IMF had to bail out investors because transnational capital interests have successfully tied their fates to that of the subordinate classes, particularly in the West. If the big multinational banks like Chase-Manhattan go under, it could bring down the entire U.S. financial system. Millions of people would lose their investments and the global economy would likely collapse. Yet the collapse of the global economy would be largely insignificant for billions of people. Their daily, marginalized lives of poverty and subsistence will continue whether the stock prices of multinational corporations rise or fall. Regarding the lessons of the peso crisis, India's *Telegraph* opined, "Western observers and their agents in India are trying hard to propagate the virtues of liberalization, globalization, and market system under the hegemony of international imperialist capital. . . . The realization of progress for the masses and the country demands a total break with the IMF–World Bank–WTO regimes and the MNCs and the FIIs" (U.S. Information Agency 1995b, 8).

A FEMINIST CUT

The feminist theoretical approach has a lot to say about IMF and World Bank policies and their effects on women. In addition to decrying the lack of women in the decision-making process, feminists claim that IMF and World Bank policies amount to balancing budgets on the backs of women (Cunningham and Reed 1995). The Mexican austerity program has a more significant impact on women. Mexican women are the first to lose their jobs, and those who do not lose their jobs have seen their wages cut. While men also experience these effects, women make less than men. Moreover, women are also engaged in child rearing. Economically, women and children are disproportionately affected by structural adjustment. Socially, women and children also suffer. Rates of domestic violence are higher during economic hard times as men take out their frustrations on their families.

Mexican austerity has caused food and energy prices to rise dramatically. Many women are responsible for providing food for themselves and their families, and higher prices make stretching the devalued peso even more difficult. Women are usually the ones who have to work harder, and they are more likely to suffer nutritionally. The reduction of government spending in the areas of health, welfare, and education directly affects the status and the social development of women in Mexico (Buchmann 1996). Children, particularly young girls, also suffer from the lack of educational and health spending. Limited family resources tend to be devoted to the males at the expense of female family members (*WIN News* 1995). Concern about the immiserization of women and children as a result of IMF and World Bank conditionality has led UNICEF to call for "adjustment with a human face."

The IMF and the World Bank sponsor projects that promote export industries because of the need to earn foreign currency. Most developing states have export industries in commodities or cash crops, which means that governments must appropriate land that was once used for subsistence farming. Unfortunately for women, who are principally involved in barter or informal trade, their livelihoods are directly threatened. Cash crops and export industries are controlled by men, which further solidifies their dominant position over women.

The IMF and the World Bank dispute any direct link between their structural adjustment programs and the impoverization of women and children. They argue that market reforms will empower women to take greater control over their lives. Citing their liberal economic models, these officials claim it is irrational for firms and governments to discriminate against women. Women must be allowed equal opportunity to education, jobs, and credit. Markets will raise the status of women because they will break down traditional patriarchal institutions that keep women down. Women must be integrated into the global economy in order to improve their social and economic status. Liberal feminists tend to agree with the IMF and World Bank but also recognize that economic opportunities continue to be denied to women in market economies.

Many socialist feminists counter that it is precisely this liberal quasi-feminist approach that diminishes the status of women. In fact, the inclusion of women in the development process has led to the global feminization of poverty (Simmons 1992; Khoury 1994). Women are now working double time, engaging in both paid and unpaid labor. Women's wages remain at 60–70 percent of men's wages. The problem with many liberal economic analyses of the effects of structural adjustment lies in their assumption that macroeconomic policies are gender-neutral. This assumption, while simplifying analyses, could not be further from the truth. According to a Women in Development Europe report, "Macroeconomic policies are biased in favour of men, for they do not take into consideration the sexual division of labour, nor the time and the energy that go into caring for children and a household—activities carried out primarily by women, even in the most 'advanced' societies" (cited in *WIN News* 1995, 32).

Liberal economic theory as a tool ignores the economic contributions of women; as a result, it yields unsatisfactory results regardless of who uses it, male or female. The Women in Development (WID) office of the World Bank is charged with ensuring that women are included in the development process. However, WID does not challenge the capitalist route to development or the gender bias of liberalism (Goebel and Epprecht 1995). Rather, it sees the problem as something internal to societies that markets can solve. WID is ethnocentric in that it promotes the West's liberal, feminist model of development while ignoring the cultural and ethnic experiences of Third World women. These experiences are dismissed as "traditional," and arguably oppressive to women. The market will incrementally incorporate traditional and informal sectors of societies, liberating women. In reality, however, this view reduces women to "resources" and wrongly implies that women in the advanced industrialized countries are progressing to positions of equality (Simmons 1992).

The IMF and World Bank emphasize the development and the enhancement of export industries, resulting in the formation of export processing zones (EPZs). This requires "flexible labor" policies, which deregulate labor by explicitly marginalizing unions and allowing companies to bypass government-sanctioned collective bargaining. This attracts foreign investment and spurs economic growth. Many argue that IMF and World Bank structural adjustment loans and NAFTA have led to the development of maquiladoras in Mexico. Maquiladoras are factories located along the Mexico-U.S. border. "These factories can import duty-free parts, semi-finished goods and other items from the U.S. These are then finished or assembled by lower-wage Mexican workers and freely re-exported to the U.S. market " (Balaam and Veseth 1996, 70).

Maquiladorization of Mexico also means that labor is becoming feminized. According to Guy Standing of the International Labor Organization, "The types of work, labor relations, income and insecurity associated with 'women's work' have been spreading, resulting not only in the notable rise of female labor force participation but in a fall in men's employment as well as a transformation—or feminization—of many jobs traditionally held by men" (1996, 405). The emergence of maquiladoras has been accompanied by increasing numbers of women in manufacturing jobs that were previously held by men. Many of these factories, characterized as "sweat shops," exploit female labor in Mexico, which is 30 to 40 percent cheaper than male labor in Mexico and 70 to 80 percent cheaper than labor in the United States. The entry of women into the workforce has increased the supply of labor and reduced labor's bargaining power. In spite of the rhetoric of empowerment and cooperative partnerships, IMF and World Bank policies place egregious burdens on women. And, as with other international organizations, women are virtually excluded from the upper echelons of decision making within the IMF and the World Bank.

CONTAGION?

The Mexican peso crisis was followed by a series of currency crises in emerging markets in Southeast Asia in 1997 and 1998. The once powerful "Asian Tigers" are now crippled by collapsing currencies and falling stock markets. Indonesia, Thailand, Malaysia, and the Philippines are in political and economic upheaval, surpassing the crisis in Mexico. Once again, the IMF has stepped in to bail out these ailing economies, providing emergency loans with strings attached. Once again, there are diverging views regarding the efficacy and role of the IMF. Many continue to view the IMF as an extension of the United States, with hostile intentions. According to Thailand's business-oriented *Krungthep Turakij*:

> Some analysts said it would be a suicidal and asinine idea for the United States to try to dominate the world by waging economic wars against other countries. . . . Nevertheless, if U.S. policy [makers] continue to be narrow-minded and short-sighted, without looking back at the Great Depression which was their own economic disaster, countries whose economies have been devastated by Washington's indifferent attitude may join forces in declaring war against the United States. (U.S. Information Agency 1998b, 7)

In a somewhat similar vein, Hong Kong's *Sing Pao Daily News* stated:

> As the biggest contributor to the International Monetary Fund (IMF), the U.S. would like to push open the Asian market as well as to increase the proportion of foreign enterprises by means of IMF loan conditions. [For] the United States . . . the Asian crisis happened to provide an excellent opportunity to get rid of trade barriers. (U.S. Information Agency 1998b, 7)

Other observers see the IMF and other international organizations as tools of the capitalists in general. According to Malaysia's *Star*, "Many international agencies are being used to open the financial markets in developing nations, with the IMF and the WTO among them. . . . Unless Malaysians are prepared for the financial bondage, they must do everything within their means not to request IMF assistance for any bail out." (U.S. Information Agency 1998b, 7). And India's centrist *Hindu* states:

> Western nations are seeking to exploit this crisis, partly induced by feudal corporate structures to enable their products and companies to make quick inroads and takeovers at undervalued prices. This could create a huge backlash in a region where, except for Japan and Thailand, every country has a history of colonization. (U.S. Information Agency 1998b, 10)

The IMF is not without its liberal defenders. According to Germany's *Sueedeutsche Zeitung*, "The IMF is necessary as a factor of stabilization and confidence," and Belgium's *Financieel-Economische* claims that "the IMF and World Bank are confronted with the difficult problem of curbing the crisis. In this, they have to maneuver between emergency aid and strict measures to keep the local economies viable" (U.S. Information Agency 1998b, 11–12). From this world view, the IMF plays a crucial and constructive role in managing economic crises.

Increasingly, however, IMF lending policies are difficult to sustain. Marxists and realists have long been vocal critics of the IMF, but they have since been joined by neoliberals in growing numbers. According to the UK's *Economist*, "The character of the IMF's new operations in Asia—notably the package of $57 billion it put together for South Korea—raises a bigger question. Should these bailouts be happening at all?" (U.S. Information Agency 1998b, 7). By bailing out the Asian economies, the IMF is encouraging irresponsible and speculative economic behavior. The following case study examines the Indonesian economic meltdown to sort out the specific causes and effects of the crisis.

CASE STUDY 8: INDONESIA*

Indonesia has 212 million people, making it the fourth most populous country in the world. It is also the largest Muslim state. Indonesia is a sprawling archipelago consisting of 13,500 islands, and its main industries are oil, gas, and tropical timber. It is considered one of the more dynamic and promising economies in Southeast Asia and had experienced impressive economic growth in the past twenty years. Dubbed as "Asian

---

*The account of the Indonesian crisis is largely drawn from the Indonesian Special Report <www.washingtonpost.com/wp/inatl/longterm/indonesia/timeline.htm>.

tiger" and as "the East Asian miracle," Indonesia served as a model of economic development for the Third World. In 1997, the value of many of the key Southeast Asian currencies fell to record lows. Beginning with the devaluation of the Thai baht, the Indonesian rupiah also fell in value. In order to prop up the rupiah, Indonesia borrowed $33 billion in short-term foreign loans and closed sixteen insolvent banks. In July 1997, Thailand requested IMF assistance to help arrest the fall of its currency and meet its balance of payments responsibilities. As the Thai baht began to lose its value, investors in all the major Southeast Asian economies began selling their assets, causing the currencies to fall even further. Instead of borrowing more money to keep the rupiah at its fixed rate, Indonesia let the rupiah float. The rupiah fell a dramatic 70 percent (*BBC* 1999).

In January 1998, the United States and the IMF launched a joint aid package of $43 billion for Indonesia. The United States and the IMF hoped to stave off a regional crisis like the one that affected much of Latin America after the fall of the Mexican peso. Indonesian President Suharto, who had been in power for over thirty years, agreed to the IMF conditions on economic reform. This involved tax reforms, restructuring of the banking system through recapitalization, loan collection, anticorruption legislation, removal of price controls, government deficit reduction, and the privatization of state-owned businesses. In March 1998, President Suharto was elected (through his usual dubious means) to his seventh five-year term as president. Violent antigovernment protests erupted as price increases went into effect as part of Indonesia's agreement with the IMF to remove price controls and subsidies. Protesters and political opponents of Suharto called for his resignation and violence broke out on the streets of Jakarta, Indonesia's capital. In May 1998, Suharto resigned and was replaced by Vice President Habibie. Habibie pledged to hold elections in 1999; however, the violent protests continued.

In June 1999, Indonesia held its first free election in forty-four years and the party Megawati Sukarnoputri won a plurality vote (the most votes but not a majority) in parliament. As in most parliamentary systems, the legislature is responsible for electing the executive, which means if no party gets a majority of the seats in the parliament then a coalition must be formed in order for the president (also called prime minister in some countries) to be elected. Sukarnoputri is the daughter of former President Sakarno, who was unceremoniously removed from office (with the blessing of the United States) in 1965. At the same time, the crisis in East Timor, a decades-old ethnic conflict on one of Indonesia's 13,500 islands, came to a peak as East Timor sought its independence. The simmering East Timor conflict has claimed more than 100,000 lives over the years and the economic crisis provided the East Timorese separatists with the opportunity to secede. Furthermore, the islands of Java, Bali, and Sumatra were also experiencing separatist unrest. By September 1999, it appeared that Indonesia might disintegrate as a political unit.

In a surprise move, the Indonesian Parliament elected Adurrahman Wahid over Sukarnoputri in October of 1999. Hailed as "a champion of tolerance, inclusion and self-respect," Wahid began to implement the reforms required by the IMF, albeit in a slow and ad hoc manner (Bresnan 2000). The reforms were met with opposition by Indonesian elites as well as by mass protests. In early 2000, East Timor again erupted in wide-scale protests that led to a UN intervention. The domestic economic situation also failed to improve and the Indonesian government began to balk at further reforms, fearing more unrest (*Xinhua News Agency* 2000). The IMF began withholding installments of the $43 billion package until it could gain compliance from Indonesia (*United Press International* 2001). By 2001, Wahid's popularity began to drop and the pace of reforms slowed to a halt. This set the stage for a political crisis that would lead to the eventual impeachment of Wahid and the election of Sukarnoputri during the summer 2001. After the election of Sukarnoputri, the IMF released a $400 million installment. The mass protests dwindled but were sparked again when the United States began bombing Afghanistan in October 2001 after the September 11 attacks. To date, the economic situation of Indonesia either in terms of increases of GDP or the ability of individuals to meet their basic human needs has not improved since the rupiah's collapse in 1997. What factors precipitated the Indonesian economic collapse? Did the IMF help or hurt the situation? Who won and who lost as a result of the IMF bailout? Whose interest did the IMF serve?

A REALIST CUT

The story of Indonesia illustrates the primacy of politics over abstract economic principles. The spectacular growth experienced by Indonesia was the result of state policies that promoted key industries and at the same time enhanced the strategic significance of the expansive archipelago. The United States has been integrally involved in Indonesia since the 1965 violent overthrow of President Sukarno, a communist-nationalist. The U.S. war in Vietnam, as well as other conflicts in Southeast Asia, made Indonesia central to Cold War Southeast Asian politics. After the *coup* against Sukarno, his replacement, President Suharto (by most accounts an authoritarian dictator), developed key national industries (oil and gas) using the foreign assistance provided by the West. The Western powers wanted to create a bulwark against communism in this troubled area. The resulting economic growth led to increased foreign direct investment which spurred the industrialization and urbanization. The Suharto government provided an attractive environment for foreign investment—a growing consumer market, tax incentives, and liberal banking policies. More important, labor unrest was easily quelled by the repressive arm of the Suharto dictatorship. The state led Indonesia to "Asian tiger" status, not an unrestrained market. It successfully parlayed its strategic geographic position and its natural resources to become a dominant power in the region. It harnessed market forces to serve and enrich the state, all with the blessing of the IMF and the United States. The Cold War significance of Indonesia cannot be underestimated. Billions of development assistance dollars poured into Indonesia because the Western powers saw Indonesia as the key to stability in Southeast Asia even after the disastrous policies of the 1970s. Using their voting power within the IMF and the World Bank, the West endowed Indonesia with the financial resources to establish industries that favored the economic development and the oil interests of the industrialized countries.

Unfortunately for Indonesia, the strategic interests of the West changed with the end of the Cold War in 1989. The Indonesian government had cooperated extensively with the United States, so much so that the United States and the UN looked the other way regarding Indonesian atrocities in East Timor. The government's violent response to the separatists was, at the very least, a gross violation of internationally recognized human rights and at worst, genocide. The UN only remained "concerned." After 1989, the bargaining position of Indonesia had changed dramatically and the United States was less willing to tolerate the corrupt Indonesian practices that had benefited U.S.

foreign direct investment in the past. Put another way, "the hegemonic structure of Cold War international relations protected Indonesia's authoritarian elite from the global pressure toward democracy and at the end of the Cold War explains why Indonesia became very exposed to this pressure during the regional economic crisis" (Kivimaki 2000, 527). U.S. and Western interests changed and so did their policies. As a result, so did the policies of the IMF and the World Bank.

The Southeast Asian crisis did not originate in Indonesia, but in Thailand. The Indonesian government made two fundamental mistakes when responding to the shockwaves. First, Indonesia did not impose capital controls when investors began selling their Indonesian assets. It was the free flow of capital (money in search of a good return) that sank the Indonesian economy (Kristof 1998, 6). Investors pulled their money out of Indonesia for no good reason other than that they panicked. India and Malaysia imposed strict capital controls and were able to ride out the economic storm. By preventing investors from getting out, the panic subsided and capital stayed invested in their economies. UNCTAD has backed the right of countries to adopt emergency capital controls to prevent panic selling; however, the IMF remains opposed. Regardless of what external agencies say, governments must take matters into their own hands to prevent economic crisis. Second, the Indonesian government listened to the IMF, an institution that represents the interests of large donor states. These same states that promoted a brutal and corrupt Suharto dictatorship because it supported their strategic interests and provided a favorable environment for investment during the Cold War now wanted Suharto out. The IMF's remedy of floating exchange rights only made the situation worse. The austerity programs angered the population and eventually forced Suharto from office. According to former IMF director Michel Camdessus, "We created the conditions that obliged President Suharto to leave his job" (Hanke 2000, 84). This amounts to the IMF creating considerable human suffering in the course of trying to accomplish a political goal (Hanke 2000, 84).

A LIBERAL CUT

State-led economic growth is unsustainable in the long run. Unless market forces are eventually allowed to discipline key sectors of the economy and force efficiency, industries will be unable to compete in the global market. The so-called "third way" between capitalism and socialism involved government planning and the formulation of industrial policy. Government officials would use tax, credit, and trade policies to encourage industrial development in key sectors, to ensure a greater equality of income distribution, and make investments in education and research and development. This strong state role in the market created the illusion of prosperity in Asia, but in fact has led to corruption and economic collapse.

Neoclassical liberals argue that the IMF should not soften the blow to the Asian economies or for foreign investors (Bartlett, Glassman, Hadar, Lindsey, Safire, and Zakaria 1998). According to these liberals the IMF created a "moral hazard." Investors poured money into over-invested industries and Western bankers made hundreds of billions of dollars in risky loans with the knowledge that they would be bailed out if things got tough. "In this case, the pattern of rushing in emergency aid to soften economic crises actually encouraged the making of bad loans that helped set up the crisis" (Bartlett, Glassman, Hadar, Lindsey, Safire, and Zakaria 1998, 64). The IMF should let the market discipline participants rather than mete out the discipline themselves through structural adjustment loans. The IMF is useful if it stays within its narrow mandate, promotes the flexible exchange rates, and helps with short-term balance of payments difficulties. (Blinder 1999). The IMF intervention should not be so dramatic as to interfere with the internal workings of the market. IMF interventionist practices have, in the words of Senator Lauch Faircloth (R-North Carolina,) "privatized profits and socialized losses" (Longman and Ahmad 1998, 37).

Liberal institutionalists argue that the IMF is the only institution that can help avert an economic crisis that affects the lives of billions of people. The IMF can restore investor confidence and economic growth even if the byproduct is that some creditors will be protected from the full consequences of their poor economic choices (Longman and Ahmad 1998). The IMF, the World Bank, and NGOs can help promote sustainable development by promoting better governance in the developing world. Good governance involves political accountability, freedom of association and participation, a sound judicial system, bureaucratic accountability, market reforms (Landell-Mills and Serageldin 1991). International organizations can provide incentives and technical knowledge that foster pluralism.

Liberal institutionalists acknowledge that structural adjustment is painful, but necessary. The reason the economic crisis in Indonesia deepened after IMF intervention is that reforms were inadequately implemented (Mussa and Hacche 1998). The IMF has helped reform monetary and fiscal policy and put the Asian economies back on track. The IMF and World Bank have also recognized that Indonesia and the other Asian countries were not solely at fault. The nature of the system itself is prone to panic and speculation, and the IMF and World Bank can help smooth out the sharp edges. The IMF and World Bank meeting in Prague 2000 heeded the warnings from many in the developing world about the excesses of unbridled capitalism (Pearlstein 2000, 13). This amounts to a recognition that some political control of the global market is fast becoming necessary. According to UNDP head, Mark Malloch-Brown, "The steamroller of economic globalism is not matched by the development of global politics that can respond to it. That is why you have anger in the street. And it's also why you have anxiety in the conference halls from Seattle to Prague" (Pearlstein 2000, 13). The coming together of different and competing perspectives can result in compromise and a new level of understanding of the complexities facing all states in a globalized world.

A MARXIST CUT

Marxists would agree with neoclassical liberals in that bailout of Indonesia by the IMF amounts to "socialism for the rich" (Longman and Ahmad 1998, 37). They differ in explaining why the wealthy benefit. Neoclassical liberals believe that the market is naturally unbiased and only becomes distorted by politics, whereas, for Marxists, the market is inherently biased and political and favors the interests of the dominant class. IMF bailouts are just another example of how the working class subsidizes the global bourgeoisie. Like the Mexican peso crisis, it is working-class people in both the advanced industrialized and the developing countries that end up paying the bills, as it is through their income and payroll taxes that their governments either contribute funds to or pay back the IMF. President Suharto and his family were not the only ones who were enriched through the kleptocratic period. Economic policies favored the former Dutch colonial administrators, Dutch MNCs, as well as its neo-imperialist successors, U.S. MNCs.

The IMF has also "strongly encouraged" Indonesia to attract foreign direct investment and to privatize government-owned industries. This amounts to allowing the same foreign banks and MNCs that made the initial bad investments to buy up lucrative sectors of the economy. This pattern has been seen in Mexico, South Korea, and Thailand (*Multinational Monitor* 1998). The banks and investment firms in Japan, Europe, and the United States are bailed out because the loans the IMF makes to developing countries in crisis are used to pay these foreign creditors. With the structural adjustment loans to liberalize the economy, these same creditors are then presented with a buying opportunity, snapping up assets at bargain-basement prices (*Multinational Monitor* 2000). These privatized factories and service operations have had their labor forces dramatically slashed and labor laws are "reformed" to give the new owners power to fire workers and hire them back at dramatically lower wages. Workers see their incomes slashed while austerity leads to rising food and fuel prices. Labor in Indonesia has been unable to organize because their original leadership was eradicated during the 1965 civil war, during which more than one million people were killed in anti-communist purges. Suharto's secret police "managed" any additional labor threats. As a result, the voice of labor was muted during the most recent crisis and the political and social instability claimed the lives of thousands of people (Kansas 1998). And in a dialectic twist, the IMF policies that are designed to save capitalism have stoked Islamic fundamentalism and ethnic conflict, which could mean capitalism's demise in Indonesia.

Indonesia also did not implement the one policy that could perhaps have eased its crisis—capital controls. Both Suharto and Wahid considered various forms of capital control, but the plans were rejected by the IMF. The IMF, and its doctrinaire position favoring the unfettered flow, pressured Indonesia to abandon capital control efforts. According to IMF managing director Horst Koehler, "the introduction of capital control would hinder a sustained and a broad economic recovery. What is needed to strengthen confidence in the rupiah, that is quite clear, is a steady and feasible implementation of the economic program" (*Xinhua News Agency*, June 5, 2000). The costs of implementing this economic program are paid for by the working poor, while the free flow of capital benefits only one group—transnational capitalists looking to maximize their return by any means necessary.

The Asian crisis represents a culmination of a systemic challenge to the "Asian model." This model placed great emphasis on a central state role that involved set wages, guarantees of lifetime employment, and a cooperative relationship among different actors (labor, business, and government) in the economy. The state was responsible for education and social welfare. This model was immensely productive during the 1970s and 1980s and represented an attractive alternative to the laissez-faire liberalism of the United States. A panic by foreign investors provided the IMF and the United States the opportunity to ideologically attack and dismantle the Asian model. In spite of the occasional lip service to the idea of political control over the global market, neoclassical liberalism is still being preached and is the only game in town. IMF practices and policies force the Asian economies to resemble the economies of the West, creating the same kind of political and social relations that exist in the West. In other words, whether or not an economy has successfully reformed is judged by its resemblance to the West. In this sense, the IMF is an agent of Western imperialism.

A Feminist Cut

IMF-imposed government austerity means that the government spends dramatically less on food and fuel subsidies, education, health care, and social welfare. As a result, women bear the brunt of austerity as they are responsible for food, fuel, education, and health care. In Indonesia, women are disproportionately illiterate, in poor health, and inadequately nourished (*WIN* 1999). The effects of IMF structural adjustment on Indonesian women are similar to those experienced by Mexican women. The structural adjustment loans lead to social unrest that manifests itself as an increase in rape and domestic violence. Men, powerless against their government and the IMF, vent their frustrations on the weak and vulnerable. The development of export industries means the displacement of rural women who engage in subsistence farming. Women who are able to find factory work face the sweat shop conditions of long hours and low pay. They receive lower wages than men and are often hired as day laborers instead of full-time permanent employees. In addition, they are subjected to sexual harassment or are forced into the sex industry. The story is repeated in all countries experiencing economic crisis and IMF structural adjustment.

In spite of the Women in Development (WID) office of the World Bank, the experience of women under structural adjustment continues to be ignored by the IMF and the World Bank. After nearly twenty years of feminist critiques, these institutions continue to disregard the impact of their policies on women. Additional feminist criticism of the IMF is considered repetitive (nagging—as postmodern feminists might highlight). Perhaps the ideological bias of these institutions centers on market reforms as the key to the liberation of women and not the cause of their plight. However, liberal feminism, that tends to agree with the IMF, still cannot explain the lack of enforcement of women's rights in developing countries. In Indonesia, women are constitutionally guaranteed the same rights, obligations, and opportunities as men; however, the government does nothing to enforce those rights. The disparity between the rights that are guaranteed in law and those that exist in fact seem to be of no concern to the IMF and the World Bank. With all their emphases on "good governance," not one IMF or World Bank loan has been withheld because of the (mis) treatment of women.

Feminists also encounter difficulty trying to organize women in Indonesia because feminism is associated with the United States. "In Indonesia, writings that question the implementation of human rights often reveal the fear that securing human rights means adopting liberalism, making people individualistic, egoistic and, thus disrupting the spirit of togetherness and solidarity" (Budianta 2000). In Indonesia, liberalism is associated with a notion of Western women that many find offensive. Motherhood, subservience, and chastity are considered sacred in Indonesia and Western notions of feminism are seen as a form of imperialism. The tension created by the collision of Western-styled capitalism with traditional Muslim culture further reduces the role of women to the margins. Women that seek equal rights or participation in the Western sense are unpatriotic and are reminded of their feminine duties to the community and family (Sunindyo 1998). Human rights activists from the West complicate matters further because they are usually culturally relative when it comes to women's rights. As a result, both liberal feminists and critical feminists are at a distinct disadvantage trying to organize Indonesian women to protest IMF and governmental "liberal" policies.

Women's groups have not given up trying. Women's NGOs have continued to document women's human rights abuses and bring them to the direction of international community. The anti-IMF riots in Jakarta were widely reported in the international media; however, rape was missing from press analysis. NGOs and the Indonesian government-sponsored National Human Rights Commission pointed out that while the IMF unrest involved the killing of protesters and the destruction of property, it also involved the systematic rape of ethnic Chinese women and girls. The actual numbers of reported rapes range from 85 to 168; however, many NGOs report that the number is probably a lot higher (*WIN* 1999). What is not in dispute is that these Chinese women and girls were targeted in an organized and coordinated manner over a three-day period. Feminist analyses show the masculine bias of the IMF and the World Bank policies, or at least their blind eye. They highlight the experience of women and how local, national, and international events impact the feminine experience.

CONCLUSION

Russia and Argentina are the latest countries to experience currency crises, and the IMF is once again challenged to manage the situation. Economic development in the South and in the former Eastern Bloc appears to be at stake. The issue of international development combines issues of colonialism, trade, and financial stability. The case studies of the Mexican peso crisis and the Indonesian economic collapse illustrate how the different theoretical approaches view the central issues of development and the role of the IMF and the World Bank in the development process. Variations of the theoretical approaches either advocate or challenge the orthodox and critical views of development. For example, traditional realists, liberals, and liberal feminists tend to have orthodox views of development. However, neorealists recognize that the uneven economic playing field enables great powers to exploit developing states through increased economic leverage. Marxists and some feminists argue that sustainable economic development, either in the orthodox or critical sense, is simply not possible under capitalist market conditions. The next chapter examines an international issue related to international development—the environment.

THE ENVIRONMENT

THE NATURAL ENVIRONMENT is composed of air, land, and water resources. From these resources, human life and biodiversity are sustained. The idea that the environment ought to be protected seems obvious, but how to manage the earth's global resources is as contentious an issue as international development. The environment directly relates to development and to the operation of the global economy. Natural elements provide food, energy, and the raw materials necessary to support the world's population, which is estimated to be nearing six billion people. The protection of global resources is controversial because the development of an advanced industrial society involves the exploitation of natural resources to produce goods and services for world markets. How are societies to balance the resource needs of industrial society with the natural environment? That is, how do societies continue to support their people in the manner to which they have become accustomed without destroying their natural habitat?

In this chapter, we examine international efforts to protect the environment and to manage global resources. We look first at collective action problems associated with environmental protection, then at the structure of IGOs involved in managing land and sea resources. NGOs that monitor and participate in international environmental protection are also surveyed. Our case studies cover the 1997 global warming treaty, which was negotiated in Kyoto, Japan, and the International Whaling Commission and its efforts to protect the whales.

THE TRAGEDY OF THE COMMONS

The difficulties in protecting the environment are often illustrated with the "tragedy of the commons" parable, first articulated by Garrett Hardin (1968). This parable shows how many individuals, each acting rationally, can destroy the very resources that sustain them all. Consider a village in which all sheep owners are entitled to use the commons (a collectively owned pasture) to graze their sheep. Each owner has an economic incentive to use the commons, grazing as many sheep as possible, because the commons is "free": Using it lowers the cost of raising the sheep, thereby increasing profit at the market. And higher profits means each owner can raise even more sheep. But as each owner adds more grazing sheep to the commons, the commons itself deteriorates. The grass, once so lush, disappears; the topsoil, denuded of roots, turns to mud in the rain; and the muddy ground washes away. Overexploited, the commons is destroyed, and with it, the community itself. A tragedy.

It seems logical, then, that community members should work together to protect the commons on which their livelihood depends. To do so, they can pursue two alternative strategies. First, they could create an authoritative body to regulate the commons. This body would determine how many sheep each person may graze, monitor the condition of the commons, and make sure that the commons is replenished. This strategy can be successful only if the interest of the authoritative body lies in preserving the commons and not in protecting the interests of the powerful sheep owners. After all, it must decide communal questions: What is a fair number of sheep for each person? What regulations are necessary? And what kinds of regulations would unduly interfere with commerce? The trouble is, even when the authoritative body is absolutely authoritative, owning both sheep and commons, the protection of the commons is not guaranteed. Consider, for example, the former communist governments in Eastern Europe and the Soviet successor states. These governments—authoritative bodies—owned both the means of production and the natural resources. Yet these governments chose to focus on industrialization, even at the expense of the environment.

The second strategy is to privatize, assigning property rights in the commons to individuals. In this case, individuals have incentives to care for their own property. Overgrazing your own land would be irrational, meaning that it would go against your individual self-interest. Your interest lies in preserving your land in the best possible condition, given your grazing needs. This strategy also has complications. In the first place, assigning property rights is an inherently political process. Who gets what and how much? And what is the rationing mechanism? Are only the rich entitled to buy and use the commons? Furthermore, an authoritative body is still needed—a body capable of assigning those property rights and enforcing them.

The tragedy of the commons allows us to understand how global "commons" are fast becoming depleted and why global actors, in seeking to use and protect the environment, are encountering difficulties. Consider fishing in international waters. International waters, which are not owned by any country, comprise a "collective good." Each fishing boat operating in international water has incentive to catch as much fish as it possibly can. However, there are many such boats, all fishing the same water, all depleting the same stock of fish; collectively, they are threatening the industry itself. Each boat individually reaps the profits yielded by a larger catch of fish, but no boat bears the whole cost of its activity. The costs of overfishing are external costs—costs borne not by the producers but by everyone.

Avoiding the tragedy of the ocean commons means dealing with the same plague of problems attending the protection of our hypothetical pasture. In fact, protecting the ocean's resources is even more difficult because multiple actors are involved. Governments, MNCs, IGOs, NGOs—each represents different interests and has diverse capabilities. Landlocked states and seafaring states compete for a share of the ocean resources. National and local fishing companies compete with MNCs. Issues remain: What, precisely, is the ocean commons and what is the territory of the state? And debates rage on the best strategies for managing the ocean resources: Many governments and MNCs seek privatization of the ocean commons, while many IGOs and NGOs seek more authoritative regulation of the environment.

Intuitively, privatization of the environment seems impossible, particularly as it relates to the oceans and atmosphere. How can individuals privately own the air or the water? You can't partition the atmosphere, outlawing breathing in private space; nor can you divide up all the fish, making them stay in privately owned sections of the ocean. Water might be privatized by creating zones; however, pollution knows no bounds, as recent oil spills have demonstrated. Privatization of "difficult to divide" natural resources usually takes the form of licenses—a license to fish or a license to pollute. That is, firms buy the rights to use the resources of the atmosphere or the ocean. As we'll see later in this chapter, pollution rights are a key feature of international efforts to counter global warming. For our current purposes, however, we simply recognize that both strategies—regulation and privatization—involve the creation of an authoritative body either to create environmental regulations or to assign and enforce property rights with regard to using natural resources. And both strategies are controversial because neither has been particularly effective at protecting the environment.

One of the principal challenges to environmental protection is that of balancing the capitalist mode of production, which involves the use and mass consumption of natural resources, with such values as preserving biodiversity and ensuring clean air, land, and water. The market cannot easily determine the price of these values; moreover, environmental protection can hurt profits and undermine industries and jobs. Environmental problems are part and parcel of economic development, so that the attending issues and controversies are intertwined. The concept of sustainable development is therefore an important one—it is used to describe efforts to maintain stable economic growth without undermining the environment and permanently depleting resources.

The theoretical approaches to international relations differ as to how to achieve sustainable development; some even question whether such a balance between the environment and economic development is possible. Much of the environmental degradation today is attributable to capitalist development in just seven or eight advanced industrialized states. These states, particularly the United States, consume the vast majority of the world's resources and account for a significant portion of the world's waste. Can the planet sustain this kind of development without experiencing a tragedy of the commons on a global scale? And can other countries, such as China, India, Russia, and Brazil, have the same consumption habits as the West? The answers to these questions depend on your theoretical lens. Realists are pessimistic about international cooperation in protecting the environment, arguing that states must do what they can to protect themselves and minimize external environmental threats. International competition for natural resources and raw materials will increase as more and more states develop. States must be able to get the resources they need, through the exercise of power if necessary. Liberals see the market as a means for promoting efficient use of raw materials. They argue that the market will force firms and individuals to use their resources wisely; otherwise they will be uncompetitive in the global economy. In that case, environmental costs—externalities that are not included in the price of goods—should be managed by international environmental regimes. Marxists see environmental protection as incompatible with capitalism. Environmental protection fetters international and domestic commercial activities and undermines profits. Environmental protection will always take a back seat to the interests of capitalists seeking to maximize profits and quarterly returns. Firms and individuals will take an "exploit and move on" approach to the environment until some entity with the power decides to stop them. Feminists tend to see current environmental protection as futile because most protection strategies are masculine in nature. This means that most strategies are informed by the idea that humans are somehow separated from their environment. The environment is something that man can control, conquer, and dominate. It is masculinist to think that science and scientific understanding will always solve environmental problems that arise from environmental exploitation.

ENVIRONMENTAL PROBLEMS

Most environmental problems revolve around pollution and resource depletion. Some problems can be corrected. Others cannot. Some kinds of pollutants can be treated, restoring land or water. But radioactive wastes and chemical pollutants in sufficient concentration can also permanently kill a body of water or render areas of land uninhabitable. Some resources are renewable, like fresh water and trees, while other resources, such as oil and coal, are not.

Five interrelated environmental problems have been of contemporary international concern—deforestation, desertification, biodiversity, ozone depletion, and global warming. Deforestation involves the clearing of forests for economic and social reasons. The most obvious reason for cutting trees down is for timber. Timber is processed into the lumber that builds houses, furniture, and the like. Another reason is to provide additional farmland for crops or grazing. Yet another reason is to provide additional living space for growing populations. These reasons are not trivial. The survival of millions of people depends on subsistence farming, which involves "slash and burn" techniques.

But the consequences of deforestation are dire. They involve soil erosion and loss of habitat for plant and animal species. More important, deforestation means the loss of the major producers of oxygen—trees. Trees are the principal mechanisms for recycling carbon dioxide into oxygen. Deforestation raises the level of carbon dioxide in the air, rendering it less breathable to animal life, and contributes to the warming of the atmosphere. The tropical rain forests in Latin America, Africa, and Asia are crucial to the ecological balance of the planet because they recycle 90 percent of the earth's carbon dioxide.

Desertification is closely related to deforestation because the removal of trees makes the topsoil unstable and robs it of the necessary nutrients that sustain vegetation. Normal rainfall patterns are disrupted, and the land becomes a desert—barren and uninhabitable. Desertification has posed a serious problem in Africa, where (normal) periodic droughts have been exacerbated to the extent that entire populations are now at risk. Desertification has created millions of environmental refugees, provoking unprecedented levels of starvation. Desertification is directly related to food security and has been linked closely with famines in Ethiopia, Somalia, and Sudan.

Biodiversity refers to the number and variety of plant and animal species. Biodiversity is considered important because local, regional, and global ecosystems depend on different species for continued existence. "Key species" are lynchpin plants and animals that are necessary for sustaining the food chain. Plankton, which is a tiny microorganism found in salt and fresh water, is just such a species. The extinction of plankton could collapse a food chain that includes salmon and trout, whales and dolphins, seals and bears. In biodiversity, more is better and protecting the "more" is better still. Thus, it is better to try to preserve biological complexity, in all its varieties, than to risk the unknown consequences of losing a species about which humans know very little. Biodiversity is tied to deforestation and desertification because the destruction of ecosystems destroys the habitat of plant and animal species. Efforts to preserve biodiversity include trying to protect species from extinction even if they have not been identified as a key species. Endangered species like the spotted owl or the humpback whale deserve to be protected for reasons that extend beyond their current economic value or the short-term costs of their protection. Long-term rewards might be indeterminable now, but the uncertainty of the costs of their loss is unbearable in an increasingly wealthy world.

Ozone depletion is the deterioration of the ozone layer caused by the release of chlorofluorocarbons (CFCs). CFCs are used extensively as propellants; they are common in refrigerating units and in aerosol preparations such as antiperspirants and hair sprays. The ozone layer is an important component of the earth's atmosphere because it provides the principal shield between the earth's surface and the sun. It protects, for example, against the harmful effects of ultraviolet (UV) light. Exposure to excessive UV can cause certain kinds of cancers and genetic mutations. Ozone depletion has been documented by a variety of international sources studying expanding atmospheric holes. While such holes are principally located over the South Pole, they have also been found in Africa, Australia, and New Zealand. From the appearance of three-legged frogs to the disappearance of entire species, many ill effects have been attributed to a combination of deforestation, desertification, and ozone depletion.

Global warming refers to the gradual increase of the earth's overall temperature. Many attribute the rising temperature to the burning of fossil fuels and the buildup of greenhouse gases (carbon dioxide, CFCs, and methane) in the earth's atmosphere. The causes and consequences of global warming for the environment and human life are disputed by scientists, economists, governments, IGOs, and NGOs. Scientists disagree as to how much the world's temperature will increase; estimates range anywhere from 3 to 12 degrees. They disagree as to whether the process of global warming can be reversed. And they disagree as to whether global warming is even a bad thing for the planet. Moreover, international efforts to address global warming are complicated by competing world views, the North–South conflict, and the continuing primacy of state sovereignty.

International efforts to protect the environment and manage the earth's natural resources have led to a proliferation of international environmental organizations, which include IGOs, MNCs, NGOs, and regimes. In the following sections, we'll outline some of those international organizations and look at the UN-sponsored conferences that are central to the interrelated environmental issues of deforestation, desertification, biodiversity, ozone depletion, and global warming.

THE STOCKHOLM CONFERENCE (1972)

The first comprehensive international conference addressing the environment was the UN Conference on the Human Environment, held in Stockholm, Sweden. The Stockholm Conference produced 26 principles and 109 recommendations regarding human settlements, natural resource management, pollution, educational and social aspects of the environment, development, and international organizations (Greene 1998, 317; Bennett 1995, 335). The Stockholm Conference is perhaps best remembered for advocating the creation of the United Nations Environmental Program (UNEP), for establishing transnational monitoring networks, and for institutionalizing the principle of the Common Heritage of Mankind.

The UNEP was created shortly after the Stockholm Conference by the General Assembly and is overseen by the ECOSOC. It is administered by a small secretariat, which organizes and promotes interagency cooperation within the UN system. The UNEP also helps coordinate the monitoring of environmental problems by UN agencies and NGOs. The UNEP is funded by the Environmental Fund, which is made up of voluntary contributions. The UNEP possesses no supranational authority and therefore must rely on the cooperation of states, UN agencies, and NGOs for fostering environmental protection.

The UNEP is central to the global monitoring of environmental conditions. This network consists of monitoring stations with links among UN offices, state agencies, and NGOs. In addition to measuring pollution and documenting the status of natural resources, this monitoring network collects data regarding potential environmental threats. Environmental NGOs play a pivotal role in helping to define environmental problems and identifying issues and strategies. NGOs also provide expertise and credible analysis of environmental conditions to governments at the local and national levels and to IGOs.

The Common Heritage of Mankind is an important principle that attempts to define the global commons. The principle seeks to clarify the extent to which specific areas belong to all the countries on the planet. These are places whose resources everyone may exploit and all have the right to use—international waters, the deep seabed, and orbital space. The Common Heritage of Mankind is fundamental. It identifies, defines, and protects the global commons. It promotes the idea that everyone should reap the benefits of the global commons, not just those with means to utilize them. As a result, the North–South conflict and development issues are inextricably intertwined with the principle of the Common Heritage of Mankind. This is illustrated clearly with efforts to manage the ocean resources.

THE UN CONFERENCE ON THE LAW OF THE SEA (UNCLOS)

UNCLOS (1973–1982) reflects the limited international understanding of rights to and protection of the oceans and their resources. UNCLOS builds upon the first modern law-of-the-sea conference, which was held in 1958. This conference attempted to reconcile two principles—state sovereignty and freedom of the high seas. Many coastal states claimed absolute sovereignty over large areas of the oceans, a claim that conflicted with the historic principle of the free navigation of the high seas. Widespread disagreements existed (and still exist) among states as to where the state's territorial jurisdiction ends and international waters begin. What is the best way to measure and define national claims of sovereignty? The 1958 conference attempted to resolve this dispute by measuring the depth as well as the breadth of the territorial sea. Traditionally, the territorial sea was defined as an area extending three miles from the shore, over which states exercised exclusive and complete jurisdiction. This three-mile marker was rooted in nineteenth-century precedent, being the average range of cannon-fire. Coastal states also claimed that sovereignty extended to the edge of the continental shelf, where the ocean floor drops off into the deep seabed.

Twentieth-century states, however, have sought to extend their sovereignty further, claiming jurisdictions of 200 beyond-shore miles, regardless of where the continental shelf ends. So more disagreements arose: Is this sovereignty absolute, does it extend to resources, or is it limited to navigation? These disagreements were particularly acute because the 200-mile zones often overlapped. Moreover, they would allow island states to extend their territory and their sovereignty considerably. The 1958 law-of-the-sea convention addressed these concerns, but was unable to resolve them among the negotiating parties.

After several failed rounds of negotiations in the 1960s, international efforts to regulate the oceans were revived in 1973, in part because of the momentum generated by the Stockholm Conference. The UNCLOS conference (1973–1982) extended the territorial sea to 12 miles where states may regulate shipping. As shipping has important environmental and security implications for nations, coastal states have the right to impose shipping regulations. UNCLOS also established a 200-mile exclusive economic zone, granting coastal states the rights to all the fishing and mineral resources within that area. We can see in the 200-mile zone an effort to privatize the commons. States have been unwilling to yield the necessary sovereignty to create a supranational body to regulate the commons. But by privatizing the commons, coastal states get the rewards and pay the costs of controlling large areas of the oceans. Theoretically, these states will behave rationally—they will protect the oceans and their resources because it's in their immediate and long-term self-interest to do so.

The UNCLOS was controversial because it ceded significant resources to coastal states, many of which are exceptionally wealthy. Many poorer and landlocked states protested the conference provisions because the public good was greatly reduced. Coastal states could exclude others from the 200-mile zone, keeping the less advantaged from exploring the deep seabed that extends beyond the zone. The conference created the International Sea Bed Authority to monitor deep-sea exploration, but it is still unclear as to whether and how deep-sea resources will be distributed. Those who capitalize on the global commons, which now lies beyond the 200-mile zone, are supposed to share the wealth with the international community; but those having the capability to exploit the deep seabed are reluctant to commit the resources for exploration if their profit margins are significantly narrowed. To complicate matters even further, some coastal states want to extend their jurisdictions even further, well beyond the 200-mile exclusive economic zone. The United States, for example, did not sign onto UNCLOS until 1994 after extracting significant concessions that many see as undermining the entire treaty. Today, coastal states continue to claim sovereignty further and further from their shores.

EFFORTS TO PROTECT BIODIVERSITY

Several unilateral, bilateral, and multilateral initiatives to protect biodiversity and natural habitat have drawn attention to the peril of sea and land mammals as well as birds. Although these efforts have met with varying degrees of success, they have all sought to save habitat and species from spoilage and economic exploitation. The following international treaties have been established to preserve habitat and protect biodiversity (Greene 1998, 316–317):

> 1971 Ramsar Convention (conserves wetlands—the natural habitat of water-fowl)
> 1972 Convention on Trade in Endangered Species
> 1972 London Dumping Convention (restricts the disposal of chemical and nuclear wastes at sea)
> MARPOL Convention (curbs oil pollution)

In addition, IGOs, such as the International Whaling Commission, have also been established to protect certain endangered species. Most efforts to protect biodiversity occur at the national level because states exercise direct jurisdiction over habitat. For example, the U.S. Endangered Species Act protects domestic species like the eagle, the spotted owl, and timber wolves, while the U.S. Marine Mammal Protection Act extends protection to sea mammals outside national jurisdiction by restricting trade with countries that harvest dolphins or whales. For the most part, habitat protection falls to states through domestic legislation.

The Rio Conference (discussed in detail later in this chapter) engendered the Convention on Biological Diversity, which was signed by 155 states. The legal framework of the treaty acknowledges the sovereign rights of states to resources within their territorial jurisdiction, but commits states to the protection of species, ecosystems, and habitats. The treaty also establishes rules for the use of genetic resources derived from plants and animals. Unsurprisingly, the North–South divide made negotiating this treaty difficult: "Developing countries were concerned that an international treaty might put unwanted limitations on the use of their natural resources, including forests. . . . Developed nations, on the other hand, wanted continued access to the plant and animal life in developing nations" (Press 1992). Money issues afforded another impediment. Developing countries wanted the richer countries to pay for conservation efforts in the developing world. The protection of fish, animals, birds, and plants together with their habitats is an expensive endeavor, requiring a significant commitment of financial resources—resources Third World states simply cannot spare. Developing states also want to share in the wealth generated from pharmaceuticals and the genetic engineering of plant and animal life originating in the Third World. The treaty recognizes that wealthy nations have a responsibility to help fund conservation internationally; however, monetary contributions are, for the most part, voluntary and remain small.

THE VIENNA CONVENTION OF THE PROTECTION OF THE OZONE AND THE MONTREAL PROTOCOL (1985)

Ozone depletion threatens biodiversity and poses a health hazard to humans. The Vienna Convention and the Montreal Protocol significantly reduce the amount of CFCs that can be released into the atmosphere and establish a schedule for their eventual elimination (Benedict 1991). The Montreal Protocol also creates a trust fund, known as the Multilateral Fund, that helps developing states acquire substitutes for CFCs and other ozone-depleting substances. The Vienna Convention and the Montreal Protocol have been widely hailed as important environmental protection successes because the gap between North and South was bridged through compromise and consensus. Most scientists were able to agree as to the causes and consequences of ozone depletion.

The principal depleting agents are relatively easy to identify and the agents have comparable, nonharmful substitutes.

The successes of the Vienna Convention and the Montreal Protocol have set an encouraging precedent for international environmental cooperation; however, implementation of the agreements has encountered domestic roadblocks in the United States. Several CFC-producing firms have filed suit in federal court, claiming that certain aspects of the treaty violate due process. Some have asked Congress to exempt CFCs that are used in inhalers for asthma. But in spite of such problems, the Vienna Convention and the Montreal Protocol show that compromise and consensus can be achieved without resorting to "the lowest common denominator" approach that has plagued other international negotiations to protect the environment.

THE RIO CONFERENCE

The UN Conference on the Environment and Development (1992) held in Rio de Janeiro, Brazil, simultaneously and systematically addressed the interrelated environmental issues of desertification, biodiversity, climate change, and deforestation. The Rio Conference, also known as the Earth Summit, was attended by more than 150 states while several hundred NGOs participated in a parallel conference. Among the attendees were more than 100 heads of state, signaling that economic development and protection of the environment are priorities of the international community in the new world order.

The Rio Conference adopted the theme of "sustainable development." First articulated in 1987 by the World Commission on Environment and Development (also known as the Brundtland Commission), sustainable development is economic development that "meets the needs of the present without compromising the ability of future generations to meet their own needs" (World Commission on Environment and Development 1987, 43). Sustainable development recognizes that the kind of economic development that has occurred in the advanced industrialized countries cannot be replicated in the Third World without grave environmental consequences. The Brundtland Commission assigned significant responsibility for environmental degradation to the advanced industrialized countries and raised important equity issues between North and South. It also considered the rights of future generations. The Rio Conference adopted the Brundtland recommendations, adding new dimensions to environmental protection and socioeconomic development.

The Rio Conference was the culmination of years of preparatory work in drafting agreements known as framework conventions (Greene 1998, 330)—international agreements that establish basic aims and principles but impose no binding obligations on states. During the Rio Conference, three principal framework conventions were adopted: the Convention on Climate Change, the Convention on Biological Diversity, and the Convention to Combat Desertification. Unfortunately, a framework convention on deforestation failed. International negotiations could generate no consensus regarding principles, norms, aims, or procedures for arresting deforestation. This setback notwithstanding, framework conventions are useful. They provide the first steps in systematically addressing interrelated and interdependent environmental problems.

The parties to framework conventions commit themselves to following up their agreements with legally binding treaties. Parties agree to cooperate on setting broad goals and to cultivate concrete strategies for achieving more narrow and specific objectives. Negotiations for developing the Conventions on Biological Diversity and Desertification have stalled; however, more than 130 nations did meet in 1997 in Kyoto, Japan, to tangibly implement the Framework Convention on Climate Change. The Framework Convention on Climate Change called on the industrialized states to cap their emissions to 1990 levels, but the parties could not agree on a timetable. The Framework Convention also establishes mechanisms for monitoring global warming and commits the advanced industrialized states to partially fund emission-control measures in the developing world (Stevens et al. 1992, 11). The Kyoto Conference, which is designed to give the international agreement on global warming treaty status, seeks to achieve emission stabilization and reduction goals. The Conference also addressed the always-controversial issue of financing, which is discussed at length in our case study on global warming.

The Rio Conference also adopted Agenda 21, which is an 800-page program for promoting sustainable development in the twenty-first century. Agenda 21 is divided into four sections. The first section deals with issues relating to social and economic development. It addresses poverty, consumption patterns, population, human settlements, and policymaking as they affect the prospects of achieving sustainable development. The second section focuses on the conservation and management of resources for development. Specifically, this section addresses protection of the atmosphere, and land and ocean resources. It outlines strategies for combating deforestation, desertification, and drought. It also addresses the use of toxic chemicals and the disposal of hazardous and radioactive wastes. The third section explores ways to strengthen the role of major sociodemographic groups such as women, youth, indigenous peoples, NGOs, workers, unions, farmers, business, industry, and scientists. The fourth section deals with ways and means of Agenda 21 implementation. This section examines financial resources, the transfer of environmentally sound technology, and promoting environmental awareness.

Agenda 21 consists of forty chapters that outline a very ambitious and forward-looking program for environmental protection and economic development. It also calls for the creation of the Commission on Sustainable Development (CSD) to help implement and monitor Agenda 21 initiatives. Created in December 1992, the CSD is a 53-member functional commission of the ECOSOC. More than a thousand NGOs are accredited to participate in the Commission's work. The CSD is charged with promoting visibility of sustainable development in UN activities and for improving the coordination of environmental and development programs among UN agencies and within and between states.

In 1997, the CSD reported to the UN General Assembly on the status of Agenda 21 implementation in "Rio+5." Progress has been slow at the national level as many countries, including the United States, encountered domestic trouble in passing the appropriate national legislation. Many of the agreements worked out and signed during the Rio convention established basic aims but did not formally bind or commit states. The language of the biodiversity treaty, for example, is sprinkled with such qualifying phrases as "where appropriate" or "subject to national legislation" or "as far as possible" (Press 1992). The CSD, seeking to keep the Rio momentum going, put forth a comprehensive document entitled "Programme for the Further Implementation of Agenda 21" (Commission on Sustainable Development 1998). States continue to be pressured domestically and internationally to pursue meaningful sustainable development policies.

Agenda 21 also addresses the financing of environmental protection and sustainable economic development. Agenda 21 calls for the Global Environmental Facility (GEF) to help finance sustainable development efforts. The GEF, which became operational in 1991, was created to facilitate concessionary financing for the Third World to assist in managing the greenhouse effect, the loss of biodiversity, and ocean pollution (Finance and Development 1991). The GEF is jointly operated by the World Bank and the United Nations Development and Environmental Fund (UNDEP). Its initial start-up $1.5 billion was provided by the advanced industrialized world.

Many consider the Rio Conference a success in that it brought most of the world's nations together to address myriad environmental and socioeconomic developmental problems. The conference brought together NGOs and IGOs, representing states, women's groups, business, industry, labor unions, scientists, and indigenous peoples. The Rio conference highlights the increasing importance of NGOs in international governance. Thousands of NGOs are involved with influencing international environmental issues. These NGOs defy any defining characteristics. They can be religious, secular, for-profit, nonprofit, private, or public. NGOs influence environmental governance by defining or redefining environmental issues, by lobbying governments, by proposing draft texts of conventions, by lobbying international agencies, and by monitoring the development and implementation of international agreements (Porter and Brown 1991, 54). These nonstate actors have carved out a central place for themselves in the formation of national and international environmental policies.

Are international efforts to protect the environment sufficient? Are they equitable? What is the best way to balance environmental protection with economic development in a global capitalist economy—an economy largely based on natural resource extraction and consumption? The complexities of environmental controversies are illustrated next in the case study on global warming. This case highlights the deep differences between rich and poor nations and deep-seated divisions over the causes and consequences of global warming. It demonstrates how competing world views make international consensus-building difficult and how different groups within and between societies seek to pass the costs of global warming on to others and even on to future generations.

CASE STUDY 9: GLOBAL WARMING

Global warming is a phenomenon, a progressive increase of the temperature of the earth's atmosphere attributable to the buildup of greenhouse gases (carbon dioxide, CFCs, and methane) trapped in the atmosphere. According to the Intergovernmental Panel on Climate Change (IPCC):

> [H]uman activities—such as the burning of coal to run industries and gasoline to fuel automobiles—are warming up the global climate. Left unchecked, the "enhanced greenhouse effect" is expected to alter the earth's climate and adversely affect human health, ecosystems, farming, forestry, water levels, and human development. (World Bank News 1997, 6)

Global warming is further exacerbated by indiscriminant land clearing, the lack of reforestation, and the expanding market for tropical timbers.

Global warming became a focal point of international environmental protection in the late 1980s as more and more scientists began to warn that global warming was real and had both immediate and long-term consequences. Rising sea levels threaten coastal and island states and their human settlements. Weather extremes, such as floods and drought, threaten hundreds of millions of lives, destroy habitat and crops, and can lead to the destruction of temperate and tropical rain forests. Increased economic development and rapid population growth ensure that global emissions of carbon dioxide will increase; meanwhile, the square acreage of forest, particularly the tropical rain forests, will decrease as the need for living space, fuel, and raw materials becomes greater. Without the forests, carbon dioxide levels will rise, increasing global temperatures.

In November 1989, sixty-eight countries met in the Netherlands to address the global warming issue. Three strategies were given consideration. First, all states should commit to stabilizing or reducing carbon dioxide emissions by a certain date in the future. Second, only the advanced industrialized countries should stabilize or reduce their greenhouse gas emissions. These countries should also pay for new technologies to help the developing world cultivate more efficient industries and energy-consumption patterns. This strategy was advocated by many Third World nations, particularly India and China, who argued that Third World states were not responsible for current global warming trends. Rather, global warming was the result of the North's industrialization process and the U.S. love affair with the automobile. Developing countries need new industries to alleviate poverty and promote economic development, which translates into an increase in energy use. Curbing greenhouse gas emissions in the Third World would put undue burdens on their economies, stifling economic growth and limiting consumption. It also makes the Third World pay the externalized costs of the economic development of the West. The third strategy, advocated by the United States, the former Soviet Union, and Japan, was to conduct more research and try to reach a scientific consensus before committing to any specific reduction or stabilization plan. These three strategies, or variations thereof, have been debated, albeit acrimoniously, at the preparatory global warming conferences in Geneva, at the Rio Conference, and at the Kyoto Conference in 1997.

The causes and the consequences of global warming are contested. Several observers question whether enough evidence exists to conclude that global warming is, in fact, a real environmental condition. Long-term temperature records are incomplete and documentation is inadequate. After all, in the 1970s, environmentalists and meteorologists warned, not of warming, but of a coming ice age. Others acknowledge that global warming exists but disagree as to its causes or its effects. Many argue that warmer temperatures are an acceptable price to pay for our current standard of living and technological advancement. A few even argue that countries in the Northern Hemisphere, like Russia and Canada, could benefit from global warming.

Several facts, however, are not in dispute. First, the United States accounts for almost 20 percent of global greenhouse gas emissions, followed by the European Union, China, and Russia. People in the industrialized countries account for less than 25 percent of the world's population, but generate 55 percent of the heat-trapping atmospheric gases (Cohen 1994, 7). But in terms of economic output, the advanced industrialized countries are far more efficient users of fossil fuels than are developing countries. Economic output refers to the metric tons of greenhouse gases emitted per million dollars of gross domestic product generated. Using this measure, China, India, Russia, and the rest of the developing world have far more "dirty industries" and are less efficient. Thus, their pollution rates are higher, given what is produced and consumed.

The Kyoto Conference was held in December 1997. The initial agreement was hammered out after eleven days of turbulent debate. The Kyoto Protocol included three major features. First, the 159 parties to the Protocol agreed to reduce worldwide emissions of greenhouse gases by 5.2 percent below 1990 levels by the year 2012. (*Online Newshour* 1997). All the parties are permitted to set their own reduction targets to achieve this goal. The EU, the United States, and Japan have agreed to reduce their emissions by 8, 7, and 6 percent below 1990 levels, respectively. Second, only the advanced industrialized states are required to meet their agreed-upon target. The Kyoto Protocol requires the 38 developed states to reduce their greenhouse gas emissions, as they tend to be the largest emitters. The developing countries are only required to set voluntary limits. Third, the Kyoto Protocol allows for the trading of emission permits. That is, developed countries could buy the right to emit greenhouse gases from countries in the developing world. This would help all nations to achieve their collective goal: Worldwide greenhouse gas emissions could dip overall while Third World industries could afford to develop greater efficiencies—efficiencies that would benefit both the developing and the developed world.

Is the Kyoto Protocol good and effective public international law? Will the Kyoto Protocol be successful at reducing greenhouse gas emissions? Who stands to gain and who stands to lose from its implementation or lack thereof? Is Kyoto a missed opportunity to build upon a framework that addresses global rather than national concerns?

A REALIST CUT

Environmental issues such as biodiversity, desertification, and global warming occupy the realm of low politics for most realists. These issues take a back seat to geostrategic and military concerns because environmental threats are distant and convoluted while environmental protection is costly. More important, the rewards of environmental protection are uncertain at best. States in the international system need to be kept apprised of potential environmental threats, but they should not sacrifice more important and more immediate interests such as a strong, healthy, and diversified economy.

Global warming is the kind of environmental issue that bumps against traditional notions of national interests. If the environmental scientists are right, global warming is the result of the human way of life. And the way humans live is a very difficult thing to change without a very good reason. In general, realists argue that "free riding" on any global warming agreement would be quite easy and highly likely. While many, if not most, states are willing to cooperate in curbing greenhouse emissions, other states—free riders—can reap the rewards of a reversal of global warming without paying the price. Free-riding states can then devote their resources to increasing their economic or military strength at the expense of the environment and the collective efforts of states to reduce greenhouse gas emissions. Free-riding states can even nullify the efforts to check global warming. The end result is quite similar to the prisoners' dilemma (Chapter 3). If everyone cooperates, the efforts to curb global warming are likely to be effective, producing the best outcome for everyone on the planet. Unfortunately, incentives to defect are great. If one large emitter, like a United States or a China, defects—or if a group of states defects—the efforts of the rest are for naught. So each state would be better off not cooperating, because chances are high someone is going to defect.

Which states are likely to be free riders? That depends on whether you're a realist from the developed world or a realist from the developing world. Realists in the North argue that any international agreement on global warming that does not include binding target reductions on countries like China, India, Mexico, and Brazil is pointless (Zengerle 1998, 10–11). Developing states are expected to account for more than 50 percent of greenhouse gas emissions by 2010. Thus, developing states are, in effect, free riding because they are permitted to increase their emissions while the developed world must fundamentally change its way of life. The U.S. Chamber of Commerce argues that the Kyoto Protocol will cost the average American family of four some $30,000 to meet the U.S. commitment (U.S. Chamber of Commerce 1998). The advanced industrialized states would be downright foolish to agree to such costly (and substantive) changes in lifestyle with no assurances of success in reducing greenhouse gas emissions from the developing world.

Realists from the developing world take another view. They argue that global warming is the fault of the advanced industrialized powers, whose status is directly related to their long history of greenhouse gas emissions. The developed states currently produce the lion's share of emissions, and will produce approximately half of them in 2010. Yet, the advanced industrialized states want to distribute the costs of global warming onto developing countries, costs they can ill afford. According to the editorial opinion in Brazil's *Folha de Sao Paulo* on December 8, 1997:

> The position of the developed countries is also comfortable. Once nature is devastated, these nations, the United States in particular, want to divide the destruction's costs worldwide. . . . But the developed countries are the major emitters of polluting gas. The United States, leading the ranking polluters, is the one that defends the slower rate for the reduction of burning of fossil fuel that produces the greenhouse effect. (U.S. Information Agency 1997b, 12)

The motives of states, particularly the powerful ones, factor into international negotiations. According to Gu Qi in China's *Jiefan Ribao*, Kyoto negotiations can be explained in a variety of ways. "One explanation for U.S. behavior is that its national interests are more important than global interests. . . . For its own economic interests, the United States is unwilling to accept restrictions, and is guilty of using various delaying tactics" (U.S. Information Agency 1997b, 3). At the same time, the United States saw the European proposal of reducing greenhouse gas emissions to 15 percent below 1990 levels as unrealistic. The Europeans knew full well that such a plan would not be considered seriously; however, the plan did allow the Europeans to take the moral high ground and engender support among developing nations.

Realists from both developed and developing states rail against the loss of state sovereignty implied by the Kyoto Convention. According to U.S. Senator Chuck Hagel (R-NE), "This is the United Nations, for the first time ever . . . having the power to dictate to a nation, to the United States, how much energy it can use, what kind of energy it can use" (cited in Zengerle 1998, 10–11). Undoubtedly, realists in developing states are equally concerned about yielding state prerogatives to international organizations.

For realists, states that cooperate with international efforts to check global warming and reduce carbon dioxide emissions face job losses, skyrocketing energy prices, and high taxes on its citizens. All of these are unacceptable costs for an environmental issue that offers uncertain rewards, if any. Some states, like Canada and Russia, stand to benefit from global warming while Southern states at or close to sea level face devastating consequences. The incentives for others to free ride could even mean that states that actively cooperate may face a relative decline of economic and military capability. The best that states can do, absent a higher authority, is to tend to their own economic and security needs and respond to environmental threats as they arise. As Senator Hagel remarked, "Meteorologists can't even tell you from forty-eight hours to forty-eight hours what kind of weather we're going to have. In Kyoto, they were talking about one-hundred-year weather patterns" (cited in Zengerle 1998, 10–11).

A LIBERAL CUT

The liberal views of global warming break down into two positions: the neoclassical economic perspective and the neoliberal institutionalist perspective. The neoclassical economic perspective is the position originally advocated by the United States at the Kyoto conference—zero reduction of greenhouse emissions, but a cap on emissions. Each state is then assigned a "right" to emit, based on its economic output. Recall that economic output refers to metric tons of greenhouse gases emitted per million dollars of gross domestic product generated. Embedded in this proposal is the right of states to buy and sell emission permits that would force economically expanding states to buy the right to emit greenhouse gases from other states. According to Britain's *Daily Telegraph* (December 10, 1997), "the U.S. proposal is based on its own successful domestic experience with tradable permits for sulphur emissions. This kind of market solution boosts efficiency and puts a ceiling on overall emissions."

   The neoclassical perspective relies heavily on the idea that the best way to protect the global commons is to privatize it. Giving states the right to pollute gives them, in effect, property rights in the atmosphere, whereby both the environment and economic development can be sustained. The U.S. proposal sought to establish an effective equilibrium between the demands of economic development and environmental protection as it relates to global warming by bringing market forces to bear upon both interests. One of the central problems of development is the externality of many environmental costs. But if firms are forced to pay as they pollute, they will come closer to bearing the true costs of economic development—and the prices of goods and services produced will reflect those costs. Assigned rights to pollute, coupled with right to buy and sell pollution permits, governments have incentives to encourage energy-efficient behaviors on the part of firms and individuals. And the more efficient states become, the more rights they can sell to less efficient states (or industries at the national level). At the same time, no artificial impediments are placed on economic growth and flexibility is built into the greenhouse gas–reducing scheme.

   One way that states can encourage energy-efficient behaviors for firms is to institute an investment tax credit for those utilizing energy-efficient technologies, both in existing and future sectors. According to Murray Weidenbaum (1992), investment tax credits have two positive effects. First, investment tax credits stimulate economic growth rates, and the increased economic output generates the resources to address environmental issues. Second, tax credits encourage the replacement of old, inefficient, pollution-generating capital equipment. The investment tax credit is thus a tangible, but nonintrusive, way for governments to use market forces to achieve both macroeconomic and macroenvironmental goals.

Neoclassical liberals are wary of environmental regulations that curb market forces or stress the role of the state. They argue that state control over industries and extensive regulation of the environment will not produce desirable environmental and economic results. As proof, they cite the former Eastern Bloc and Soviet successor states, where both the environment and industry suffered severe, and possibly irreparable, harm when market forces were eliminated through excessive bureaucratic regulation. The Soviet Union—a managed economy—left a legacy of "ecocide," the result of its efforts to become an agricultural and industrial giant (Sneider 1992, 10–11). The old Soviet territory, once rich in natural resources, is now massively contaminated by industrial pollution, pesticides, chemical fertilizers, and nuclear waste. Thus, states should have a limited role, lest bureaucratic inefficiencies undermine both the economy and the environment.

The neoliberal institutional approach specifies a much more prominent role for governments and international organizations. Rather than merely assigning and monitoring property rights, then letting markets govern the rest, the institutionalists maintain that national governments and international organizations are essential to international environmental governance absent a world government. The international environmental regime consists of states, IGOs, nonprofit NGOs, businesses, and the scientific community. These different actors represent both congruent and competing interests—interests that must be addressed openly and systematically in international forums. While all interests may not be equitably addressed and bargaining power may vary, the balance of all these interests will approximate an international public good. This dynamic brings about a consensus among a variety of groups and leads to the formation of knowledge-based groups known as epistemic communities.

The neoliberal institutionalist perspective is further divided between centralized and decentralized approaches. The centralized approach reflects the arguments associated with the advocates of some kind of world government. The centralized approach is based on the idea that governments should agree to a "set of actions calibrated to achieve the desired reduction in emissions" (Cooper 1998, 72). The best way for governments to achieve a reduction in greenhouse gas emission is to tax the offending activity. This so-called carbon tax would be monitored by the IMF, which could report to the body that implements the global warming treaty. While Kyoto is a long, long way from an international tax, many advocated a central role for international organizations. This centralized view was never seriously considered at Kyoto, as the United States, a virtual veto state, strenuously pursued the neoclassical view.

The decentralized view of international governance as it relates to global warming considers the local, municipal, subnational, national, regional, and international activities of all the different actors affected by global warming. It acknowledges a complex web of actors, each pursuing different goals and aims. However, unlike the neoclassical approach, it would not unleash unfettered market forces on firms and individuals to reduce greenhouse gas emission. Rather, it would marshal ideas. That is, divergent interests would compete in an international marketplace of ideas—an open atmosphere in which a variety of interests and arguments can be heard. This process, in turn, would further the advancement of knowledge. Competing interests within and between states, within and between industries, within and between NGOs, and within and between scientific communities clash in this intellectual market . . . such a clash will force a rethinking and redefining of previously held positions, prompting more rigorous debate.

The knowledge process, while arduous, can achieve global environmental protection without undermining individual, local, or national interests. The Kyoto Protocol, which builds upon the Framework Convention for Climate change, is far from perfect. But perfection was never the goal. International environmental protection will never be easy in an international arena where politics are influenced heavily by competitive nation-states. As stated in an editorial by *The Guardian* (December 11, 1997):

> We have seen the same old divisions setting developed nations against the developing with the same last-minute concessions and late night fudges. The result, assuming it can be pinned down and ratified, is acknowledged on all sides to be only a tentative stab attacking a problem already soaring out of control. All concerned, including environmental lobbyists, say that a defective accord is better than none. Wearily, we must accept the logic of this argument. (U.S. Information Agency 1997b, 8)

Pragmatism and process are the best routes to solutions that address competing concerns. These competing concerns are reflected in the World Bank's assessment of Kyoto and its own role in building the capacity and the economic resources of states to ensure economic development and environmental protection. To this end, the World Bank is working to mainstream renewable energy policies, to integrate climate change externalities, and to identify climate-friendly options in the World Bank Group Portfolio (*World Bank News* 1997). The World Bank strongly supports the compromise at Kyoto, which exempts developing states from mandatory greenhouse gas reduction targets. The World Bank, building upon neoclassical economic analysis, views economic development as necessary in order to create the wealth required to adequately address global warming. From international to local levels, economic development and environmental protection are pursued incrementally to the mutual benefit of individuals, firms, nations, and the world.

In sum, the distinguishing features of any liberal view of environmental protection are the prominent roles of markets (political and/or economic) and the behavior of nonstate actors, particularly firms and NGOs. Environmental NGOs have created an expansive network of agencies that monitor environmental problems and lobby governments and IGOs for rules and regulations that protect the environment. Firms are also important because they are the ones generating wealth, and environmental regulation affects their interests. Governments are also involved in that they respond to domestic constituencies and enforce property rights (in this case, the right to pollute). Any environmental regime that addresses global warming must have the cooperation of states to enforce international rules and norms.

A MARXIST CUT

Marxists point out that international efforts to protect the environment reveal widening differences between rich and poor. These differences relate to the causes of environmental degradation and the best strategies for environmental protection. Like realists from the developing world, many Marxists see global warming as a consequence of the economic development of the North. However, Marxists emphasize that it is the economic development of the advanced industrialized countries that has caused the current crisis in global warming. The capitalist mode of production, with its emphasis on private property, wage labor, and markets has undermined the natural environment. Hence, the Marxist lens focuses on capitalism and the mass consumer societies of the North as the principal culprit. Northern societies benefited from the unrestricted use of their own resources and access to resources in colonies in the South. They cleared millions of square kilometers of forest without any regard to the environmental consequences. The global capitalist economy is based on the consumption of fossil fuels by industries and consumers. To many Marxists, the UN emphasis on "sustainable development" is just a euphemism for sustaining the privileges of the dominant capitalist states or classes (Seabrook 1993). Radio commentary on *Westdeutscher Rundfunk* of Cologne stated that the U.S. position at the Kyoto conference reflected its privileged status: "This is a climate policy according to the decisions of the lord of the manor" (U.S Information Agency 1997b, 10).

The negotiations of the Kyoto protocol represent the continuing dominance of neoclassical liberal economic thought. Gramscian Marxists point out that market solutions are near dogma at the IMF and the World Bank. Even decidedly liberal observers have recognized that these multilateral financial institutions and the regional development banks have yet to internalize "sustainable development" in evaluating loan applications and in their general lending practices (Porter and Brown 1991, 47–49). These international organizations stand in the way of significant environmental protection. To many Marxist-inspired observers, the recent emphasis of multilateral financial institutions on environmental protection is more "rhetoric" than "reality" (Rich 1993; Foster 1993). They continue to fund industry at the expense of the environment and they limit the participation of NGOs in development and environmental projects (*Earth Island Journal* 1992, 20). The now infamous "Summers's Memo," written by then–World Bank official Lawrence Summers, recommended that developing states should relax or discourage environmental regulations to lure industries from developed states (Rauber 1992). While this recommendation makes perfect sense from a neoclassical standpoint, it bodes ill for the environment.

The Kyoto Protocol is a victory for capitalism and international industries because it accomplishes very little, which is precisely what industry wants. Industries that are able to externalize their pollution costs are able to achieve higher rates of profits for their owners and shareholders. Industries are only concerned about their quarterly reports and prospects for growth. The furthest thought from the minds of most CEOs is the temperature of the earth's atmosphere and the environmental consequences one hundred years from now. It is not surprising that the largest multinational corporations lobbied against strengthening the Clean Air Act in the United States, the world's largest emitter of greenhouse gases. These powerful and influential actors included, but are not limited to, Allied Chemical, Chevron, Dow Chemical, Dupont, Exxon, General Electric, General Motors, Getty Oil, Kaiser Aluminum & Chemical Corporation, Mobil Oil, Standard Oil, and Texaco.

The oil and automobile industries' displeasure with environmental regulation translated into direct and decisive influence on the U.S. position at Kyoto. According to an editorial in Japan's *Mainichi* on December 9, 1997, "About 50 U.S. senators and members of Congress as well as petroleum and auto officials are assembled at the conference site to keep close watch on Washington's insistence on a 'zero percent' reduction to the last. Isn't this the imposition of an environmental 'Pax Americana' on the rest of the world?" (U.S. Information Agency 1997b, 2). To many observers of the Kyoto negotiations, the U.S. position was untenable. As Italy's *La Repubblica* stated, "The United States . . . will not accept meaningful changes in its ways of production and consumption" (U.S. Information Agency 1997b, 9). Denmark's *Information* editorialized, "The United States won a victory for the global market economy at the historic meeting in Kyoto. A precedent has been created where the most dangerous greenhouse gases will become trading commodities. The climate will not be the winner" (U.S. Information Agency 1997b, 10).

Marxists see environmental degradation as a contradiction of capitalism. The level of economic development of the capitalist core has come at the expense of the environment and the developing world. As the *Brundtland Report* states, future economic development cannot take place without grave consequences to the environment, which is why Kyoto is as much a conference on international equity, social justice, and economic ideology as it is about global warming. *Le Pays*, Burkina Faso's principal newspaper, declared:

> A tip of the hat to the Group of 77 that from now on wants to break from the triumphant capitalism, the all-powerful gospel of competition in the name of which the United States behaves, not only as the universal principal polluter, but also as transforming our countries into tubs for toxic wastes. It is true that the poor countries are the first victims of the destruction of the environment, the devastation of resources, the accumulation of noise pollution, the over-consumption of the rich, the economic system based on monopolizing profit, and the arrogance of civilization experts. (U.S. Information Agency 1997b, 9)

A FEMINIST CUT

The Rio Conference brought many women's issues to the forefront of the international agenda. The roles of women in sustainable development are argued to be central to the success of Agenda 21. One role of women is that of "environmental managers" (Cohen 1994). Women, especially those who live in the developing world with traditional and subsistence economies, are users and conservers of their immediate environment. They are "the major food producers and marketers, water and fuel wood gatherers, and overseers of domestic sanitation and waste disposal" (Cohen 1994, 8). Women are also the reproducers of the human population. Population growth translates into more energy consumers and the need for additional living space, both of which contribute significantly to global warming.

Many see rapid population growth as undermining the environment and the local and national economies (*Finance and Development* 1991). Women obviously play a critical role in promoting stable population growth because they can influence family size. Environmentalists, population advocates, and feminists all agree that improving the status of women globally is the most important means for controlling population growth. They argue that women must be allowed more control over their lives. Women must be politically and economically enfranchised, and they must have access to birth control and other reproductive services.

Yet cultural and religious impediments remain, as does outright sexism. These features are prevalent both in the developed and the developing world. Many feminists are wary of government population policies because they have led to forced abortion and sterilization at one extreme (China and India) and the criminalization of birth control and forced child bearing on the other (Ireland). Feminists argue that population policies that are implemented without specific and guaranteed protection of the individual rights of women are catastrophic for women. They argue that a bottom-up approach that allows women control over their bodies and their lives will enable effective family planning and stable population growth. Only then will population pressures on the world's reserves of food, water, and other natural resources be alleviated.

While population growth is directly related to global consumption patterns, women are also important consumers of energy and gatherers of wood fuel. Taxes that attempt to restrict energy consumption put additional burdens on women. Global warming and international efforts to curb its effects have both positive and negative effects for women. On the positive side, women in developing countries are permitted to continue their energy consumption without formal restrictions. On the negative side, women will bear the brunt of substantial cutbacks in greenhouse gas emissions in the future. The irony of global warming is that its natural effects impact men and women without discrimination. However, masculine solutions to the problems associated with global warming will likely pass the cost on to the most vulnerable in the international community. Feminists argue that a more local, horizontal, cooperative approach toward global warming is likely to be more effective than any global approach.

Ecofeminists have sought to redefine women's roles in environmental protection beyond the "women as environmental managers" (Peterson and Runyan 1993, 145). This includes demanding full participation by women in the formulation of policy at all government levels and redefining development that recognizes women's work, bartering, and informal sectors of the economy. Development must also be reconceptualized to include environmental costs and the costs of environmental restoration. Feminists also argue that the North–South divide that permeates much of international politics also affects feminist unity regarding global warming. Feminists have found themselves divided between liberal feminists and socialist feminists because of their theoretical differences. Socialist feminists criticize the consumption patterns in the West and the market-oriented strategies for addressing global warming. They see the market as a cause of global warming, not a solution.

GLOBAL WARMING: A POSTSCRIPT

In March 2001, the Bush administration announced that the United States would reject the Kyoto Protocol. The Bush administration stated that the treaty would hurt the U.S. economy and was inherently unfair because developing countries were excused from binding emission cuts. The U.S. withdrawal from the treaty dealt a significant blow to further multilateral negotiations. Having the largest greenhouse gas emitter on the sidelines has caused other important industrialized states to reconsider their efforts (Revkin 2001, A8). Nevertheless, the international community led by the EU continued to negotiate curbs on greenhouse gas emissions. In November 2001, binding rules for the Kyoto Protocol were hammered out. Termed the "Marrakech rules" after the city in Morocco where they were negotiated, the 165 nations agreed to the following points (*Associated Press* 2001, A15):

- Industrialized countries are to cut or limit greenhouse gas emissions by an average of 5.2 percent from 1990 levels by 2012.
- Countries may offset requirements or earn credit by properly managing carbon sinks (forests and farm lands that absorb carbon dioxide).
- Emissions trading using permits to buy and sell the right to pollute.
- Countries that do not meet their target emissions will face mandatory punishment.

- In order for the treaty to take force, it must be ratified by 55 countries responsible for 55 percent of the greenhouse gas emissions.

The Marrakech rules are the culmination of difficult negotiations between the competing interests of nation-states, and represent the desire of the vast majority of nations to address global warming. The United States has chosen to "free-ride," which could ultimately mean the failure of Kyoto. With the United States on the sidelines, all of the advanced industrialized countries will have to ratify the treaty in order to reach the requisite 55 percent of the worldwide greenhouse gas emissions. Still, environmental experts say that the Marrakech rules represent an important event in industrial history (Revkin 2000, A8) Observers still hold out hope that international cooperation in the "war on terrorism" might spill over into multilateral approaches to environmental protection. The Bush administration states that the United States remains committed to solving the problems of global warming, but in its own way and at its own pace (Revkin 2001, A8).

Case Study 10: Whaling

The International Whaling Commission (IWC) was created by the International Convention for the Regulation of Whaling (ICRW) in 1946. The ICRW recognized that the story of whaling was one of overfishing that had led to a dangerous depletion of whale stocks. At the same time, it recognized that whaling is an important industry for some countries and an important source of food for many indigenous people. The IWC created by Article III of the ICRW was designed to promote the interests of whaling states by preserving whaling stocks. Specifically the IWC is responsible for the proper conservation of whale stocks and the orderly development of the whaling industry.

The IWC currently has forty members, with each state having one vote. Membership is open to any state wishing to sign on to the ICRW. IWC decisions are made on the basis of a simple majority except that a two-thirds majority is required when determining the following:

1. Protected and unprotected species
2. Open and closed seasons
3. Open and closed waters, including the designation of sanctuary areas
4. Size limits for each species
5. Time, methods, and intensity of whaling (including the maximum catch of whales to be taken in any one season)
6. Types and specification of gear and apparatus and appliance that may be used

The IWC meets annually, is supported by a small secretariat, and is represented by the secretary-general. The work of the IWC is divided between three committees: the Scientific, Technical, and Finance and Administration. This division of labor within the IWC allows each committee to specialize and develop expertise in their areas. For example, the Technical committee deals with Aboriginal Subsistence Whaling and researches the patterns of whale consumption by aboriginal peoples like the Inuit in Alaska. In general, the IWC is charged with protecting endangered species, designating whale sanctuaries, setting quotas on whale kills, specifying hunting seasons, and regulating the capture of female whales with suckling calves. Moreover, the IWC is responsible for measuring and maintaining whale stocks, as well as conducting scientific research.

The IWC is an example of an international organization being created in order to avoid the tragedy of the commons. In this case, the IWC is supposed to protect whaling stocks and the livelihoods of whaling states. After WWII, when food supplies were low, the United States encouraged Japanese whaling to stave off famine. Whale hunting and whale products are integral parts of Russian, Icelandic, and Norwegian heritage. However, industrialization and technological innovations led to the mass killing and processing of whales, nearly to the point of extinction. The fourteen founding members of the IWC were countries that had sizable whaling industry and/or interests and their goal was to protect the resource that sustained them all. Yet, the whale population had continued to declined. In spite of over forty years of IWC management, the whale population was decimated as whaling states exceeded their quotas and industrial pollution poisoned their habitat. Since the IWC is principally a scientific body and not an enforcement agency, it could only warn of impending disaster. Like many other IGOs, the ICW relies on the voluntary cooperation of member states.

By the 1970s, its membership had expanded to include more than thirty members, many of whom opposed whaling on moral and ethical grounds. In 1982, IWC issued a fifteen-year moratorium on all commercial whaling, while permitting whaling for indigenous groups and scientific research. This was accomplished by setting the quota for commercial whaling at zero. The former Soviet Union, Japan, Iceland, and Norway opposed the moratorium, which went into effect in 1986, but only Norway formally objected to the moratorium. Japan was granted an exemption to kill whales for scientific purposes. In 1994, the IWC placed an indefinite moratorium on commercial whaling over the formal objections of Japan and Norway. Article V, section 3, of the ICRW allows objections from members to IWC rules, which means the regulations adopted by the IWC are not binding on the objecting state. Hence, Norway and Japan are not bound by the moratorium and have continued whaling.

At the 2001 meeting, IWC members discussed two major issues—the revised management scheme and additional whale sanctuaries. The revised management scheme would lift the moratorium on commercial whaling and assign Norway and Japan whale-kill quotas. The creation of whale sanctuaries in the South Pacific and the South Atlantic was also at issue. When the IWC designates a certain area of the ocean a sanctuary, most types of whaling in that area are prohibited. The meeting of the IWC pitted pro-whaling states against conservationist states and ended in deadlock. The creation of the two new whale sanctuaries was blocked, as conservationists could not get the requisite two-thirds majority. The moratorium remains in place; however, IWC rules allow exemptions for objecting states. Hence, the whaling activities of objecting states are largely unregulated. Several questions are raised about the efficacy of the IWC. Is the IWC an effective institution of international governance? Whose interests does the IWC serve? What influences IWC decisions? What is the future of the IWC?

A REALIST CUT

Issues such as whaling and efforts to "save the whales" occupy the realm of low politics. The depletion and extinction of animal resources are nothing new as they are often the unfortunate consequences of human interaction with other species. However, the case of IWC does present several lessons regarding sovereignty over natural resources and the role of bargaining power in influencing the decisions made by international organizations. The creation of the IWC was part of the post–WWII flurry of institution-building under U.S. hegemony. The goal was for the whaling states to manage whale stocks and thereby preserve their national heritage and identity. States have sovereignty over their natural resources and may utilize them as they see fit. By signing on to the ICRW, whaling states agreed to monitor and take steps to preserve whale stocks; however, they did not agree to put themselves out of business. As membership in the IWC expanded it became clear that these new members, along with the United States, were interested in protecting "whale stocks" by eliminating the whaling industry altogether. Led by the United States, members such as Australia, New Zealand, the Netherlands, France, Germany, and the UK used the bargaining power within the IWC to establish the moratorium. These conservationist states, influenced by their own domestic environmental movements, saw the killing of whales as an immoral act. To these states, whales are majestic creatures deserving of special protection and they used the IWC to achieve that goal. Whaling states were forced to either issue formal objections with the IWC or withdraw from it (as Iceland did). Norway simply exercised its sovereign right to object under the ICRW and has continued to whale in its own waters (Chadwick 2001). Japan was forced to bow to U.S. pressure and accept the moratorium in 1984, but was able to negotiate the "scientific research" loophole that would allow it to keep hunting whales. Within the IWC structure, the wealthy, more powerful states were able to influence the organization to achieve its environmental goals.

Whaling states have a choice between two strategies in securing their national interests with regard to whaling. First, they can seek to change the current balance of power within the IWC. Japan and Norway have been able to enlist the support of many small, developing states to create an obstructionist bloc. With eight or nine developing states, the whaling states can prevent the two-thirds vote necessary for regulations affecting their interests. Japan has specifically tied increases in development assistance to several Caribbean countries in order to gain their favorable votes within the IWC (*BBC News*, July 4, 2000; Young 2001). Not surprisingly, this bloc of states was able to vote down the formation of additional whale sanctuaries at the 2001 meeting. They were also able to block efforts to more closely regulate "scientific" whaling. The pro-whaling faction is likely to get stronger if Iceland rejoins the IWC. Also not surprising then, Iceland's petition to rejoin the IWC was rejected by the conservationist states at the 2001 meeting.

Second, whaling states could abandon the IWC altogether. Unless the moratorium on commercial whaling is lifted, the industry and the communities sustained by them could face extinction. The High North Alliance, a pro-whaling group with members from Canada, the Faroe Islands, Greenland, Iceland, and Norway have lobbied their government to withdraw from the IWC. Whaling states are looking toward the North Atlantic Marine Mammal Commission (NAMMCO) as a new vehicle of international cooperation. The NAMMCO seeks to reinstate commercial whaling and further the interests of whaling states (*BBC News*, July 4, 2000). Whaling states still have incentives to stay with IWC. First, "scientific whaling" is just as good as commercial whaling. All whaling states need to do is conduct a few tests and then process their scientific subjects for commercial use. It might mean some legal maneuvering around the Convention of Trade in Endangered Species, but it could be done. Second, states that have violated the moratorium on whaling face only international condemnation, but no real economic or political consequences. Until the conservationists are willing to put some teeth into the moratorium, whaling states have good reasons not to completely abandon the IWC.

After all, the conservationist states are not going to risk their economic and political relationships with Japan, Norway, or Iceland over some whales.

A LIBERAL CUT

Absent a higher authority in international relations, the IWC is the best alternative, balancing the needs of environmentalists, the whales, the whaling industry, whaling states, and conservationist states. Liberal interpretations of the IWC have several variants. One stresses the role of science. The IWC is based on a scientific foundation that seeks to preserve whale stock by learning about their migratory and birthing patterns. The problem with the IWC is that it is politically driven and has ignored the scientific findings of its professional and competent staff. From its inception until the 1970s, the IWC ignored its scientific analyses and predictions and presided "over the mass destruction of one great whale population after another" (Aron 2000). Today, the voice of science is again being ignored, "this time to prevent the taking of whales, regardless of their population abundance "(Aron 2000). Science does not take any moral position on whether it is right or wrong to hunt whales. Science provides decision makers with the facts about whale populations, migration, and reproduction (Schweder 2000). It is up to political actors to use the information in a manner that was mutually agreed upon. If whaling as an industry is to be permitted, there are several species, like the minke and sperm whales, that have sufficient populations for culling. The neoclassical liberal argument suggests that one way to protect the whales and whaling industry is to assign hunting rights; however, this only works if the interests of both the whales and the industry are considered. If the industry is condemned, then property rights and markets will not solve the problem.

Another and perhaps opposing variant of liberalism highlights the protection of whales and development of shared values regarding the consumption of whale products. Without the IWC moratorium on commercial whaling, the whale population could have been decimated and several types of whales could have become extinct. The moratorium was the first step to the preservation of the whales as a species. The values of the international community have evolved to include an almost complete consensus against whaling as an industry. The community has been willing to accept limited whaling on the part of indigenous peoples so that they can retain their independence and identity. However, the international community is almost universally opposed to whaling for commercial purposes and mass consumption. The market for whale products is small and borne out of nationalism and tradition. This niche market does not give whaling states the right to ignore their international obligations, engage in vote-buying, and slaughter whales. The IWC may not have the teeth to enforce the moratorium on commercial whaling; however, coupled with international efforts to protect biodiversity and prohibit trade in endangered species, it can expose deviant states. The whaling "regime" informs consumers about the practices of Japan, Norway, Russia, and Iceland and allows them to make educated choices regarding their consumer choices.

A MARXIST CUT

The plight of the whales and those who have taken up their cause illustrates the spectacular failure of the liberal promise of markets, science, technology, and shared values in solving, or even effectively managing, international problems. The market for whale products is not a niche, but a large one that is culturally based in northeast Asia and their extended relatives in Northern Europe and North America. If markets were allowed to decide the fate of the whales, then the days of whales are numbered. Does the rational self-interest of the whaling industry include the preservation of the resource that sustains them all? No, the whaling industry will hunt until every whale is "harvested." Their interests are immediate and short-term—how much they kill and how much they can earn bringing the kill in. Through the process of subcontracting of whale services from hunting to processing to marketing, responsibility for the destruction of the whales is diffused. Whether the whales become extinct in five, ten, or fifty years is irrelevant to whalers. IWC has only provided the illusion of whale protection.

Scientific inquiry does little to help the situation. Every side in the dispute is able to marshall numerous scientific studies to support their position and dispute any findings from opposing viewpoints. The so-called unbiased science becomes so muddled that no one can agree as to whether scientific findings are valid and all sides accuse each other of manipulating science to serve their own ends. Scientific uncertainty is used to politicize issues before the IWC. Japan has used "scientific whaling" to serve its commercial whaling interests, and while countries have called this commercial whaling in disguise, who is to say that countries that have a tradition of consuming whale meat and products are not interested in preserving this resource through scientific research? Whaling communities suspect the science that finds that whale meat may be unfit to eat. In 1999, after testing samples of whale meat in Japanese restaurants, American and Japanese scientists found that half of the meat held concentrations of heavy metals, dioxins, and PCBs. This finding can easily be seen as a scare tactic to try to get consumers to abandon whale meat. Similarly, scientific studies of the Inuit have found that they have been contaminated with PCBs and pesticides from eating whale meat (Edwards 1998).

Technology has been of little use, unless one considers technology of mass killing a positive contribution. The IWC has, throughout its fifty-three-year history, tried to promote the most efficient and humane way of killing whales. This translates into many dead whales, killed in an industrial yet humane manner. Has this technology been used to promote the fertility and the proliferation of whales? Has technology been used to track and document the activity of whaling ships and poachers? The vast majority of the research and development under the IWC is devoted to the "humane" killing of whales.

The idea of "shared values" of the "international community" is also absurd. The conservationist states oppose whaling because their culture finds it abhorrent and offensive and they are trying to impose their cultural values on others (*New Scientist* 2001). Yet these same countries have no problem with mass killing of cows, chickens, pigs, or kangaroos even though other cultures find those practices inhumane, offensive, or profane. Certain values cannot be distributed by the "marketplace of ideas" as that results in the lowest common denominator approach. That, in turn, means the demise of the whales—an outcome that both whalers and conservationists would like to avoid.

A FEMINIST CUT

A significant contribution of the feminist perspective is the question: Where are the women? Whaling has been and continues to be a manly pursuit. The whaling industry is controlled exclusively by men. It is men who captain the whaling ships and hunt the whales. Women are conspicuously absent at most levels of decision making within the industry or the IWC. Female scientists have conducted a few studies for the IWC; however, their influence is diluted because of the debate regarding scientific uncertainty relating to whale populations. Whaling is a masculine endeavor, lionized in fiction and folklore. This, in turn, perpetuates the hunting of whales.

The market for whale products is extensive and includes more than just whale for human consumption. However, the niche market of whale meat in the trendy, upscale sushi bar and restaurants in Japan is the domain of Japanese men (*Time International* 2001). Whale is considered a rare treat to be shared with male colleagues, like a fine scotch or handrolled Cuban cigars in the United States. Whale meat is also believed to cure impotence and enhance sexual prowess and virility. In fact, the continued trade of many types of endangered species is spurred by the belief that by consuming certain body parts, male sexual performance is enhanced. At the very least, the male's gender role as hunter contributes to the need to hunt animals in the wild that has led the whales to the verge of extinction. In this sense, the feminist perspective problematizes the masculine when trying to explain the inability of the international community to prevent the decimation of the whale population.

This is not to say that women do not consume whale; however, they do so in large numbers only as members of indigenous people. And whale consumption has not been kind to their children. A study of the peoples of the Faroe Islands, north of Scotland, has showed brain and liver damage higher than normal in children whose mothers had eaten whale meat (Chadwick 2001). Studies have also shown that breast-feeding Inuit mothers can damage the health of their babies, as their milk contains ten time more chlordane than that of mothers in southern Canada (Edwards 1998).

Women have been active in anti-whaling NGOs such as Greenpeace and Save the Whales. They also have been at the forefront of conservation efforts and have taken whaling states to task in international and national fora. New Zealand Prime Minister Helen Clark has publicly insisted that Japan explain its vote-buying in the IWC (Department of Conservation July 19, 2001). She also publicly denounced Norway when it announced that it would lift its ban on whale exports. New Zealand Conservation Minister Sandra Lee led the 2001 campaign to establish a whale sanctuary in the South Pacific (Department of Conservation June 28, 2001). Women's voices are among the more strident and determined in banning whaling and establishing a new industry for the whales—whale watching.

CONCLUSION

Environmental problems like deforestation, desertification, global warming, and biodiversity are intractable and inseparable from the issues of equity and development. The theoretical frameworks of realism, liberalism, Marxism, and feminism approach equity and environmental protection quite differently. How these problems are to be managed will be debated, tabled, and readdressed in the decades to come. Each approach raises valid and legitimate points about the values that ought to be pursued with regard to global warming and whaling. Each approach seeks to order priorities according to their preferences and precepts. The challenge for environmental protection is how to determine which values will prevail and which arguments warrant substantive review. These are the roles and the politics of international organizations in the realm of environmental protection.

10

SOCIAL AND HUMANITARIAN ISSUES

INTERNATIONAL ORGANIZATIONS play crucial roles relating to social and humanitarian issues. IGOs like the UN, EU, and the Arab League deliver humanitarian and emergency assistance to societies in crisis. NGOs (often functioning as subcontractors) work with IGOs to provide food aid and health, education, and legal services. Social and humanitarian crises are intertwined with political violence, environment degradation, and gross violations of human rights. In this chapter, we examine two social/humanitarian issues—refugee protection and human rights. We will look at the international law and international organizations that directly address these issues and we will see how they shape the contemporary international political landscape. The case studies investigate the UN response to the Rwanda genocide in 1994 and the creation of a war crimes tribunal for the former Yugoslavia in 1995.

REFUGEES

One of the more destabilizing events threatening international peace and security is the mass movement of people across international boundaries. World War II forced millions of Europeans and Africans from their homes. The 1948 Arab–Israeli War displaced millions of Palestinians. The Cold War and the rise of Soviet-styled regimes caused many to flee communist oppression. The decolonization process generated tens of millions of additional refugees in Africa and Southeast Asia in the 1960s and 1970s. In the 1980s, the civil unrest in Central America and Haiti caused many to flee their homeland. During the 1990s, the Balkan crisis and the breakdown of civil order in many African countries once again put millions on the move. The twenty-five-year Afghanistan crisis has sent millions of Afghans into neighboring countries and abroad. Currently, more than twenty million persons are in "refugee-like" situations. Refugee movements create unimaginable hardship on individuals fleeing crisis and can destabilize neighboring countries as millions of people stream across borders seeking asylum, safety, or just food and water.

The international community has done much to protect "stateless" persons and to provide humanitarian assistance. The UN responded to many of the post–WWII refugee movements by creating the United Nations High Commissioner for Refugees (UNHCR) in 1950 by a General Assembly resolution. The UNHCR is charged with co-ordinating multilateral aid and seeking "durable solutions" to the plight of refugees. It attempts to establish a permanent settlement for each refugee situation and responds with emergency relief and care. More important, the UNHCR facilitates international cooperation among UN members, a task that is not easily accomplished because its scope and mandate extend well beyond the legal obligations of states.

The legal obligation of states is set out in the 1951 Convention Relating to the Status of Refugees and the 1967 Protocol. Article I of the Convention defines a refugee as someone who has a

> well-founded fear of being persecuted for reasons of race, religion, nationality, membership to a particular social group or political opinion, is outside the country of his nationality and is unable or, owing to such fear, is unwilling to avail himself of the protection of that country; or, who, not having a nationality and being outside the country of his habitual residence as a result of such events, is unable or, owing to such fear, is unwilling to return to it.

States that are party to the Convention have a legal obligation not to return refugees or those seeking such status back to a situation of persecution. This principle of no return is called *nonrefoulement* and it is through this principle that refugees are ultimately protected. The process of obtaining legal refugee status involves a series of administrative steps. First, the individual enters the territory of the state and applies for asylum. The right to grant asylum is a sovereign right of states. If asylum is granted, the individual is registered with the UNHCR and is considered a legal or *de jure* refugee. Arrangements are then made to find a more permanent or "durable" solution through one of three mechanisms—voluntary repatriation, resettlement, or assimilation. Voluntary repatriation is often impossible as the conditions in the refugee's country of origin are not likely to have changed in the short term. Resettlement in third countries usually depends on the ties between the individual and the third country, such as whether the individual has family in the third country or a particular skill. Assimilation, therefore, is the usual course of action. The refugee is usually given an opportunity, after a certain period of time, to apply for citizenship.

On the surface, the definition of a refugee seems sufficiently broad to include a wide range of persecution. However, the definition refers to *individual* persecution. Excluded are those who flee because of foreign occupation, generalized violence, civil war, civil disorder, and civil unrest. Also excluded are victims of extreme poverty or natural disaster. People who flee these conditions do not qualify because these conditions affect the general population as a whole. Asylum seekers must prove that they are individual targets of persecution. Many countries interpret "well-founded fear" as meaning the individual is more likely than not to face persecution upon return. In this sense, the definition of a refugee is quite narrow and the burden of proof quite high.

To complicate matters further, the mandate of the UNHCR has expanded to include more than just assisting and protecting *de jure* refugees. Unrest in Asia and the colonization process in Africa resulted in large-scale disorder and violence, producing large numbers of people resembling refugees, yet not qualifying under the narrow definition of the 1951 Convention. In 1957, the General Assembly authorized the UNHCR to use its good offices to assist those in Hong Kong regardless of the controversy surrounding their exact status (Gordenker 1987, 39–48). This allowed the UNHCR to use funds donated by governments to assist Chinese asylum seekers even though they did not meet the statutory requirements of the Convention. The UNHCR's mandate was expanded further as a result of its involvement during and after the Algerian revolt against France. The brutal counterguerrilla campaign by France sent tens of thousands of Algerians across the border into Tunisia and Morocco. The UNHCR moved to assist the Algerians and the General Assembly later approved the UNHCR's actions. The UNHCR was also called into action in Cyprus after the 1972 *coup d'etat* and invasion by Turkey caused large-scale internal displacements. Under the good office umbrella, the mandate of UNHCR expanded to those who flee foreign occupation, civil war, and generalized violence, as well as those who are internally displaced and unable to flee. As was noted earlier, international law prescribes a rather narrow definition of a refugee and levies a legal obligation on states not to return refugees to situations of persecution. However, the scope of the UNHCR mandate extends far beyond the conventional framework. This discrepancy is at the heart of the current dilemma concerning the protection of *de jure* refugees and those who are likewise assisted by the UNHCR, *de facto* refugees. The role of the UNHCR has evolved to address "refugee-like" while the legal framework formalizing state obligations has not.

The UNHCR spends anywhere from $400 million to $1 billion annually, depending on refugee situations and the generosity of UN members. The UNHCR budget is voluntary and contributions largely come from the United States, Japan, Germany, and other industrialized countries. The UNHCR budget is used to assist *de jure* and *de facto* refugees in developing countries that are unable to foot the bill alone. The UNHCR also works closely with other UN agencies assisting in refugee situations. The World Food Program (WFP) was established in 1963 to serve as the central UN agency for the distribution of food aid within the UN system. The agency has the dual role of providing emergency food aid in crisis situations and supporting economic and social development. The World Food Program provides for the basic food needs of refugees worldwide. The WFP responds with emergency food aid when population movements suddenly occur and works with the UNHCR on self-sufficiency projects.

The UNHCR also works closely with the World Health Organization (WHO). WHO is the primary agency responsible for the health needs of refugees. WHO provides vaccinations for polio, measles, chicken pox, and other infectious diseases. Programs also include pre- and postnatal care for refugee women, as well as infant care. WHO provides instruction regarding AIDS and cancer prevention. Finally, WHO responds to outbreaks of malaria and typhoid fever, which can occur in densely populated refugee camps.

The activities of the UNHCR and other UN agencies are complicated by the fact that the refugee crises are rooted in international and civil war, and the breakdown of civil order. These tensions are exacerbated by environmental conditions such as drought or flooding, which results in famine and disease. Very few meet the *de jure* definition of a refugee. UN agencies deal almost exclusively with *de facto* refugees and are often caught between warring parties, all of whom are willing to use humanitarian assistance to refugees as a form of leverage or even a weapon of war. UN personnel and property have become targets of violence. Durable solutions to these crises involve more than just responding with humanitarian assistance as the situation disintegrates into chaos. It involves early warning mechanisms and state-building after the crisis. Increasingly, international peace and security are linked to respect for human rights.

Like the environment, human rights have taken center stage in international politics in recent years. Human rights violations and refugee crises in Chechnya, Iraq, Bosnia, Somalia, Kosovo, Rwanda, and Burundi have generated a great deal of international concern and, in some cases, even intervention. Historically, the relationship between the government and its citizens has been an internal matter, falling well within the sovereign domain of states. However, beginning in 1945 and accelerating since 1970, human rights have become increasingly internationalized (Forsythe 1991a). Human rights are now legitimate values to be pursued through international politics. Chapter I, Article 1(3) of the UN Charter explicitly identifies promotion of human rights as a central concern of the UN. One purpose of the UN is "to achieve international cooperation in solving international problems of an economic, social, cultural, humanitarian character, and in promoting and encouraging respect for human rights and for fundamental freedoms for all without distinction to race, sex, language or religion." Chapter IX, Articles 55 and 56 of the UN Charter restate the UN's responsibility for encouraging universal respect for human rights and levy a legal duty on states to cooperate in both the promotion and the protection of human rights. Beginning with the UN Charter, a proliferation of international human rights agreements has detailed civil, political, economic, social, and cultural rights. Human rights commissions and monitoring systems have been developed to implement these accords. Other treaties pertaining to genocide, racial discrimination, the rights of women, torture, and collective bargaining have also been negotiated. Like the environment, human rights generate significant controversy. While no one is against human rights or the environment, there are vehement disagreements regarding definition and implementation. Human rights are contentious because they challenge the principle of sovereignty and may even invite international intervention.

MAJOR HUMAN RIGHTS AGREEMENTS

In addition to the UN Charter, several international agreements pertaining to human rights have been reached. In 1948, the Universal Declaration of Human Rights was passed by the UN General Assembly without a dissenting vote, although South Africa, the USSR, and several Eastern Bloc states abstained from the resolution. The Universal Declaration of Human Rights lists thirty basic principles that are considered fundamental to human dignity. The Universal Declaration on Human Rights is not legally binding on states; however, it serves as an authoritative guide to interpretation of the UN Charter and represents the sense of the international community (Brownlie 1994, 21). It spells out political and civil rights, including the rights to life, liberty, personal security, and political participation. It also addresses economic and social rights, such as the right to work, to form unions, and to a standard of living adequate for health and well-being. In addition to these individual human rights, the Universal Declaration contains collective rights, such as the right to self-determination and development. The drafters of the resolution intended to follow up the Universal Declaration with a binding treaty or covenant that would have imposed specific duties and obligations on states (Donnelly 1993, 10).

The Universal Declaration of Human Rights explicitly links respect for human rights with international peace. According to the preamble, the foundation of freedom, justice, and peace in the world is the recognition of the dignity and equality of all human beings and their inalienable rights. Human rights are essential for promoting friendly relations between states and respect between individuals. In many respects, the Universal Declaration of Human Rights is revolutionary because it challenges state sovereignty and represents a higher moral authority.

Transforming rhetoric into reality has proven difficult. The binding international law that was supposed to follow the Universal Declaration of Human Rights was impeded by Cold War tensions and the attendant quarrels over social and economic rights versus political and civil rights (Donnelly 1993, 7–10; Pollis and Schwab 1979, 1–18; Forsythe 1991, 121–127). The human rights debate was and is complex. It centers on three political arguments rooted in the historic East–West conflict, the continuing North–South conflict, and the ongoing debate between universalism and cultural relativism (Vincent 1988). The West, led by the United States, has emphasized civil and political rights over economic and social rights. The West used civil and political human rights to criticize the Soviet Union and to justify Cold War policies. The Soviet Union criticized racial discrimination in the United States and accentuated economic and social rights—rights to which the United States has paid little attention.

Developing states sought to actualize cultural and collective rights in addition to many economic rights. The North–South conflict, which focuses on the disparities between rich and poor in the international community, highlighted the inconsistencies in U.S. and European foreign policies. On the one hand, the West criticized the East for systematically denying civil and political rights, yet supported brutal colonial regimes, then authoritarian governments, as bulwarks against communism. The North systematically ignored the basic needs of people in the developing world and has denied that any "right to development" exists.

In the debate over universality versus cultural relativism, the question is fundamental: Are human rights universal—applicable to all—or must they be understood in the light of culture? Proponents of the cultural relativist approach argue that human rights, as conceptualized by the UN, are eurocentric. That is, the notions of political, civil, economic, social, and cultural rights found in Western European political and economic thought ignore non-Western approaches to human rights. Even economic rights, which are more closely associated with Marxism, are Western in origin. The philosophic and religious traditions of the Middle East, the Indian subcontinent, China, and Southeast Asia are ignored or marginalized by the human rights discourses. The inherent biases of human rights laws demand a relative approach to their implementation, lest the West impose its culture on the rest of the world.

The lag between the Universal Declaration and more binding international law was the result of the very real political divisions within the United Nations. Two treaties were negotiated to set international standards and to implement human rights—the International Covenant on Economic, Social and Cultural Rights and the International Covenant on Civil and Political Rights. These treaties were opened for signatures in 1966 after nearly twenty years of heated, contentious debate. The International Covenant on Economic, Social and Cultural Rights recognizes and details the several important economic rights: the right to work, the right to fair remuneration, the right to safe working conditions, the right to form and join unions, and the right to strike. Special protection is also extended to working mothers before and after childbirth. This covenant also includes social rights such as the right to food, housing, and education. Cultural rights include the right to participate in the cultural life of a society and the right to benefit from scientific progress. The International Covenant on Civil and Political Rights recognizes the right to life, liberty, freedom of movement, equality under the law, and the presumption of innocence. It details the rights of association as well as the freedom of religion and conscience. It lists the right to free elections, universal suffrage, and the right to have access to public service. More than half of the member states have since become parties to both of the International Covenants.

The slow process of creating formal, legal obligations for human rights is a direct result of deep-seated disagreements about the definition and implementation of human rights. The lists of human rights are extensive and ambitious, and different states have different preferences about which rights ought to be actively pursued. East–West and North–South factions emerged. The United States wanted civil and political rights to take precedence over economic and social rights. Rooted in liberal ideology, the U.S. argument centered on the idea that if individuals are armed with civil and political rights, they can actualize for themselves their economic and social rights. American suspicions of intrusive government, particularly in the marketplace, have focused U.S. human rights efforts on promoting civil and political rights. Only after these rights are guaranteed can individuals pursue a family, a home, or an education. The former socialist countries and many developing countries have argued that economic and social rights are necessary in order for individuals to participate in the political and civil life of the community. The state appropriately has a role in securing minimum standards of living, even if it means intervention in the economy. Non-Western societies expressed concern about Western conceptions of individual and gender equality. The promotion, protection, and implementation of human rights became an exceptionally politicized process in the highly charged environment of the Cold War. States were very slow to sign on to the international covenants; the treaties did not receive the requisite ratifications until 1976.

In spite of the political controversies surrounding human rights, the proliferation of international human rights agreements has continued. Some of the more notable agreements are the Declaration on the Granting of Independence to Colonial Countries and Peoples (1960), the Convention on the Prevention and Punishment of the Crime of Genocide (1948), the Convention Against Torture and Other Cruel, Inhuman, or Degrading Treatment or Punishment (1984), and the Convention on the Rights of the Child (1989). In 1993, the Vienna Declaration and Programme of Action for Human Rights resulted from the World Conference on Human Rights. The Vienna Declaration emphasized the universality of human rights and stressed that the right to development, the rights of women, and the rights of indigenous peoples need particular attention. Special attention was also paid to the largely post–Cold War problems of ethnic cleansing, and to the systematic rape of women in violent conflicts. The continuing proliferation of values and norms has led to a proliferation of actors involved in implementing and monitoring international agreements on human rights.

UN AGENCIES AND HUMAN RIGHTS

Several UN bodies and agencies are integrally involved in promoting and protecting human rights. The UN Commission on Human Rights, which reports to the ECOSOC, was created shortly after the inception of the UN itself. This Commission drafted the 1948 Universal Declaration on Human Rights and actively worked to institutionalize the International Covenants. The Covenants themselves establish elaborate procedures and monitoring bodies to supervise their implementation. The Covenant on Civil and Political Rights creates the Committee on Human Rights to review state reports on their human rights records and to report to the ECOSOC and the General Assembly. The Committee may investigate individual complaints from citizens of states that have consented to this kind of oversight. This right of individual petition exists in very few countries. The Committee spends most of its time reviewing the implementation of the Covenant on Civil and Political Rights without any real authority to challenge signatories with weak human rights records.

The Covenant on Economic, Social and Cultural Rights gives the ECOSOC the authority to oversee its implementation. The ECOSOC originally created the Committee on Government Experts to review state reports, but this body was unable to effect a serious commitment to social, economic, and cultural rights. In 1985 the ECOSOC replaced the Committee on Government Experts with the Committee on Individual Experts. This new committee has been instrumental in establishing national guidelines for signatories regarding standards for adequate food, shelter, health care, and other rights (Weiss, Forsythe, and Coate 1994, 139). In addition to reviewing state reports, the Committee on Individual Experts also receives reports from NGOs and IGOs.

The 1993 Vienna Declaration and Programme for Human Rights called for the creation of the United Nations High Commissioner for Human Rights (UNHCHR). The General Assembly obliged by creating the office, which became fully functional in 1994. This office was given responsibility to diplomatically promote and protect human rights, to provide advisory and technical assistance to states, and to coordinate UN education and public information programs. The UNHCHR is also charged with playing an active role in removing obstacles to the full realization of human rights and preventing the continuation of human rights violations. The UNHCHR can engage states in a dialog in order to secure respect for human rights; however, the High Commissioner can do little to force states to observe internationally recognized human rights. The vague language of the UNHCHR mandate falls far short of empowering the High Commissioner to confront the grave human rights situations in the post–Cold War world. The Organization of Islamic Conference (OIC) followed the Vienna Conference by issuing the Cairo Declaration. The Islamic world used the Cairo Declaration to serve as the basis of the Islamic world's interpretations of human rights. The Islamic world views human rights as being defined by Allah and the Shari'a, or Islamic law. It posits different rights for women and men and highlights colonialism and racism as grave violations of human rights (*UNESCO Courier* 1994).

The Vienna Declaration and Programme of Action also raised the issue of women's rights as human rights. The international community has long looked the other way as women have been systematically denied their basic human rights. The Vienna Declaration reaffirmed that the rights of women and girls formed an inalienable and indivisible part of internationally recognized human rights. The UN Conference on Women in Beijing (1996) reaffirmed women's rights as human rights, but stressed that the status of women's rights was not significantly improving vis à vis the rights of men. The very fact that such an imbalance exists between men's "human" rights and women's "human" rights suggests that rights are, in large part, culturally determined.

The International Labor Organization (ILO) was established in 1919 as an autonomous agency of the League of Nations. This independent yet cooperative relationship was maintained with the creation of the United Nations in 1945. The ILO consists of three bodies: The International Labor Conference (a plenary body), the Governing Body (an executive committee), and the International Labor Office (the bureaucratic arm). The ILO's central purpose is to set international labor standards and to improve the rights of workers globally. In the post–World War II era, the ILO sponsored the following treaties relating to social, economic, and cultural human rights: The Freedom of Association and Protection of the Right to Organize Convention (1948); Right to Organize and Collective Bargaining Convention (1949); Equal Remuneration Convention (1951); Convention Concerning the Abolition of Forced Labor (1957); Discrimination Convention (1958); Equality of Treatment Convention (1962); Social Policy Convention (1962); Employment Policy Convention (1964); and the Convention Concerning Indigenous and Tribal Peoples in Independent Countries (1989). The ILO is the principal body in promoting economic, social, and cultural rights in a political arena that has emphasized civil and political rights, even at the expense of other human rights.

REGIONAL HUMAN RIGHTS ACCORDS AND AGENCIES

Regional accords also recognize, promote, and protect internationally recognized human rights. The European human rights regime is the most advanced and institutionalized of the regional arrangements. This regime is organized around the European Convention on Human Rights (1953). This convention contains several protocols that outline many, if not most, of the rights contained in the Universal Declaration on Human Rights, including civil and political rights as well as economic, social, and cultural rights. The convention also creates the European Commission on Human Rights, which functions as an ombudsman for individual complaints. The European Commission investigates petitions and seeks to negotiate an acceptable resolution for the parties involved. If such a resolution cannot be reached, the petition can go to the European Court of Human Rights, which consists of one judge from each of the members of the Council of Europe. One of the ironies of human rights protection is that areas that have the most comprehensive institutional arrangements are also areas that have good human rights records in the first place. As a result, very few cases have been brought before the European Commission and even fewer have been brought before the European Court.

The Inter-American human rights regime is quite similar to its European counterpart in terms of organization. This regime, anchored by the Organization for American States (OAS), is based on three parts: The Inter-American Convention on Human Rights, The Inter-American Commission on Human Rights, and the Inter-American Court of Human Rights. The Inter-American Convention principally focuses on promoting and protecting civil and political rights, although the Convention devotes Article 26 to detailing social and economic rights. The Commission and the Court have the authority to investigate and adjudicate human rights claims. Unfortunately for human rights activists, this authority exists only in legal theory. In practice, these organizations have been ignored or bypassed by member states. The legal framework exists; but, because of the poor human rights records of many members, states have lacked the political will to make the law more effective. To a lesser extent, human rights have also been integrated in African and Middle Eastern regional arrangements. The Organization of African Unity (OAU) has sponsored several conferences and declarations on the end of colonialism and white rule in Southern Africa (then-Rhodesia,

South Africa, Swaziland). The OAU has also sought an end to racial discrimination internationally, including in the United States, and an immediate end to apartheid by whites in South Africa. In 1981, the African Charter on Human and People's Rights was passed; it emphasized these collective rights in addition to individual human rights. This Charter creates a Commission that has the power to collect documents and to undertake studies on African human and people's rights. The commission may hear complaints and make recommendations to governments on strategies for resolving disputes. The African human rights regime does not significantly empower the Commission in theory or practice because of fears of intervention and violations of state sovereignty. These fears nixed plans for an African human rights court and have limited the regional institutionalization of human rights.

NGOs and Human Rights

A proliferation of human rights NGOs has accompanied the proliferation of human rights agreements and monitoring agencies. NGOs have come to play important roles in identifying and investigating human rights violations. They are also influential in pressuring governments and IGOs to meet their international obligations to promote and protect human rights. Several NGOs are particularly noteworthy. The first is the International Committee for the Red Cross (ICRC). The ICRC mission is to aid the victims of war, mainly civilians and prisoners of war. The ICRC is not directly linked to a human rights treaty, although its mandate does extend to human rights during war. The ICRC has "observer status" at the UN, the only NGO to be an official member. The ICRC heads a world federation of national Red Cross and Red Crescent units that are active in delivering humanitarian assistance in national emergencies.

The mission and legal status of the ICRC arise from the Geneva Conventions relating to international war. While the ICRC status in internal conflicts is unclear at best, the ICRC has played a role in the delivery of humanitarian assistance in many internal conflicts, including those in Ethiopia, Sudan, Bosnia, and Chechnya. The ICRC stresses that human rights remain human rights, even during war and violent conflict. Governments, military units, and civilians have the responsibility to meet their international obligations under international law and other humanitarian rules. The ICRC commands a great deal of international respect for its neutral competence and impartiality. The ICRC is independent of governments and international organizations and prides itself on championing the needs of victims of armed conflict and internal violence.

ICRC generally takes a "quiet diplomacy" approach to promoting and protecting human rights during war. Other NGOs rely on publicity and domestic and international political pressure to remind governments of their international obligations. Amnesty International is such an organization.* Started in 1961, Amnesty International today has more than a million members, nearly five thousand local chapters, in more than a hundred countries. Its mission consists of four focal points: To free all prisoners of conscience; to ensure fair and prompt trials of political prisoners; to abolish the death penalty, torture, and other cruel forms of punishment; and to end extrajudicial executions and disappearances.

---

*The discussion and description of Amnesty International is drawn from its Web page <www.amnesty.org>.

Amnesty International pursues several strategies. First, it engages in worldwide campaigns that involve lobbying governments and international organizations, reporting on human rights issues, and educating officials regarding human rights abuses. These publicity efforts raise awareness of human rights and expose violations. Second, it assists individuals who are prisoners of conscience or have been detained without trial, providing legal assistance and social support. Third, it maintains an Urgent Action network for individuals who are in immediate danger of torture and execution. Government officials and media outlets are flooded with appeals and protests on behalf of those at risk. Fourth, Amnesty International sustains a specialized network of medical and legal professionals, as well as specialists in women's, children's, and workers' rights.

Human Rights Watch is another NGO that investigates and publicizes human rights violations. These activists have extensive networks that monitor the status of human rights and also attempt to hold nonstate actors responsible for their abuse. These nonstate actors include national and multinational corporations, guerrilla groups, and crime organizations such as drug cartels. Human Rights Watch also engages in special initiatives such as academic freedom, domestic violence, and prison conditions. Human Rights Watch compiles annual reports on the human rights records of states; its reputation is such that its reports are used in congressional or parliamentary hearings and by executive and ministerial agencies. Human Rights Watch is also willing to take on unpopular causes against powerful states. In 1998, they were one of the few groups willing to take on the United States and the way the U.S. states disenfranchise voters. In Florida, people are denied the right to vote because they have a criminal record. This has led to the disenfranchisement of one in every three African American males in Florida (Davies 1998, 1A). According to a national study, 3.9 million Americans have lost the right to vote because of their criminal records, which includes 13 percent of the male population (Davies 1998, 1A).

Doctors Without Borders (Médecins Sans Frontieres) is an NGO whose two thousand–plus volunteers come from more than forty-five nations (Doctors Without Borders 1998). Established in 1971, it has offices in nineteen countries and operations in more than seventy countries. Doctors Without Borders is committed to providing medical relief to populations in crisis regardless of ideology or national origin. Like the ICRC, Amnesty International, and Human Rights Watch, Doctors Without Borders is independent of governments and IGOs and is committed to impartiality. Doctors Without Borders attempts to work with the consent of parties involved but has, on occasion, delivered medical assistance without the approval of military or civilian authorities.

NGOs play central roles in the protection of internationally recognized human rights. They have consultative status and report to the International Commission on Human Rights (Weiss, Forsythe, and Coate 1994, 163). Their people on the ground investigate alleged human rights abuses and provide legal representation to prisoners of conscience. NGOs also organize at the grassroots level to apply domestic political pressure to respect human rights and to get more individuals actively involved in the implementation of all human rights including economic, social, and cultural rights.

In spite of the proliferation of human rights accords, agencies, and NGOs, gross violations of human rights continue to occur on a large scale. Instances of mass killings, deliberate starvation, ethnic cleansing, systematic rape, summary execution, and genocide are far too common in the post–Cold War order. Economic, social, and cultural rights are routinely denied in the developing world and under attack in the developed countries. Forced labor, child labor, and below-subsistence wages are commonplace in many areas, and the ability of workers to unionize has been compromised. The gross violations of human rights have generated renewed international interest in alternative ways to ensure respect for human rights.

HUMANITARIAN INTERVENTION

Traditionally, recognition, promotion, and protection of human rights have involved the use of diplomacy and political pressure to persuade and challenge states to improve their human rights records. Since the end of the Cold War, however, international enforcement of human rights has emerged as a controversial feature in international politics. UN humanitarian actions in Iraq (on behalf of Iraqi Kurds), Somalia, and Bosnia renewed interest in the notion of "humanitarian intervention." Broadly speaking, humanitarian intervention refers to "dictatorial interference" in the internal affairs of a sovereign state to secure and enforce human rights. Dictatorial interference can include both nonforcible and forcible measures. The former includes such measures as economic sanctions, withholding of aid, and the funding of opposition parties (Damrosch 1989). The latter refers to the use of military units within the territorial jurisdiction of a target state without the government's consent.

The controversy surrounding humanitarian intervention revolves around a central question: When is it permissible for international organizations to override state sovereignty to provide or protect internationally recognized human rights? The broad definition of intervention as "dictatorial interference" makes it difficult to draw a distinction between impermissible intervention and permissible political activities because it includes both forcible and nonforcible measures. Recall that Article 2(7) of the UN Charter contains the companion principle of sovereignty, the principle of nonintervention. The UN is enjoined from intervening in the domestic jurisdiction of member states, and no member is required to submit such matters to the UN for settlement. In 1965, the UN General Assembly attempted to clarify what nonintervention meant with Resolution 2131:

> No State has the right to intervene, directly or indirectly, for any reason whatever in the internal or external affairs of any other state. Consequently, armed intervention and all other forms of interference or attempted threats against the personality of the State or against its political, economic, or cultural elements are condemned.
>
> No State may use or encourage the use of economic, political, or any other type of measure to coerce another state in order to obtain from it the subordination of the exercise of its sovereign rights, or to secure from it advantages of any kind. Also no state shall organize, assist, foment, finance, invite or tolerate subversive terrorist or armed activities directed towards the violent overthrow of the regime of any other state or interfere in the civil strife in another state. (UN Doc A/6014, December 21, 1965)

This same interpretation of nonintervention was included in another General Assembly Resolution 2625 titled the Declaration on Principles of International Law Concerning Friendly Relations and Cooperation Among States (1970). Article 2(7), UN General Assembly Resolutions 2131 and 2625 contain the usual exception that nothing in these sections shall be construed as affecting UN Charter provisions relating to the maintenance of international peace and security.

Unfortunately, these provisions do little to define what precisely constitutes dictatorial interference. International politics involves trying to get actors to do things they might not do otherwise; this means applying political pressure and providing negative, as well as positive, inducements. Under the General Assembly construction of intervention, however, economic sanctions and political lobbying are impermissible. Developing states are concerned that human rights will be used to deny them development loans. The World Bank cut off assistance to Malawi and restricted loans to Kenya because of their human rights violations in 1992 (Riding 1992, A6). World Bank loans to China were scaled back in 1989 after the government's crackdown on a prodemocracy demonstration in Tiananmen Square (American Banker 1990, 18; Mann and Pine 1990, A1). Developing states argue that the World Bank is politicizing development loans, in contravention of the World Bank Charter, which commits the institution to political neutrality.

There is some question of jurisdiction with respect to human rights. According to China's former Premier Li Peng, for example, "The issue of human rights falls within the sovereignty of each country. A country's human rights situation should not be judged in total disregard of its history and national conditions. . . . China . . . is opposed to interference in the internal affairs of other countries using the human rights issue as an excuse" (*New York Times* 1992). Most developing states are sympathetic to this position. It is, after all, their sovereignty that is at stake: The UN has neither the will nor the capability to override the sovereignty of powerful states. UN intervention is possible only against the weaker members—members that lack the political protection of a permanent member of the Security Council. Powerful states may ignore their allies' human rights violations while seeking to punish political foes for committing the same violations. Developing countries, worried about this double standard, also stress another: While violations of civil and political rights tend to prompt UN intervention, violations of economic and social rights do not. The World Bank and IMF freely demand structural adjustments in return for their loans—adjustments that interfere with the economic and social rights of their citizens.

Countering this view of human rights and intervention is the argument that human rights are proper international subject matters, despite the many disagreements over definition and implementation (Forsythe 1991). Many states have become formal legal parties to human rights treaties, thereby internationalizing human rights. As the Permanent Court of International Justice stated in Nationalities Decrees in Tunis and Morocco (1923), "The question of whether a certain matter is or is not solely within the jurisdiction of a state is an essentially relative question; it depends on the development of international relations." Human rights are just as much an international concern as slavery and colonialism are. Both slavery and colonialism were once internal affairs, but no longer; neither is permissible state behavior, under any circumstances (Szasz 1983, 345). States and the UN have every right and the responsibility to oppose states engaging in slavery or colonialism.

The record of multilateral humanitarian intervention is rather sketchy. In 1966 and 1968, the UN Security Council authorized mandatory economic sanctions against Rhodesia (now Zimbabwe), after the white minority government declared independence from the United Kingdom and implemented minority rule. Recall that Chapter VII, Article 39, of the UN Charter states that the Security Council can "determine the existence of any threat to the peace, breach of the peace, or act of aggression and shall make recommendations or decide what measures shall be taken . . . to maintain or restore international peace and security." Security Council decisions are legally binding and member states of the UN have a duty to "accept and carry out'" these decisions. Security Council resolutions regarding Rhodesia, particularly the 1968 decision, identify the human rights situation as a threat to peace (Van Dyke 1970). If the Security Council links human rights violations to international peace and security, then both forcible and nonforcible measures are technically permissible.

The Rhodesia case is a "fuzzy" precedent for nonforcible intervention because Rhodesia was not a recognized sovereign state and the Security Council resolutions did not clarify the precise legal basis for its authoritative review. South Africa represents a similar case. In 1977, the Security Council mandated an arms embargo against South Africa, which was then ruled by a white minority government and practiced apartheid, a policy that enforced a comprehensive segregation of races. The resolution never articulated what triggered its authoritative action aside from "the situation in South Africa" (S/RES/418, 1977).

Forcible intervention raises different questions regarding multilateral actions. Mandating economic sanctions or an arms embargo is one thing; using military force and other forms of violence is quite another. The first clearly identifiable, forcible UN intervention occurred during the Persian Gulf Crisis. After the cessation of hostilities between UN and Iraqi forces, the Iraqi government began a brutal campaign to suppress rebelling Kurds in northern Iraq and Shi'ite Muslims in southern Iraq. In 1991, the Security Council explicitly linked human rights violations occurring materially within a sovereign state to international peace and security. According to Resolution 688:

> The Security Council, mindful of its duties and its responsibilities under the Charter of the United Nations for the maintenance of international peace and security . . .
>
> 1. Condemns the repression of the Iraqi civilian population in many parts of Iraq, including most recently in Kurdish populated areas, the consequences of which threaten international peace and security in the region;
> 2. Demands that Iraq, as a contribution to removing the threat to international peace and security in the region, immediately end this repression and expresses the hope in the same context that an open dialogue will take place to ensure that the human and political rights of all Iraqi citizens are respected;
> 3. Insists that Iraq allow immediate access by international humanitarian organizations to all those in need of assistance in all parts of Iraq and to make available all necessary facilities for their operations. (S/RES/688)

The UN subsequently sent military units into northern Iraq without the consent of the Iraqi government to create a safe-haven zone for the Iraqi Kurds.

Iraq represents a unique case because it was part of a collective security action involving traditional security issues and concerns. A vanquished Iraq had little choice but to accept the UN action in northern Iraq. Even so, Resolution 688 was far from unanimous. China and India abstained from the vote on the resolution. Cuba, Zimbabwe, and Yemen voted against the resolution, claiming it was an unacceptable disregard for state sovereignty. In spite of Iraq's pariah status, developing states were sensitive to the precedent that denigrates traditional sovereign rights.

Many developing states are concerned that alleged human rights violations will be used as an excuse to mask other motives. Unilateral uses of force are almost always condemned because they represent clear violations of Article 2(4), which prohibits the threat or use of force in international relations. International organizations may sanction the use of force purportedly to correct human rights, but that does not necessarily justify the intervention or make it permissible. The Organization of Eastern Caribbean States sanctioned the U.S. intervention in Grenada to protect the lives of American medical students and restore civil and political rights. Yet many in the international community and the General Assembly condemned the action. As long as international organizations must rely on the armed forces of member states to carry out resolutions, they will be vulnerable to the charge that they are motivated by the interests of powerful member states, not by concern for the rights and welfare of persons at risk.

As a result of the North–South divide on the issue of humanitarian intervention, the international community is forced to address human rights situations on a case-by-case basis. The breakdown of civil order in Somalia put a large segment of the population at immediate risk of starvation and disease. In 1992, the UN Security Council deemed the situation in Somalia a threat to international peace and security and authorized "all means necessary" to deliver humanitarian assistance. The Security Council also stated that anyone interfering in the delivery of humanitarian assistance could be guilty of a war crime, which was a direct warning to the warring rival factions. The UN action in Somalia was a success in providing immediate assistance, but it did little to create a political environment that could sustain peace. The UN was virtually chased out of Somalia, raising questions about the efficacy of using force to protect human rights. Is it possible to use force and maintain a neutral position within the existing domestic political arena?

The humanitarian crisis in Somalia triggered UN authoritative action while others went relatively unnoticed. Grave human rights situations in Burundi, Mozambique, East Timor, North Korea, Afghanistan, and Sudan did not prompt multilateral action, even though these crises were, at the very least, as dire as the Somali crisis. No clear pattern has emerged as to what kinds of human rights, and on what scale, might trigger authoritative review. During the Cold War, the political paralysis of the Security Council prevented any serious review of situations in Cambodia, Guatemala, El Salvador, Chile, and Ethiopia. After the Cold War, humanitarian action occurred in Iraq, Somalia, and the former Yugoslavia. The humanitarian crisis in Rwanda serves as our next case study because it shows the difficulties in building an international coalition to confront gross violations of human rights.

CASE STUDY 11: RWANDA*

In April 1994, the tiny country of Rwanda took a disastrous turn toward genocide that would claim more than 800,000 lives in a mere 100 days. The victims were members of the Tutsi minority and moderate Hutus who were murdered with machetes and small arms in just a few weeks. The perpetrators of the genocide were roaming gangs of the ethnic majority Hutus consisting mostly of men; however, large numbers of women and children also took part in the carnage.

The genocidal killing began on April 6 after the airplane carrying Rwanda Hutu President Juvenal Habyarimana and Burundi President Cyprien Ntaryamira was shot down by a rocket in Tanzania. The two had been attending a peace conference that was

---

*The chronology of the events in Rwanda was compiled by Reuters and distributed by Tribunal Watch <ubvm.cc.buffalo.edu>.

geared toward building a lasting peace in the Great Lakes Region of Central Africa. This region has experienced wide-scale political unrest and violence, most of which stemmed from the ethnic conflict between Tutsis and Hutus. In 1993, the UN Security Council created and deployed a small, lightly armed peacekeeping force called the UN Assistance Mission for Rwanda (UNAMIR). UNAMIR's mandate was to help implement the ceasefire between the Hutu government and Tutsi rebels as part of the Arusha Peace Agreement. UNAMIR's 2,500 blue helmets represented the international community's commitment to the peace process and consisted of troops from Belgium, Ghana, and Pakistan. Within hours after the downing of President Habyarimana's plane, the Rwanda presidential guard began hunting down the Tutsi and Hutu opponents of the president and killing them. On April 7, Rwanda's first female Prime Minister Agathe Uwilingiyimana (and Habyarimana critic) was raped and murdered. The ten Belgian peacekeepers assigned to protect her were tortured, brutalized, and killed.

The UNAMIR commander was informed by Hutu government insiders that Hutu extremists intended to kill all the Tutsis. UNAMIR commanders wanted to move quickly to seize weapons that had been stockpiled, but were told by then-head of UN peacekeeping Kofi Annan that weapons seizures would not be supported and that UNAMIR was not to take any action without further authorization. In the meantime, Hutu gangs were on the move committing mass murder of the Tutsi minority. Rwanda radio incited the violence by directing killers to where Tutsis were hiding and filling the airways with hateful propaganda. More moderate leaders were murdered, as UN peacekeepers stepped aside. Thousands of Tutsis, fleeing the machetes, went to UN camps for protection.

The Tutsi rebel force, known as the Rwanda Popular Front (RPF), launched an offensive to seize power and stop the killing. The approaching Tutsi force caused hundreds of thousands of Hutus to flee Kigali, the Rwanda capital. The mass movements of Tutsis and Hutus created a humanitarian disaster in the border regions, especially in Tanzania. The UNHCR and the WFP struggled to avoid famine and disease. Several Western countries also sent special forces to Rwanda; however, their mission was to evacuate foreign nationals out of Rwanda. The Tutsi employees of the Western embassies were not evacuated even though they faced certain death. On April 22, the UN Secretary-General recommended that the UN Security Council either beef up and heavily arm UNAMIR or withdraw the peacekeepers from harm's way. The Security Council voted to reduce UNAMIR to a token presence of 270 people. As the UN withdrew from Rwanda, Hutu extremists overran the camps and slaughtered the inhabitants.

By July, Kigali fell to the RPF and over one million Hutus fled to neighboring countries. A new coalition government was formed with Tutsis prominently represented. The genocide was effectively ended. In November, the UN Security Council announced the creation of an international criminal court to try the Rwanda "war" criminals. In November 1996, the UNAMIR mission was officially concluded. What factors precipitated the crisis? What factors influenced the behavior of the UN? What role did the UN play in the crisis?

A REALIST CUT

The end of the Cold War effectively signaled the demise of the great powers' engagement of the Great Lakes Region and their interest in Africa in general. During the Cold War, the outcome of political and ethnic conflicts in the region were of strategic importance to the superpowers in their ideological and territorial battle. The United States, European states, and the former Soviet Union meddled in African wars of independence, each trying to influence events in their favor. The end of the Cold War greatly diminished the strategic importance of Africa, and African states were left to themselves to solve their political and ethnic conflicts that had been inflamed and exacerbated by years of Cold War tensions. In short, by 1994 the great powers had no compelling national interests in Rwanda.

Unfortunately for the Rwandans massacred in the genocide, the UN's first post–Cold War foray into Africa was a disaster for U.S. armed forces. The U.S.-led UN intervention into Somalia in 1992 was to deliver humanitarian food and medical aid to the millions of Somalis at risk. Once that mission was accomplished, U.S. forces began the difficult task of state-building by trying to create a coalition government among hostile warlords. U.S. forces had to track down renegade warlords and attempt to disarm exceptionally well-armed militias. Nineteen U.S. "peacekeepers" were brutally killed and their bodies were dragged through the streets of Mogiadishu, the capital of Somalia. The U.S. peacekeepers were on the same kind of mission that UNAMIR initially requested to undertake in Rwanda as the genocide began to unfold. With that experience, the United States was reluctant to expand UNAMIR's mission because it would likely have involved a commitment of U.S. troops in another remote region of Africa. As a result, UNAMIR was denied the authorization to take decisive steps to seize the weapons that could have at least stalled the genocide.

The United States had a policy not to intervene in Rwanda and, therefore, the UN did not intervene (Forsythe 2000, 15). U.S. State Department officials were instructed not to use the word "genocide" even though it was clear to officials that the genocide was occurring (*Frontline* 1999). Rwanda even had a nonpermanent seat on the Security Council but no one asked the Rwanda representative to explain what was happening or even to assure Security Council members that the activities merely amounted to a "breach of the peace." Neither the United States nor the UN would use the word "genocide" because genocide demands a response and the United States was committed to nonintervention (Lewis 2001, A5).

Where were the Europeans, the Belgians in particular? Belgium's historical and political ties to Rwanda suggests that perhaps they might have done something. The Belgian government, however, was reeling from the death of their peacekeepers. The Belgian government went on an extensive lobbying campaign to pull the UNAMIR force out of Rwanda. The Belgians did not want to lose face by pulling only their troops out so they lobbied Security Council members behind the scenes to pull out the entire peacekeeping force (*Frontline* 1999). They found a very sympathetic ear from the United States, who was still licking its Somalian wounds. The Hutus knew from the lessons of Somalia that "if you kill a few" they will leave and that is exactly what happened. After all, the conflict between the Tutsis and Hutus was not the fight of the Americans, the French, or the Belgians. Therefore, it was not the fight of the UN. Why should these countries risk the lives of their soldiers where they have no compelling national interest worth dying for? The Tutsis made a monumental mistake by hoping the UN would prevent their slaughter. It was the Rwanda Popular Front and its mere 600 troops that halted the genocide, and they did so with relative ease. The UN peacekeepers were better armed and trained than the RPF, yet they did nothing to halt the killings.

A LIBERAL CUT

The Rwanda Genocide is a story of good intentions, missed opportunities, and institutional weaknesses that resulted in UN paralysis. And the echo of the Jewish Holocaust remains, "All it takes for evil to triumph is for good people to do nothing." The UN involvement in Rwanda and the Great Lakes Region was motivated by a desire for a lasting peace and humanitarian concern for those living in the area. UN agencies and UNAMIR were there to help promote social and political stability and to build confidence between the ethnic groups (Waters 2001, 5–16). The UNHCR, the WFP, the WHO, and UNICEF operate extensive programs designed to help Rwanda, not to hurt it. International organizations play positive and constructive roles in mitigating ethnic conflict; however, they are caught between traditional norms of sovereignty and demands for humanitarian intervention which inevitably involves taking sides (Esman and Telhami 1995). Peacekeeping missions and international agencies have limited mandates and resources and must proceed with the consent of the parties involved.

The descent into genocide happened so quickly and was precipitated by an event that no one could predict (the downing of President Habyarimana's plane). The initial shock and disbelief as to what was happening paralyzed UN officials on the ground. The perpetrators of the Rwanda genocide have proven themselves particularly vicious and committed and were willing to murder anyone standing in their way. UN personnel were also victimized and brutalized. The UN has a responsibility to protect its people or pull them out of harm's way. Tragically for the Rwanda people, the UN had no choice but to pull them out as the members were unwilling to militarily confront the Hutu extremists.

The UN did miss a few opportunities that might have averted the catastrophe or at least mitigated it. First, the UN could have authorized the seizure of weapon stockpiles to keep them out of the hands of Hutu extremists. However, given the murkiness of what was happening on the ground and the dangers of the mission, it was difficult for UN decision makers in New York to authorize a risky mission that could cost the lives of hundreds of peacekeepers and lead to a further deterioration of the situation. Given conflicting reports and a lack of political will for expanded peacekeeping, UN decision makers made a judgment call that, in hindsight, may have cost tens of thousands of lives. A second missed opportunity on the part of the UN was failing to call the genocide, "genocide." The reluctance of UN officials to use the term allowed members to drag their feet and avoid taking action. By falling back on protocol and norms of diplomacy, the UN did not speak up against the slaughter.

According to an independent report commissioned by the Security Council (SC/6842 April 14, 2000), the failure to stop or prevent the genocide in Rwanda was a failure of the UN system as a whole. "The fundamental failure was the lack of resources and political commitment devoted to developments in Rwanda and the United Nations presence there. There was a persistent lack of political will by member states to act, or to act assertively enough, which affected the Secretariat's response, the Security Council's decision making and the difficulties in getting troops for the United Nations Assistance Mission for Rwanda" (UNAMIR). Genocides and other horrors are likely to continue until UN members find the political will and the resources for preventive action. UN missions into troubled areas need to have clear rules of engagements and must have a mandate to disarm belligerents, by force if necessary, and to raid arms caches. Just because the UN failed Rwanda does not mean it is evil and must be scrapped. The UN and its members must learn hard lessons, make the necessary changes, and try not to let this kind of horror happen again.

A Marxist Cut

The ethnic conflict between Hutus and Tutsis in the Great Lakes Region defies national boundaries. This ethnic conflict has manifested itself in wide-scale violence in Uganda, Congo (Zaire), Burundi and Tanzania, as well as Rwanda. Ethnic hatreds might date back centuries; however, they are often used by colonizing powers to maintain political control over a country's resources and labor. Rwanda was a Belgian colony from 1918 to 1962. The Belgian government favored the Tutsi minority and created a Tutsi aristocracy to help them rule over the Hutu majority. This aristocracy was based on the racial superiority of taller, leaner Tutsis and that notion of superiority was nurtured and fostered by Belgium (*Frontline* 1999). The Tutsis received preferential treatment in education and employment and many were welcomed in white colonial circles. The discriminatory treatment and marginalization of the Hutus under Belgian rule barely raised an eyebrow on the UN Trusteeship Council. Recall from Chapter 2 that the Trusteeship Council was responsible for overseeing the decolonization process. Yet it was comprised of the colonial powers, which was the equivalent of having the fox guard the chicken coop.

In 1959, Tutsi King Charles Mutara Rudghiwa died, creating a power struggle within Rwanda. Hutus and Tutsis clashed violently for more than two years until Hutus finally took power in 1961 and declared their independence in 1962. Rwanda became a member of the United Nations on September 18, 1962. With the Hutu in power, the Tutsi minority, once the elite of Rwanda society (next to the white colonialists, of course), were now persecuted. In 1963 a failed Tutsi invasion from Burundi (also a former Belgian colony and ruled by the Tutsi minority) resulted in more deaths of thousands. Many Tutsis fled to neighboring countries or to Belgium. In 1972, a Tutsi minority government in Burundi massacred tens of thousands of Hutus in order to retain their political control. The Rwanda Hutu government responded in kind and expelled more Tutsis. It is against this colonial heritage and rocky independence that the Rwanda genocide is to be understood.

The "racialization" of the Hutu–Tutsi difference took place under colonialism and is at the root of the 1994 genocide (Mamdani 2001, 76–102). The feudal system created under Belgian rule created almost complete dependence of the Hutu majority on the Tutsi minority. Hutus were kept extremely poor and uneducated, creating an inferiority complex. The Tutsi Lords collaborated with their colonial benefactors in extracting most of the precious metals from Rwanda. Tutsis benefited greatly from Belgian rule in that they were rewarded financially and politically. Very little in the way of development took place under Belgian "trusteeship" and Rwanda has been and remains among the poorest of the poor. The ethnic tensions exacerbated by Belgian colonial rule and mistreatment laid the groundwork for the desperately impoverished Hutus to commit genocide.

The UN and its aid agencies are suspect in that they are seen as part of the problem, not the solution. Belgium still has limited economic ties to Rwanda and is the largest donor of foreign aid. That gives Belgium considerable leverage. Belgians compromised the leadership of the peacekeeping force. The good intentions of the UN have caused nothing but disaster for Rwanda. The independent report commissioned by the Security Council recognizes the very limited credibility of the UN among Rwandans. The UN apology for not halting the genocide is hollow and meaningless, for the conditions that gave rise to the genocide remain. Only now, after the 2001 genocide trial of four Rwandans in Belgium, are questions being raised about the former colonial power's responsibility for the atrocities (*BBC*, June 7, 2001).

A FEMINIST CUT

According to liberal feminism, women are just as capable of brutality and violence as men. And the Rwanda genocide supports this assertion. The role of Hutu women in the genocide is not widely publicized. Women, who held positions in the civil service, who were teachers, nurses, and nuns were directly and indirectly involved with the mass murder of Tutsis (Summerfield 1996, 1816). While some women did participate directly in the killings, most women were involved with inciting the violence. "Some acted as cheerleaders, ululating the killers into action, and stripped the dead and the barely living of their jewelry, money, and clothes. They betrayed their own neighbors, friends and relatives to the militia" (Summerfield 1996, 1816). Many women who took part in the genocide were also staffers for international aid agencies. A few months before the genocide, these women were helping the UN and NGOs deliver humanitarian assistance to Rwanda's impoverished.

Women in leadership positions also joined in the genocide. Two Roman Catholic nuns were convicted of genocide in Belgium for providing petrol and leading militants to where Tutsis were hiding. Two women ministers in the Hutu government also actively promoted genocide. One of the women, Pauline Nyiramushuko, the Minister for Women and the Family, visited refugee camps and supervised the murder of Tutsi men (Summerfield 1996, 1816). She later found work with a UN aid agency after the genocide, helping the victims until she was charged, along with six others, with genocide by the International Criminal Tribunal for Rwanda, a body created by the UN after the genocide to try the perpetrators.

Rape was another important feature of the Rwanda genocide. Over 250,000 women were raped and, as is common with rigidly patriarchal societies, they and their children are now shunned by society (Royte 1997, 37). These women have not received counseling or health care. Many are now infected with HIV, the virus that causes AIDS. This amounts to a slow-motion genocide against Tutsi women. Once again the UN appears paralyzed, claiming a lack of resources and will, and the West, which turned a blind eye to the slaughter, is now unwilling to donate the drugs that might add many quality years to their lives. If the UN was really sorry for their inaction, they would help mitigate the consequences of their inaction on the living victims.

The unexamined gender relations of Rwanda society also contributed to the violence. The rapes of the Tutsi women were particularly violent and brutal, as the Hutu men saw them as too proud and somehow above them (*Win News* 1998, 34). The subordination, or feminization, of Hutu males to Tutsis, especially Tutsi women, led them to treat their rape victims in an exceptionally horrific manner. Women's groups have asserted that the UN has failed to punish the rapists or extend help to their victims (*Win News* 1998, 34).

Essentialist feminism highlights the close connection between sex and violence. The fact that men could find it within themselves to commit systematic rape in the midst of machetes and body parts indicates that part of the problem of violence might stem from the essential nature of men. Rwanda is not an isolated incident. Men have historically used rape as a weapon to demoralize their male opponents by raping their mothers, wives, and daughters. However, essentialist feminism points out that physical arousal is required to commit rape. If violence triggers a sexual arousal in men then international organizations need to take this into account if they are going address systematic rape in the future. If the rape cannot be prevented, then at least have the tools in place to help the victims come to terms with their ordeal and help them pick up the pieces of their lives. The UN has done little to help the raped women of Rwanda and they have been able to blame their inaction on the culture of patriarchal African society that shuns even discussion of women's "dishonor."

The genocides in Rwanda and the former Yugoslavia have prompted the international community to create criminal courts to prosecute those accused of the most egregious kinds of human right violations: genocide, war crimes, and crimes against humanity. The International Criminal Tribunal for the former Yugoslavia was selected because it is more institutionalized and has had more "success" than its Rwanda counterpart.

CASE STUDY 12: THE INTERNATIONAL CRIMINAL TRIBUNAL FOR THE FORMER YUGOSLAVIA

As we explored in Chapter 5, the origins and causes of the violent conflict in the former Yugoslavia are complex and interdependent. When the multiethnic state of Yugoslavia broke apart, with several republics declaring independence, war ensued across the Balkans. As a result of the attempted dismemberment of Bosnia, Muslims became victims of the worst violence. The Bosnian Muslims were without the diplomatic and military protection of neighboring states that was enjoyed by Bosnian Serbs and Bosnian Croats. The disintegration of the former Yugoslavia gave rise to a virulent form of nationalism that has led to gross violations of human rights. The UN was challenged by many in the developing world to address the crisis in Bosnia. The UN was certainly willing to intervene militarily in Third World countries (Iraq and Somalia); however, extreme and systematic violence against Muslims in the heart of Europe generated only "grave concern." UN inaction left it open to the charge of applying a double standard. The Bosnian government asked for Security Council intervention; however, none of the members was willing to commit the armed forces necessary to stop the violence. The Bosnian state claimed that it was under attack from within and without. Croatia and Serbia were aiding Bosnian Croats and Bosnian Serbs; therefore, the crisis in Bosnia was not an internal affair. The governments of Croatia and Serbia were contributing to, if not actually causing, the ethnic cleansing in Bosnia.

The UN response was rather muted. The UN offered to send peacekeeping forces (UNPROFOR) with the consent of the parties involved. The UN also offered humanitarian assistance to those who were internally displaced. The UN created safe havens for Bosnian civilians and sought to mediate a negotiated settlement with the Serbs and the Croats. The UN also instituted an arms embargo on the region and placed economic sanctions against Serbia. To many, the UN's attempts to remain neutral played into the hands of Serbia, which continued its aggression in Croatia and Bosnia. Western powers indicated that effective UN action was hampered by the Russian protection of Serbia; however, it is likely that the UN was reluctant to get involved because none of the member states was willing to bear the costs of an expensive and dangerous ground presence in Bosnia. The situation in Bosnia continued to deteriorate until 1995 when Serbian forces overran several UN safe-haven zones, committing mass murder of Muslim men and systematic rape of Muslim women. In spite of their past military successes, Serbian forces also suffered significant human losses in both Croatia and Bosnia.

The UN arms embargo did not completely stem the flow of weapons to Bosnia, as many Arab and Muslim states provided military assistance to the Bosnian government. In spite of UN declarations affirming Serb aggression, the UN maintained an embargo to the entire region and against all parties. Many European representatives argued that allowing arms for the Muslims would only add fuel to the nationalist fires. One does not put out a fire by adding gasoline. On the other hand, many developing states argued that the arms embargo only served to keep arms from the Muslims, as Serbia continued to receive assistance from Russia and Croatia received assistance from other former Eastern Bloc countries. The Muslims were victimized by the embargo while Serbs and Croats stood to gain from Muslim vulnerability. Winter 1995 marked a watershed in the Bosnian crisis. First, after four years of sustained and intense conflict, the UN, led by the United States, intervened decisively. NATO forces attacked Serb positions in Bosnia, particularly around the besieged city of Sarajevo, with UN authorization. Second, the G-7 announced that it would sponsor and support the creation of two war crimes tribunals: one for the former Yugoslavia and one for Rwanda. The 1994 Rwanda genocide went largely unnoticed by the international community when it happened, but the UN was intent on prosecuting the perpetrators after the fact. That tribunal is located in Arusha, Tanzania, and has tried and convicted several war criminals. The Yugoslav tribunal, located in the Hague, began hearing evidence of war crimes allegedly committed by Serb, Croat, and Muslim officials. By starting these judicial proceedings, the UN sought to apply as much political pressure as possible on the belligerents without rewarding the aggressors. Given that most of the war crimes were committed by Bosnian Serbs, the UN also wanted to divide the Serbian leadership by isolating the Bosnian Serb leader Radovan Karadijc and his lead general Ratko Mladic from Serbian President Slobodan Milosevic. Milosevic was later charged in 1999 for alleged crimes in Kosovo and was charged in 2001 with genocide.

After the UN issued indictments against Karadijc and Mladic, along with lower ranking Croats and Serb officials, the United States and the UN invited the official Croat, Serb, and Bosnian leadership to meet in Dayton, Ohio, to hammer out a peace plan that would end the hostilities in Bosnia. The Dayton Accords called for an immediate cease-fire and an exchange of prisoners of war. All the parties agreed that indicted war criminals would be taken into custody and brought to trial at The Hague. Bosnian civilians would be allowed to return to their homes without fear of reprisals. The UN authorized the placement of 60,000 NATO troops (IFOR) in Bosnia to implement these provisions.

The Dayton Accords reaffirmed Bosnia as a multiethnic state, but did little to tangibly reintegrate the ethnic groups. Large sections of Bosnia are still controlled by Serbs, whose leadership is still under indictment for war crimes and genocide. Muslims are understandably reluctant to return to their homes in Serb-held areas. Most observers recognize that the peace in Bosnia is tenuous at best. The central dilemma for mediators was how to stop the violence without using violence. Using force to protect human rights runs the risk of violating human rights. War is not a precise business and "collateral damage" would mean even more deaths. Very few situations lend themselves to a neat humanitarian intervention. The focus of the enforcement of human rights has come in the form of international criminal courts. Do these courts serve a useful purpose in international affairs? Whose interests do they serve? Who stands to win and who stands to lose? The theoretical approaches generate different interpretations regarding the efficacy of international criminal courts.

A REALIST CUT

Realists, particularly those from powerful states, do not take international criminal courts seriously. International criminal courts, like the temporary courts set up for Rwanda and the former Yugoslavia, and the permanent International Criminal Court created in August of 1998, will only be effective against junior-level suspects offered up as sacrificial lambs, if at all. While human rights violations offend the human conscience, states have more pressing national interests relating to security and the balance of power. The Bosnian crisis is no exception. Most states are interested in international stability, and most would have preferred to maintain the status quo. Very few countries, save for Slovenia, Croatia, and Bosnia, wanted to see the disintegration of Yugoslavia. Most states would have tolerated political repression as long as the former Yugoslavia remained intact; however, with its implosion, the best the international community can hope to do is manage the transition.

Transitionary periods in international politics tend to be characterized by violence. Conflicts on the scale and intensity of Bosnia are common as states break apart and new allegiances are formed. Most of today's nation-states were formed in the fires of violent conflict. To charge anyone with "war crimes" during times of war is like handing out speeding tickets at the Indy 500.* Whether a particular action is just or right is irrelevant because for realists, might makes right. The victors write the history books and they never portray themselves in an overly harsh or critical light. Similarly, international law is made by the powerful to control the weak. If human rights violations are ever raised during war, then it only amounts to a "victors' justice." Only the vanquished are brought before an international court to answer for their crimes, as German and Japanese officials discovered at the Nuremberg and Tokyo tribunals after World War II. During the Cold War, no one was ever prosecuted for "grave breaches" as identified in Article 147 of the Geneva Convention on the Protection of Civilian Persons in Time of War (1949). According to Article 147, grave breaches include

> [w]illful killing, torture or inhumane treatment, including biological experiments, willfully causing great suffering or serious injury to body or health, unlawful deportation or transfer or unlawful confinement of a protected person, compelling a protected person to serve in forces of a hostile Power, or willfully depriving a protected person of the rights of fair and regular trial prescribed in the present Convention, taking of hostages and extensive destruction and appropriation of property, not justified by military necessity and carried out unlawfully and wantonly.

Ironically, these words are quite vague and subject to political interpretations. States must have compelling national or collective security interests to enforce this law because charging heads of state and other high-ranking government officials with war crimes

---

*This analogy was articulated in Francis Ford Coppola's *Apocalypse Now* (1979).

is tricky business. In the first place, the Court must have a reasonable chance of taking the person into custody, which is not likely if the state in question retains its territorial integrity. Second, violent conflict usually requires a negotiated settlement, and mediators need somebody to talk to—someone who is not under indictment. Hence, those who wish to punish state officials accused of committing war crimes and grave offenses must have not only the capability, but the political will to do so.

The Bosnian crisis illustrates why human rights and justice take a backseat to other political considerations. Even though Serbian Leader Slobodan Milosevic was eventually indicted by the Yugoslav war crimes tribunal (1999) and brought to trial (2000), his indictment went through only when the West allowed it. How could the man who, presumably, gave the orders—the man who provided military assistance to Bosnian Serbs—not be charged with war crimes until 1999? The man was at an air force base in Ohio in 1995 and the United States negotiated a deal with him. The United States did not arrest him. The simple and short answer is that Milosevic was a formal head of state and, as such, he was necessary to restore peace and stability in the Balkans. Although a prima facie case could easily have been made for indicting the president of the Republic of Serbia for war crimes, it was not prudent to indict the very individual who is crucial to negotiating a peace settlement. Only when NATO launched a massive air campaign against Serbia did they decide he was, in fact, a war criminal. The timing of indictment shows how easily the ICTY was manipulated by the West. At best, the war crime tribunals pay lip service to the rule of law, but they do little to punish aggressors or deter future gross violations of human rights.

Applying the rule of law includes more than being able to get ahold of perpetrators. It also involves the resolve of the international community, particularly the members of the UN Security Council. Both France and Russia have expressed sympathy for the Serbian position. Russia has historically been allied with fellow Slavs, and France remembers Serb resistance against Nazi aggression during World War II. Germany has made no secret of its support for Croatia. Croatia has ethnic German ties, and Croatian officials collaborated with the Germans during World War II. The UK and the United States sympathized with the plight of Bosnian Muslims, largely because of their allies in the Arab world, particularly Saudi Arabia. Russia and China both have domestic human rights situations (Chechnya and Tibet, respectively) that they would rather keep from outside scrutiny. Given these political divisions on the Security Council, solutions to the Balkans crisis are likely to be elusive, and as illusory as justice.

When the G-7 announced its support for the Yugoslav war crimes tribunal in 1995, it was met with considerable skepticism. According to the UK's *Independent*, "The UN appears to be creating a tactical nightmare for itself. On the one hand it is trying to deliver peace in the former Yugoslavia, on the other it is threatening those with whom it has to negotiate that peace with long jail sentences" (U.S. Information Agency 1995a, 5). According to Germany's *Die Welt*, "[T]he increasingly absurd situation in Bosnia seems to support the view that the UN's plan to hold war crimes trials in The Hague . . . is about as likely to succeed as the League of Nations would have been if it had demanded the extradition of Hitler, Himmler, Goering, and Goebbels from Germany in 1943. The UN—and individual nations like Germany—are running the risk of losing even more credibility. . . . Nobody is talking about the main culprit Milosevic" (U.S. Information Agency 1995a, 5). Saudi Arabia's *Al Riyadh* reflects on the difference between war criminals and historic national heroes:

> Such a condemnation was previously leveled at many of the Zionist leaders: Begin, Shamir, Sharon, and others. However, they became, after the creation of Israel and the 1967 war victories, heroes in the view of those who earlier condemned their actions in the name of human rights. This is exactly what will happen to persons such as Saddam Hussein, the leaders of the Serbs and Rwanda and others. (U.S. Information Agency 1995a, 6)

The pessimism regarding the efficacy of the Yugoslav tribunal has proven to be justified. Six years after Karadijc and Mladic were indicted, they remain at large in Bosnia. NATO forces have made no effort to arrest the suspects in spite of having several clear opportunities. Only a few junior officers and soldiers have been prosecuted and sentenced to jail terms. Political expediency again trumps the enforcement of human rights and the pursuit of justice. The existence of the Yugoslav tribunal has not deterred Serb aggression. The brutal assault on Kosovo suggests that Milosevic was not particularly concerned with the threat of indictment. What is more important, the United States has unsigned the treaty creating the International Criminal Court (ICC), a permanent war crimes tribunal to replace ad hoc commissions after their mandates expire. The United States wanted prosecutions in the ICC to be approved by the Security Council, subject to permanent member veto. Opponents of the U.S. position hold that all states must be held to the same standard, including the great powers. According to Italy's *La Repubblica* (July 16, 1998):

> In reality, what is really at stake here is the balance of power which emerged out of the second World War. As a matter of fact, the "no" alignment group is led by four of the five permanent UNSC members. More than a concern about the exploitation of the court, they seem concerned about a projected "revision" of the entity: no longer an autonomous tribunal, but a new tool in the hands of the powerful of the earth, to use according to their political needs both as stick and carrot. (U.S. Information Agency 1998c, 7)

The United States was unsuccessful at pushing through its demand of Security Council control and found itself in strange company, isolated from its allies. As Belgium's conservative *La Libre Belgique* opined, "It is most paradoxical that the great Western nation whose obstinacy made the Nuremberg trials possible, found itself in Rome on the same line as Iraq, Algeria and Libya, where human rights are still anathematized" (U.S. Information Agency 1998c, 9). For realists, this is not really a paradox. It exemplifies a state maximizing its power and national interest at Nuremberg and Rome. The company the United States keeps, be it Iraq or France, is determined by its national interests, not by shared values regarding human rights.

A LIBERAL CUT

The creation of criminal courts to prosecute gross violations of human rights is one way to promote and protect human rights. These courts can isolate those accused of violating human rights and function as a deterrent for those that might take the same path in order to achieve their aims. The war crimes tribunal for the former Yugoslavia ensures that the perpetrators of the Bosnian genocide and war crimes do not go unpunished. Liberals stress that these courts are far from perfect and are constrained by other political considerations. This does not mean, however, that human rights are marginalized. Human rights are obviously of concern to states and other international actors or else the UN and/or NATO would not have become involved in Rwanda, Burundi, and Bosnia.

The crisis in the former Yugoslavia is a crisis because of the loss of human life and dignity. It is not a crisis because of any dramatic shift in the balance of power or Serbian dominance in Central Europe. Even realists recognize that none of the great powers has any compelling interest, yet the UN and NATO have committed significant resources and human capital to resolving the conflict. This is not misguided altruism. It represents a fundamental change in the nature and dynamics of international politics. Even given the worst-case scenario, in which no high-ranking officials are ever tried, the criminal courts serve the basic purpose of publicizing human rights abuses. Those charged with genocide and war crimes in Bosnia and Rwanda can never be accepted back into the international community until they have answered those charges. They cannot travel freely to other countries, nor can they amass personal fortunes. They are virtual prisoners in their own countries. Human rights are not marginalized. Rather, those who engage in gross human rights violations are the ones marginalized in international politics.

Liberals argue that a true revolution has occurred as it relates to human rights. The international community has every right to review human rights situations and to act if those situations threaten international peace and security. The human suffering caused by gross violations causes instability by displacing huge populations internally. Millions are also forced across borders, creating crises in neighboring countries. Whether or not the crisis in Bosnia is an internal or international affair is a question of semantics rather than a tangible distinction. According to the UN Secretary-General Javier Perez de Cuéllar:

> It is now increasingly felt that the principle of non-interference within the essential domestic jurisdiction of states cannot be regarded as a protective barrier behind which human rights could be massively or systematically violated with impunity. The fact that diverse situations in the United Nations have not been able to prevent atrocities cannot be accepted as an argument, legal or moral, against the necessary corrective action, especially when peace is threatened. (UN Doc. A/461, 1991)

The creation of the Yugoslav and Rwanda tribunals demonstrated the international community's resolve to challenge those who commit genocide and war crimes, even if the community cannot make the parties comply with their international commitments. As Saudi Arabia's internationally circulated *Al-Sharq Al-Aswat* claimed:

> [T]he decision of the Hague international war crimes tribunal . . . comes as an unexpected and pleasant surprise. Although the chances of arresting and bringing to trial the leader of the Serbs and the commander of their armed forces are slight, still the initiative remains an important political announcement during the coming round of the war. . . . Even if the court failed to achieve any progress on the ground, it has at least provided a verdict in the dirty war of Bosnia. (U.S. Information Agency 1995a, 6)

Liberals point out that human rights are among the principal values challenging the primacy of sovereignty and affecting the national interests of states. However, they recognize that sovereignty and political exigencies hamper the promotion, protection, and enforcement of human rights. A central factor determining whether international criminal courts will become important, institutionalized features of the international political landscape depends on hegemonic leadership. Unfortunately, the United States has shown that it is not willing, for a variety of reasons, to assume that leadership role.

According to Italy's *La Repubblica*, "By refusing to sign the treaty on the birth of the International Court, following its previous refusal regarding a ban against land mines, the United States has given up its role of moral leader of the world. . . . In both cases, Clinton's America has privileged domestic policy concerns and its national interest over those of the international community" (U.S. Information Agency 1998c, 5). Liberal institutionalists acknowledge that hegemonic leadership is a requisite for the creation of international organizations and the hegemon is not going to support every institution-building effort.

A Marxist Cut

Marxists stress the hypocrisy of Western concerns with war crimes and human rights violations in the former Yugoslavia. Millions of people die every day because they lack adequate nutrition or access to clean water. What about their human rights? Why do civil and political rights warrant criminal prosecution and socioeconomic deprivations barely raise the eyebrows of the West? The Marxist lens, like the realist's, is focused on the pessimistic. The West's creation of the Yugoslav war crimes tribunal has, according to Slovenia's *Dnevnik*, only "quieted its conscience" (U.S. Information Agency 1995a, 4). They question the West's seriousness about prosecuting alleged war criminals. According to the Netherlands' *Algemeen Dagblad*, "Fearing revenge, the United States decided to back down. . . . The hunt is over. Karadijc and Mladic, responsible for the ethnic cleansing in Srebrenica, are going free. This is too cynical to be true. The two war criminals have made a fool of the entire world community and the world's strongest superpower. Justice can no longer be done" (U.S. Information Agency 1998a, 9).

Marxists also wonder if ethnic and religious biases affect the West's resolve to effective human rights enforcement. The West's historic suspicions of Muslims makes the Muslims less sympathetic as victims of Serb aggression. According to Pakistan's *Muslim*:

> The United States bears a historic responsibility for these acts against the Kosovar Muslims especially since it voted against the International Criminal Court [ICC]: Ironically more than 100 countries voted in favor of ICC with the full blessing of the United Nations. . . . In the ultimate analysis, the United States is encouraging people like Milosevic to continue to act as criminals of wars and to crimes against humanity. . . . If no action is taken to save the Kosovar Muslims, the Muslims are doomed. (U.S. Information Agency 1998a, 12)

The U.S. insistence that the ICC be subject to Security Council review indicates its penchant for exempting itself from the same rules that it imposes on everyone else. According to Germany's *Berliner Zeitung*, "An ICC that depends on the blessing of the permanent members of the UNSC is, in reality, not an independent court. . . . It would mean open discrimination of all other states and would strengthen the antiquated special rights of the veto powers, thus undermining necessary reform of the UN constitution" (U.S. Information Agency 1998c, 3). International criminal courts serve to reinforce, rather than challenge, the status quo. Human rights enforcement centers on civil and political rights and ignores economic, social, and cultural rights. Like the realists, Marxists argue that only the weak and vanquished are likely to be prosecuted while crimes committed by the capitalist states and their allies will be overlooked.

A Feminist Cut

Feminists identify several positive and negative aspects of human rights enforcement in the former Yugoslavia. On a positive note, many feminists applaud the role of then–U.S. Ambassador to the UN, Madeleine Albright. Ambassador Albright was a leading advocate of creating the Yugoslav tribunal. Albright has argued that in spite of the pessimism expressed by many in the international community, the Yugoslav war crimes tribunal is necessary for peace in the Balkans and for strengthening international law (Albright 1994, 209). Feminists, particularly liberal feminists, place special emphasis on women operating outside their traditional gender roles. Albright's leadership was instrumental in the tribunal's creation and should receive recognition for challenging the status quo.

Feminists also stress the importance of the Yugoslav war crimes tribunal in publicizing rape as a war crime. Rape has historically been overlooked as a violation of human rights and as a war crime. Rape used to be considered one of the "spoils" of war. Women were the fruits of war, to be plundered by occupying armies. The systematic rape of women in Bosnia raised awareness that rape is a form of genocide and ethnic cleansing. Rape has been used to terrorize and demoralize Bosnian Muslims and Bosnian Croat civilians. In other words, rape is a weapon of war used against the most vulnerable. The Yugoslav war crimes tribunal has brought violence against women to the forefront of human rights issues. Also important is the 2000 conviction of several for their participation in rape camps in Bosnia.

The feminist world view focuses on the role of women and the effects of war on women. Feminists are discouraged by the apparent impotence of NATO. The inability of NATO to stand up and arrest the leaders who are most responsible for the atrocities in the former Yugoslavia is troubling. The tens of thousands of women who have been raped and killed will not have justice. It seems that justice is not worth the costs to the men who make the decisions. It is ironic that men who are armed "to the teeth" with the most sophisticated weapons are afraid of the consequences of arresting rapists and murderers. According to Denmark's *Politiken*, "The [U.S.] military was responsible for making the decision, despite the fact that leading American diplomats—Holbrooke included—have long called for the arrests to be made. Clinton is not a president who is able to go against the wishes of the military. They do not think that the 'purely moral nature' of the action is worth risking the life of a single military soldier" (U.S. Information Agency 1998a, 9). The so-called realist priorities are really masculinist priorities that put the interests of men over the interests of women.

Conclusion

International efforts to promote, protect, and enforce human rights have met with varying degrees of success. Human rights both challenge and reinforce the status quo. This statement is not contradictory if it is analyzed using the different theoretical frameworks. Human rights violations have been identified by the Security Council as a threat to international peace and security. Human rights violations have led to domestic instability and civil war. The nature of international conflict in the twenty-first century suggests that human rights will remain controversial in international relations. Disagreements regarding definition and implementation are inevitable. What is certain is that human rights will remain permanent features in twenty-first century world politics.

11

GLOBAL GOVERNANCE IN 2075

PREDICTION IN POLITICS is always hazardous, and international politics is no exception. What role will international organizations play in the governance of twenty-first-century international affairs? Will new international organizations be created or will existing organizations be significantly transformed? What are the prospects for international peace and cooperation? How will international organizations behave in "the new world order?" International relations have multiple futures with multiple interpretations.

A REALIST CUT

Realists predict continuity, both in international relations and in the nature of international governance. States remain the principal and most important actors in international relations, and international organizations are subordinate to the dominant powers of the day. The international system will still be defined as anarchy characterized by some kind of balance of power. International organizations will continue to play secondary roles in the management of international affairs. War, violence, and conflict will remain at the forefront of the international stage. What will change, according to realists, is the distribution of capabilities among states. There is nothing inevitable about the world order created under U.S. hegemony. The values, norms, and rules regarding state behavior in the year 2075 will be decided by the powerful. The behavior and interests of IGOs will reflect that underlying balance of power.

Even if the UN is still a viable organization, collective security will continue to be a politically motivated and power-driven endeavor. Collective security will be triggered only when the geostrategic, military, and economic interests of all the great powers are engaged and those interests are congruent. A congruence of great-power interests will be just as difficult to achieve, if not more so, in the late twenty-first century as it was during the twentieth century. Liberal principles of justice and international law will not prompt UN action, only great-power interests. Whether or not the UN will continue to exist will be determined in large part by the answers to two questions.

1. *Can war between the great powers be avoided?* The historical record suggests that war is an inevitable part of international relations. States that want peace must always be

prepared for war. Nuclear weapons may create a particular kind of balance of power that renders war between the great powers obsolete, but that is no guarantee against devastating terrorist attacks. War remains a likely possibility, particularly if the current international order experiences a crisis or some kind of breakdown. A global depression or a regional conflict that spins out of control could erode U.S. leadership capabilities to the extent that a revisionist challenger will seek to change the system. The United States could fight or abandon its leadership role. A new world leader, possibly China, may create international organizations that institutionalize its dominant role and legitimize its leadership position. The UN may meet the same fate as the League of Nations, finding itself on the trash heap of failed experiments. Even if global war can be averted, the United States or some other state (or a group of states) must be willing to commit the resources necessary to keep the UN operating. Chances are that great-power indecision and neglect will prove fatal to the UN.

2. *Can the UN adapt to the changing power distributions among states?* If nuclear weapons generate an effective stalemate among the great powers, then the UN must change to reflect the shifting distributions of conventional military and economic capabilities. The original composition of the Security Council reflected the balance of power after World War II. However, after the Cold War, the permanent members of the Security Council have resisted reforms that would include rising states and states from the developing world on the Council. The permanent members have rejected any change in the veto provision or other substantive decision-making procedures. The Security Council will likely remain a great-power concert in that the members will balance each other but will permit the great powers to intervene militarily in their own spheres of influence. The great-power cooperation that occurred during the 1990s was more an aberration than the birth of true collective security.

The Security Council of the late twenty-first century will be just as paralyzed as it always has been. The optimism of the 1990s quickly eroded as its collective security initiatives in Somalia and the former Yugoslavia proved disastrous. The sobering conflicts of interest and power realities have prevented effective collective security. As an institutional framework, collective security does little to curb unilateral uses of force by the permanent members. These states will continue to use violence to secure their national interests, which include forcibly changing the governments of other states and carrying out military reprisals. The proliferation of nuclear weapons will create multiple "cold wars" as adversaries stand off. The Security Council will likely become paralyzed, unable to act.

The nature of conflict in the twenty-first century does not lend itself to traditional collective security of the kind envisioned by the UN architects after World War II. Collective security in the twentieth century was designed to guard against the traditional land grab and the territorial expansion of states through force. International conflict in the twenty-first century has internal sources and is low in intensity but prolonged. Terrorism is also a persistent threat. International conflict occurs in the marginalized areas of the world where the permanent members have few interests. Marginalized states have disintegrated along ethnic and religious lines. Only strong states continue to survive internal and external challenges. International security between strong states at the end of the twenty-first century will be achieved through a balance of power, just as it has been achieved for the last 500 years. The UN Security Council will either reflect that balance of power or it will become obsolete.

Regional security arrangements such as NATO are not likely to fare any better. Absent a major war or systemic threat, NATO is likely to be disbanded or become moribund. If NATO has not been disbanded, then it is no longer a security alliance but a political organization like the OCSE or the WEU. In other words, it is an alliance on paper only. Without a common enemy or clearly defined military objectives, alliances either shift or dissolve. NATO is no exception. The defense policies of European states are likely to be renationalized, with each European member maintaining a military sufficient for its own national defense.

NATO may become a central IGO in European affairs as a military alliance if a new cold war emerges in Europe. Communism is far from dead in Russia and may once again guide that nation's economic and foreign policy. This cold war may not have any symmetry with the twentieth-century Cold War. Any number of states in Europe have great-power aspirations and may seek to establish their own sphere of influence. Russia, Ukraine, Georgia, Serbia, Turkey, all have impressive capabilities that may require some form of containment policy to curb their influence or geographic expansion. The Central Asian Republics, with their oil and natural gas reserves, are also potential sources of power and instability. However, in order for NATO or any military alliance to be effective, an engaged hegemon will be required. The United States is not likely to have the capability or the will to commit the necessary resources. If the United States does not lead, then who will? Will other European countries follow the lead of France or a rearmed Germany? For realists, the question of the role of international organizations is not at issue. Rather, the issues center on which states will have power and therefore create and control international organizations. International security organizations, whether collective security or traditional military alliances, may be created by a new hegemon, or existing organizations will be transformed to reflect some new dominant power. Otherwise, they will fall by the wayside, discarded tools that are no long useful. In short, they will become anachronistic institutions, relics of the past.

IGOs that relate to trade will meet the same fate as security IGOs. The WTO, which is based on free trade principles, will be effective only as long as the major powers stand to benefit from free trade. States will ignore any WTO decisions that go against their important national interests. And they will abandon free trade if they begin to lose significant national wealth. States will erect barriers to trade in order to arrest their decline or maximize economic advantages. They simply will be more clever, paying lip service to the benefits of free trade, all the while managing their trade to their own strategic advantages. States that engage in managed and strategic trade will take advantage of those that pursue free trade policy. Their firms and state industries will have access to the markets of others while keeping their markets closed to international competition. Firms that have the full backing of their governments will have a competitive advantage because they do not have to worry about going out of business. They can sell the products or services below cost, driving competitors out of business and establishing a monopoly or oligopoly. These firms and their countries will control the leading sectors of the economy. Japan and China have become the dominant economic powers in the twenty-first century.

Realists point out that globalization is neither inevitable nor new. International relations are whatever states decide they are. And states have the power to implement policies that control the forces of globalization. States can, and will, put controls on trade, currency, and capital if it suits their national interests. "Globalization" and "a new world order" are hardly new ideas. U.S. presidents ranging from Wilson to Nixon to Bush to Clinton have all spoken of a new world order based on democracy and liberal economic principles. That vision has not been sustained by the historical record, nor have international relations fundamentally changed. According to Nicholas D. Kristof:

> [G]lobalization . . . may not be quite as fresh as it sometimes seems. Since at least the 13th century, when Florentine merchants lent to the English to pay for King Edward's wars, international capital has roamed the world in search of highest returns. (The start was inauspicious: England defaulted causing the collapse of two Florentine banks.) What has changed . . . is the scale of capital flows and their ability to capsize small nations—even large ones. (1998, 6)

International organizations that deal with the substantive economic issues, such as trade and finance, are likely to experience serious crises. The WTO has already been under attack for undermining national interests, jobs, and national industries. In the twenty-first century, states will seek to regain control over their borders in order to curb job losses and to keep certain industries within their territorial boundaries. While the WTO will continue to promote neoclassical views of trade, states will subvert WTO rulings that compromise their national interest. A global economic recession may even cause the failure of the WTO, as states are forced to regroup and reassure their concerned citizenship that they can deliver economic prosperity. States must once again be responsible for ensuring a certain standard of living, which inevitably involves state intervention in the market and making the market subservient to the state. Realists argue that the logic of the market artificially puts individual and firm interests over national interests. Individuals and firms must recognize and promote the interests of the state because the state will ultimately protect and defend them. This recognition must be more than just patriotic lip service and the waving of national flags. States and industries must work together to improve and provide the best quality of life for citizens.

Economic development in the Third World is likely to undergo a crisis. Developing countries realize that the nature of economic relations is, in many respects, a zero-sum game and they are on the short end of the stick. Developing states need to take responsibility for their own national development and not rely on foreign capital and foreign assistance. Economic development in the Third World has been arrested by ballooning external debt and currency crises. Free flows of capital have created speculative bubbles that can burst, taking entire economies with them. Again, according to Kristof:

> Most governments imposed capital controls early in this century and then lifted them in the 1970s and 1980s, and limitations on changing money came to be seen as quaint. Paradoxically, it is the holdouts on capital controls, like China and India, that have weathered the financial crisis much better than others, because they were not vulnerable to a sudden exodus of capital. (1998, 6)

In spite of stopgap measures implemented at the end of the twentieth century, the international monetary order will move toward a global crisis in the twenty-first century as more and more currencies become vulnerable to speculators. The logic of the market may indicate the creation of a single global currency, but that currency will not emerge spontaneously. The dominant power of a hegemon is necessary, coupled with some kind of catastrophic collapse.

Unfortunately, U.S. leadership capabilities in the global economy have waned considerably in the twenty-first century, and its strategy has been to find "market" solutions to cover its inability to provide a stable international monetary order. The international monetary system is an inherently political creature, and the creation of a global or regional currency will favor some at the expense of others. States will be reluctant to accept a global currency unless they stand to gain substantially. Any transformation of the international monetary system will reflect the relative power of states and the vision of the new leader of the global economy. Realists also point out that the international economy may not be based on liberal principles at all. Absent a liberal hegemon, the global economy could break apart into regional blocs that are intensely competitive and hostile.

The environment in 2075 will have degraded extensively. States have taken steps to renew their resources such as forests and fresh water; however, global warming and ozone depletion will have taken their toll. Whales are virtually extinct. Coastal and equatorial states have experienced the devastating effects of global warming. These states have lost territory due to the increase in sea levels, and they are subject to periodic and catastrophic floods. Historically, states have been both blessed and cursed by geography. Coastal and equatorial states will either have prepared for the effects global warming or will have suffered the consequences. While it is not fair or just, states must respond and adjust to the changing environmental reality. Similarly, states will have to prepare and educate their citizens for the effects of ozone depletion. Humans will have to adjust their lifestyles, which will include spending more time indoors. While outside, humans will have to wear hats, sunglasses, sunscreen, long sleeves, and long pants.

On a positive note, the principal cause of global warming, the burning of fossil fuels, is no longer a factor. The world's supply of oil, natural gas, and coal have been depleted and replaced with other forms of energy, including a supercell that harnesses electricity generated by solar, nuclear, or hydroelectric sources. Technology will solve some of the environmental problems of the twenty-first century, but states must actively develop and utilize that technology. Responsible states will have pursued alternative energy strategies, not so much because of global warming, but because world supplies are limited and nonrenewable.

The protection, promotion, and enforcement of human rights remain in the realm of low politics in the twenty-first century. States will remain appalled by gross violations of human rights in other countries, but they are not likely to intervene unless significant national interests are at stake. Hence, international enforcement of human rights is a politically motivated endeavor—a noble mask for the not-so-noble interests of the intervening states. Given impending economic and energy crises, many states will use economic, social, and collective rights to reassert control over their borders and to manage these crises. Many states, particularly in Europe and the developing world, will use their responsibility to protect and promote human rights of their citizens to reassert their sovereignty over trade and monetary issues.

The International Criminal Court created in 1998 to prosecute those committing war crimes and other gross violations of human rights will fall quickly to the wayside. The harsh reality is that the Court will not apply to the powerful, which means that other states will not ratify the Court's charter. The Yugoslav and Rwanda war crimes tribunals demonstrated that only the vanquished will be prosecuted, and then only when it is politically expedient. In the twenty-first century, the promotion and protection of human rights will be largely voluntary and not a high priority of states. Definition and implementation of human rights will be determined by the powerful and will be used to manipulate and control the weak.

A LIBERAL CUT

International relations in the twenty-first century are fundamentally different from those obtaining in prior centuries. International politics is conducted within the framework of a global society consisting of a variety of international actors tied together by computer and information technologies. This global society is founded on individual human rights and the global marketplace. The international system is characterized by a complex interdependence that significantly decreases the utility of military force to achieve goals. States have become transnationalized in that they are inextricably tied to the global economy and global civil society. Other actors such as MNCs, NGOs, and even individuals are part and parcel of global civil society. The UN framework will have been transformed into some loose form of federal world government, albeit a quasi-government, in which all international actors are allowed to participate.

The international system will not exactly be "perpetual peace" in the twenty-first century. International (global) peace and stability face several complex threats. These threats emanate from within states as certain segments of society resist change and globalization. Many societies will experience some form of "tribalism" as a reaction to global integrative forces. Some segments will revert to religious fundamentalism or virulent nationalism. This tribalism can threaten international stability, particularly if tribalist forces take over governments and disrupt markets. These tribalist governments can also represent a traditional territorial threat to transnationalized states and will require some kind of containment.

This containment will be conducted through collective security provisions of the UN. By the year 2075, China will have been fully integrated into the global economy and will share the values of the Western members. The Security Council veto will have been abandoned and more democratic procedures for membership and decision making will be instituted. The UN will likely have a standing multinational military force that can be dispatched in emergencies. Military force will not be particularly useful, either because of a military stalemate or because the problems defy military solutions. Nonviolent means of leverage will become important and appropriate for responding to international security threats.

NATO was transformed into the defense pillar of the European Union in the early twenty-first century, and has since been transformed into a global collective security arrangement under the UN. The NATO successor, perhaps called the Democratic Treaty Organization (DTO), assembles the most sophisticated military and technological capability, which it will bring to bear against any physical threat to members. DTO members must be democratic, have civilian control of the military, and renounce the use of military force in their international relations. DTO will largely be a military institution under the civilian control of a democratically elected Security Council. Security will be based globally with some regional overlap.

The UN and DTO assist states in addressing domestic violence and crimes, although the line between domestic and international has been erased for all intents and purposes. Government decisions may no longer reach to all segments of society, and governments are unable to enforce their own laws. Criminal syndicates will also have transnational activities, requiring transnational approaches. The UN and DTO will help national governments by providing social and economic assistance. They will still engage in peacekeeping and peacemaking when appropriate. They will help provide social welfare and humanitarian assistance to global society's disadvantaged.

The international economy has become truly global. The production of goods and services takes place on a global scale. The concept of a national economy is obsolete; rather, the economy is divided between global and local. The local economy consists of local services such as taxi driving, hair styling, child care, and lawn services. Most other goods and services will be produced and provided globally. The WTO has been successful in liberalizing trade in almost all areas of the economy. It now functions as a laissez-faire entity enforcing trade rules, copyrights, and intellectual property rights. This is a crucial function of the WTO in the maturing stage of the technological revolution. Growth in the global economy is still in the areas of information, telecommunication, transportation, and aerospace technologies. The global economy has also been transformed by the depletion of fossil fuels and the switch to solar, hydroelectric, and nuclear energy. Adaptation is easier in the global economy because individuals and firms, not states and complicated bureaucracies, make private and public choices. Because the global market is allowed to operate, innovation is spontaneous and benefits are more easily diffused.

The international monetary system experienced a systemic breakdown in the early part of the twenty-first century. The crisis affected all the national currencies and caused a global economic recession. However, all the democratic states worked together, relying on negotiations and compromise, to create a single global currency controlled by the IMF. Paper money exists only in museums. Money is electronic and transactions are direct. The creation of a cashless global society means that money no longer has any national significance, not even as a symbol. The single global currency is created because it is necessary for the smooth functioning of the global economy. Necessity is the mother of all invention. Even though no state possesses hegemony, states, MNCs, and NGOs can cooperate under existing international organizations to solve global monetary problems.

The global market now encompasses what was known as the "developing world" or the "South" during the twentieth century. Now practically indistinguishable from the "developed world" or the "North," these areas experienced significant economic growth and investment during their transition from traditional society into modern and postmodern consumer society. The market has caused the diffusion of wealth, technology, values, investment, and capital. Liberals argue that this does not mean that the developing world has become Westernized. Rather, market forces work to sort out the best of all worlds, transforming both North and South, developed and underdeveloped.

Of course, not all liberals are this optimistic, despite their agreement that market forces are generally positive. They acknowledge that the gap between rich and poor will not disappear, as the market affords an uneven playing field. Nevertheless, they argue, individuals must have the opportunity to participate in the market. Gender, nationality, or race should not be allowed to interfere with the market, nor should individuals be excluded from the market for these reasons. The developing world of the twentieth century will become the developed world of the twenty-first century, and everyone in the South will have access to the same amenities as everyone else. They will have access to health care, education, clean water, electricity, sanitation, computers, and some form of telecommunications. But access will not level the fundamental playing field. Thus, the UN, NGOs, and states of the twenty-first century will be needed to protect and assist those who fall between the cracks or fail to compete in the new global economy. However, the UN must emphasize individual initiatives, helping individuals help themselves. Given the scale of the global economy in the twenty-first century, the UN will only be able to provide for a minimum safety net. Individuals will have more control over their lives in the twenty-first century than they have ever had in human history.

The environmental threats identified at the end of the twentieth century continue to worsen in the early twenty-first century. International treaties and organizations are strengthened to address these problems and help bridge the gap between North and South. The expansion of global markets encourages more efficient industrial production, and new technology transforms dirty industries into cleaner industries. NGOs continue to play a crucial role in identifying and monitoring international environmental problems. They will continue to hold the feet of states, industries, and MNCs to the fire regarding environmental protection. NGOs will also offer plausible solutions to environmental problems. Since environmental problems affect all, without respect to geography or nationality, all states will be forced to cooperate and work together to solve these problems.

Like the international monetary system, the ecosystem permits no choice: Environmental issues must be addressed head-on. Collective international learning will help states overcome collective action problems. Most liberals argue that market forces should be allowed to prevail, but environmental costs should not be externalized. International organizations can help states and other actors ensure that environmental costs are included in the price of goods and services, thereby affecting demand via the price mechanism. The market remains the most efficient way to utilize and distribute resources. It is also the principal source of innovation. The twenty-first century has seen the rise of an entire eco-industry that provides environmentally friendly technology, goods, and services. Environmental education has created consumer demands that protect the natural environment and place considerable value on biodiversity. The economic development of the South has allowed their governments and citizens to obtain the financial and human resources necessary to environmental protection.

The international environmental regime that emerged in the late twentieth century is now a global regime, led by supranational organizations with the authority to privatize much of the global commons. Orbital space and extraterrestrial bodies are important and controversial aspects of the commons in 2075, with states and MNCs vying for property rights to these areas. The supranational authorities are charged with weighing the global society's rights, balancing them with the rights of individuals, firms, and states. The disparities between rich and poor remain important obstacles to global cooperation with regard to managing "out-of-earth" resources both effectively and efficiently.

Human rights form the foundation of the legal system of global society. Local, provincial, national, and international law, all recognize and implement the Universal Declaration of Human Rights. Civil and political rights are specifically guaranteed by the UN. Individuals will be able to appeal to the UN or UN-sponsored agencies to seek redress for wrongs, particularly when national or regional petitions fail. Violators of human rights can be held civilly liable and criminally responsible for their acts. Those accused of committing gross violations of human rights or war crimes can be brought before the International Criminal Court for justice. Those found guilty of such crimes would receive lengthy prison terms. The death penalty has been outlawed in most areas and it is actionable as a human rights violation under international law.

Economic, social, and collective rights are not institutionalized on a par with civil and political rights because they do not form the foundation of global civil society. The UN is incapable of delivering such rights as the provision of health care and education to individuals. Rather, individuals working in their own communities must actualize for themselves their economic, social, and cultural rights. Collective rights remain elusive because it is hard to define the collective in the twenty-first century, outside of a generalized global citizenship. The rights to a clean environment and development are relative to the age. These rights mean quite different things in 2075 than they did in 1998.

International relations have fundamentally changed owing to the expansion of markets, human rights, and democratic forms of governments. The world in 2075 is far from perfect and serious inequities remain. Nevertheless, the quality of life for everyone on the planet is better than that in previous generations. International war is virtually obsolete, and violent conflict is seen as inappropriate for settling disputes. The rule of law is a norm that has been institutionalized. Law that is made by the people, for the people, through their elected representatives is the best way to promote justice and the peaceful settlement of disputes. International actors are expected to compromise, mediate, arbitrate, and adjudicate; but they will not use violence. After centuries of war, the international system has finally evolved into a stable and peaceful order. These conditions are not the result of a nuclear stalemate. They are the result of the evolution of human society and the natural collective learning process.

A MARXIST CUT

Dickens, that other nineteenth-century thinker (contemporary with Marx), said it all: "It was the best of times, it was the worst of times" (*Tale of Two Cities*). And in 2075, that much, at least, has not changed—the dialectic nature of change. Thus the international system is still characterized by the persistence of class struggle; and if capitalism remains the dominant mode of production, it has become different from the late twentieth-century variety. Capitalism has transformed to the extent that many economic and environmental contradictions have been averted. However, human beings are no better off than they were in previous generations. While approximately 1.5 billion people enjoy an impressive standard of living, the quality of life for the remaining 12.5 billion people remains poor. This majority is still impoverished, even by the twentieth century's primitive standards. Most of the world's population has missed the technological revolution and benefits little from the new celestial resources.

Absent a catastrophic failure of capitalism, the global economy is still guided by retro-neoclassical economic principles. Capitalism underwent a series of mini-crises in the early twenty-first century. The social and environmental consequences of unrestricted, highly mobile capital were felt during the contagion currency crises and the resulting economic depression. States, once guided by Keynesian economic principles, were either unable to reimpose capital controls or ideologically unwilling to do so.

Transnational capital was able to solidify its dominant position in the new global economy by tying the fate of many workers to their own. Workers received part of their wages and most of their retirement payments in the form of stocks and bonds. States (principally core states) and the IMF had no choice but to bail out investors or face a full-scale depression. Of course, the bailout of investors and MNCs was paid for by national, as well as international, taxes. At the same time, transnational capital was able to use the relative immobility of labor and national rivalries to their own advantage. The relative wages and benefits of workers, save for a few high-tech industries, have declined globally.

International conflict is rooted in economic inequity and is exacerbated by ethnicity and nationalism in 2075. But in spite of the emergence of a "global society," international political and military institutions remain weak. The tribalism predicted by many liberals is a fact but is far more than a sporadic, violent accident of globalism. Rather, tribalism is a systemic challenge, representing a pervasive contradiction to global market forces. International violence takes several forms. Unilateral uses of force continue in the twenty-first century, principally to protect key economic interests and ensure the safety of investments. Revisionist states or states that have adopted strong forms of socialism or corporatism are challenged, and their governments are removed by force if necessary. Terrorism remains a problem as religious fundamentalists and fringe groups challenge the status quo. The UN Security Council has done little to curb such unilateral uses of force. States and international organizations will intervene for "humanitarian" purposes as groups within and between states pursue the right of self-determination.

The globalization of production has provided opportunities as well as challenges to subordinate classes. The so-called tribes can be quite disruptive, particularly if they have access to or control of important resources. Strikes at a single plant can shut down global production. The technological revolution provides ample opportunity for serious failure and even sabotage. The twenty-first century started out with a technological glitch that cost billions of dollars and caused virtual computer chaos. The speed, complexity, and volatility of the global market have caused many in the twenty-first century to question whether global markets should be valued by humankind.

Regional cooperation and security under NATO have given way to capitalist competition. The collapse of the Soviet Union and former Eastern Bloc in the twentieth century provided additional investment opportunities, balanced by additional instability risks. By 2075, Russia, Central Europe, and Central Asia have disintegrated along ethnic or tribal lines. Serious divisions between rich and poor have been intensified by economic recession. NATO continues to foster some military cooperation in Western Europe but has done little to stop internal violence eastward. In fact, NATO has done more to stabilize the domestic situations of its original members in Europe. NATO now functions to contain tribalism in the twenty-first century, as it once contained communism.

Although useful in addressing tribalism, NATO remains a weak political and military institution. Weak political institutions help capitalism expand and evolve. But trade and monetary organizations have increased their power and authority. The WTO continues to be guided by neoclassical principles of free trade. It reviews local, provincial, national, and regional laws and regulations to determine whether or not they interfere with free trade. In the twenty-first century, almost every aspect of private and public life

has become "commodified" and subjected to international competition. The Multilateral Agreement on Investment (MAI) was ratified after the global economic recession
in the early twenty-first century. The MAI was presented as the only way to stimulate the
global economy and promote international investments after the recession.

The international monetary order collapsed during the early twenty-first century,
which prompted global recession. The IMF and the liberal capitalist economies then
developed a single international currency, which is now issued and monitored by the
IMF. The global currency signals the final subordination of national interest to the
transnational interest in a stable monetary order. Currency speculators no longer exist
because currencies (or their values) are no longer bought and sold like commodities.
The transition from national currencies to a single global currency was extremely disruptive and tumultuous. The initial value of the global currency vis à vis the national
currency was difficult to set. The hard currencies, which were valued higher, were given
preferential treatment by the IMF. The soft currencies lost most of their market value
before the transition, which deepened the recession in the South. This situation gave
the MNCs a great advantage because they could more easily afford the developing
world's assets and resources.

Global economic development is a tale of two worlds. In the core, economic and
technological development races on at an impressive pace. However, the rest of the
world is mired in grinding poverty. The gap between the richest and poorest continues to widen. Development in the twenty-first century is also distinguished by a dramatic
increase of poverty among citizens of the "developed" world. More and more people
in the North have been marginalized by technology and capital mobility. While poverty in the North is not as life-threatening as poverty in the South, it remains an important source of violent conflict. The average citizen struggles for adequate shelter,
nutrition, and education. The technological revolution has left most people behind.
They do not have the education or the skills to survive in the very competitive twenty-
first century global labor force.

The status of the earth's natural resources is also grim. Biodiversity has been diminished drastically, as has the square acreage of tropical rain forest. The temperature of the atmosphere has risen by about ten degrees, wreaking havoc on low-lying
coastal regions. Countries like Haiti, Jamaica, Sri Lanka, Bangladesh, Malaysia, and Indonesia have taken devastating losses in terms of property and territory. More important, millions of people have lost their lives, causing many in the developing world to
claim that environmental genocide is being perpetrated against these countries.

Environmental conditions in the North have also deteriorated. Countries like Sweden, Canada, and Germany have been forced to lower their environmental standards
in order to attract capital investments and to help their firms compete globally. The
competition for capital has lowered environmental standards worldwide, causing the
destruction of habitat and the depletion of resources. With oil reserves depleted, the
new powerful MNCs are those that have harnessed solar energy effectively. The technological revolution, like the industrial revolution, has come with considerable environmental cost. While technology has made hard industries more efficient, the disposal
of waste and technology byproducts has proven problematic and expensive.

Marxists agree with liberals that human rights will be increasingly cast as civil and
political rights. Economic rights, save for the right to own property, cannot be sustained by the markets or states. Firms cannot remain competitive if they have to pay a

minimum wage, use unionized labor, or provide health insurance. The state is in no position to provide for these rights. Save for the tribal state, which is constantly being challenged from within and without, most governments have a laissez-faire approach to health, education, environmental regulations, and consumer safety. The threat to human rights in the twenty-first century is not the government per se, but governmental neglect.

A FEMINIST CUT

Liberal feminists see improvements in the status of women in the twenty-first century. By 2075, more women are participating in national and international decision-making circles. Liberal states and international organizations have heightened sensitivities to women's issues, and those sensitivities are reflected in their policies. The technological revolution has opened many doors for women in traditionally male-dominated positions, including combat roles in the military. The globalization of markets has released women from their traditional roles, empowering them economically and allowing them to control their lives (Bergman 1986). As a result, the poverty rates among women are declining and women's human rights are respected.

Socialist feminists and essentialist neofeminists are not so confident that the lives of women will improve in the twenty-first century. This picture is darker. War is still a permanent feature, and women still bear the brunt of international violence. The technological revolution allows men to press a button and rain death upon a society hundreds, if not thousands, of miles away. The military is an inherently masculine institution—one that has not changed just because women have been allowed to join. Rather, women are expected to act like men and pursue the same strategies as men. International security continues to be conceptualized in masculine ways, and men continue to control decision making in states and most international organizations. IGO, MNCs, and many NGOs still reflect patriarchy, subjugating women and trivializing the female experience.

The global economy threatens the gains made by women in the twentieth century. Entire sectors of the global economy are increasingly feminized. In 2075, women, who must still work in the home, must also work in the global economy—and they are still making less than men. Women's wages are 85 percent of men's in the developed countries and the percentage is even less in the developing world. Global markets have made jobs far more competitive and driven wages down. Women also suffer more from environmental degradation. Worse, they are seen as the source of environmental problems. Women, many of whom remain disenfranchised, are part of forced population-control programs to curb population growth. Without proper vigilance, the global population in 2075 can even become unnaturally skewed because males are more valued than females. The forced population-control policies can lead to an increase in infanticide among girls. Genetic engineering in 2075 allows couples to fix the sex of their child prior to conception. Unlike liberals, who assume a scientific tendency toward equilibrium, many feminists argue that patriarchy can have ill effects when coupled with the technological revolution.

The rights of women vis à vis those of men have far from equal status in 2075. Men's rights are still more respected and better recognized than women's, although women in the core have made great strides. Economic, social, and cultural rights of women are almost nonexistent, as state social welfare programs have been drastically cut back. In spite of the strides made by the women's movement in the twentieth century, women's rights have suffered some setbacks quantitatively and qualitatively in the twenty-first century. The weakening of the state has meant that no entity exists to enforce antidiscrimination laws or equality issues. The market determines wages, and women's wages are, for whatever reason, lower than men's. Ironically, just as women have gained the right to participate in government through voting and office holding, the state has waned in importance—it no longer serves as a vehicle for improving the lives of citizens. In 2075 women must now gain access to the IGOs responsible for global governance.

CONCLUSION

The theoretical approaches to international relations allow us to improve our understanding of the nature of international governance and the behavior of international organizations. For many, international governance is based on a great-power concert, or balance of power, which is facilitated by international organizations. For others, it is based on democratic cooperation and collective action, which is institutionalized and perpetuated by liberal international organizations. For still others, international governance is founded on capitalist exploitation, in which case international organizations are mechanisms of capitalist exploitation. Most international organizations are dominated by men, and according to feminists, reflect masculine values. But if we ask which of these world views is right, we are asking the wrong question. There's a better question: What does each have to teach us about the nature of international governance and about the source of the policies emanating from international organizations?

APPENDICES

APPENDIX A: COVENANT OF THE LEAGUE OF NATIONS*

THE HIGH CONTRACTING PARTIES,

In order to promote international cooperation and to achieve international peace and security

by the acceptance of obligations not to resort to war,

by the prescription of open, just and honorable relations between nations,

by the firm establishment of the understandings of international law as the actual rule of conduct among Governments, and

by the maintenance of justice and a scrupulous respect for all treaty obligations in the dealings of organized peoples with one another,

Agree to this Covenant of the League of Nations.

ARTICLE 1. MEMBERSHIP AND WITHDRAWAL

1. The original Members of the League of Nations shall be those of the Signatories which are named in the Annex to this Covenant and also such of those other States named in the Annex as shall accede without reservation to this Covenant. Such accessions shall be effected by a declaration deposited with the Secretariat within two months of the coming into force of the Covenant. Notice thereof shall be sent to all other Members of the League.

2. Any fully self-governing State, Dominion or Colony not named in the Annex may become a Member of the League if its admission is agreed to by two-thirds of the Assembly, provided that it shall give effective guaranties of its sincere intention to observe its international obligations, and shall accept such regulations as may be prescribed by the League in regard to its military, naval and air forces and armaments.

3. Any Member of the League may, after two years' notice of its intention so to do, withdraw from the League, provided that all its international obligations and all its obligations under this Covenant shall have been fulfilled at the time of its withdrawal.

---

*Amendments are in italics.

ARTICLE 2. MAJOR ORGANS

The action of the League under this Covenant shall be effected through the instrumentality of an Assembly and of a Council, with a permanent Secretariat.

ARTICLE 3. ASSEMBLY

1. The Assembly shall consist of representatives of the Members of the League.
2. The Assembly shall meet at stated intervals and from time to time, as occasion may require, at the Seat of the League or at such other place as may be decided upon.
3. The Assembly may deal at its meetings with any matter within the sphere of action of the League or affecting the peace of the world.
4. At meetings of the Assembly each Member of the League shall have one vote and may have not more than three Representatives.

ARTICLE 4. COUNCIL

1. The Council shall consist of representatives of the Principal Allied and Associated Powers, together with Representatives of four other Members of the League. These four Members of the League shall be selected by the Assembly from time to time in its discretion. Until the appointment of the Representatives of the four Members of the League first selected by the Assembly, Representatives of Belgium, Brazil, Greece and Spain shall be Members of the Council.
2. With the approval of the majority of the Assembly, the Council may name additional Members of the League, whose Representatives shall always be Members of the Council; the Council with like approval may increase the number of Members of the League to be selected by the Assembly for representation on the Council.
2. bis. *The Assembly shall fix by a two-thirds' majority the rules dealing with the election of the non-permanent Members of the Council, and particularly such regulations as relate to their term of office and the conditions of re-eligibility.*
3. The Council shall meet from time to time as occasion may require, and at least once a year, at the Seat of the League, or at such other place as may be decided upon.
4. The Council may deal at its meetings with any matter within the sphere of action of the League or affecting the peace of the world.
5. Any Member of the League not represented on the Council shall be invited to send a Representative to sit as a member at any meeting of the Council during the consideration of matters specially affecting the interests of that Member of the League.
6. At meetings of the Council, each Member of the League represented on the Council shall have one vote, and may have not more than one Representative.

ARTICLE 5. VOTING AND MEETING PROCEDURES

1. Except where otherwise expressly provided in this Covenant or by the terms of the present Treaty, decisions at any meeting of the Assembly or of the Council shall require the agreement of all the Members of the League represented at the meeting.
2. All matters of procedure at meetings of the Assembly or of the Council, including the appointment of the Committees to investigate particular matters, shall be regulated by the Assembly or by the Council and may be decided by a majority of the Members of the League represented at the meeting.
3. The first meeting of the Assembly and the first meeting of the Council shall be summoned by the President of the United States of America.

ARTICLE 6. SECRETARIAT, SECRETARY-GENERAL AND EXPENSES

1. The permanent Secretariat shall be established at the Seat of the League. The Secretariat shall comprise a Secretary-General and such secretaries and staff as may be required.
2. The first Secretary-General shall be the person named in the Annex; thereafter the Secretary-General shall be appointed by the Council with the approval of the majority of the Assembly.
3. The secretaries and the staff of the Secretariat shall be appointed by the Secretary-General with the approval of the Council.
4. The Secretary-General shall act in that capacity at all meetings of the Assembly and of the Council.
5. *The expenses of the League shall be borne by the Members of the League in the proportion decided by the Assembly.*

ARTICLE 7. SEAT, QUALIFICATIONS AND IMMUNITIES

1. The Seat of the League is established at Geneva.
2. The Council may at any time decide that the Seat of the League shall be established elsewhere.
3. All positions under or in connection with the League, including the Secretariat, shall be open equally to men and women.
4. Representatives of the Members of the League and officials of the League when engaged on the business of the League shall enjoy diplomatic privileges and immunities.
5. The buildings and other property occupied by the League or its officials or by Representatives attending its meetings shall be inviolable.

ARTICLE 8. REDUCTION OF ARMAMENTS

1. The Members of the League recognize that the maintenance of peace requires the reduction of national armaments to the lowest point consistent with national safety and the enforcement by common action of international obligations.
2. The Council, taking account of the geographical situation and circumstances of each State, shall formulate plans for such reduction for the consideration and action of the several Governments.
3. Such plans shall be subject to reconsideration and revision at least every ten years.
4. After these plans shall have been adopted by the several Governments, the limits of armaments therein fixed shall not be exceeded without the concurrence of the Council.
5. The Members of the League agree that the manufacture by private enterprise of munitions and implements of war is open to grave objections. The Council shall advise how the evil effects attendant upon such manufacture can be prevented, due regard being had to the necessities of those Members of the League which are not able to manufacture the munitions and implements of war necessary for their safety.
6. The Members of the League undertake to interchange full and frank information as to the scale of their armaments, their military, naval and air programs and the condition of such of their industries as are adaptable to warlike purposes.

ARTICLE 9. PERMANENT MILITARY, NAVAL AND AIR COMMISSION

A permanent Commission shall be constituted to advise the Council on the execution of the provisions of Articles 1 and 8 and on military, naval and air questions generally.

ARTICLE 10. GUARANTIES AGAINST AGGRESSION

The Members of the League undertake to respect and preserve as against external aggression the territorial integrity and existing political independence of all Members of the League. In case of any such aggression or in case of any threat or danger of such aggression the Council shall advise upon the means by which this obligation shall be fulfilled.

ARTICLE 11. COLLECTIVE ACTION

1. Any war or threat of war, whether immediately affecting any of the Members of the League or not, is hereby declared a matter of concern to the whole League, and the League shall take any action that may be deemed wise and effectual to safeguard the peace of nations. In case any such emergency should arise the Secretary-General shall on the request of any Member of the League forthwith summon a meeting of the Council.

2. It is also declared to be the friendly right of each Member of the League to bring to the attention of the Assembly or the Council any circumstance whatever affecting international relations which threatens to disturb international peace or the good understanding between nations upon which peace depends.

ARTICLE 12. DISPUTES

1. The Members of the League agree that, if there should arise between them any dispute likely to lead to a rupture, they will submit the matter either to arbitration *or judicial settlement* or to inquiry by the Council, and they agree in no case to resort to war until three months after the award by the arbitrators *or the judicial decision,* or the report by the Council.

2. In any case under this Article the award of the arbitrators *or the judicial decision* shall be made within a reasonable time, and the report of the Council shall be made within six months after the submission of the dispute.

ARTICLE 13. ARBITRATION OR JUDICIAL SETTLEMENT

1. The Members of the League agree that, whenever any dispute shall arise between them which they recognize to be suitable for submission to arbitration *or judicial settlement,* and which can not be satisfactorily settled by diplomacy, they will submit the whole subject-matter to arbitration *or judicial settlement.*

2. Disputes as to the interpretation of a treaty, as to any question of international law, as to the existence of any fact which, if established, would constitute a breach of any international obligation, or as to the extent and nature of the reparation to be made for any such breach, are declared to be among those which are generally suitable for submission to arbitration *or judicial settlement.*

3. *For the consideration of any such dispute, the court to which the case is referred shall be the Permanent Court of International Justice, established in accordance with Article 14, or any tribunal agreed on by the parties to the dispute or stipulated in any convention existing between them.*

4. The Members of the League agree that they will carry out in full good faith any award *or decision* that may be rendered, and that they will not resort to war against a Member of the League which complies therewith. In the event of any failure to carry out such an award *or decision,* the Council shall propose what steps should be taken to give effect thereto.

ARTICLE 14. PERMANENT COURT OF INTERNATIONAL JUSTICE

The Council shall formulate and submit to the Members of the League for adoption plans for the establishment of a Permanent Court of International Justice. The Court shall be competent to hear and determine any dispute of an international character which the parties thereto submit to it. The Court may also give an advisory opinion upon any dispute or question referred to it by the Council or by the Assembly.

ARTICLE 15. DISPUTES NOT SUBMITTED TO ARBITRATION OR JUDICIAL SETTLEMENT

1. If there should arise between Members of the League any dispute likely to lead to a rupture, which is not submitted to arbitration *or judicial settlement* in accordance with Article 13, the Members of the League agree that they will submit the matter to the Council. Any party to the dispute may effect such submission by giving notice of the existence of the dispute to the Secretary-General, who will make all necessary arrangements for a full investigation and consideration thereof.

2. For this purpose, the parties of the dispute will communicate to the Secretary-General, as promptly as possible, statements of their case with all the relevant facts and papers, and the Council may forthwith direct the publication thereof.

3. The Council shall endeavor to effect a settlement of the dispute, and, if such efforts are successful, a statement shall be made public giving such facts and explanations regarding the dispute and the terms of settlement thereof as the Council may deem appropriate.

4. If the dispute is not thus settled, the Council either unanimously or by a majority vote shall make and publish a report containing a statement of the facts of the dispute and the recommendations which are deemed just and proper in regard thereto.

5. Any member of the League represented on the Council may make public a statement of the facts of the dispute and of its conclusions regarding the same.

6. If a report by the Council is unanimously agreed to by the Members thereof other than the Representatives of one or more of the parties to the dispute, the Members of the League agree that they will not go to war with any party to the dispute which complies with the recommendations of the report.

7. If the Council fails to reach a report which is unanimously agreed to by the members thereof, other than the Representatives of one or more of the parties to the dispute, the Members of the League reserve to themselves the right to take such action as they shall consider necessary for the maintenance of right and justice.

8. If the dispute between the parties is claimed by one of them, and is found by the Council, to arise out of a matter which by international law is solely within the domestic jurisdiction of that party, the Council shall so report, and shall make no recommendation as to its settlement.

9. The Council may in any case under this Article refer the dispute to the Assembly. The dispute shall be so referred at the request of either party to the dispute, provided that such request be made within 14 days after the submission of the dispute to the Council.

10. In any case referred to the Assembly, all the provisions of this Article and of Article 12 relating to the action and powers of the Council shall apply to the action and powers of the Assembly, provided that a report made by the Assembly, if concurred in by the Representatives of those Members of the League represented on the Council and of a majority of the other Members of the League, exclusive in each case of the Representatives of the parties to the dispute, shall have the same force as a report by the Council concurred in by all the members thereof other than the Representatives of one or more of the parties to the dispute.

ARTICLE 16. SANCTIONS AND EXPULSION

1. Should any Member of the League resort to war in disregard of its covenants under Articles 12, 13, or 15, it shall *ipso facto* be deemed to have committed an act of war against all other Members of the League, which hereby undertake immediately to subject it to the severance of all trade or financial relations, the prohibition of all intercourse between their nationals and the nationals of the covenant-breaking State, and the prevention of all financial, commercial or personal intercourse between the nationals of the covenant-breaking State and the nationals of any other State, whether a Member of the League or not.

2. It shall be the duty of the Council in such case to recommend to the several Governments concerned what effective military, naval or air force that Members of the League shall severally contribute to the armed forces to be used to protect the covenants of the League.

3. The Members of the League agree, further, that they will mutually support one another in the financial and economic measures which are taken under this Article, in order to minimize the loss and inconvenience resulting from the above measures, and that they will mutually support one another in resisting any special measures aimed at one of their number by the covenant-breaking State, and that they will take the necessary steps to afford passage through their territory to the forces of any of the Members of the League which are cooperating to protect the covenants of the League.

4. Any Member of the League which has violated any covenant of the League may be declared to be no longer a Member of the League by a vote of the Council concurred in by the Representatives of all the other Members of the League represented thereon.

ARTICLE 17. DISPUTES INVOLVING NON-MEMBERS

1. In the event of a dispute between a Member of the League and a State which is not a Member of the League, or between States not Members of the League, the State or States not Members of the League shall be invited to accept the obligations of membership in the League for the purposes of such dispute, upon such conditions as the Council may deem just. If such invitation is accepted, the provisions of Articles 12 to 16 inclusive shall be applied with such modifications as may be deemed necessary by the Council.

2. Upon such invitation being given, the Council shall immediately institute an inquiry into the circumstances of the dispute and recommend such action as may seem best and most effectual in the circumstances.

3. If a State so invited shall refuse to accept the obligations of membership in the League for the purposes of such dispute, and shall resort to war against a Member of the League, the provisions of Article 16 shall be applicable as against the State taking such action.

4. If both parties to the dispute when so invited refuse to accept the obligations of membership in the League for the purposes of such dispute, the Council may take such measures and make such recommendations as will prevent hostilities and will result in the settlement of the dispute.

ARTICLE 18. REGISTRATION AND PUBLICATION OF TREATIES

Every treaty or international engagement entered into hereafter by any Member of the League shall be forthwith registered with the Secretariat and shall as soon as possible be published by it. No such treaty or international engagement shall be binding until so registered.

ARTICLE 19. REVIEW OF TREATIES

The Assembly may from time to time advise the reconsideration by Members of the League of treaties which have become inapplicable, and the consideration of international conditions whose continuance might endanger the peace of the world.

ARTICLE 20. ABROGATION OF INCONSISTENT OBLIGATIONS

1. The Members of the League severally agree that this Covenant is accepted as abrogating all obligations or understandings *inter se* which are inconsistent with the terms thereof, and solemnly undertake that they will not hereafter enter into any engagements inconsistent with the terms thereof.

2. In case any Member of the League shall, before becoming a Member of the League, have undertaken any obligations inconsistent with the terms of this Covenant, it shall be the duty of such Member to take immediate steps to procure its release from such obligations.

ARTICLE 21. ENGAGEMENTS THAT REMAIN VALID

Nothing in this Covenant shall be deemed to affect the validity of international engagements, such as treaties of arbitration or regional understandings like the Monroe doctrine, for securing the maintenance of peace.

ARTICLE 22. MANDATES SYSTEM

1. To those colonies and territories which as a consequence of the late war have ceased to be under the sovereignty of the States which formerly governed them and which are inhabited by peoples not yet able to stand by themselves under the strenuous conditions of the modern world, there should be applied the principle that the well-being and development of such peoples form a sacred trust of civilization and that securities for the performance of this trust should be embodied in this Covenant.

2. The best method of giving practical effect to this principle is that the tutelage of such peoples should be intrusted to advanced nations who by reason of their resources, their experience or their geographical position can best undertake this responsibility, and who are willing to accept it, and that this tutelage should be exercised by them as Mandatories on behalf of the League.

3. The character of the mandate must differ according to the stage of the development of the people, the geographical situation of the territory, its economic conditions and other similar circumstances.

4. Certain communities formerly belonging to the Turkish Empire have reached a stage of development where their existence as independent nations can be provisionally recognized subject to the rendering of administrative advice and assistance by a Mandatory until such time as they are able to stand alone. The wishes of these communities must be a principal consideration in the selection of the Mandatory.

5. Other peoples, especially those of Central Africa, are at such a stage that the Mandatory must be responsible for the administration of the territory under conditions which will guarantee freedom of conscience and religion, subject only to the maintenance of public order and morals, the prohibition of abuses such as the slave trade, the arms traffic and the liquor traffic, and the prevention of the establishment of fortifications or military and naval bases and of military training of the natives for other than police purposes and the defense of territory, and will also secure equal opportunities for the trade and commerce of other Members of the League.

6. There are territories, such as South West Africa and certain of the South Pacific islands, which, owing to the sparseness of their population, or their small size, or their remoteness from the centers of civilization, or their geographical contiguity to the territory of the Mandatory, and other circumstances, can be best administered under the laws of the Mandatory as integral portions of its territory, subject to the safeguards above mentioned in the interests of the indigenous population.

7. In every case of mandate, the Mandatory shall render to the Council an annual report in reference to the territory committed to its charge.

8. The degree of authority, control or administration to be exercised by the Mandatory shall, if not previously agreed upon by the Members of the League, be explicitly defined in each case by the Council.

9. A permanent Commission shall be constituted to receive and examine the annual reports of the Mandatories and to advise the Council on all matters relating to the observance of the mandates.

ARTICLE 23. SOCIAL RESPONSIBILITIES

Subject to and in accordance with the provisions of international conventions existing or hereafter to be agreed upon, the Members of the League:

(a) will endeavor to secure and maintain fair and humane conditions of labor for men, women and children, both in their own countries and in all countries to which their commercial and industrial relations extend, and for that purpose will establish and maintain the necessary international organizations;

(b) undertake to secure just treatment of the native inhabitants of territories under their control;

(c) will intrust the League with the general supervision over the execution of agreements with regard to the traffic in women and children, and the traffic in opium and other dangerous drugs;

(d) will intrust the League with the general supervision of the trade in arms and ammunition with the countries in which the control of this traffic is necessary in the common interest;

(e) will make provision to secure and maintain freedom of communications and of transit and equitable treatment for the commerce of all Members of the League. In this connection, the special necessities of the regions devastated during the war of 1914–1918 shall be borne in mind;

(f) will endeavor to take steps in matters of international concern for the prevention and control of disease.

ARTICLE 24. INTERNATIONAL BUREAUS

1. There shall be placed under the direction of the League all international bureaus already established by general treaties if the parties to such treaties consent. All such international bureaus and all commissions for the regulation of matters of international interest hereafter constituted shall be placed under the direction of the League.

2. In all matters of international interest which are regulated by general conventions but which are not placed under the control of international bureaus or commissions, the Secretariat of the League shall, subject to the consent of the Council and if desired by the parties, collect and distribute all relevant information and shall render any other assistance which may be necessary or desirable.

3. The Council may include as part of the expenses of the Secretariat the expenses of any bureau or commission which is placed under the direction of the League.

ARTICLE 25. PROMOTION OF RED CROSS

The Members of the League agree to encourage and promote the establishment and cooperation of duly authorized voluntary national Red Cross organizations having as purposes the improvement of health, the prevention of disease and the mitigation of suffering throughout the world.

ARTICLE 26. AMENDMENTS

1. Amendments to this Covenant will take effect when ratified by the Members of the League whose Representatives compose the Council and by a majority of the Members of the League whose Representatives compose the Assembly.
2. No such amendment shall bind any Member of the League which signifies its dissent therefrom, but in that case it shall cease to be a Member of the League.

ANNEX I. ORIGINAL MEMBERS OF THE LEAGUE OF NATIONS, SIGNATORIES OF THE TREATY OF PEACE

United States of America*	Guatemala
Belgium	Haiti
Bolivia	Hedjaz*
Brazil	Honduras
British Empire	Italy
Canada	Japan
Australia	Liberia
South Africa	Nicaragua
New Zealand	Panama
India	Peru
China	Poland
Cuba	Portugal
Czechoslovakia	Romania
Ecuador**	Serb-Croat-Slovene State [Yugoslavia]
France	Siam
Greece	Uruguay

States Invited to Accede to the Covenant

Argentine Republic	Persia
Chile	Salvador
Colombia	Spain
Denmark	Sweden
Netherlands	Switzerland
Norway	Venezuela
Paraguay	

ANNEX II. FIRST SECRETARY-GENERAL OF THE LEAGUE OF NATIONS THE HONORABLE SIR JAMES ERIC DRUMMOND, K.C.M.G., C.B.

---

*Did not ratify.
**Did not ratify peace treaty but was admitted to membership in 1934.

Appendix B: Charter of the United Nations

Preamble to the Charter of the United Nations

WE THE PEOPLES OF THE UNITED NATIONS DETERMINED

to save succeeding generations from the scourge of war, which twice in our lifetime has brought untold sorrow to mankind, and

to reaffirm faith in fundamental human rights, in the dignity and worth of the human person, in the equal rights of men and women and of nations large and small, and

to establish conditions under which justice and respect for the obligations arising from treaties and other sources of international law can be maintained, and

to promote social progress and better standards of life in larger freedom,

AND FOR THESE ENDS

to practice tolerance and live together in peace with one another as good neighbours, and

to unite our strength to maintain international peace and security, and

to ensure, by the acceptance of principles and the institution of methods, that armed force shall not be used, save in the common interest, and

to employ international machinery for the promotion of the economic and social advancement of all peoples,

HAVE RESOLVED TO COMBINE OUR EFFORTS TO ACCOMPLISH THESE AIMS

Accordingly, our respective Governments, through representatives assembled in the city of San Francisco, who have exhibited their full powers found to be in good and due form, have agreed to the present Charter of the United Nations and do hereby establish an international organization to be known as the United Nations.

CHAPTER I: PURPOSES AND PRINCIPLES

Article 1

The Purposes of the United Nations are:

1. To maintain international peace and security, and to that end: to take effective collective measures for the prevention and removal of threats to the peace, and for the suppression of acts of aggression or other breaches of the peace, and to bring about by peaceful means, and in conformity with the principles of justice and international law, adjustment or settlement of international disputes or situations which might lead to a breach of the peace;

2. To develop friendly relations among nations based on respect for the principle of equal rights and self-determination of peoples, and to take other appropriate measures to strengthen universal peace;

3. To achieve international co-operation in solving international problems of an economic, social, cultural, or humanitarian character, and in promoting and encouraging respect for human rights and for fundamental freedoms for all without distinction as to race, sex, language, or religion; and

4. To be a centre for harmonizing the actions of nations in the attainment of these common ends.

Article 2

The Organization and its Members, in pursuit of the Purposes stated in Article 1, shall act in accordance with the following Principles.

1. The Organization is based on the principle of the sovereign equality of all its Members.

2. All Members, in order to ensure to all of them the rights and benefits resulting from membership, shall fulfill in good faith the obligations assumed by them in accordance with the present Charter.

3. All Members shall settle their international disputes by peaceful means in such a manner that international peace and security, and justice, are not endangered.

4. All Members shall refrain in their international relations from the threat or use of force against the territorial integrity or political independence of any state, or in any other manner inconsistent with the Purposes of the United Nations.

5. All Members shall give the United Nations every assistance in any action it takes in accordance with the present Charter, and shall refrain from giving assistance to any state against which the United Nations is taking preventive or enforcement action.

6. The Organization shall ensure that states which are not Members of the United Nations act in accordance with these Principles so far as may be necessary for the maintenance of international peace and security.

7. Nothing contained in the present Charter shall authorize the United Nations to intervene in matters which are essentially within the domestic jurisdiction of any state or shall require the Members to submit such matters to settlement under the present Charter; but this principle shall not prejudice the application of enforcement measures under Chapter VII.

CHAPTER II: MEMBERSHIP

Article 3

The original Members of the United Nations shall be the states which, having participated in the United Nations Conference on International Organization at San Francisco, or having previously signed the Declaration by United Nations of 1 January 1942, sign the present Charter and ratify it in accordance with Article 110.

Article 4

1. Membership in the United Nations is open to all other peace-loving states which accept the obligations contained in the present Charter and, in the judgment of the Organization, are able and willing to carry out these obligations.
2. The admission of any such state to membership in the United Nations will be effected by a decision of the General Assembly upon the recommendation of the Security Council.

Article 5

A Member of the United Nations against which preventive or enforcement action has been taken by the Security Council may be suspended from the exercise of the rights and privileges of membership by the General Assembly upon the recommendation of the Security Council. The exercise of these rights and privileges may be restored by the Security Council.

Article 6

A Member of the United Nations which has persistently violated the Principles contained in the present Charter may be expelled from the Organization by the General Assembly upon the recommendation of the Security Council.

CHAPTER III: ORGANS

Article 7

1. There are established as the principal organs of the United Nations: a General Assembly, a Security Council, an Economic and Social Council, a Trusteeship Council, an International Court of Justice, and a Secretariat.
2. Such subsidiary organs as may be found necessary may be established in accordance with the present Charter.

Article 8

The United Nations shall place no restrictions on the eligibility of men and women to participate in any capacity and under conditions of equality in its principal and subsidiary organs.

CHAPTER IV: THE GENERAL ASSEMBLY

COMPOSITION

Article 9

1. The General Assembly shall consist of all the Members of the United Nations.
2. Each Member shall have not more than five representatives in the General Assembly.

FUNCTIONS AND POWERS

Article 10

The General Assembly may discuss any questions or any matters within the scope of the present Charter or relating to the powers and functions of any organs provided for in the present Charter, and, except as provided in Article 12, may make recommendations to the Members of the United Nations or to the Security Council or to both on any such questions or matters.

Article 11

1. The General Assembly may consider the general principles of co-operation in the maintenance of international peace and security, including the principles governing disarmament and the regulation of armaments, and may make recommendations with regard to such principles to the Members or to the Security Council or to both.

2. The General Assembly may discuss any questions relating to the maintenance of international peace and security brought before it by any Member of the United Nations, or by the Security Council, or by a state which is not a Member of the United Nations in accordance with Article 35, paragraph 2, and, except as provided in Article 12, may make recommendations with regard to any such questions to the state or states concerned or to the Security Council or to both. Any such question on which action is necessary shall be referred to the Security Council by the General Assembly either before or after discussion.

3. The General Assembly may call the attention of the Security Council to situations which are likely to endanger international peace and security.

4. The powers of the General Assembly set forth in this Article shall not limit the general scope of Article 10.

Article 12

1. While the Security Council is exercising in respect of any dispute or situation the functions assigned to it in the present Charter, the General Assembly shall not make any recommendation with regard to that dispute or situation unless the Security Council so requests.

2. The Secretary-General, with the consent of the Security Council, shall notify the General Assembly at each session of any matters relative to the maintenance of international peace and security which are being dealt with by the Security Council and shall similarly notify the General Assembly, or the Members of the United Nations if the General Assembly is not in session, immediately the Security Council ceases to deal with such matters.

Article 13

1. The General Assembly shall initiate studies and make recommendations for the purpose of:
    a. promoting international co-operation in the political field and encouraging the progressive development of international law and its codification;
    b. promoting international co-operation in the economic, social, cultural, educational, and health fields, and assisting in the realization of human rights and fundamental freedoms for all without distinction as to race, sex, language, or religion.

2. The further responsibilities, functions and powers of the General Assembly with respect to matters mentioned in paragraph 1 (b) above are set forth in Chapters IX and X.

Article 14

Subject to the provisions of Article 12, the General Assembly may recommend measures for the peaceful adjustment of any situation, regardless of origin, which it deems likely to impair the general welfare or friendly relations among nations, including situations resulting from a violation of the provisions of the present Charter setting forth the Purposes and Principles of the United Nations.

Article 15

1. The General Assembly shall receive and consider annual and special reports from the Security Council; these reports shall include an account of the measures that the Security Council has decided upon or taken to maintain international peace and security.

2. The General Assembly shall receive and consider reports from the other organs of the United Nations.

Article 16

The General Assembly shall perform such functions with respect to the international trusteeship system as are assigned to it under Chapters XII and XIII, including the approval of the trusteeship agreements for areas not designated as strategic.

Article 17

    1.   The General Assembly shall consider and approve the budget of the Organization.

    2.   The expenses of the Organization shall be borne by the Members as apportioned by the General Assembly.

    3.   The General Assembly shall consider and approve any financial and budgetary arrangements with specialized agencies referred to in Article 57 and shall examine the administrative budgets of such specialized agencies with a view to making recommendations to the agencies concerned.

VOTING

Article 18

    1.   Each member of the General Assembly shall have one vote.

    2.   Decisions of the General Assembly on important questions shall be made by a two-thirds majority of the members present and voting. These questions shall include: recommendations with respect to the maintenance of international peace and security, the election of the non-permanent members of the Security Council, the election of the members of the Economic and Social Council, the election of members of the Trusteeship Council in accordance with paragraph 1(c) of Article 86, the admission of new Members to the United Nations, the suspension of the rights and privileges of membership, the expulsion of Members, questions relating to the operation of the trusteeship system, and budgetary questions.

    3.   Decisions on other questions, including the determination of additional categories of questions to be decided by a two-thirds majority, shall be made by a majority of the members present and voting.

Article 19

A Member of the United Nations which is in arrears in the payment of its financial contributions to the Organization shall have no vote in the General Assembly if the amount of its arrears equals or exceeds the amount of the contributions due from it for the preceding two full years. The General Assembly may, nevertheless, permit such a Member to vote if it is satisfied that the failure to pay is due to conditions beyond the control of the Member.

PROCEDURE

Article 20

The General Assembly shall meet in regular annual sessions and in such special sessions as occasion may require. Special sessions shall be convoked by the Secretary-General at the request of the Security Council or of a majority of the Members of the United Nations.

Article 21

The General Assembly shall adopt its own rules of procedure. It shall elect its President for each session.

Article 22

The General Assembly may establish such subsidiary organs as it deems necessary for the performance of its functions.

Chapter V: The Security Council

COMPOSITION

Article 23

    1.   The Security Council shall consist of fifteen Members of the United Nations. The Republic of China, France, the Union of Soviet Socialist Republics, the United Kingdom of Great Britain and Northern Ireland, and the United States of America shall

be permanent members of the Security Council. The General Assembly shall elect ten other Members of the United Nations to be Non-permanent members of the Security Council, due regard being specially paid, in the first instance to the contribution of Members of the United Nations to the maintenance of international peace and security and to the other purposes of the Organization, and also to equitable geographical distribution.

2. The non-permanent members of the Security Council shall be elected for a term of two years. In the first election of the non-permanent members after the increase of the membership of the Security Council from eleven to fifteen, two of the four additional members shall be chosen for a term of one year. A retiring member shall not be eligible for immediate re-election.

3. Each member of the Security Council shall have one representative.

FUNCTIONS AND POWERS

Article 24

1. In order to ensure prompt and effective action by the United Nations, its Members confer on the Security Council primary responsibility for the maintenance of international peace and security, and agree that in carrying out its duties under this responsibility the Security Council acts on their behalf.

2. In discharging these duties the Security Council shall act in accordance with the Purposes and Principles of the United Nations. The specific powers granted to the Security Council for the discharge of these duties are laid down in Chapters VI, VII, VIII, and XII.

3. The Security Council shall submit annual and, when necessary, special reports to the General Assembly for its consideration.

Article 25

The Members of the United Nations agree to accept and carry out the decisions of the Security Council in accordance with the present Charter.

Article 26

In order to promote the establishment and maintenance of international peace and security with the least diversion for armaments of the world's human and economic resources, the Security Council shall be responsible for formulating, with the assistance of the Military Staff Committee referred to in Article 47, plans to be submitted to the Members of the United Nations for the establishment of a system for the regulation of armaments.

VOTING

Article 27

1. Each member of the Security Council shall have one vote.

2. Decisions of the Security Council on procedural matters shall be made by an affirmative vote of nine members.

3. Decisions of the Security Council on all other matters shall be made by an affirmative vote of nine members including the concurring votes of the permanent members; provided that, in decisions under Chapter VI, and under paragraph 3 of Article 52, a party to a dispute shall abstain from voting.

PROCEDURE

Article 28

1. The Security Council shall be so organized as to be able to function continuously. Each member of the Security Council shall for this purpose be represented at all times at the seat of the Organization.

2. The Security Council shall hold periodic meetings at which each of its members may, if it so desires, be represented by a member of the government or by some other specially designated representative.

3. The Security Council may hold meetings at such places other than the seat of the Organization as in its judgment will best facilitate its work.

Article 29

The Security Council may establish such subsidiary organs as it deems necessary for the performance of its functions.

Article 30

The Security Council shall adopt its own rules of procedure, including the method of selecting its President.

Article 31

Any Member of the United Nations which is not a member of the Security Council may participate, without vote, in the discussion of any question brought before the Security Council whenever the latter considers that the interests of that Member are specially affected.

Article 32

Any Member of the United Nations which is not a member of the Security Council or any state which is not a Member of the United Nations, if it is a party to a dispute under consideration by the Security Council, shall be invited to participate, without vote, in the discussion relating to the dispute. The Security Council shall lay down such conditions as it deems just for the participation of a state which is not a Member of the United Nations.

CHAPTER VI: PACIFIC SETTLEMENT OF DISPUTES

Article 33

1. The parties to any dispute, the continuance of which is likely to endanger the maintenance of international peace and security, shall, first of all, seek a solution by negotiation, enquiry, mediation, conciliation, arbitration, judicial settlement, resort to regional agencies or arrangements, or other peaceful means of their own choice.

2. The Security Council shall, when it deems necessary, call upon the parties to settle their dispute by such means.

Article 34

The Security Council may investigate any dispute, or any situation which might lead to international friction or give rise to a dispute, in order to determine whether the continuance of the dispute or situation is likely to endanger the maintenance of international peace and security.

Article 35

1. Any Member of the United Nations may bring any dispute, or any situation of the nature referred to in Article 34, to the attention of the Security Council or of the General Assembly.

2. A state which is not a Member of the United Nations may bring to the attention of the Security Council or of the General Assembly any dispute to which it is a party if it accepts in advance, for the purposes of the dispute, the obligations of pacific settlement provided in the present Charter.

3. The proceedings of the General Assembly in respect of matters brought to its attention under this Article will be subject to the provisions of Articles 11 and 12.

Article 36

1. The Security Council may, at any stage of a dispute of the nature referred to in Article 33 or of a situation of like nature, recommend appropriate procedures or methods of adjustment.

2.   The Security Council should take into consideration any procedures for the set-
     tlement of the dispute which have already been adopted by the parties.

3.   In making recommendations under this Article the Security Council should also
     take into consideration that legal disputes should as a general rule be referred by
     the parties to the International Court of Justice in accordance with the provisions
     of the Statute of the Court.

Article 37

1.   Should the parties to a dispute of the nature referred to in Article 33 fail to settle it
     by the means indicated in that Article, they shall refer it to the Security Council.

2.   If the Security Council deems that the continuance of the dispute is in fact likely
     to endanger the maintenance of international peace and security, it shall decide
     whether to take action under Article 36 or to recommend such terms of settle-
     ment as it may consider appropriate.

Article 38

Without prejudice to the provisions of Articles 33 to 37, the Security Council may, if all the parties to any dispute so request, make recommendations to the parties with a view to a pacific settlement of the dispute.

CHAPTER VII: ACTION WITH RESPECT TO THREATS TO THE PEACE, BREACHES OF THE PEACE, AND ACTS OF AGGRESSION

Article 39

The Security Council shall determine the existence of any threat to the peace, breach of the peace,
or act of aggression and shall make recommendations, or decide what measures shall be taken in
accordance with Articles 41 and 42, to maintain or restore international peace and security.

Article 40

In order to prevent an aggravation of the situation, the Security Council may, before making the
recommendations or deciding upon the measures provided for in Article 39, call upon the parties concerned to comply with such provisional measures as it deems necessary or desirable.
Such provisional measures shall be without prejudice to the rights, claims, or position of the
parties concerned. The Security Council shall duly take account of failure to comply with such
provisional measures.

Article 41

The Security Council may decide what measures not involving the use of armed force are to be
employed to give effect to its decisions, and it may call upon the Members of the United Nations
to apply such measures. These may include complete or partial interruption of economic relations and of rail, sea, air, postal, telegraphic, radio, and other means of communication, and
the severance of diplomatic relations.

Article 42

Should the Security Council consider that measures provided for in Article 41 would be inadequate
or have proved to be inadequate, it may take such action by air, sea, or land forces as may be necessary to maintain or restore international peace and security. Such action may include demonstrations, blockade, and other operations by air, sea, or land forces of Members of the United Nations.

Article 43

1.   All Members of the United Nations, in order to contribute to the maintenance of
     international peace and security, undertake to make available to the Security Coun-
     cil, on its call and in accordance with a special agreement or agreements, armed
     forces, assistance, and facilities, including rights of passage, necessary for the pur-
     pose of maintaining international peace and security.

2. Such agreement or agreements shall govern the numbers and types of forces, their degree of readiness and general location, and the nature of the facilities and assistance to be provided.

3. The agreement or agreements shall be negotiated as soon as possible on the initiative of the Security Council. They shall be concluded between the Security Council and Members or between the Security Council and groups of Members and shall be subject to ratification by the signatory states in accordance with their respective constitutional processes.

Article 44

When the Security Council has decided to use force it shall, before calling upon a Member not represented on it to provide armed forces in fulfillment of the obligations assumed under Article 43, invite that Member, if the Member so desires, to participate in the decisions of the Security Council concerning the employment of contingents of that Member's armed forces.

Article 45

In order to enable the United Nations to take urgent military measures, Members shall hold immediately available national air-force contingents for combined international enforcement action. The strength and degree of readiness of these contingents and plans for their combined action shall be determined within the limits laid down in the special agreement or agreements referred to in Article 43, by the Security Council with the assistance of the Military Staff Committee.

Article 46

Plans for the application of armed force shall be made by the Security Council with the assistance of the Military Staff Committee.

Article 47

1. There shall be established a Military Staff Committee to advise and assist the Security Council on all questions relating to the Security Council's military requirements for the maintenance of international peace and security, the employment and command of forces placed at its disposal, the regulation of armaments, and possible disarmament.

2. The Military Staff Committee shall consist of the Chiefs of Staff of the permanent members of the Security Council or their representatives. Any Member of the United Nations not permanently represented on the Committee shall be invited by the Committee to be associated with it when the efficient discharge of the Committee's responsibilities requires the participation of that Member in its work.

3. The Military Staff Committee shall be responsible under the Security Council for the strategic direction of any armed forces placed at the disposal of the Security Council. Questions relating to the command of such forces shall be worked out subsequently.

4. The Military Staff Committee, with the authorization of the Security Council and after consultation with appropriate regional agencies, may establish regional sub-committees.

Article 48

1. The action required to carry out the decisions of the Security Council for the maintenance of international peace and security shall be taken by all the Members of the United Nations or by some of them, as the Security Council may determine.

2. Such decisions shall be carried out by the Members of the United Nations directly and through their action in the appropriate international agencies of which they are members.

Article 49

The Members of the United Nations shall join in affording mutual assistance in carrying out the measures decided upon by the Security Council.

Article 50

If preventive or enforcement measures against any state are taken by the Security Council, any other state, whether a Member of the United Nations or not, which finds itself confronted with special economic problems arising from the carrying out of those measures shall have the right to consult the Security Council with regard to a solution of those problems.

Article 51

Nothing in the present Charter shall impair the inherent right of individual or collective self-defence if an armed attack occurs against a Member of the United Nations, until the Security Council has taken measures necessary to maintain international peace and security. Measures taken by Members in the exercise of this right of self-defence shall be immediately reported to the Security Council and shall not in any way affect the authority and responsibility of the Security Council under the present Charter to take at any time such action as it deems necessary in order to maintain or restore international peace and security.

CHAPTER VIII: REGIONAL ARRANGEMENTS

Article 52

1. Nothing in the present Charter precludes the existence of regional arrangements or agencies for dealing with such matters relating to the maintenance of international peace and security as are appropriate for regional action provided that such arrangements or agencies and their activities are consistent with the Purposes and Principles of the United Nations.
2. The Members of the United Nations entering into such arrangements or constituting such agencies shall make every effort to achieve pacific settlement of local disputes through such regional arrangements or by such regional agencies before referring them to the Security Council.
3. The Security Council shall encourage the development of pacific settlement of local disputes through such regional arrangements or by such regional agencies either on the initiative of the states concerned or by reference from the Security Council.
4. This Article in no way impairs the application of Articles 34 and 35.

Article 53

1. The Security Council shall, where appropriate, utilize such regional arrangements or agencies for enforcement action under its authority. But no enforcement action shall be taken under regional arrangements or by regional agencies without the authorization of the Security Council, with the exception of measures against any enemy state, as defined in paragraph 2 of this Article, provided for pursuant to Article 107 or in regional arrangements directed against renewal of aggressive policy on the part of any such state, until such time as the Organization may, on request of the Governments concerned, be charged with the responsibility for preventing further aggression by such a state.
2. The term enemy state as used in paragraph 1 of this Article applies to any state which during the Second World War has been an enemy of any signatory of the present Charter.

Article 54

The Security Council shall at all times be kept fully informed of activities undertaken or in contemplation under regional arrangements or by regional agencies for the maintenance of international peace and security.

CHAPTER IX: INTERNATIONAL ECONOMIC AND SOCIAL CO-OPERATION

Article 55

With a view to the creation of conditions of stability and well-being which are necessary for peaceful and friendly relations among nations based on respect for the principle of equal rights and self-determination of peoples, the United Nations shall promote:

a. higher standards of living, full employment, and conditions of economic and social progress and development;

b. solutions of international economic, social, health, and related problems; and international cultural and educational cooperation; and

c. universal respect for, and observance of, human rights and fundamental freedoms for all without distinction as to race, sex, language, or religion.

Article 56

All Members pledge themselves to take joint and separate action in co-operation with the Organization for the achievement of the purposes set forth in Article 55.

Article 57

1. The various specialized agencies, established by intergovernmental agreement and having wide international responsibilities, as defined in their basic instruments, in economic, social, cultural, educational, health, and related fields, shall be brought into relationship with the United Nations in accordance with the provisions of Article 63.

2. Such agencies thus brought into relationship with the United Nations are hereinafter referred to as specialized agencies.

Article 58

The Organization shall make recommendations for the co-ordination of the policies and activities of the specialized agencies.

Article 59

The Organization shall, where appropriate, initiate negotiations among the states concerned for the creation of any new specialized agencies required for the accomplishment of the purposes set forth in Article 55.

Article 60

Responsibility for the discharge of the functions of the Organization set forth in this Chapter shall be vested in the General Assembly and, under the authority of the General Assembly, in the Economic and Social Council, which shall have for this purpose the powers set forth in Chapter X.

CHAPTER X: THE ECONOMIC AND SOCIAL COUNCIL

COMPOSITION

Article 61

1. The Economic and Social Council shall consist of fifty-four Members of the United Nations elected by the General Assembly.

2. Subject to the provisions of paragraph 3, eighteen members of the Economic and Social Council shall be elected each year for a term of three years. A retiring member shall be eligible for immediate re-election.

3. At the first election after the increase in the membership of the Economic and Social Council from twenty-seven to fifty-four members, in addition to the members elected in place of the nine members whose term of office expires at the end of that year, twenty-seven additional members shall be elected. Of these twenty-seven additional members, the term of office of nine members so elected shall expire

at the end of one year, and of nine other members at the end of two years, in accordance with arrangements made by the General Assembly.

4.   Each member of the Economic and Social Council shall have one representative.

FUNCTIONS AND POWERS

Article 62

1.   The Economic and Social Council may make or initiate studies and reports with respect to international economic, social, cultural, educational, health, and related matters and may make recommendations with respect to any such matters to the General Assembly to the Members of the United Nations, and to the specialized agencies concerned.

2.   It may make recommendations for the purpose of promoting respect for, and observance of, human rights and fundamental freedoms for all.

3.   It may prepare draft conventions for submission to the General Assembly, with respect to matters falling within its competence.

4.   It may call, in accordance with the rules prescribed by the United Nations, international conferences on matters falling within its competence.

Article 63

1.   The Economic and Social Council may enter into agreements with any of the agencies referred to in Article 57, defining the terms on which the agency concerned shall be brought into relationship with the United Nations. Such agreements shall be subject to approval by the General Assembly.

2.   It may co-ordinate the activities of the specialized agencies through consultation with and recommendations to such agencies and through recommendations to the General Assembly and to the Members of the United Nations.

Article 64

1.   The Economic and Social Council may take appropriate steps to obtain regular reports from the specialized agencies. It may make arrangements with the Members of the United Nations and with the specialized agencies to obtain reports on the steps taken to give effect to its own recommendations and to recommendations on matters falling within its competence made by the General Assembly.

2.   It may communicate its observations on these reports to the General Assembly.

Article 65

The Economic and Social Council may furnish information to the Security Council and shall assist the Security Council upon its request.

Article 66

1.   The Economic and Social Council shall perform such functions as fall within its competence in connexion with the carrying out of the recommendations of the General Assembly.

2.   It may, with the approval of the General Assembly, perform services at the request of Members of the United Nations and at the request of specialized agencies.

3.   It shall perform such other functions as are specified elsewhere in the present Charter or as may be assigned to it by the General Assembly.

VOTING

Article 67

1.   Each member of the Economic and Social Council shall have one vote.

2.   Decisions of the Economic and Social Council shall be made by a majority of the members present and voting.

PROCEDURE

Article 68

The Economic and Social Council shall set up commissions in economic and social fields and for the promotion of human rights, and such other commissions as may be required for the performance of its functions.

Article 69

The Economic and Social Council shall invite any Member of the United Nations to participate, without vote, in its deliberations on any matter of particular concern to that Member.

Article 70

The Economic and Social Council may make arrangements for representatives of the specialized agencies to participate, without vote, in its deliberations and in those of the commissions established by it, and for its representatives to participate in the deliberations of the specialized agencies.

Article 71

The Economic and Social Council may make suitable arrangements for consultation with non-governmental organizations which are concerned with matters within its competence. Such arrangements may be made with international organizations and, where appropriate, with national organizations after consultation with the Member of the United Nations concerned.

Article 72

1. The Economic and Social Council shall adopt its own rules of procedure, including the method of selecting its President.
2. The Economic and Social Council shall meet as required in accordance with its rules, which shall include provision for the convening of meetings on the request of a majority of its members.

CHAPTER XI: DECLARATION REGARDING NON–SELF-GOVERNING TERRITORIES

Article 73

Members of the United Nations which have or assume responsibilities for the administration of territories whose peoples have not yet attained a full measure of self-government recognize the principle that the interests of the inhabitants of these territories are paramount, and accept as a sacred trust the obligation to promote to the utmost, within the system of international peace and security established by the present Charter, the well-being of the inhabitants of these territories, and, to this end:

a. to ensure, with due respect for the culture of the peoples concerned, their political, economic, social, and educational advancement, their just treatment, and their protection against abuses;

b. to develop self-government, to take due account of the political aspirations of the peoples, and to assist them in the progressive development of their free political institutions, according to the particular circumstances of each territory and its peoples and their varying stages of advancement;

c. to further international peace and security;

d. to promote constructive measures of development, to encourage research, and to co–operate with one another and, when and where appropriate, with specialized international bodies with a view to the practical achievement of the social, economic, and scientific purposes set forth in this Article; and

e. to transmit regularly to the Secretary-General for information purposes, subject to such limitation as security and constitutional considerations may require, statistical and other information of a technical nature relating to economic, social, and educational conditions in the territories for which they are respectively responsible other than those territories to which Chapters XII and XIII apply.

Article 74

Members of the United Nations also agree that their policy in respect of the territories to which this Chapter applies, no less than in respect of their metropolitan areas, must be based on the general principle of good-neighbourliness, due account being taken of the interests and well-being of the rest of the world, in social, economic, and commercial matters.

CHAPTER XII: INTERNATIONAL TRUSTEESHIP SYSTEM

Article 75

The United Nations shall establish under its authority an international trusteeship system for the administration and supervision of such territories as may be placed thereunder by subsequent individual agreements. These territories are hereinafter referred to as trust territories.

Article 76

The basic objectives of the trusteeship system, in accordance with the Purposes of the United Nations laid down in Article 1 of the present Charter, shall be:

    a.   to further international peace and security;

    b.   to promote the political, economic, social, and educational advancement of the inhabitants of the trust territories, and their progressive development towards self-government or independence as may be appropriate to the particular circumstances of each territory and its peoples and the freely expressed wishes of the peoples concerned, and as may be provided by the terms of each trusteeship agreement;

    c.   to encourage respect for human rights and for fundamental freedoms for all without distinction as to race, sex, language, or religion, and to encourage recognition of the interdependence of the peoples of the world; and

    d.   to ensure equal treatment in social, economic, and commercial matters for all Members of the United Nations and their nationals, and also equal treatment for the latter in the administration of justice, without prejudice to the attainment of the foregoing objectives and subject to the provisions of Article 80.

Article 77

    1.   The trusteeship system shall apply to such territories in the following categories as may be placed thereunder by means of trusteeship agreements:

        a.   territories now held under mandate;

        b.   territories which may be detached from enemy states as a result of the Second World War; and

        c.   territories voluntarily placed under the system by states responsible for their administration.

    2.   It will be a matter for subsequent agreement as to which territories in the foregoing categories will be brought under the trusteeship system and upon what terms.

Article 78

The trusteeship system shall not apply to territories which have become Members of the United Nations, relationship among which shall be based on respect for the principle of sovereign equality.

Article 79

The terms of trusteeship for each territory to be placed under the trusteeship system, including any alteration or amendment, shall be agreed upon by the states directly concerned, including the mandatory power in the case of territories held under mandate by a Member of the United Nations, and shall be approved as provided for in Articles 83 and 85.

Article 80

    1.   Except as may be agreed upon in individual trusteeship agreements, made under Articles 77, 79, and 81, placing each territory under the trusteeship system, and

until such agreements have been concluded, nothing in this Chapter shall be construed in or of itself to alter in any manner the rights whatsoever of any states or any peoples or the terms of existing international instruments to which Members of the United Nations may respectively be parties.

2. Paragraph 1 of this Article shall not be interpreted as giving grounds for delay or postponement of the negotiation and conclusion of agreements for placing mandated and other territories under the trusteeship system as provided for in Article 77.

Article 81

The trusteeship agreement shall in each case include the terms under which the trust territory will be administered and designate the authority which will exercise the administration of the trust territory. Such authority, hereinafter called the administering authority, may be one or more states or the Organization itself.

Article 82

There may be designated, in any trusteeship agreement, a strategic area or areas which may include part or all of the trust territory to which the agreement applies, without prejudice to any special agreement or agreements made under Article 43.

Article 83

1. All functions of the United Nations relating to strategic areas, including the approval of the terms of the trusteeship agreements and of their alteration or amendment shall be exercised by the Security Council.

2. The basic objectives set forth in Article 76 shall be applicable to the people of each strategic area.

3. The Security Council shall, subject to the provisions of the trusteeship agreements and without prejudice to security considerations, avail itself of the assistance of the Trusteeship Council to perform those functions of the United Nations under the trusteeship system relating to political, economic, social, and educational matters in the strategic areas.

Article 84

It shall be the duty of the administering authority to ensure that the trust territory shall play its part in the maintenance of international peace and security. To this end the administering authority may make use of volunteer forces, facilities, and assistance from the trust territory in carrying out the obligations towards the Security Council undertaken in this regard by the administering authority, as well as for local defence and the maintenance of law and order within the trust territory.

Article 85

1. The functions of the United Nations with regard to trusteeship agreements for all areas not designated as strategic, including the approval of the terms of the trusteeship agreements and of their alteration or amendment, shall be exercised by the General Assembly.

2. The Trusteeship Council, operating under the authority of the General Assembly shall assist the General Assembly in carrying out these functions.

CHAPTER XIII: THE TRUSTEESHIP COUNCIL

COMPOSITION

Article 86

1. The Trusteeship Council shall consist of the following Members of the United Nations:
    a. those Members administering trust territories;

b.   such of those Members mentioned by name in Article 23 as are not admin-
     istering trust territories; and

c.   as many other Members elected for three-year terms by the General Assem-
     bly as may be necessary to ensure that the total number of members of the
     Trusteeship Council is equally divided between those Members of the Unit-
     ed Nations which administer trust territories and those which do not.

2.   Each member of the Trusteeship Council shall designate one specially qualified
     person to represent it therein.

FUNCTIONS AND POWERS

Article 87

The General Assembly and, under its authority, the Trusteeship Council, in carrying out their
functions, may:

a.   consider reports submitted by the administering authority;

b.   accept petitions and examine them in consultation with the administering au-
     thority;

c.   provide for periodic visits to the respective trust territories at times agreed upon
     with the administering authority; and

d.   take these and other actions in conformity with the terms of the trusteeship agree-
     ments.

Article 88

The Trusteeship Council shall formulate a questionnaire on the political, economic, social, and
educational advancement of the inhabitants of each trust territory, and the administering authority for each trust territory within the competence of the General Assembly shall make an annual report to the General Assembly upon the basis of such questionnaire.

VOTING

Article 89

1.   Each member of the Trusteeship Council shall have one vote.

2.   Decisions of the Trusteeship Council shall be made by a majority of the members
     present and voting.

PROCEDURE

Article 90

1.   The Trusteeship Council shall adopt its own rules of procedure, including the
     method of selecting its President.

2.   The Trusteeship Council shall meet as required in accordance with its rules, which
     shall include provision for the convening of meetings on the request of a major-
     ity of its members.

Article 91

The Trusteeship Council shall, when appropriate, avail itself of the assistance of the Economic
and Social Council and of the specialized agencies in regard to matters with which they are respectively concerned.

CHAPTER XIV: THE INTERNATIONAL COURT OF JUSTICE

Article 92

The International Court of Justice shall be the principal judicial organ of the United Nations.
It shall function in accordance with the annexed Statute, which is based upon the Statute of the
Permanent Court of International Justice and forms an integral part of the present Charter.

Article 93

   1.   All Members of the United Nations are ipso facto parties to the Statute of the International Court of Justice.

   2.   A state which is not a Member of the United Nations may become a party to the Statute of the International Court of Justice on conditions to be determined in each case by the General Assembly upon the recommendation of the Security Council.

Article 94

   1.   Each Member of the United Nations undertakes to comply with the decision of the International Court of Justice in any case to which it is a party.

   2.   If any party to a case fails to perform the obligations incumbent upon it under a judgment rendered by the Court, the other party may have recourse to the Security Council, which may, if it deems necessary, make recommendations or decide upon measures to be taken to give effect to the judgment.

Article 95

Nothing in the present Charter shall prevent Members of the United Nations from entrusting the solution of their differences to other tribunals by virtue of agreements already in existence or which may be concluded in the future.

Article 96

   1.   The General Assembly or the Security Council may request the International Court of Justice to give an advisory opinion on any legal question.

   2.   Other organs of the United Nations and specialized agencies, which may at any time be so authorized by the General Assembly, may also request advisory opinions of the Court on legal questions arising within the scope of their activities.

Chapter XV: The Secretariat

Article 97

The Secretariat shall comprise a Secretary-General and such staff as the Organization may require. The Secretary-General shall be appointed by the General Assembly upon the recommendation of the Security Council. He shall be the chief administrative officer of the Organization.

Article 98

The Secretary-General shall act in that capacity in all meetings of the General Assembly, of the Security Council, of the Economic and Social Council, and of the Trusteeship Council, and shall perform such other functions as are entrusted to him by these organs. The Secretary-General shall make an annual report to the General Assembly on the work of the Organization.

Article 99

The Secretary-General may bring to the attention of the Security Council any matter which in his opinion may threaten the maintenance of international peace and security.

Article 100

   1.   In the performance of their duties the Secretary-General and the staff shall not seek or receive instructions from any government or from any other authority external to the Organization. They shall refrain from any action which might reflect on their position as international officials responsible only to the Organization.

   2.   Each Member of the United Nations undertakes to respect the exclusively international character of the responsibilities of the Secretary-General and the staff and not to seek to influence them in the discharge of their responsibilities.

Article 101

1. The staff shall be appointed by the Secretary-General under regulations established by the General Assembly.

2. Appropriate staffs shall be permanently assigned to the Economic and Social Council, the Trusteeship Council, and, as required, to other organs of the United Nations. These staffs shall form a part of the Secretariat.

3. The paramount consideration in the employment of the staff and in the determination of the conditions of service shall be the necessity of securing the highest standards of efficiency, competence, and integrity. Due regard shall be paid to the importance of recruiting the staff on as wide a geographical basis as possible.

CHAPTER XVI: MISCELLANEOUS PROVISIONS

Article 102

1. Every treaty and every international agreement entered into by any Member of the United Nations after the present Charter comes into force shall as soon as possible be registered with the Secretariat and published by it.

2. No party to any such treaty or international agreement which has not been registered in accordance with the provisions of paragraph 1 of this Article may invoke that treaty or agreement before any organ of the United Nations.

Article 103

In the event of a conflict between the obligations of the Members of the United Nations under the present Charter and their obligations under any other international agreement, their obligations under the present Charter shall prevail.

Article 104

The Organization shall enjoy in the territory of each of its Members such legal capacity as may be necessary for the exercise of its functions and the fulfillment of its purposes.

Article 105

1. The Organization shall enjoy in the territory of each of its Members such privileges and immunities as are necessary for the fulfillment of its purposes.

2. Representatives of the Members of the United Nations and officials of the Organization shall similarly enjoy such privileges and immunities as are necessary for the independent exercise of their functions in connexion with the Organization.

3. The General Assembly may make recommendations with a view to determining the details of the application of paragraphs 1 and 2 of this Article or may propose conventions to the Members of the United Nations for this purpose.

CHAPTER XVII: TRANSITIONAL SECURITY ARRANGEMENTS

Article 106

Pending the coming into force of such special agreements referred to in Article 43 as in the opinion of the Security Council enable it to begin the exercise of its responsibilities under Article 42, the parties to the Four-Nation Declaration, signed at Moscow, 30 October 1943, and France, shall, in accordance with the provisions of paragraph 5 of that Declaration, consult with one another and as occasion requires with other Members of the United Nations with a view to such joint action on behalf of the Organization as may be necessary for the purpose of maintaining international peace and security.

Article 107

Nothing in the present Charter shall invalidate or preclude action, in relation to any state which during the Second World War has been an enemy of any signatory to the present Charter, taken or authorized as a result of that war by the Governments having responsibility for such action.

CHAPTER XVIII: AMENDMENTS

Article 108

Amendments to the present Charter shall come into force for all Members of the United Nations when they have been adopted by a vote of two thirds of the members of the General Assembly and ratified in accordance with their respective constitutional processes by two thirds of the Members of the United Nations, including all the permanent members of the Security Council.

Article 109

1. A General Conference of the Members of the United Nations for the purpose of reviewing the present Charter may be held at a date and place to be fixed by a two-thirds vote of the members of the General Assembly and by a vote of any nine members of the Security Council. Each Member of the United Nations shall have one vote in the conference.

2. Any alteration of the present Charter recommended by a two-thirds vote of the conference shall take effect when ratified in accordance with their respective constitutional processes by two thirds of the Members of the United Nations including all the permanent members of the Security Council.

3. If such a conference has not been held before the tenth annual session of the General Assembly following the coming into force of the present Charter, the proposal to call such a conference shall be placed on the agenda of that session of the General Assembly, and the conference shall be held if so decided by a majority vote of the members of the General Assembly and by a vote of any seven members of the Security Council.

CHAPTER XIX: RATIFICATION AND SIGNATURE

Article 110

1. The present Charter shall be ratified by the signatory states in accordance with their respective constitutional processes.

2. The ratifications shall be deposited with the Government of the United States of America, which shall notify all the signatory states of each deposit as well as the Secretary-General of the Organization when he has been appointed.

3. The present Charter shall come into force upon the deposit of ratifications by the Republic of China, France, the Union of Soviet Socialist Republics, the United Kingdom of Great Britain and Northern Ireland, and the United States of America, and by a majority of the other signatory states. A protocol of the ratifications deposited shall thereupon be drawn up by the Government of the United States of America which shall communicate copies thereof to all the signatory states.

4. The states signatory to the present Charter which ratify it after it has come into force will become original Members of the United Nations on the date of the deposit of their respective ratifications.

Article 111

The present Charter, of which the Chinese, French, Russian, English, and Spanish texts are equally authentic, shall remain deposited in the archives of the Government of the United States of America. Duly certified copies thereof shall be transmitted by that Government to the Governments of the other signatory states.

IN FAITH WHEREOF the representatives of the Governments of the United Nations have signed the present Charter.

DONE at the city of San Francisco the twenty-sixth day of June, one thousand nine hundred and forty-five.

Appendix C: Universal Declaration of Human Rights

Adopted and proclaimed by General Assembly resolution 217 A (III) of 10 December 1948

Preamble

Whereas recognition of the inherent dignity and of the equal and inalienable rights of all members of the human family is the foundation of freedom, justice and peace in the world,

Whereas disregard and contempt for human rights have resulted in barbarous acts which have outraged the conscience of mankind, and the advent of a world in which human beings shall enjoy freedom of speech and belief and freedom from fear and want has been proclaimed as the highest aspiration of the common people,

Whereas it is essential, if man is not to be compelled to have recourse, as a last resort, to rebellion against tyranny and oppression, that human rights should be protected by the rule of law,

Whereas it is essential to promote the development of friendly relations between nations,

Whereas the peoples of the United Nations have in the Charter reaffirmed their faith in fundamental human rights, in the dignity and worth of the human person and in the equal rights of men and women and have determined to promote social progress and better standards of life in larger freedom,

Whereas Member States have pledged themselves to achieve, in cooperation with the United Nations, the promotion of universal respect for and observance of human rights and fundamental freedoms,

Whereas a common understanding of these rights and freedoms is of the greatest importance for the full realization of this pledge,

Now, therefore,

The General Assembly,

Proclaims this Universal Declaration of Human Rights as a common standard of achievement for all peoples and all nations, to the end that every individual and every organ of society, keeping this Declaration constantly in mind, shall strive by teaching and education to promote respect for these rights and freedoms and by progressive measures, national and international, to secure their universal and effective recognition and observance, both among the peoples of Member States themselves and among the peoples of territories under their jurisdiction.

Article 1

All human beings are born free and equal in dignity and rights. They are endowed with reason and conscience and should act towards one another in a spirit of brotherhood.

Article 2

Everyone is entitled to all the rights and freedoms set forth in this Declaration, without distinction of any kind, such as race, colour, sex, language, religion, political or other opinion, national or social origin, property, birth or other status.

Furthermore, no distinction shall be made on the basis of the political, jurisdictional or international status of the country or territory to which a person belongs, whether it be independent, trust, non-self-governing or under any other limitation of sovereignty.

Article 3

Everyone has the right to life, liberty and security of person.

Article 4

No one shall be held in slavery or servitude; slavery and the slave trade shall be prohibited in all their forms.

Article 5

No one shall be subjected to torture or to cruel, inhuman or degrading treatment or punishment.

Article 6

Everyone has the right to recognition everywhere as a person before the law.

Article 7

All are equal before the law and are entitled without any discrimination to equal protection of the law. All are entitled to equal protection against any discrimination in violation of this Declaration and against any incitement to such discrimination.

Article 8

Everyone has the right to an effective remedy by the competent national tribunals for acts violating the fundamental rights granted him by the constitution or by law.

Article 9

No one shall be subjected to arbitrary arrest, detention or exile.

Article 10

Everyone is entitled in full equality to a fair and public hearing by an independent and impartial tribunal, in the determination of his rights and obligations and of any criminal charge against him.

Article 11

Everyone charged with a penal offence has the right to be presumed innocent until proved guilty according to law in a public trial at which he has had all the guarantees necessary for his defence.

No one shall be held guilty of any penal offence on account of any act or omission which did not constitute a penal offence, under national or international law, at the time when it was committed. Nor shall a heavier penalty be imposed than the one that was applicable at the time the penal offence was committed.

Article 12

No one shall be subjected to arbitrary interference with his privacy, family, home or correspondence, nor to attacks upon his honour and reputation. Everyone has the right to the protection of the law against such interference or attacks.

Article 13

Everyone has the right to freedom of movement and residence within the borders of each State.

Everyone has the right to leave any country, including his own, and to return to his country.

Article 14

Everyone has the right to seek and to enjoy in other countries asylum from persecution.

This right may not be invoked in the case of prosecutions genuinely arising from non-political crimes or from acts contrary to the purposes and principles of the United Nations.

Article 15

Everyone has the right to a nationality.
No one shall be arbitrarily deprived of his nationality nor denied the right to change his nationality.

Article 16

Men and women of full age, without any limitation due to race, nationality or religion, have the right to marry and to found a family. They are entitled to equal rights as to marriage, during marriage and at its dissolution.

Marriage shall be entered into only with the free and full consent of the intending spouses. The family is the natural and fundamental group unit of society and is entitled to protection by society and the State.

Article 17

Everyone has the right to own property alone as well as in association with others.

No one shall be arbitrarily deprived of his property.

Article 18

Everyone has the right to freedom of thought, conscience and religion; this right includes freedom to change his religion or belief, and freedom, either alone or in community with others and in public or private, to manifest his religion or belief in teaching, practice, worship and observance.

Article 19

Everyone has the right to freedom of opinion and expression; this right includes freedom to hold opinions without interference and to seek, receive and impart information and ideas through any media and regardless of frontiers.

Article 20

Everyone has the right to freedom of peaceful assembly and association.

No one may be compelled to belong to an association.

Article 21

Everyone has the right to take part in the government of his country, directly or through freely chosen representatives.

Everyone has the right to equal access to public service in his country.

The will of the people shall be the basis of the authority of government; this will shall be expressed in periodic and genuine elections which shall be by universal and equal suffrage and shall be held by secret vote or by equivalent free voting procedures.

Article 22

Everyone, as a member of society, has the right to social security and is entitled to realization, through national effort and international co-operation and in accordance with the organization and resources of each State, of the economic, social and cultural rights indispensable for his dignity and the free development of his personality.

Article 23

Everyone has the right to work, to free choice of employment, to just and favourable conditions of work and to protection against unemployment.

Everyone, without any discrimination, has the right to equal pay for equal work.

Everyone who works has the right to just and favourable remuneration ensuring for himself and his family an existence worthy of human dignity, and supplemented, if necessary, by other means of social protection.

Everyone has the right to form and to join trade unions for the protection of his interests.

Article 24

Everyone has the right to rest and leisure, including reasonable limitation of working hours and periodic holidays with pay.

Article 25

Everyone has the right to a standard of living adequate for the health and well-being of himself and of his family, including food, clothing, housing and medical care and necessary social services, and the right to security in the event of unemployment, sickness, disability, widowhood, old age or other lack of livelihood in circumstances beyond his control.

Motherhood and childhood are entitled to special care and assistance. All children, whether born in or out of wedlock, shall enjoy the same social protection.

Article 26

Everyone has the right to education. Education shall be free, at least in the elementary and fundamental stages. Elementary education shall be compulsory. Technical and professional education shall be made generally available and higher education shall be equally accessible to all on the basis of merit.

Education shall be directed to the full development of the human personality and to the strengthening of respect for human rights and fundamental freedoms. It shall promote understanding, tolerance and friendship among all nations, racial or religious groups, and shall further the activities of the United Nations for the maintenance of peace.

Parents have a prior right to choose the kind of education that shall be given to their children.

Article 27

Everyone has the right freely to participate in the cultural life of the community, to enjoy the arts and to share in scientific advancement and its benefits.

Everyone has the right to the protection of the moral and material interests resulting from any scientific, literary or artistic production of which he is the author.

Article 28

Everyone is entitled to a social and international order in which the rights and freedoms set forth in this Declaration can be fully realized.

Article 29

Everyone has duties to the community in which alone the free and full development of his personality is possible.

In the exercise of his rights and freedoms, everyone shall be subject only to such limitations as are determined by law solely for the purpose of securing due recognition and respect for the rights and freedoms of others and of meeting the just requirements of morality, public order and the general welfare in a democratic society.

These rights and freedoms may in no case be exercised contrary to the purposes and principles of the United Nations.

Article 30

Nothing in this Declaration may be interpreted as implying for any State, group or person any right to engage in any activity or to perform any act aimed at the destruction of any of the rights and freedoms set forth herein.

APPENDIX D: PURPOSES OF THE INTERNATIONAL MONETARY FUND

ARTICLE I

Purposes

The purposes of the International Monetary Fund are:

(i) To promote international monetary cooperation through a permanent institution which provides the machinery for consultation and collaboration on international monetary problems.

(ii) To facilitate the expansion and balanced growth of international trade, and to contribute thereby to the promotion and maintenance of high levels of employment and real income and to the development of the productive resources of all members as primary objectives of economic policy.

(iii) To promote exchange stability, to maintain orderly exchange arrangements among members, and to avoid competitive exchange depreciation.

(iv) To assist in the establishment of a multilateral system of payments in respect of current transactions between members and in the elimination of foreign exchange restrictions which hamper the growth of world trade.

(v) To give confidence to members by making the general resources of the Fund temporarily available to them under adequate safeguards, thus providing them with opportunity to correct maladjustments in their balance of payments without resorting to measures destructive of national or international prosperity.

(vi) In accordance with the above, to shorten the duration and lessen the degree of disequilibrium in the international balances of payments of members.

The Fund shall be guided in all its policies and decisions by the purposes set forth in this Article.

BIBLIOGRAPHY

Adelman, Irma, and J. Edward Taylor. 1989. Is Structural Adjustment with a Human Face Possible? The Case of Mexico. *Journal of Development Studies* 26 (April): 388–407.

Agra Europe. 1999. EU Judge Rejects French GM Ban. November 26: 11.

———. 2000. Public Ignorant of GM Issues. April 28: 5–7.

———. 2000. Thailand Files First GMO Complaint at WTO. September 29: 9.

Ahmad, Feroz. 1991. Arab Nationalism, Radicalism, and the Specter of Neocolonialism. *Monthly Review* 42 (February): 30–35.

Ahmed, Leila. 1984. *Early Feminist Movements in the Middle East in Muslim Women.* Ed. Freda Hussain. New York: St. Martins Press.

Ahsan, Abdullan. 1988. *The Organization of Islamic Conference.* The International Institute of Islamic Thought.

Albright, Madeleine. 1994. *Bosnia in Light of the Holocaust: War Crimes Tribunals.* U.S. Department of State Dispatch 5 (April 18): 209(4).

———. 1997. Enlarging NATO: Why Bigger Is Better. *The Economist* 342 (February 15): 21(3).

Alger, Chadwick F. 1996. Thinking About the Future of the UN System. *Global Governance* 2 (December–January): 335–360.

Allison, Graham. 1971. *The Essence of Decision.* Boston, MA: Little Brown.

Al-Radi, Selma. 1995. Iraqi Sanctions—A Postwar Crime. *The Nation* 260 (March 27): 416(2).

Alvarez, Jose. 1995. The Once and Future of the Security Council. *Washington Quarterly* 18 (spring): 5–20.

Alvarez, Sonia E. 1997. Contradictions of a "Women's Space" in a Male-Dominant State: The Political Role of the Commission on the Status of Women in Postauthoritarian Brazil. In *Women, International Development, and Politics: The Bureaucratic Mire,* ed. Kathleen Staudt. Philadelphia, PA: Temple University Press, 59–100.

Ambrose, Stephen E. 1988. *The Rise to Globalism: American Foreign Policy Since 1938.* New York: Penguin Books.

American Banker. 1990. Full Resumption of Lending to China Seen as Unlikely. 155 (June 13): 18.

Amin, Samir. 1977. *Imperialism and Uneven Development.* New York: Monthly Review Press.

Anderson, Roy R., Robert F. Seibert, and Jon G. Wagner. 1998. *Politics and Change in the Middle East.* Upper Saddle River, NJ: Prentice Hall.

APS Diplomat Recorder. 2000. Arab Affairs. Cairo Summit Decisions. 53 (October 28): NA.

———. 2001. Arab Affairs: Leagues FMs Give PA $40m/Month. 54 (March 17): NA.

———. 2001. Arab Affairs: PA Appeals to Arab League. 54 (May 26): NA.

Aron, William. 2000. The International Whaling Commission—A History of Malignant Neglect. Microbehavior and Macroresults. <www.orst.edu>

Ascher, William. 1990. The World Bank and U.S. Control. In *The United States and Multilateral Institutions: Patterns of Changing Instrumentality and Influence*, ed. Margaret P. Karns and Karen A. Mingst. Boston, MA: Unwin Hyman, 115–140.

Ascherio, Alberto, et al. 1992. Effect of the Gulf War on Infant and Child Mortality in Iraq. *New England Journal of Medicine* 327 (September 24): 931(6).

Ashworth, Lucian M., and Larry A. Swatuk. 1998. Masculinity and the Fear of Emasculation in International Relations Theory. In *The "Man" Question in International Relations*, ed. Marysia Zalewski and Jane Parapart. Boulder, CO: Westview Press, 73–92.

Associated Press. 2001. 165 Nations Agree to Rules for Pact Cutting Back Carbon Emissions. *The St. Louis Post Dispatch*, November 11, A15.

Aubrey, Lisa. 1997. *The Politics of Development Cooperation: NGOs, Gender, and Partnership in Kenya.* New York: Routledge.

Balaam, David N., and Michael Veseth. 1996. *Introduction to International Political Economy.* Upper Saddle River, NJ: Prentice Hall.

Baldwin, David, ed. 1993. *Neorealism and Neoliberalism.* New York: Columbia University Press.

Barnett, Michael N., and Martha Finnemor. 1999. The Politics, Power and Pathologies of International Organizations. *International Organization* 53 (autumn): 698–747.

Bartlett, Bruce, et al. 1998. Asia Unravels: Could This be the Sequel to Fall of the Berlin Wall? *The American Enterprise* 9 (May–June): 58–64.

Bayne, Nicholas. 1997. What Governments Want from International Institutions and How They Get It. *Government and Opposition* 31 (summer): 361–380.

BBC News. 1999. Indonesia and IMF near Agreement. April 3. <www.bbc...co..uk>

———. 2001. Rwanda Trial Opens Belgians' Eyes. June 7. <www.news.bbc.co. uk>

———. 2000. Whaling Commission Struggles to Survive. July 4. <www.news.bbc.uk>

Bedjaoui, Mohammed. 1994. *The New World Order and the Security Council: Testing the Legality of Its Acts.* Dordrecht, Netherlands: Nijhoff Publishers.

Beelman, Maude S. 1996. Fingerprints: Arms to Bosnia, The Real Story. *The New Republic* 215 (October 28): 26–29.

Benedict, Richard E. 1991. *Ozone Diplomacy.* Cambridge, MA: Harvard University Press.

Bennett, A. LeRoy. 1991. *International Organizations: Principles and Issues.* 5th ed. Upper Saddle River, NJ: Prentice Hall.

———. 1995. *International Organizations: Principles and Issues.* 6th ed. Upper Saddle River, NJ: Prentice Hall.

Bennett, Andrew, and Joseph Lepgold. 1993. Reinventing Collective Security After the Cold War and Gulf Conflict. *Political Science Quarterly* (summer): 213–238.

Bennis, Phyllis. 1996. *Calling the Shots: How Washington Dominates Today's UN.* New York: Olive Branch Press.

Bentham, Jeremy. 1961. *An Introduction to the Principles of Morals and Legislation.* Garden City, NY: Double Day.

Bergeron, Suzanne L. 1999. Imperialism. In *Elgar Companion to Feminist Economics*, ed. Meg Lewis and Janice Peterson. Brookfield, VT: Edward Elgar Publishing.

Bergman, Barbara. 1986. *The Economic Emergence of Women.* New York: Basic Books.

Biersteker, Thomas J. 1978. *Distortion or Development? Contending Perspectives on the Multinational Corporation.* Cambridge, MA: MIT Press.

Binmore, Ken. 1992. *Fun and Games: A Text on Game Theory.* Lexington, MA: D. C. Heath.

Blinder, Alan S. 1999. Eight Steps to a New Financial Order. *Foreign Affairs* 78 (September–October): 50–63.

Boyer, Gabriela. 1994. GATTastrophe. *The Nation* 268 (June 13): 821(1).

Brecher, Jeremy, and Tim Costello. 1994. *Global Village or Global Pillage: Economic Reconstruction from the Bottom Up.* Boston, MA: South End Press.

Bresnan, John. 2000. Indonesia in Aftershock. *Great Decisions.* <www.fpa.org>

Brown, Bartram S. 1992. *The United States and the Politicization of the World Bank: Issues of International Law and Policy.* London: Kegan Paul International.

Brown, Lester, and Hal Kane. 1994. *Full House, Reassessing the Earth's Population Carrying Capacity.* New York: W. W. Norton.

Brownlie, Ian. 1994. *Basic Documents on Human Rights.* Oxford, UK: Clarendon Press.

Buchmann, Claudia. 1996. The Debt Crisis, Structural Adjustment and Women's Education; Implications for Status and Social Development. *International Journal of Comparative Sociology* 37 (June): 5–31.

Buckley, William F. 1996. Has the WTO Threatened U.S.? *National Review* 48 (February 26): 70–71.

Budianta, Melani. 2000. Double Text. *Representing American* and *Discussing Women's Issues in Indonesia.* American Studies International 38 (October): 47–54

Budhoo, Davidson. 1994. IMF/World Bank Wreak Havoc on Third World. Pp. 20–23 in *50 Years Is Enough: The Case Against the World Bank and the International Monetary Fund,* ed. Kevin Danaher. Boston, MA: South End Press.

Butcher, Tim. 1998. Defence Chiefs Warn Against Enlarging NATO. *UK News Issue* 1076 (May 6). <www.telegraph.co.uk>

Cahn, Steven M. 1997. *Classics of Modern Political Theory.* New York: Oxford University Press.

Callahan, Daniel. 2000. Food for Thought. *Commonweal* 127 (April 7): 7–10.

Campbell, Horace, and Howard Stein, eds. 1992. *Tanzania and the IMF: The Dynamics of Liberalization.* Boulder, CO: Westview Press.

Cardoso, Fernando H., and Enzo Faletto. 1979. *Dependency and Development in Latin America.* Berkeley, CA: University of California Press.

Carpenter, Ted Galen. 1997. The Mirage of Global Collective Security. Pp. 13–28 in *Delusions of Grandeur: The United Nations and Global Intervention,* ed. Ted Galen Carpenter. Washington, D.C.: Cato Institute.

Castleman, Barry, and Richard Lemen. 1998. Corporate Junk Science: Corporate Influence at International Science Organization. *Multinational Monitor* 19 (January–February): 28(3).

CBS News. 2001. Islamic Conference Condemns Terror. October 10. <www.cbsnews.com>

Chadwick, Douglas H. 2001. Pursuing the Minke. *National Geographic* 199 (April): 58.

Chemical Week. 2001. Brussels Maintains GMO Ban. 163 (January 24): 8.

Christopher, Warren. 1997. NATO: Future Partnership for Peace. *Vital Speeches* 63 (January 1): 162(4).

Clark, Mark T. 1995. The Trouble with Collective Security. *Orbis* 39 (spring): 237(22).

Claude, Inis. 1993. The Gulf War and Prospects for World Order by Collective Security. Pp. 23–38 in *The Persian Gulf Crisis: Power in the Post–Cold War World,* ed. Robert F. Helms II and Robert H. Dorff. Westport, CT: Praeger.

Clausewitz, Carl Von. 1968. *On War.* Translated by J. J. Graham. New York: Barnes & Noble.

Cockburn, Alexander, and Ken Silverstein. 1995. The Demands of Capital. *Harper's Magazine* 290 (May): 66–68.

Cockcroft, James D. 1996. *Latin America: History, Politics, and U.S. Policy.* Chicago, IL: Nelson Hall Publishers.

Cohen, Benjamin J. 1986. *In Whose Interest? International Banking and American Foreign Policy.* New Haven, CT: Yale University Press.

Cohen, Roger. 1999. European Crisis Paves Way for More Accountability. *New York Times,* March 17.

Cohen, Susan. 1994. Competition or Consensus? Women, Population and the Planet. *Populi* (July/August): 7–9.

Commission on Sustainable Development, 1998. General Information. April 6. <www. un.org/esa/sustdev/csdgen.htm>

Connors, Jane. 1996. NGOs and the Human Rights of Women at the United Nations. Pp. 147–180 in *"The Conscience of the World": The Influence of Nongovernmental Organizations in the UN System,* ed. Peter Willetts. Washington, D.C.: Brookings Institution.

Cook, Alice, and Gwyn Kirk. 1983. *Greenham Women Everywhere.* Boston, MA: South End Press.

Cook, Helena. 1997. Amnesty International and the United Nations. Pp. 181–213 in *"The Conscience of the World": The Influence of Nongovernmental Organizations in the UN System,* ed. Peter Willetts. Washington, D.C.: Brookings Institution.

Cooper, Richard N. 1998. Toward a Real Global Warming Treaty: Implications of the 1997 Kyoto Conference. *Foreign Affairs* 77 (March–April): 66–80.

Cornwall, Rupert. 1995. A Global Money Crisis: The Sinking of the Greenback. *World Press Review* 42 (May): 8–10.

Cox, Robert W. 1987. *Production, Power, and World Order. Social Forces in the Making of History.* New York: Columbia University Press.

Crane, George T., and Alba Amawi. 1997. *The Theoretical Evolution of International Political Economy.* New York: Oxford University Press.

Crossette, Barbara. 1998. Kofi Annan's Astonishing Facts. *New York Times*, September 27.

———. 1999. UN Details Its Failure to Stop '95 Bosnia Massacre. *New York Times*, November 16, A3

Crow, Patrick. 1996. Defending the WTO. *Oil and Gas Journal* 94 (March 18): 37.

Crozier, Brian. 1991. Handling the United Nations: Bush's Triumph. *National Review* 43 (April 1): 40–42.

Cunningham, Shea, and Betsy Reed. 1995. Balancing the Budgets on Women's Backs: The World Bank and the 104th Congress. *Dollars and Sense* 202 (November–December): 22–26.

D'Amico, Francine. 1999. Women Workers in the United Nations: From Margin to Mainstream. Pp. 19–40 in *Gender Politics in Global Governance*, ed. Elizabeth Prugl and Mary K. Meyer. Boston, MA: Rowman & Littlefield.

Damrosch, Lori Fisler. 1989. Politics across Borders: Nonintervention of Nonforcible Influence over Domestic Affairs. *American Journal of International Law* 83 (January): 1–50.

Danaher, Kevin, ed. 1994. *Third World. 50 Years Is Enough: The Case Against the World Bank and the International Monetary Fund.* Boston, MA: South End Press.

Davies, Frank. 1998. Florida Leads in Stripping of Voting Rights. *Miami Herald*, October 230, 1A.

Department of Conservation. 2001. Media Statement from the Office of the Prime Minister of New Zealand. July 19. <www.doc.govt.nz>

———. 2001. South Pacific Whale Sanctuary Issue Sparks Renewed International Interest in the IWC. June 28. <www.doc.govt.nz>

Doctors Without Borders. 1998. General Information. September 24. <www.dwb.org/intro.htm>

Donini, Antonio. 1996. The Bureaucracy and the Free Spirits: Stagnations and Innovations in the Relationship between the UN and NGOs. Pp. 83–102 in *NGOs, the UN, and Global Governance*, ed. Thomas Weiss and Leon Gordenker. Boulder, CO: Lynne Rienner Press.

Donnelly, Jack. 1993. *International Human Rights.* Boulder, CO: Westview Press.

Duffield, John S. 1992. International Regimes and Alliance Behavior: Explaining NATO Conventional Force Levels. *International Organizations* 46 (fall): 819–855.

———. 1994a. Explaining the Long Peace in Europe: The Contributions of Regional Security Regimes. *Review of International Studies* 20 (October): 369–388.

———. 1994b. NATO's Functions After the Cold War. *Political Science Quarterly* 109 (winter): 763(25).

———. 1998. NGO Relief in War Zones: Toward an Analysis of a New Aid Paradigm. Pp. 139–159 in *Beyond UN Subcontracting: Task-Sharing with Regional Security Arrangements and Service-Providing NGOs*, ed. Thomas G. Weiss. New York: St. Martin's Press.

Earth Island Journal. 1992. Angry Activists Vandalize World Bank Booth. 7 (summer): 20.

———. 2001. UN Team Calls WTO a Nightmare. 16 (autumn): 17.

Economist, The. 1986. Voter Power: Japan and the World Bank. 229 (April 19): 83.

———. 1991. Forgive Us Our Debt. 321 (October 12): S23–28.

———. 1995a. A Fork in the IMF's Road: The Fund Has a Credibility Problem That Cannot Be Dithered Away. 334 (January 28): 14.

———. 1995b. Hazardous Morals: The Mexican Affair Has Left the IMF with Some Hard Thinking to Do. 334 (February 11): 19–21.

———. 1998a. Back from the Brink. Mexico's Financial Crisis Was Different from Asia's but It Holds Valuable Lessons. 346 (March 7): S8(3).

———. 1998b. Food Fights: Genetically Modified Plants are Already Commonplace in America. Europeans Would Be Better Off If They Embraced Them with Equal Enthusiasm (June 13): 79–81.

———. 2000. Briefs in a Twist; WTO; The WTO Tries Too Hard (December 9): 6.

Edwards. Rob. 1998. Unfit to Eat. *New Scientist* (September 26): 13.

Eldridge, Philip J. 1995. *Non-government Organizations and Democratic Participation in Indonesia.* New York: Oxford University Press.

Enloe, Cynthia. 1990. *Bananas, Beaches, and Bases: Making Sense of International Politics.* Berkeley, CA: University of California Press.

Enloe, Cynthia. 1993. *The Morning After: Sexual Politics at the End of the Cold War.* Berkeley, CA: University of California Press.

Esman, Miltion J., and Shibley Telhami, eds. 1995. Ithaca, NY: Cornell University Press.

Europa World Year Book. 1990. Brussels: European Publications.

European Report. 2000. EU/UN: France Hosts First Meeting Under the Biosafety Protocol. December 23: 504.

European Report. 2001. Eurobarometer Confirms Indifference of EU Citizens Towards the EU. July 21: 102.

Evans, Peter. 1979. *Dependent Development: The Alliance of Multinational, State and Local Capital in Brazil*. Princeton, NJ: Princeton University Press.

Feld, Werner J., Robert S. Jordan, and Leon Hurwitz. 1994. *International Organizations: A Comparative Approach*. Westport, CT: Praeger.

Feminist Review. 1998. When the Earth Is Female and the Nation Is Mother. 58 (spring): 1–22.

Ferber, Marianne, and Julie A. Nelson. 1993. Introduction: The Social Construction of Economics and the Social Construction of Gender. Pp. 1–22 in *Beyond Economic Man: Feminist Theory and Economics*, ed. Marianne Ferber and Julie A. Nelson. Chicago, IL: Chicago University Press.

Finance and Development. 1991. The Global Environmental Facility. 28 (March): 24.

Flynn, Gregory, and David J. Scheffer. 1990. Limited Collective Security. *Foreign Policy* 80 (fall): 77–102.

Force Comparison. 1987. Brussels: NATO Information Office.

Foreign Policy. 2001. An NGO by Any Other Name. (July): 18.

Forsythe, David P. 1990. *The Politics of International Law*. Boulder, CO: Lynne Rienner Press.

———. 1991a. Human Rights in the Post–Cold War World. *The Fletcher Forum* 15 (summer): 55–70.

———. 1991b. *The Internationalization of Human Rights*. Lexington, MA: D. C. Heath.

———. 1993. *Human Rights and Peace: International and National Dimensions*. Lincoln, NE: University of Nebraska Press.

———. 1998. The International Court of Justice at Fifty. Pp. 385–405 in *The International Court of Justice*. The Hague: Kluwer Law International.

———. 2000. *Human Rights in International Relations*. Cambridge, UK: Cambridge University Press.

Foster, John Belamy. 1993. Let Them Eat Pollution: Capitalism and the World Environment. *Monthly Review* 44 (January): 10–21.

Fowler, Penny, and Simon Heap. 1998. Learning from the Marine Stewardship Council: A Business-NGO Partnership for Sustainable Marine Fisheries. *Greener Management International* (winter): 77–97.

Frank, Andre Gunder. 1979. *Dependent Accumulation and Underdevelopment*. New York: Monthly Review Press.

Friedman, Thomas L. 1999. Senseless in Seattle. *New York Times*, December 1, A31.

Friend, Theodore. 2000. South East Asia. *Asia Times Online*, February 19. <www.atimes.com>

Frontline. 1999. The Triumph of Evil. *PBS*, aired January 26.

GA/9228 (Press Release). 1997. Assembly President Proposes Increase in Security Council. 20 March 1997.

Gardam, Judith Gail. 1993. Proportionality and Force in International Law. *American Journal of International Law* 87 (July): 391–413.

Garthoff, Raymond L. 1987. *Policy Versus the Law: The Reinterpretation of the ABM Treaty*. Washington, D.C.: Brookings Institution.

German Information Center. 1995. German Support for the Reform Process in the Former Soviet Union and the Countries of Central, Southeastern, and Eastern Europe. New York: German Information Center.

Gill, Stephen. 1991. *American Hegemony and the Trilateral Commission*. Cambridge, UK: Cambridge University Press.

Gilpin, Robert. 1981. *War and Change in World Politics*. Cambridge, UK: Cambridge University Press.

———. 1987. *The Political Economy of International Relations*. Princeton, NJ: Princeton University Press.

Gluck, Sherna Berger. 1995. Palestinian Women: Gender Politics and Nationalism. *Journal of Palestine Studies* 24 (spring): 5–16.

Goebel, Allison, and Marc Epprecht. 1995. Women and Employment in Sub-Saharan Africa: Testing the World Bank and the WID Models with a Lesotho Case Study. *African Studies Review* 38 (April): 1–22.

Goetz, Anne Maire. 1997. *Getting Institutions Right for Women in Development*. New York: ZED Books.

Goldstein, Joshua. 1996. *International Relations*. 2nd ed. New York: Harper Collins.

Goodby, James E., and Daniel B. O'Connor. 1993. *Collective Security: An Essay on Its Limits and Possibilities After the Cold War*. Washington, D.C.: United States Institute for Peace.

Gordenker, Leon. 1987. *Refugees in International Politics*. London: Croom Helm, Ltd.

Gowa, Joanne. 1988. Rational Hegemons, Excludable Foods, and Small Groups: An Epitaph for Hegemonic Stability Theory. *World Politics* 41 (April): 307–324.

Greene, Owen. 1998. *Environmental Issues: The Globalization of World Politics: An Introduction to International Relations*. Oxford, UK: Oxford University Press.

Greenhouse, Steven. 2001. Report Outlines the Abuse of Foreign Domestic Workers. *New York Times*, June 14, A16.

Greenpeace. 1999. The Food Industry's Secret Ingredient. *Greenpeace* (winter): 22–24.

Grogan, John, and Cheryl Long. 2000. The Problem with Genetic Engineering. *Organic Gardening* 47 (January): 42–55.

Grotius, Hugo. 1984. *The Law of War and Peace*. Birmingham, AL: Legal Classics Library, Division of Gryphon Editions.

———. 1995. *The Law of Prize and Booty*. Buffalo, NY: Hein.

Haas, Ernst. 1958. *Uniting Europe*. Stanford, CA: Stanford University Press.

———. 1964. *Beyond the Nation-State*. Stanford, CA: Stanford University Press.

Hale, Angela. 1997. Trade Liberalization and Women Workers. *The Ecologist* 27 (May–June): 87(2).

Halford, Nigel. 2001. Agricultural Biotechnology. *Chemistry and Industry* (August 20): 505–508.

Hamilton, Alexander. Report on Manufactures. Pp. 37–47 in *The Theoretical Evolution of Economy: A Reader*, ed. George T. Crane and Abla Amawi. New York: Oxford University Press.

Hanke, Steve H. 2000. Abolish the IMF. *Forbes* (April 17): 84.

Hanley, Delinda. 2001. Women in Black Hold Solidarity Vigil. *Washington Report on Middle East Affairs* 20 (August): 96.

Hardin, Garrett. 1968. The Tragedy of the Commons. *Science* 162 (December 16): 1,243–1,248.

Harris, Marcelite. 1997. Recognizing the Role of Women in NATO's Military Forces. *NATO Review* 45 (September–October): 25–26.

Hawke, Steve H. 1995. Bob Rubin, Meet C. N. Parkinson. *Forbes* 155 (March 13): 110.

Haynes, Jeff. 2001. Transnational Religious Actors and International Politics. *Third World Quarterly* 22 (April): 143(16).

Hedges, Chris. 1996. Bosnia Reported to be Smuggling Heavy Arms. *New York Times*, November 8, A1.

Hegel, Georg Wilhelm Friedrich. 1967. *The Philosophy of Right*. Translated with notes by T. M. Knox. Oxford: Clarendon Press.

Heilbroner, Robert L. 1986. *The Worldly Philosophers*. 6th ed. New York: Simon and Schuster.

Heilbroner, Robert L. 1992. *The Worldly Philosophers: The Lives, Times, and Ideas of the Great Economic Thinkers*. New York: Simon and Schuster.

Helm, Carsten. 1996. Transboundary Environmental Problems and New Trade Rules. *National Forum* 78 (summer): 29(17).

Henderson, Caspar. 1997. What Price Free Trade. *New Scientist* 154 (June 2): 14.

Herbener, Jeffrey. 1995. A Bail-Out of Third World Bureaucrats. *Insight on the News* 11 (July 31): 5–37.

Heredia, Carlos, and Mary Purcell. 1996. Structural Adjustment and the Polarization of Mexican Society. Pp. 273–284 in *The Case Against the Global Economy and for a Turn Toward the Local*, ed. Jerry Mander and Edward Goldsmith. San Francisco, CA: Sierra Club.

Heyzer, Noeleen, Sushma Kapoor, and Joanne Sandler, eds. 1995. *A Commitment to the World's Women: Perspectives on Development for Beijing and Beyond*. New York: UNIFEM.

Hilderbrand, Robert C. 1990. *Dumbarton Oaks: The Origins of the United Nations and the Search for Postwar Security*. Chapel Hill, NC: University of North Carolina Press.

Hoare, Quentin, and Geoffrey N. Smit, eds. 1971. *Selections from the Prison Notebooks*. London: Lawren and Wishart.

Hobbes, Thomas. 1996. *Leviathan*. Ed. Richard Tuck. Cambridge, NY: Cambridge University Press.

Howard, Michael. 1990. The UN and International Security. Pp. 31–46 in *United Nations, Divided*

World: The UN's Roles in International Relations, ed. Adam Roberts and Benedict Kingsbury. Oxford, UK: Clarendon Press.

Hudnall, Shannon. 1996. Towards a Greener International Trade System: Multilateral Environmental Agreements and the World Trade Organization. *Columbia Journal of Law and Social Problems* 29 (winter): 175–215.

Hurd, Douglas. 1994. NATO's New Horizons. Policy Statement PS51/94. New York: British Information Services.

International Herald Tribune. 2000. UN Backs Women as Peacekeepers, November 1, 7.

Isaak, Robert A. 1995. *Managing World Economic Change.* 2nd ed. Upper Saddle River, NJ: Prentice Hall.

Jacobson, Harold. 1984. *Networks of Interdependence: International Organization and the Global Political System.* 2nd ed. New York: Knopf.

Joffe, Josef. 1995. Is There Life After Victory? What NATO Can and Cannot Do. *National Interest* 41 (fall): 19–36.

Journal of Environmental Health. 2000. National Research Council Weighs in on Transgenic Plants. 63 (July): 40–43.

Kahler, Miles. 1985. Politics and International Debt. Explaining the Debt Crisis. *International Organization* 39 (fall): 357–382.

Kahn, Joseph. 2000. Protestors Battle Police in Prague. *International Herald Tribune,* September 27, 1.

Kansas, Dave. 1998. Indoamnesia. *The New Republic* 218 (February 2): 12–14.

Kant, Immanuel. 1939. *Perpetual Peace.* New York: Columbia University Press.

Kapstein, Ethan B. 1996. Shockproof: The End of the Financial Crisis. *Foreign Affairs* 74 (January–February): 2–9.

Karl, Marilee. 1995. *Women and Empowerment: Participation and Decision-Making.* London: Zed Books.

Kegley, Charles W., and Gregory A. Raymond. 1990. *When Trust Breaks Down: Alliance Norms and World Politics.* Columbia, SC: University of South Carolina Press.

Kennedy, Elizabeth T., et al. 1998. The New Gemeinschaft: Individual Initiative and Business-NGO-University Partnership. *Greener Management International* (winter): 32–43.

Kennedy, Paul, and Bruce Russet. 1995. Reforming the United Nations. *Foreign Affairs* 74 (September–October): 56–71.

Keohane, Robert O. 1984. *After Hegemony: Cooperation and Discord in the World Political Economy.* Princeton, NJ: Princeton University Press.

———. 1989. International Relations Theory: Contributions of a Feminist Standpoint. *Millennium* 18 (summer): 245–253.

Keohane, Robert O., and Lisa L. Martin. 1994/95. The Promise of Institutionalist Theory. *Journal of International Security* 19 (winter): 39–52.

Keohane, Robert O., and Joseph M. Nye Jr. 1977. *Power and Interdependence: World Politics in Transition.* Boston, MA: Little Brown.

Khor, Martin. 1996. Colonialism Redux: Reconquering the World with Protocols instead of Gunboats. *The Nation* 263 (July 15): 18–21.

Khoury, Inge. 1994. The World Bank and the Feminization of Poverty. Pp. 121–123 in *Fifty Years Is Enough: The Case Against the World Bank and the International Monetary Fund,* ed. Kevin Danaher. Boston, MA: South End Press.

Kivimaki, Timo. 2000. U.S.-Indonesian Relations during the Economic Crisis: Where Has Indonesia's Bargaining Power Gone? 22 (December): 527–550.

Klare, Michael T. 1995. Going South. *In These Times* 19 (May 1): 22–24.

Klare, Michael T. 1996. The Guns of Bosnia. *The Nation* 262 (January 22): 23–25.

Klotter, Jule. 2001. How Safe are Genetically-Engineered Crops? *Townsend Letter for Doctors and Patients* (October): 14.

Knickerbocker, Brad. 1992. The World from Rio de Janeiro. *Christian Science Monitor* (June 10): 3.

Koechlin, Tim, 1995. NAFTA's Footloose Plants Abandon Workers. *Multinational Monitor* 16 (April): 25–27.

Kole, William J., and Aida Cerkez-Robinson. 2001. UN Accused of Sex-Trade Cover-Up in Bosnia. *The Burlington Free Press,* June 14, 5A.

Kolko, Joyce, and Gabriel Kolko. 1972. *The Limits of Power: The World and United States Foreign Policy, 1945–1954.* New York: Harper Row.

Krasner, Stephen. 1983. *International Regimes.* Ithaca, NY: Cornell University Press.

———. 1985. *Structural Conflict: Third World Against Global Liberalism.* Berkeley, CA: University of California Press.

———. 1991. Global Communication and National Power: Life and the Pareto Frontier. *World Politics* 43 (April): 336–366.

Kratochwil, Friedreich, and John Gerald Ruggie. 1986. International Organization: A State of the Art or an Art of the State. *International Organization* 40 (autumn): 753–775.

Kristof, Nicholas D. 1998. As Free-Flowing Capital Sinks Nations, Experts Prepare to "Rethink System." *New York Times,* September 20, 6.

Kuchment, Anna, and Malcolm Beith. 2000. Just Say No. *Newsweek International,* October 9, 5.

Kudlow, Lawrence A. 1994. Manana Is Another Day: Mexico Can No Longer Afford PRI Politics as Usual—Nor IMF Austerity as Usual. *National Review* 46 (June 27): 46–49.

Kumar, Krishna, ed. 2001. *Women and Civil War: Impact, Organizations, and Action.* Boulder, CO: Lynne Rienner Press.

Laarman, Peter. 1996. Gattcha. *Dissent* 43 (spring): 12(2).

Lakatos, Imre. 1970. Falsification and the Methodology of Scientific Research Programmes. Pp. 91–138 in *Criticism and the Growth of Knowledge,* ed. Imre Lakatos and Alan Musgrave. Cambridge, UK: Cambridge University Press.

Lal, Deepak. 1996. The Misconceptions of "Development Economics." Pp. 29–36 in *The Political Economy of Development and Underdevelopment.* 6th ed., ed. Kenneth P. Jameson and Charles K. Wilber. New York: McGraw-Hill.

Lambrecht, Bill. 2001. Europe's Concerns Over Biotech Foods Don't Seem Likely to Be Assuaged Soon. *St. Louis Post-Dispatch,* November 4, A8.

Landell-Mills, Pierre, and Ismail Serageldin. 1991. Governance and the Development Process. *Finance and Development* 28 (September): 14–18.

Langer, Gary. 2001. Behind the Label: Many Skeptical of Bio-Engineered Food. June 19. <abcnews.go.com>

Lane, Charles. 1995. The Fall of Srebrenica. *The New Republic* 213 (August 14): 14(4).

Lewis, Neil A. 2001. Papers Show U.S. Knew of Genocide in Rwanda. *New York Times,* August 23, A5.

Li, Darryl. 2000. Anatomy of a Balkan Massacre. *Harvard International Review* 22 (fall): 34–44.

Lincoln, Edward J. 1997. A U.S.-Japan Trade Agenda. *Brookings Review* 15 (summer): 32–35.

Locke, John. 1998. Second Treatise of Government. In *Philosophy of the Classics,* ed. Nigel Warburton. London; New York: Routledge.

Longman, Phillip J., and Shaheena Ahmad. 1998. The Bailout Backlash: How to Think about the IMF and Its Critics. *U.S. News and World Report* 124 (February): 37–39.

Lustig, Nora. 1995. The Outbreak of Pesophobia. *Brookings Review* 13 (spring): 46.

Lyons, Gene M. 1995. International Organizations and National Interests. *International Social Science Journal* 47 (June): 261–277.

Machiavelli, Niccolo. 1952. *The Prince.* Translated by Luigi Ricci. New York: Oxford University Press.

Mackinlay, John, and Jarat Chopra. 1997. Second Generation Multinational Operations. In *The Politics of Global Governance: International Organization in an Interdependent World.* Boulder, CO: Lynne Rienner Press.

Maksoud, Covis. 1995. Diminished Sovereignty, Enhanced Sovereignty: United Nations-Arab League at 50. *The Middle East Journal* 49 (autumn): 582(13).

Mamdani, Mahmood. 2001. *When Victims Become Killers: Colonialism, Nativism, and the Genocide in Rwanda.* Princeton, NJ: Princeton University Press.

Mann, Jim, and Art Pine. 1990. U.S. to Oppose World Bank Loans to China. *Los Angeles Times,* January 10, A1.

Martin, Andrew. 1952. *Collective Security.* Paris: UNESCO.

Marx, Karl, and Friedrich Engels. 1965. *The Communist Manifesto.* Ed. Joseph Katz. New York: Washington Square Press.

Maynard, Cindy. 2000. Biotech at the Table. *Current Health* 2 (November): 22–25.

McFeely, Tom. 2000. The UN's Uncivil Society. *Alberta Report* (May 8): 14.

Mearsheimer, John J. 1990. Back to the Future: Instability in Europe After the Cold War. *International Security* 15 (summer): 5–56.

————. 1994/5. The False Promise of International Institutions. *International Security* 19 (winter): 5–49.

————. 1995. A Realist Theory. *International Security* 20 (summer): 82–104.

MEED Middle Eastern Economic Digest. 2001. Arabs Opt for Token Action. 45 (April 6): 3.

Meigs, A. James. 1997. Mexican Monetary Lessons. *The Cato Journal* 14 (spring–summer): 35–73.

Mikesell, Raymond. 1972. The Emergence of the World Bank as a Development Institution. Pp. 70–84 in *Bretton Woods Revisited*, ed. A. L. Acheson, J. F. Chant, and Martin Prachowny. Toronto, ONT: Toronto University Press.

Mitrany, David. 1948. The Functional Approach to World Organization. *International Affairs* 24 (July): 350–363.

————. 1966. *A Working Peace System.* Chicago, IL: Quadrangle Books.

Modelski, George. 1978. The Long Cycle of Global Politics and the Nation-State. *Comparative Studies in Society and History* 20 (April): 214–235.

Moinuddin, Hasan. 1987. *The Carter of the Islamic Conference and the Legal Framework of Economic Cooperation among Its Member States.* Oxford, UK: Clarendon Press.

Multinational Monitor. 1996. The WTO Strikes. 17 (January–February): 5.

————. 1998. Lessons from the Asian Meltdown. 19 (January–February): 5–7.

————. 2000. 20 Question on the IMF. 21 (April): 22.

Murphy, Craig N. 1994. *International Organization and Industrial Change.* New York: Oxford University Press.

Mussa, Micheal, and Graham Hacche. 1998. The Asian Economic Crisis—Its Origin and the Way Out. *New Perspectives Quarterly* 15 (winter): 30–32.

Naito, Yosuke. 1997. Kyoto Could Have Achieved Much More, Expert Says. *Japan Times*, December 12. <www.japantimes.co.jp/cop3>

NATO Handbook. 1995. Brussels: NATO Office of Information and Press.

Nelan, Bruce W. 1998. A Popular Bad Idea: Expanding NATO Comes with Risks As Well As Costs. *Time* 151 (May 11). <pathfinder.com/time/magazine...511/world>

Nelson, Julie A. 1996. *Feminism, Objectivity, and Economics.* New York: Routledge.

Nemeth, Mary. 1990. The Map-Makers' Legacy: Arabs Blame the Crisis on Colonial Powers. *Maclean's* 103 (August 27): 30.

New Republic. 1999. The Whole and Awful Truth. (December 13): 9.

New Scientist. 2001. Cruel to Be Kind. 171 (August 4): 3.

New York Times. 1992. Excerpts from Speeches by Leaders of the Permanent Members of UN Council 141 (February 1): A5.

————. 1994. Islamic Group Offering UN a Force of 10,000 for Bosnia. 143 (February 11): A6.

————. 1998. The Sea Turtle's Warning. 147 (April 10): A18.

————. 2000. 50 Multinationals Sign UN Compact on Rights and Environment. (July 27): A1.

Nincic, Miroslav. 1992. *Democracy and Foreign Policy: The Fallacy of Political Realism.* New York: Columbia University Press.

Nissen, Jill L. 1997. Achieving a Balance Between Trade and the Environment: The Need to Amend the WTO/GATT to Include Multilateral Environmental Agreements. *Law and Policy in International Business* 28 (spring): 901–928.

Niva, Steve. 1998. Tough and Tender: New World Order Masculinity and the Gulf War. Pp. 109–128 in *The "Man" Question in International Relations*, ed. Marysia Zalewski and Jane Parpart. Boulder, CO: Westview Press.

Noel, Emile. 1994. *Working Together—The Institutions of the European Community.* Luxembourg: Office for the Official Publications of the European Communities.

Nye, Joseph. 1990. *Bound to Lead: The Changing Nature of American Power.* New York: Basic Books.

Off Our Backs. 1992. Occupation: Women Pay First. 22 (February): 2–6.

O'Hanlon, Michael. 1996. Arms Control and Military Stability in the Balkans. *Arms Control Today* 26 (August): 3(6).

Oil and Gas Journal. 1996. The WTO's Gasoline Ruling. 94 (July 8): 21.

Olsen, Elizabeth. 2000. Members Call for Change in WTO Dispute System. *International Herald Tribune*, October 23, 9.

Oneal, John R., and Bruce M. Russet. 1997. The Classical Liberals Were Right: Democracy, Interdependence and Conflict, 1950–1985. *International Studies Quarterly* 41 (June): 267–294.

Online Newshour. 1997. Airing It Out. December 8. <www.pbs.org.newshour.bb.environment. july-dec97/eu-12-8.html>

Paarlberg, Robert L. 2001. *The Politics of Precaution: Genetically Modified Crops in Developing Countries.* Baltimore, MD: Johns Hopkins Press.

Packenham, Robert A. 1992. *The Dependency Movement: Scholarship and Politics in Dependency Studies.* Cambridge, MA: Harvard University Press.

Paz, Reuven. 2001. From Tehran to Beirut to Jerusalem: Iran and Hizballah in the Palestinian Uprising. The Washington Institute for Near East Policy. *Peace Watch* 313 (March 26). <www.caionet.org>

Pearlstein, Steven. 2000. World Bank Quest: New Ideas to Help Poor. *International Herald Tribune,* September 14, 17.

———. 2000. In Prague, Capitalism with a Human Face. *International Herald Tribune,* October 2, 13.

Pease, Kelly-Kate S., and David P. Forsythe. 1993. Human Rights, Humanitarian Intervention, and World Politics. *Human Rights Quarterly* 15 (May): 290–314.

Penrose, Angela, and John Seaman. 1996. The Save the Children Fund and Nutrition for Refugees. Pp. 241–269 in *"The Conscience of the World": The Influence of Nongovernmental Organizations in the UN System,* ed. Peter Willetts. Washington, D.C.: Brookings Institution.

Peteet, Julie M. 1991. *Gender in Crisis: Women and the Palestinian Resistance Movement.* New York: Columbia University Press.

Peterson, V. Spike, ed. 1992. *Gendered States: Feminist (Re)vision of International Relations Theory.* Boulder, CO: Lynne Rienner Press.

Peterson, V. Spike, and Anne Sisson Runyan. 1993. *Global Gender Issues.* Boulder, CO: Westview Press.

Pettman, Jan Lindy. 1998. Gender Issues. Pp. 483–497 in *The Globalization of World Politics: An Introduction to International Relations,* ed. John Bayliss and Steve Smith. Oxford, UK: Oxford University Press.

Phillips, Andrew. 1990. An Economy-in-Exile: Kuwaiti Exiles Keep Their Nation Alive. *Maclean's* 103 (October 1): 32–33.

Pires-O'Brien, Joaquina. 2000. GM Foods in Perspective. *Contemporary Review* 276 (January): 19–24.

Pollack, Andrew. 2000. Montreal Talks Agree on Rules for Biosafety. *New York Times,* January 20, 1 and 6.

Pollis, Adamantia, and Peter Schwab. 1979. Human Rights with Limited Applicability. Pp. 1–26 in *Human Rights: Cultural and Ideological Perspectives,* ed. Adamantia Pollis and Peter Schwab. New York: Praeger.

Porter, Gareth, and Janet Welsh Brown. 1991. *Global Environmental Politics.* Boulder, CO: Westview Press.

Press, Robert M. 1992. Biodiversity Pact Ready for Ink at Earth Summit. *Christian Science Monitor,* May 26.

Pulse. 2000. Pulse Study: Americans Uncertain about Genetically Modified Foods. December 15. <pulse.oxygen.com>

Rabkin, Jeremy. 1994. Trading in Our Sovereignty. *National Review* 46 (June 13): 34(3).

Ralph, Philip Lee, Robert E. Lerner, Standish Meacham, and Edward McNall Burns. 1991. *World Civilizations.* 8th ed., vol. 2. New York: W. W. Norton.

Ramirez, Miguel D. 1996. The Latest IMF-Sponsored Stabilization Program: Does It Represent a Long-Term Solution of Mexico's Economy? *Journal of Interamerican Studies and World Affairs* 38 (winter): 129–157.

Rauber, Paul. 1992. World Bankruptcy: The World Bank and the Environment. *Sierra* 77 (July–August): 34–35.

Reich, Robert B. 1991. *The Work of Nations: Preparing Ourselves for Twenty-First-Century Capitalism.* New York: Simon and Schuster.

Reuters. 2000. Report for UN Labels WTO a Nightmare. *International Herald Tribune,* August 12–13, 13.

Revkin, Andrew C. 2001. Deals Break Impasse on Global Warming Treaty. *New York Times,* November 11, A8.

Reynolds, Robert. 1998. For Russia, NATO a Bitter Pill. *MSNBC,* March 2. <www.msnbc.com/news/147829.asp>

Ricardo, David. 1965. *The Principles of Political Economy and Taxation.* London: Dent; New York: Dutton.

Rich, Bruce M. 1993. The Greening of the Development Banks: Rhetoric and Reality. *The Ecologist* 19 (March–April): 44–53.

Riding, Alan. 1992. West Drops Malawi's Aid Over Rights: World Bank and Leading Western Donor Nations Stop Economic Aid Over Human Rights Records. *New York Times*, May 14, A6.

Riggs, Robert E., and Jack C. Plano. 1994. *The United Nations: International Organization and World Politics.* 2nd ed. Belmont, CA: Wadsworth.

Rochester, J. Martin. 1986. The Rise and Fall of International Organization as a Field of Study. *International Organization* 40 (autumn): 777–813.

Roett, Riordan, ed. 1997. *The Mexican Peso Crisis: International Perspectives.* Boulder, CO: Lynne Rienner Press.

Rohde, David. 1998. *Endgame: The Betrayal and the Fall of Srebrenica.* New York: Westview Press.

Rostow, Walt. 1971. *Stages of Economic Growth.* London: Cambridge University Press.

Royte, Elizabeth. 1997. The Outcasts. *New York Times Magazine*, January 19, 37.

Ruggie, John Gerald. 1982. International Regimes, Transactions, and Change: Embedded Liberalism in the Post–Cold War Economic Order. *International Organization* 36 (Special Issue): 379–415.

Runyan, Anne Sisson, and V. Spike Peterson. 1990. The Radical Future of Realism: Feminist Subversions of IR Theory. *Alternatives* 16: 67–106.

Runyan, Curtis. 1999. Action on the Front Lines. *World Watch* 12: 12.

Rupp, Leila J. 1998. *Worlds of Women: The Making of an International Women's Movement.* Princeton, NJ: Princeton University Press.

Russett, Bruce M. 1993. *Grasping the Democratic Peace: Principles for a Post–Cold War World.* Princeton, NJ: Princeton University Press.

Salinger, Pierre. 1995. The United States, the United Nations, and the Gulf War. *Middle Eastern Journal* 49 (autumn): 595–614.

Sanford, Jonathan E. 1988. The World Bank and Poverty: The Plight of the World's Impoverished Is Still a Major Concern of the International Agency. *The American Journal of Economies and Sociology* 47 (July): 257–75.

Sanger, David E. 1998. Trade Arbiter Favors U.S. in Key Ruling. *New York Times*, February 6, C1.

Sassoon, Anne Showstack. 1982. *Approaches to Gramsci.* London: Writers and Readers.

Satlof, Robert. 2001. The Arab League Summit. Opportunities Amid the Vitriol? The Washington Institute of Near East Policy. *Peace Watch* 314 (March 25). <www.ciaonet.org>

Schmemann, Serge. 2001. Annan Urges New Methods to Fight Terrorism. *New York Times*, September 25, B3.

Schmitt, Eric. 1999. Deal on U.N. Dues Breaks an Impasse and Draws Critics. *New York Times*, November 16, A3.

Schoenbaum, Thomas J. 1997. International Trade and Protection of the Environment: The Continuing Search for Reconciliation. *American Journal of International Law* 91 (April): 268–313.

Schrope, Mark. 2001. UN Backs Transgenic Crops for Poorer Nations. *Nature* 412 (July 12): 109–110.

Schweder, Tore. 2000. Distortion of Uncertainty in Science: Antarctic Fin Whales in the 1950s. *Journal of International Wildlife Law and Policy* 3 (spring): 73–94.

Schweller, Randall L., and David Preiss. 1997. A Tale of Two Realisms: Expanding the Institutions Debate. *Mershon International Studies Review* 41 (May): 1–32.

Seabrook, Jeremy. 1993. *Victims of Development: Resistance and Alternatives.* London: Verso.

Sen, Amartya. 1996. Development. Which Way Now? Pp. 1–28 in *The Political Economy of Development and Underdevelopment.* 6th ed., ed. Kenneth P. Jameson and Charles K. Wilber. New York: McGraw-Hill.

Shahin, Mariam. 2001. Digging In or Bailing Out. *The Middle East* (September): 7.

Shiva, Vandana. 1989. *Staying Alive.* London: Zed Books.

———. 1997. *Biopiracy: The Plunder of Nature and Knowledge.* Boston, MA: South End Press.

———. 1999. *Stolen Harvest: The Highjacking of the Global Food Supply.* Boston, MA: South End Press.

Simmons, Pam. 1992. Women in Development: A Threat to Liberation. *The Ecologist* 22 (January–February): 16–21.

Simon, Roger. 1982. *Gramsci's Political Thought.* London: Lawrence Wishart.

Siverson, Randolph, and Michael R. Tennefoss. 1984. Power, Alliance, and the Escalation of International Conflict, 1815–1965. *American Political Science Review* 78 (spring): 1,057–1,069.

Smith, Adam. 1971. *The Wealth of Nations.* New York: Dutton.

Smith, Steve. 1998. Unacceptable Conclusions and the Man Question: Masculinity, Gender, and International Relations. Pp. 54–72 in *The "Man" Question in International Relations*, ed. Marysia Zalewski and Jane Parpart. Boulder, CO: Westview Press.

Sneider, Daniel. 1992. The Soviet "Ecocidal" Legacy. *Christian Science Monitor* (January 11): 10–11.

Snow, Donald M. 1993. *Distant Thunder: Third World Conflict in the New World Order.* New York: St. Martin's Press.

Standing, Guy. 1996. Global Feminization Through Flexible Labor. Pp. 405–430 in *The Political Economy of Development and Underdevelopment,* 6th ed., ed. Kenneth P. Jameson and Charles K. Wilber. New York: McGraw-Hill.

Stanley Foundation. 1997. *The Pros and Cons of NATO Expansion: Defining U.S. Goals and Options.* Warrenton, VA: Stanley Foundation.

Staudt, Kathleen, ed. 1997. *Women, International Development, and Politics: The Bureaucratic Mire.* Philadelphia, PA: Temple University Press.

Steinberg, Richard H. 1997. Trade-Environment Negotiations in the EU, NAFTA, and WTO: Regional Trajectories of Rule Development. *American Journal of International Law* 91 (April): 231–267.

Stevens, Scott, et al. 1992. Global Resources and System at Risk. *Christian Science Monitor* (June 2): 10–11.

Stienstra, Deborah. 1994. *Women's Movements and International Organizations.* New York: St. Martin's Press.

Strange, Susan. 1983. Cave Hic Dragones. Pp. 337–354 in *International Regimes*, ed. Stephen Krasner. Ithaca, NY: Cornell University Press.

Stuart, Douglas, and William Tow. 1990. *The Limits of Alliance: NATO Out-of-Area Problems Since 1949.* Baltimore, MD: Johns Hopkins University Press.

Summerfield, Derek. 1996. Rwanda: When Women Become Killers. *The Lancet* 347 (June 29): 1,816–1,818.

Sunindyo, Saraswati. 1998. When the Earth Is Female and the Nation Is Mother: Gender, the Armed Forces, and Nationalism in Indonesia. *Feminist Review* 58 (spring): 1–22.

Swedburg, Richard. 1986. The Doctrine of Economic Neutrality of the IMF and the World Bank. *Journal of Peace Research* 23 (December): 377–390.

Szasz, Paul. 1983. The Role of the United Nations in Internal Conflicts. *Georgia Journal of International Law* 13 (winter): 345–354.

Taylor, Paul. 1998. The United Nations and International Organization. Pp. 264–283 in *The Globalization of World Politics: An Introduction to International Relations*, ed. John Bayliss and Steve Smith. Oxford, UK: Oxford University Press.

Taylor, Paul, and A. J. R. Groom. 1988. *International Institutions at Work.* New York: St. Martin's Press.

Taylor, Phillip. 1984. *Nonstate Actors in International Politics: From Transregional to Substate Organizations.* Boulder, CO: Westview Press.

Thomas, Caroline. 1998. Poverty, Development, and Hunger. Pp. 449–467 in *The Globalization of World Politics: An Introduction to International Relations*, ed. John Bayliss and Steve Smith. New York: Oxford University Press.

Thucydides. 1963. The Peloponnesian Wars. Translated by Benjamin Jowett. New York: Washington Square Press.

Tickner, J. Ann. 1988. Hans Morgenthau's Principles of Realism: A Feminist Reformulation. *Millennium* 17 (winter): 429–440.

Time International. 2001. Wailing Over Whales. 158 (August 6): 26–28.

Timmerman, Kenneth R. 1996. Iran-Bosnia Green Light. *The American Spectator* 29 (August): L28–33.

Tribunal Watch. 1996. Rwanda Genocide Chronology <twatch-l@ubvm.cc.buffalo.edu>.

Tuchman, Barbara W. 1984. *The March of Folly.* New York: Knopf.

UN Chronicle. 1997. Flashback. 4 (spring): 31–32.

UN Chronicle. 2000. UNRWA Pioneer Microfinance Programme Benefitting Women and Men. 37 (winter): 56.

UN Commission on Sustainable Development. 1998. General Information. April 6. <www.un. org/esa/sustdev/csdgen.htm>

UNESCO Courier. 1994. The Cairo Declaration. (March 1994): 44–46.

UN General Assembly. 1999. The Fall of Srebrenica. November 15: A/54/549.

U.S. Chamber of Commerce. 1998. UN Climate Treaty? <www.chamber.org/policy/Climate Change>

United Press International. 2001. IMF-Indonesia Deal Sets Bank Sell-Off. August 27: 1008239u9086.

———. IMF: Indonesia Must Push Sell-Off. October 24: p1008277u3959.

UN Secretary General. 2001. Organization of Islamic Conference Has Central Role in Devising Effective Strategy to Combat Terrorism. October 9 (SG/SM/7989 AFG 154).

UN Security Council. 2000. Press Release: Chairman of Independent Inquiry into United Nations Actions During 1994 Rwanda Genocide Presents Report to Security Council. April 14 (SC/6843).

U.S. Department of State, International Information Programs. 2001. Arab/Muslim Media Welcome Bush Gestures, Still Distrust Coalition. September 27. <www.uninfo.state.gov>

U.S. Department of State Dispatch. 1995. U.S. Global Leadership Responsibilities: The G-7 and Beyond (President Bill Clinton, June 16, 1995). (July 6): 4–6.

U.S. Information Agency, Office of Research and Media Reaction. 1995a. The Hague War Crimes Tribunal: A "Verdict," or an "Empty Gesture." April 26. <www.usia.gov>

———, 1995b. Mexico: Financial, Political Stress. March 17. <www.usia.gov>

———. 1997a. Iraq: Regional Views Diverge—But Most Agree Crisis Is Not Over. November 26. <www.usia.gov>

———. 1997b. Kyoto Conference on Global Warming: A Defective Accord Better Than None. December 11. <www.usia.gov>

———. 1997c. NATO: Enlargement Debate Intensifies. March 12. <www.usia.gov>

———. 1997d. WTO: A Miracle Year? December 17. <www.usia.gov>

———. 1998a. Former Yugoslavia: Criticism of International Role. July 29. <www.usia.gov>

———. 1998b. Indonesia's Crisis Mounts: IMF's Prescription Evaluated. January 9. <www.usia.gov>

———. 1998c. International Criminal Court: U.S. Opposition Criticized. July 21. <www.usia.gov>

Usher, Graham. 1993. Palestinian Women, the Intifada, and the State of Independence. *Race and Class* 34 (January–March): 31(13).

Valenzuela, J. Samuel, and Arturo Valenzuela. 1978. Modernization and Dependency: Alternative Perspectives in the Study of Latin American Underdevelopment. *Comparative Politics* 10 (July): 535–537.

van der Pijl, Kees. 1984. *The Making of the Atlantic Ruling Class.* London: Verso Press.

Van Dyke, Vernon. 1970. *Human Rights, the United States, the World Community.* New York: Oxford University Press.

Vasquez, Ian. 1997. The IMF Through a Mexican Lens. *ORBIS* 41 (spring): 259–277.

Vincent, R. J. 1988. *Human Rights and International Relations.* Cambridge, UK: Cambridge University Press.

Viotti, Paul R., and Mark V. Kauppi. 1993. *International Relations Theory: Realism, Pluralism, and Globalism.* 2nd ed. New York: Macmillan Publishing Company.

Vuorela, Ulla. 1992. The Informal Sector, Social Reproduction and the Impact of the Economic Crisis on Women. Pp. 125–146 in *Tanzania and the IMF: The Dynamics of Liberalization,* ed. Horace Campbell and Howard Stein. Boulder, CO: Westview Press.

Wallerstein, Immanuel. 1980. *The Modern World System.* New York: Academic Press.

Walt, Stephen M. 1987. *The Origins of Alliances.* Ithaca, NY: Cornell University Press.

Waltz, Kenneth N. 1959. *The Man, State and War: A Theoretical Analysis.* New York: Columbia University Press.

Warwick, Hugh. 2000. Terminator Too. *The Ecologist* 30 (May): 50.

Washington Post. 1999. Indonesia Timeline. June. <www.washingtonpost.com>

Washington Report on the Middle East Affairs. 2001. OIC Condemns Raids on Iraq. 20 (April): 38

———. 2001. Using a New Language. 20 (October): 41.

Waters, Tony. 2001. *Bureaucratizing the Good Samarian: The Limitations of Humanitarian Relief Operations.* Boulder, CO: Westview Press.

Webb, Steven V., and Heidi Zia. 1990. Lower Birth Rate = Higher Saving in LDCs. *Finance and Development* 27 (June): 12(3).

Weidenbaum, Murray. 1992. A Different View of Global Warming. *Christian Science Monitor* (May 21): 3.

Weiss, Thomas G., David P. Forsythe, and Roger A. Coate. 1994. *The United Nations and Changing World Politics.* Boulder, CO: Westview Press.

Weiss, Thomas G., and Leon Gordenker, eds. 1996. *NGOs, the UN, and Global Governance.* Boulder, CO: Lynne Rienner Press.

Weissman, Robert. 1994. Secrets of the WTO. *Multinational Monitor* 15 (October): 9.

Welch, Susan, et al. Rigdon. 1997. *American Government.* 6th ed. Belmont, CA: Wadsworth.

Weston, Burns H. 1991. Security Council Resolution 678 and Persian Gulf Decision Making: Precarious Legitimacy. *American Journal of International Law* 85 (July): 516–535.

Whitworth, Sandra. 1994. *Feminism and International Relations: Toward a Political Economy of Gender in Interstate and Nongovernmental Institutions.* Basingstoke, UK: Macmillan Press.

Wiarda, Howard, J. 1995. After Miami: The Summit, The Peso Crisis, and the Future of U.S.–Latin American Relations. *Journal of InterAmerican Studies and World Affairs* 37 (spring): 43–69.

Wide. 1998. A Primer on the WTO. November. <www.eurosur.org/IEPALA/wide/weng>

Willetts, Peter, ed. 1996. *"The Conscience of the World": The Influence of Nongovernmental Organizations in the UN System.* Washington, D.C.: Brookings Institution.

Williams, Mariama M. 1996. Trade Liberalization, Society, and the Environment. *Ecumenical Review* 48 (July): 345(9).

WIN News. 1995. World Bank Structural Adjustment and Gender Policies. 21 (spring): 31–33.

———. 1998. Violence in Rwanda: A Women's Perspective. 24 (summer): 34–35.

———. 1999. Indonesia. 25 (spring): 17–19.

Winslow, Anne, ed. 1995. *Women, Politics, and the United Nations.* Westport, CT: Greenwood Press.

Wolff, Richard, and Stephen Resnick. 1987. *Economics: Marxian and Neoclassical.* Baltimore, MD: Johns Hopkins Press.

World Bank News. 1997. Climate Change Debates Heats Up in Kyoto. December 4. <www.worldbank.org/html/extdr/extcs/w120497e.htm#kyoto>

World Commission on Environment and Development. 1987. *Our Common Future.* New York: Oxford University Press.

World Watch. 1999. NGO Friend or Foe. (March–April): 2.

Wren, Christopher S. 1999. U.S. Told It Must Pay $550 Million or Risk Losing U.N. Vote. *New York Times*, A6.

Wright, Robert. 1995. Let Them Eat Hate. *New Republic* 212 (April 24): 4.

WTO, 1999. <www.wto.org>

Xinhua News Agency. 2000. Indonesia, IMF Agree Not to Introduce Capital Control. June 5: 1008157h8953.

———. 2001. Jakarta Complains at Being Pushed Too Hard by the IMF. February 15: 1008046h8085.

Yamamoto, Tadashi. 1996. *Emerging Civil Society in the Asia Pacific Community: Nongovernmental Underpinnings of the Emerging Asia Pacific Regional Community: A Twenty-Fifth Anniversary Project of JCIE.* Singapore: Institute of Southeast Asian Studies.

Zacher, Mark. 1979. *International Conflicts and Collective Security, 1946–77.* New York: Praeger Publishers.

Zalewski, Marysia, and Jane Parpart, eds. 1998. *The "Man" Question in International Relations.* Boulder, CO: Westview Press.

Zengerle, Jason. 1998. Hagelianism. *The New Republic* 218 (February 9): 10–12.

Zimmerman, Tim. 1996. Pricing a Bigger NATO. *U.S. News and World Report* 120 (April 29): 14.

INDEX